Shojo Beat

STROBE EDGE

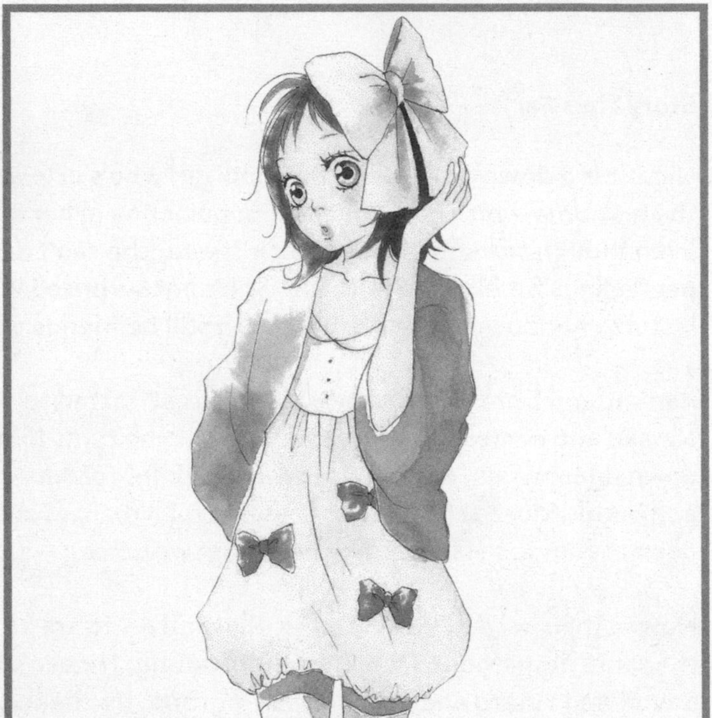

Vol. 8

Story & Art by

Io Sakisaka

STROBE EDGE

Volume 8
CONTENTS

Story Thus Far

Ninako is a down-to-earth high school girl who's in love for the first time—with Ren, the most popular boy in her grade. Even though she knows he has a girlfriend, she can't deny her feelings for him and tells him. She's not surprised when he turns her down and asks if they can still be friends.

Ren's friend from middle school, Ando, is attracted to Ninako and confesses his love for her, but she turns him down. Meanwhile, Ren starts to have feelings for Ninako, and his girlfriend, Mayuka, notices. Mayuka realizes she's been changing herself, so she breaks up with Ren.

Now in their second year, Ninako, Ren and Ando are all in the same homeroom. During a school outing, Ninako, Ren, Sayuri and Yutaro end up in the same group. By chance, it's revealed that Sayuri and Yutaro used to date. The two had been unable to let go of their past but finally achieve closure. In the midst of all this, Ando's ex-girlfriend turns up at their school...!

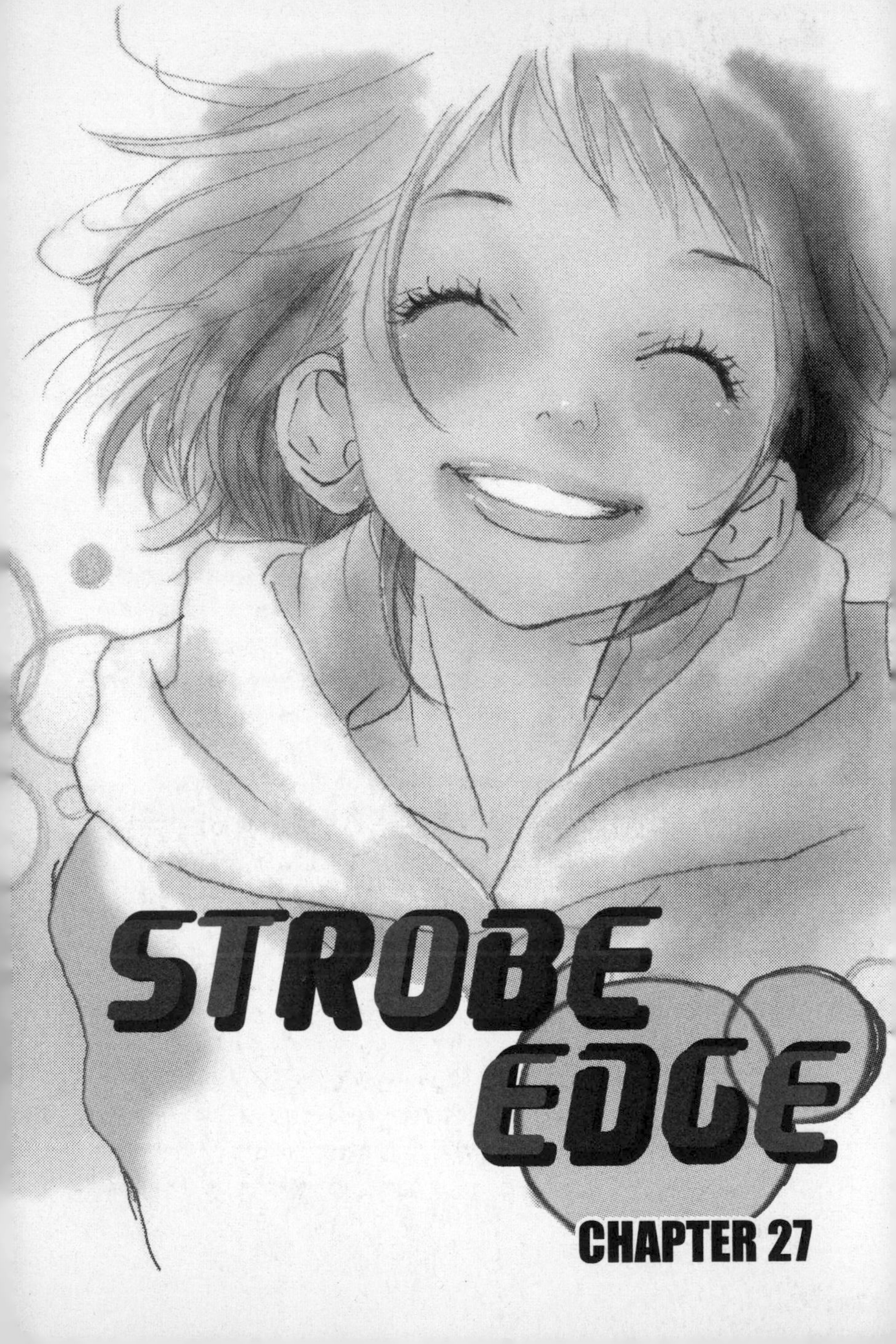
STROBE EDGE
CHAPTER 27

GREETINGS★

Hello! ★ Io Sakisaka here. Thank you so much for picking up a copy of *Strobe Edge* volume 8!

Serenity is a tremendously important thing for me when it comes to my job. When I feel unstable, I can't think straight and I panic over nothing, which hurts my work. That's just me! But that means I try hard to stay upbeat and lighthearted, and I aspire to be quick to laugh.

That said, I'm only human, and my natural inclination is toward pessimism. I have to keep an eye on that, or I begin sliding into whininess and feelings of uselessness. But when that happens, I take out the letters you've all sent me and reread them. Having your kind words fresh in my mind makes me remember how great people can be, and it restores me to where I want to be.

It's truly amazing. You're all incredible, and you've rescued me over and over again. Thanks to your kindness and support, I managed to finish this volume! I hope you all enjoy *Strobe Edge* volume 8, and that you can see my gratitude in every page.

★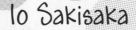

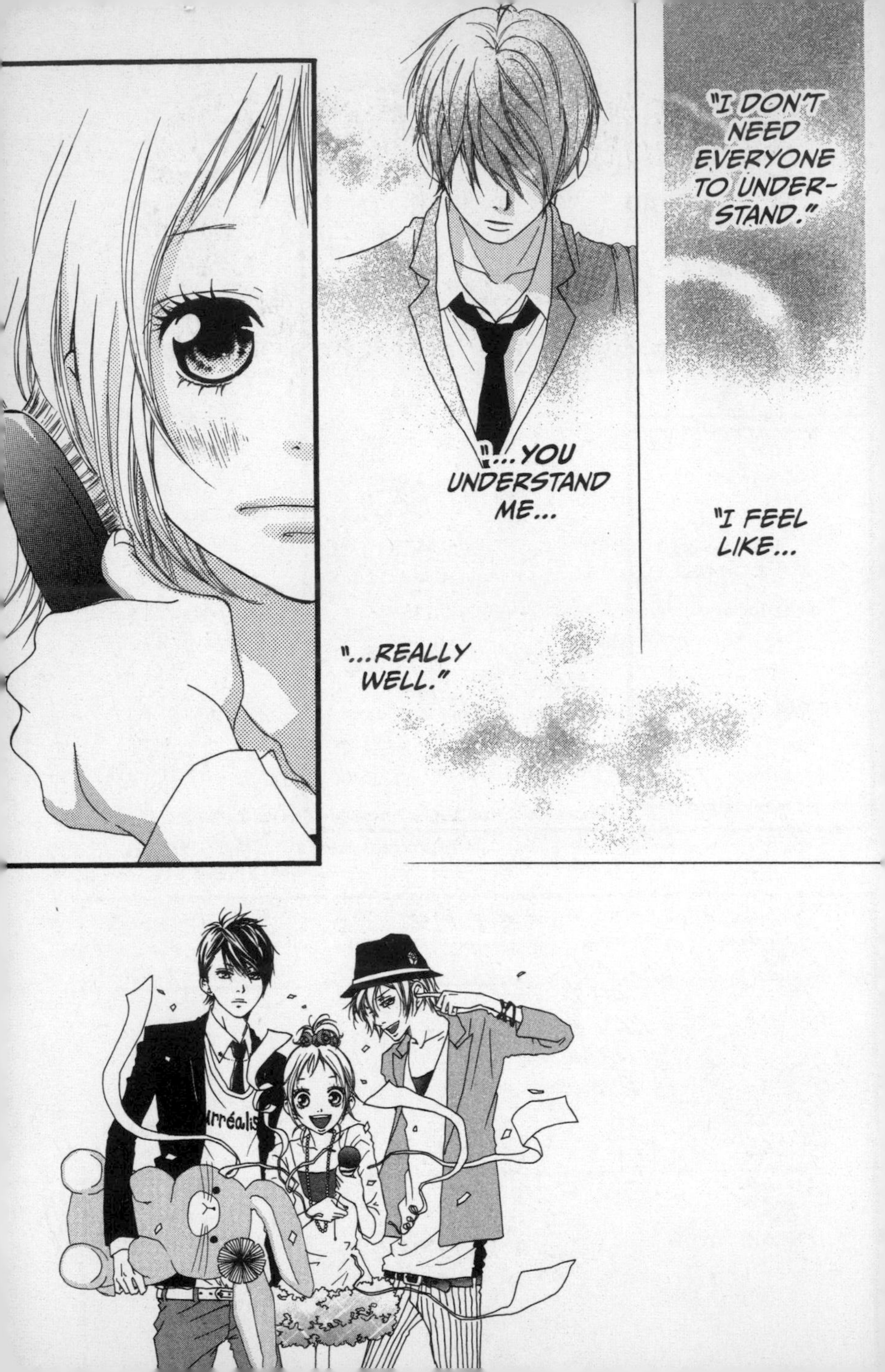
"I DON'T NEED EVERYONE TO UNDER-STAND."
"I FEEL LIKE...
"...YOU UNDERSTAND ME...
"...REALLY WELL."

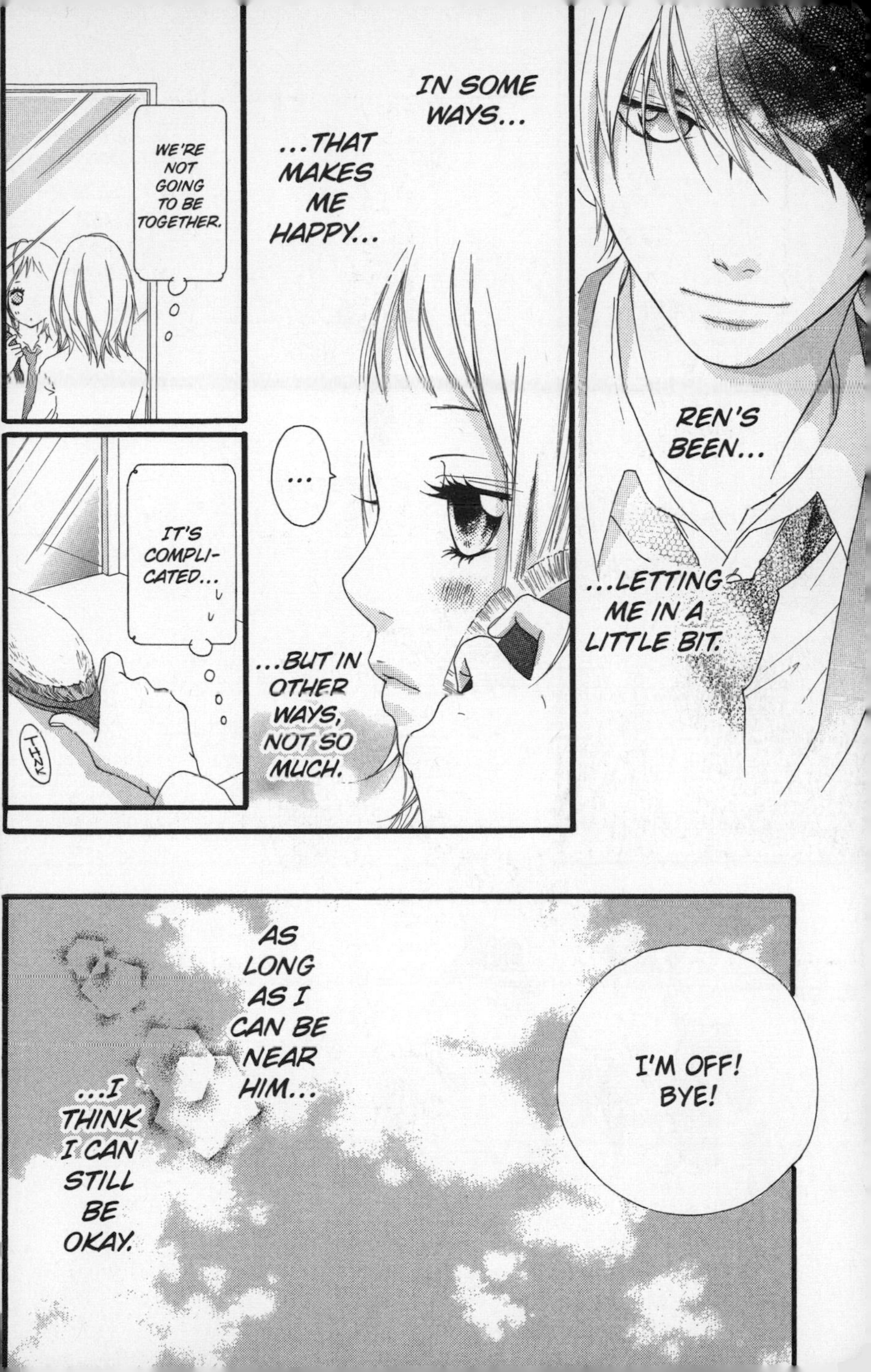
REN'S BEEN...
...LETTING ME IN A LITTLE BIT.
IN SOME WAYS...
...THAT MAKES ME HAPPY...
...
...BUT IN OTHER WAYS, NOT SO MUCH.
WE'RE NOT GOING TO BE TOGETHER.
IT'S COMPLICATED...
THNK
I'M OFF! BYE!
AS LONG AS I CAN BE NEAR HIM...
...I THINK I CAN STILL BE OKAY.

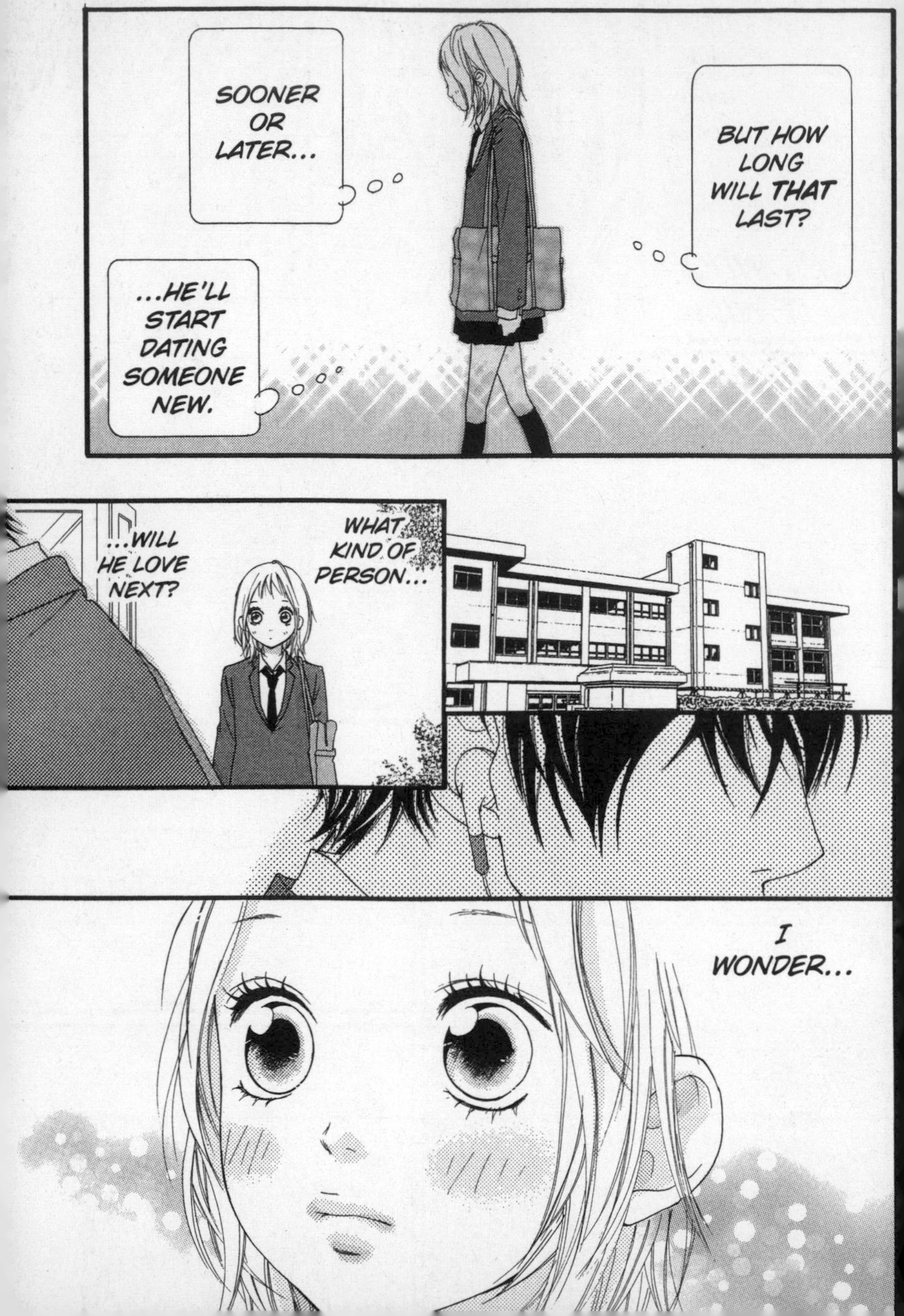
SOONER OR LATER...
...HE'LL START DATING SOMEONE NEW.
BUT HOW LONG WILL THAT LAST?
WHAT KIND OF PERSON...
...WILL HE LOVE NEXT?
I WONDER...

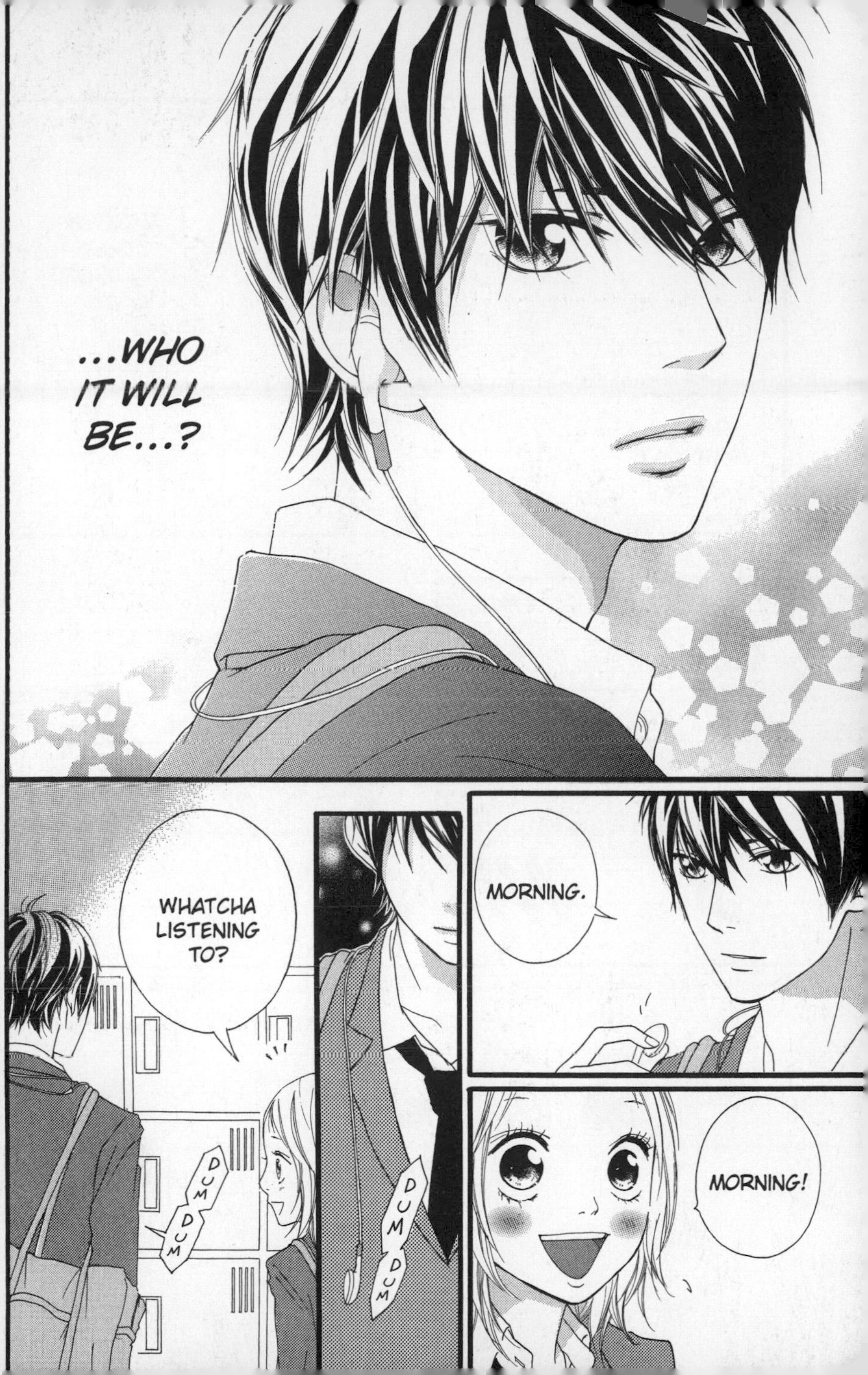
...WHO IT WILL BE...?
MORNING.
MORNING!
DUM DUM DUM
WHATCHA LISTENING TO?
DUM DUM DUM

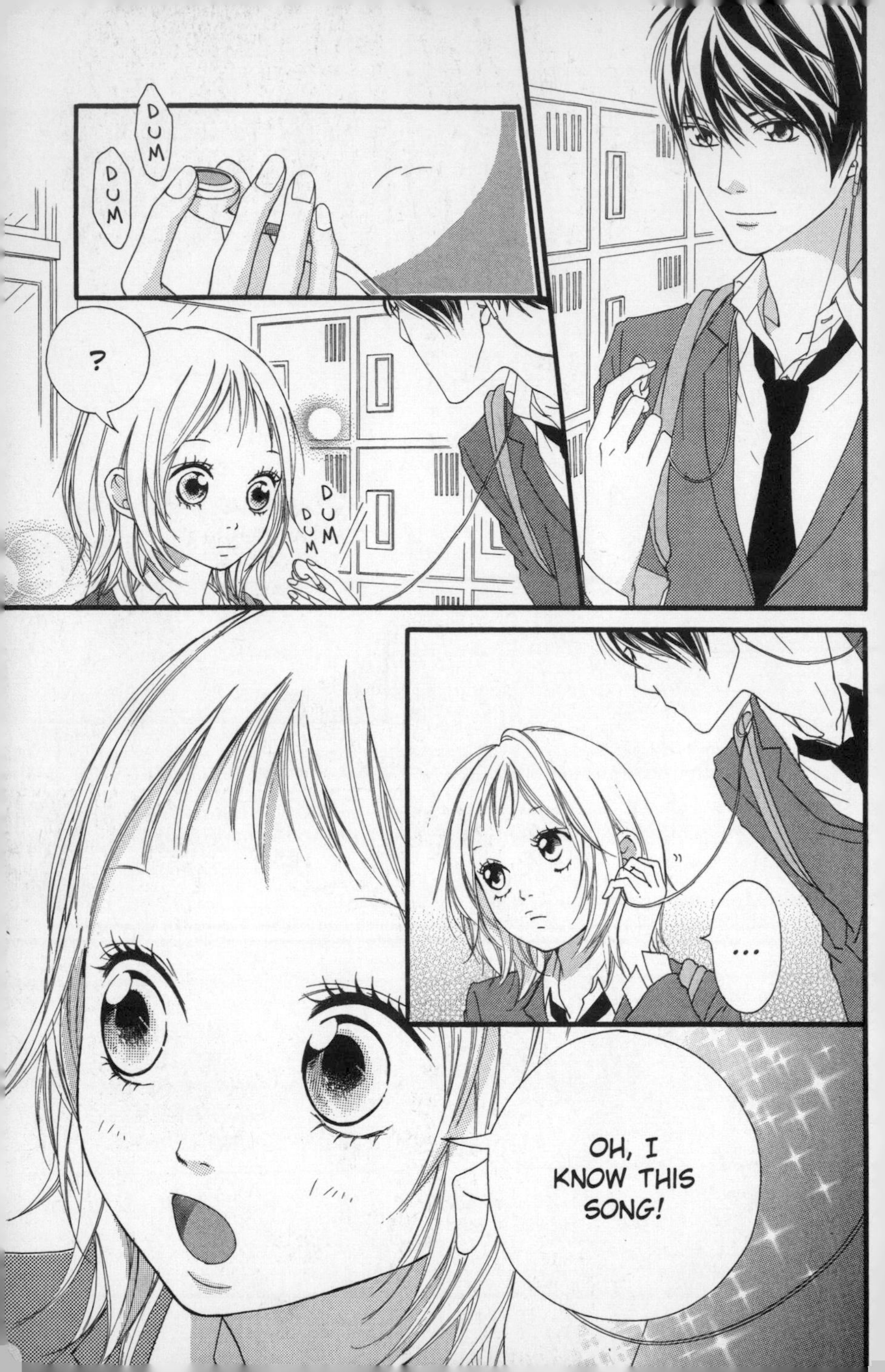
DUM
DUM
?
DUM
DUM
...
OH, I KNOW THIS SONG!

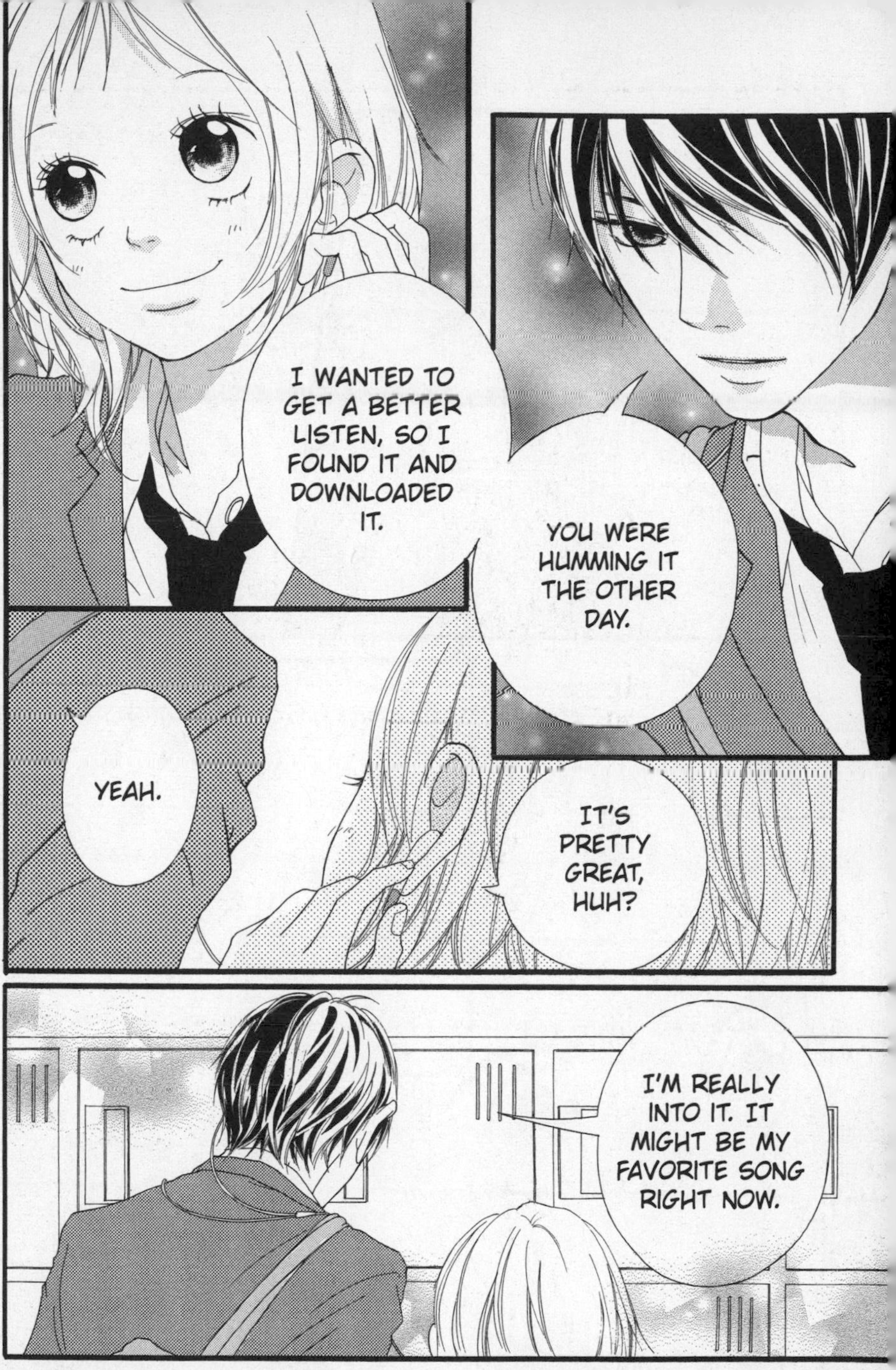
YOU WERE HUMMING IT THE OTHER DAY.
I WANTED TO GET A BETTER LISTEN, SO I FOUND IT AND DOWNLOADED IT.
IT'S PRETTY GREAT, HUH?
YEAH.
I'M REALLY INTO IT. IT MIGHT BE MY FAVORITE SONG RIGHT NOW.

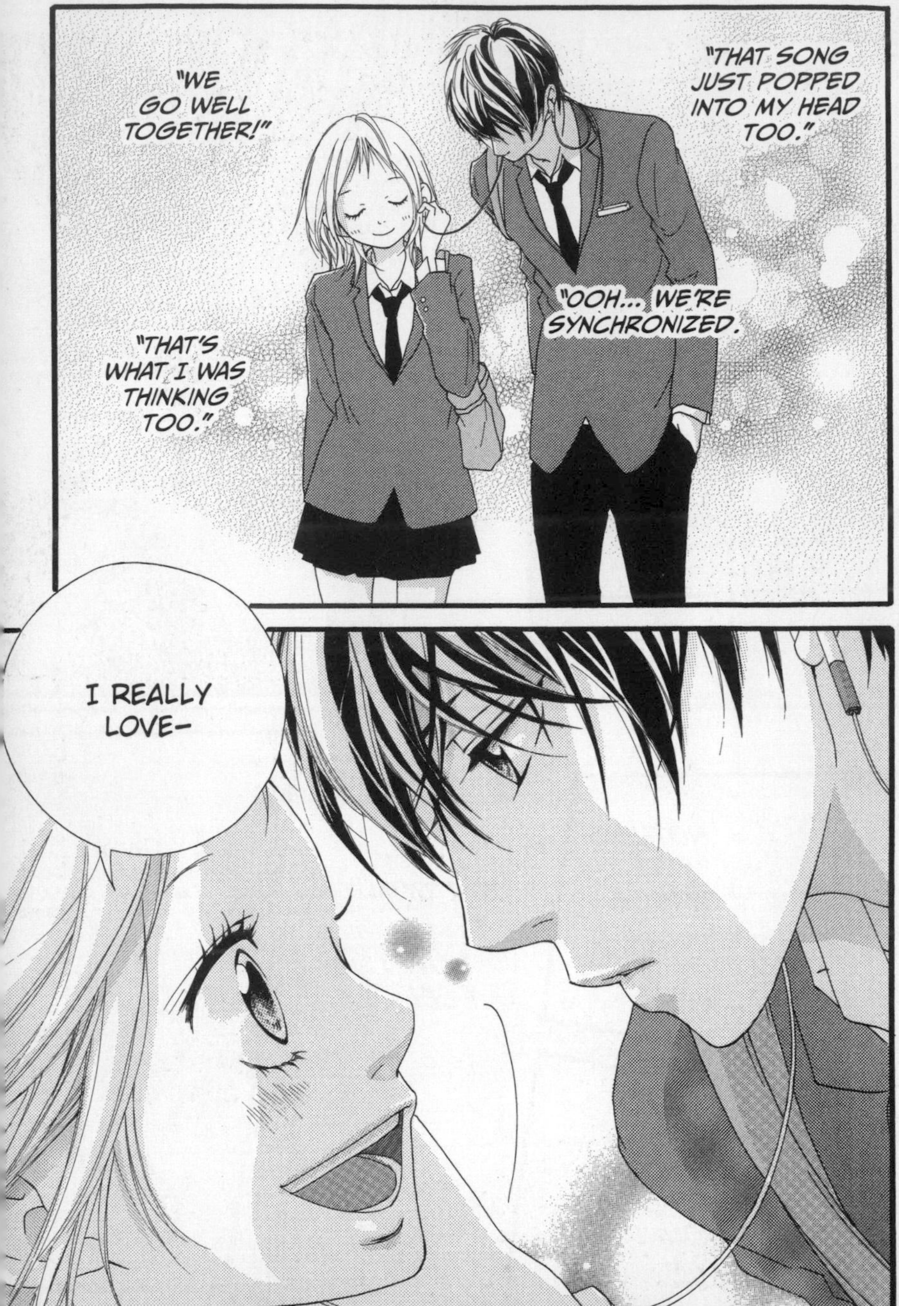
"THAT SONG JUST POPPED INTO MY HEAD TOO."
"WE GO WELL TOGETHER!"
"OOH... WE'RE SYNCHRONIZED.
"THAT'S WHAT I WAS THINKING TOO."
I REALLY LOVE–

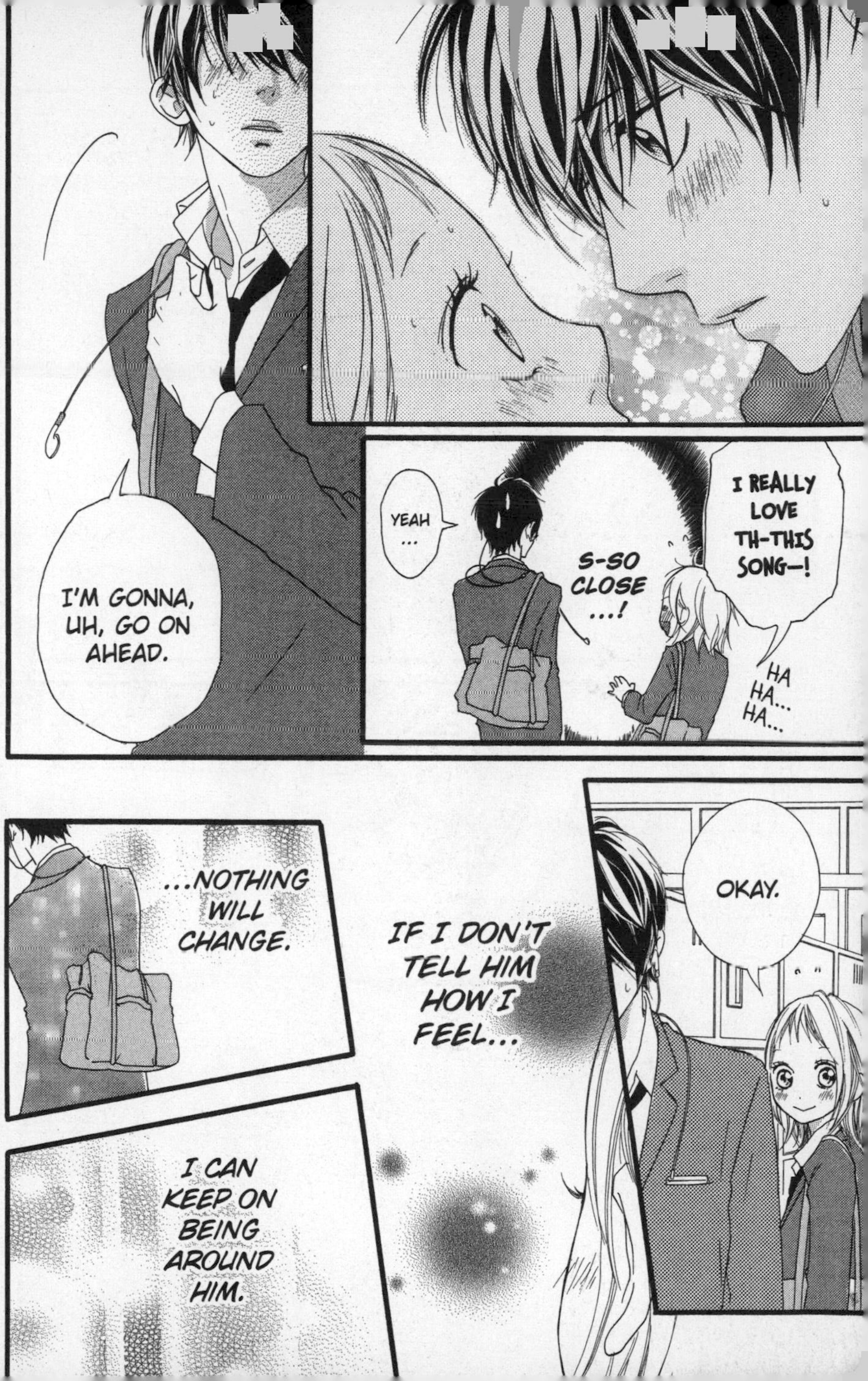
I REALLY LOVE TH-THIS SONG—!
YEAH...
S-SO CLOSE...!
HA HA... HA...
I'M GONNA, UH, GO ON AHEAD.
OKAY.
IF I DON'T TELL HIM HOW I FEEL...
...NOTHING WILL CHANGE.
I CAN KEEP ON BEING AROUND HIM.

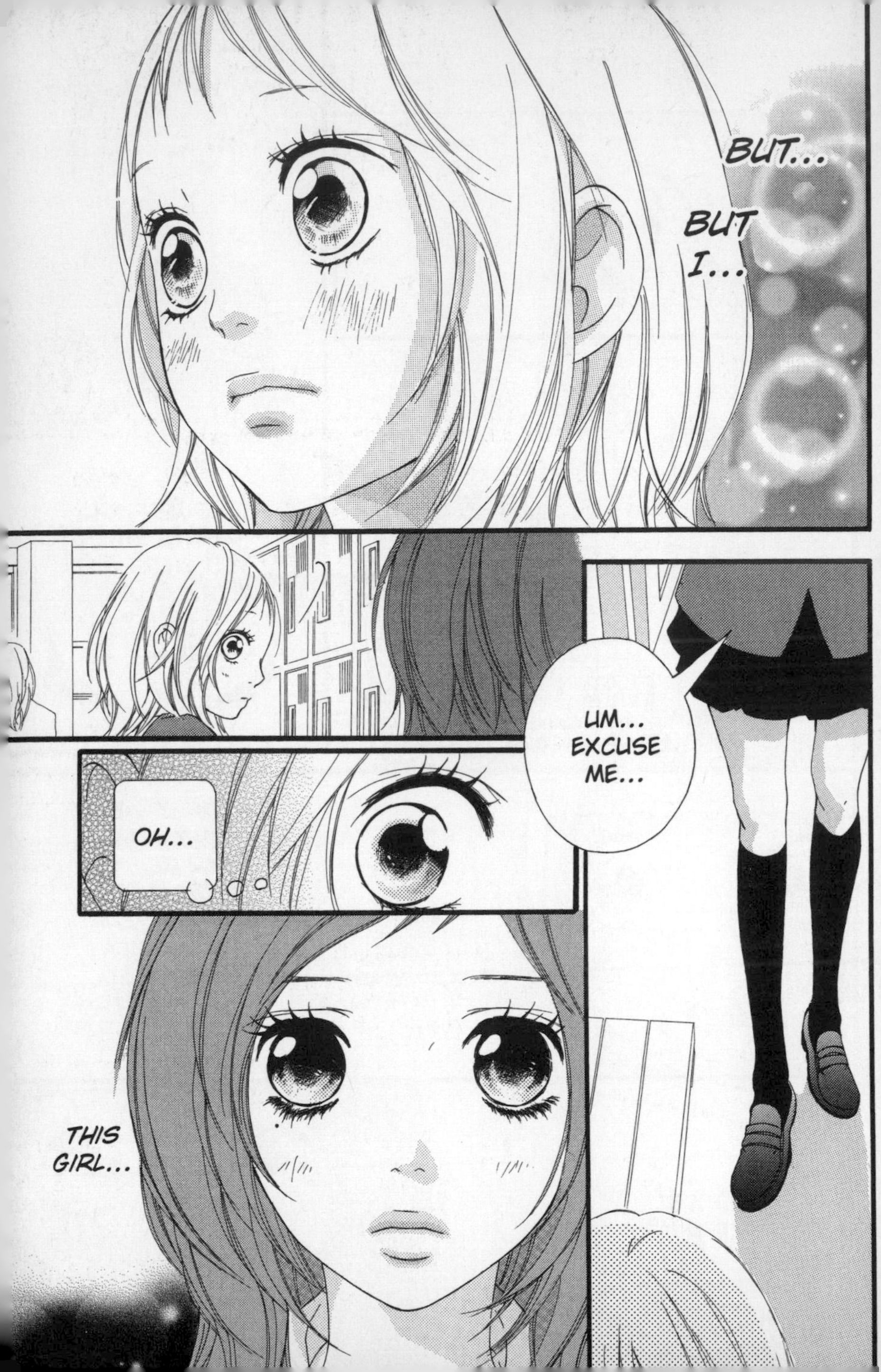
BUT...
BUT I...
UM... EXCUSE ME...
OH...
THIS GIRL...

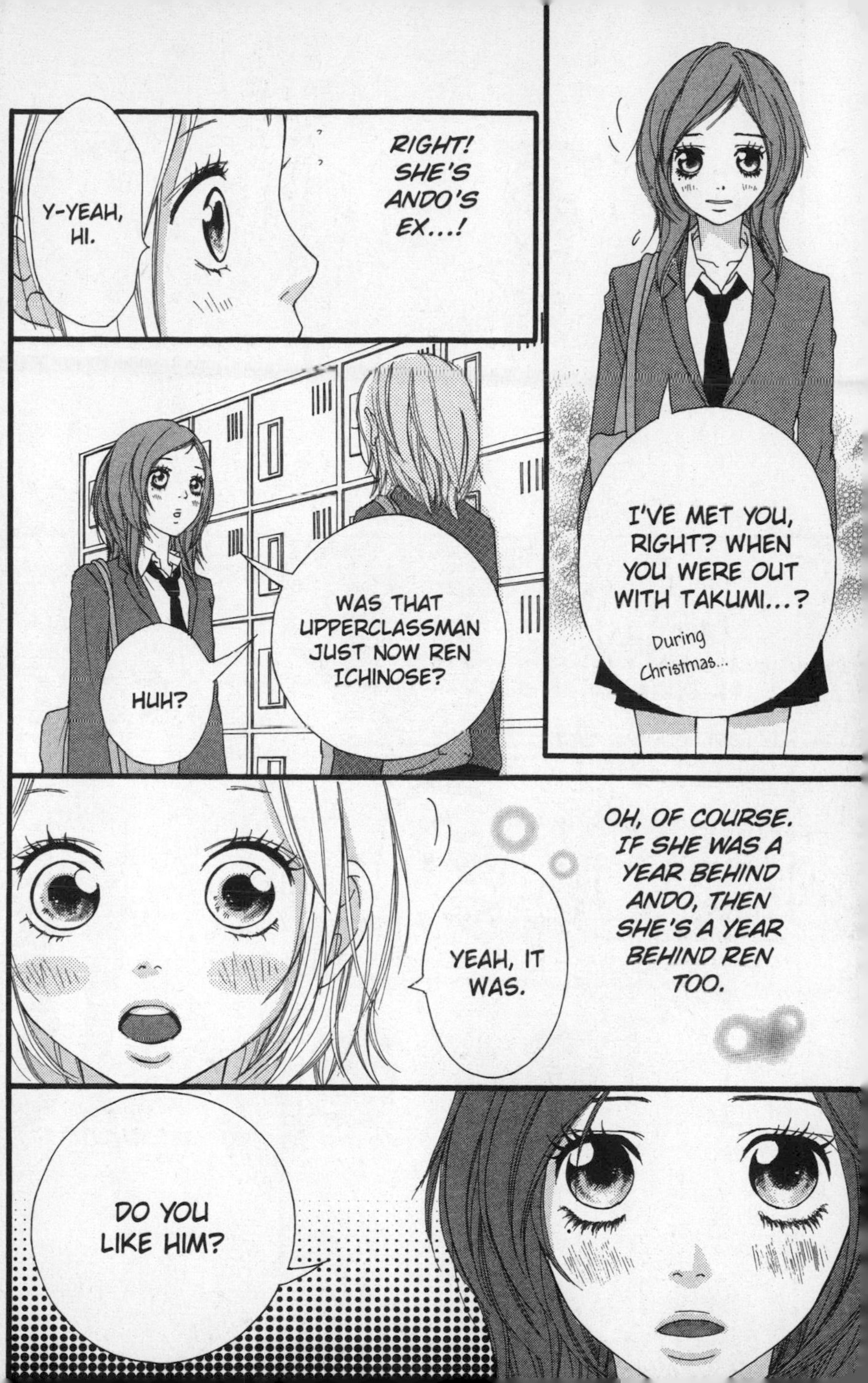
I'VE MET YOU, RIGHT? WHEN YOU WERE OUT WITH TAKUMI...?
During Christmas...
RIGHT! SHE'S ANDO'S EX...!
Y-YEAH, HI.
WAS THAT UPPERCLASSMAN JUST NOW REN ICHINOSE?
HUH?
OH, OF COURSE. IF SHE WAS A YEAR BEHIND ANDO, THEN SHE'S A YEAR BEHIND REN TOO.
YEAH, IT WAS.
DO YOU LIKE HIM?

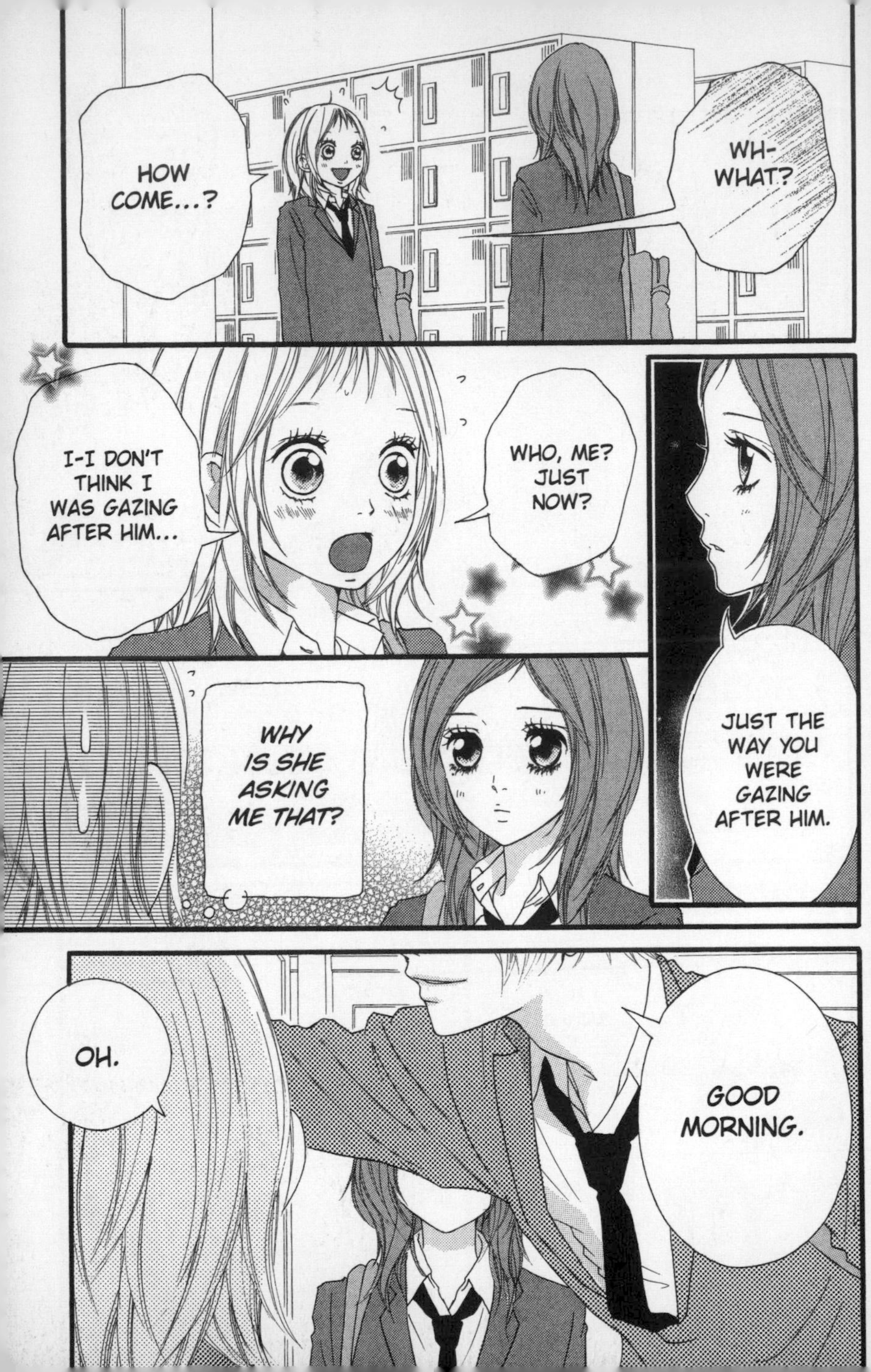
WH-WHAT?
HOW COME...?
JUST THE WAY YOU WERE GAZING AFTER HIM.
WHO, ME? JUST NOW?
I-I DON'T THINK I WAS GAZING AFTER HIM...
WHY IS SHE ASKING ME THAT?
GOOD MORNING.
OH.

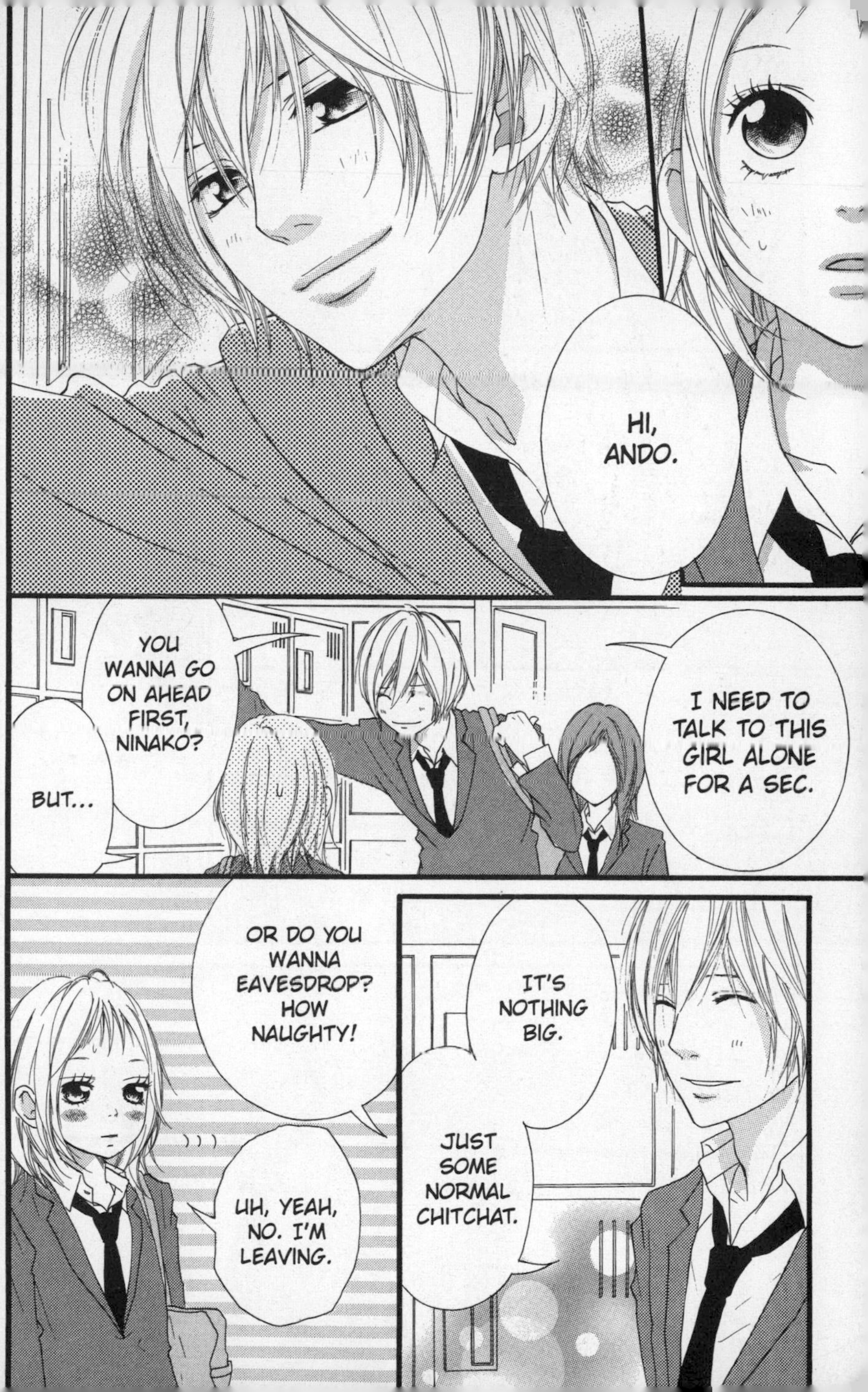
HI, ANDO.
I NEED TO TALK TO THIS GIRL ALONE FOR A SEC.
YOU WANNA GO ON AHEAD FIRST, NINAKO?
BUT...
IT'S NOTHING BIG.
JUST SOME NORMAL CHITCHAT.
OR DO YOU WANNA EAVESDROP? HOW NAUGHTY!
UH, YEAH, NO. I'M LEAVING.

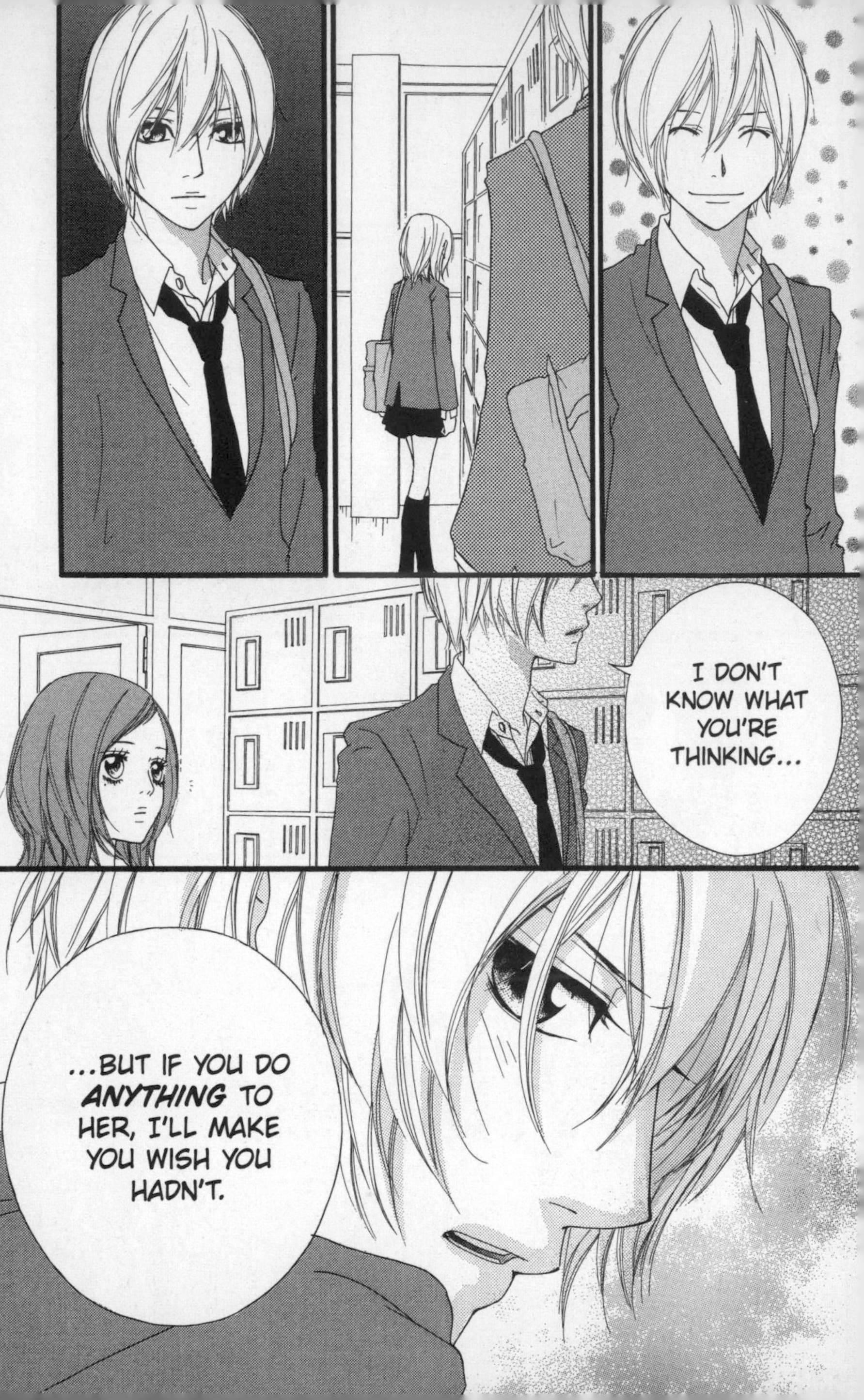
I DON'T KNOW WHAT YOU'RE THINKING...
...BUT IF YOU DO *ANYTHING* TO HER, I'LL MAKE YOU WISH YOU HADN'T.

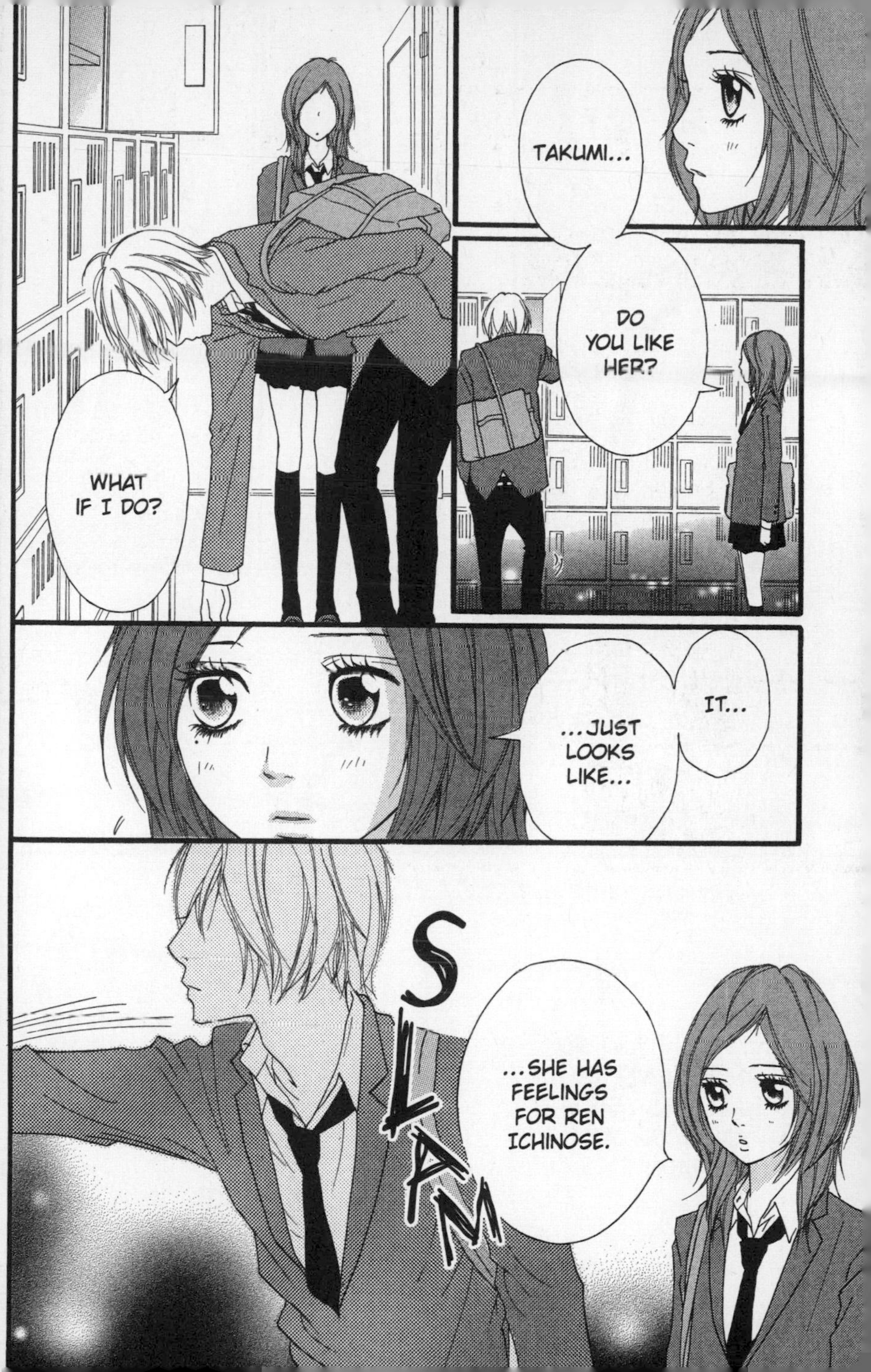
TAKUMI...
DO YOU LIKE HER?
WHAT IF I DO?
IT...
...JUST LOOKS LIKE...
...SHE HAS FEELINGS FOR REN ICHINOSE.
SLAM

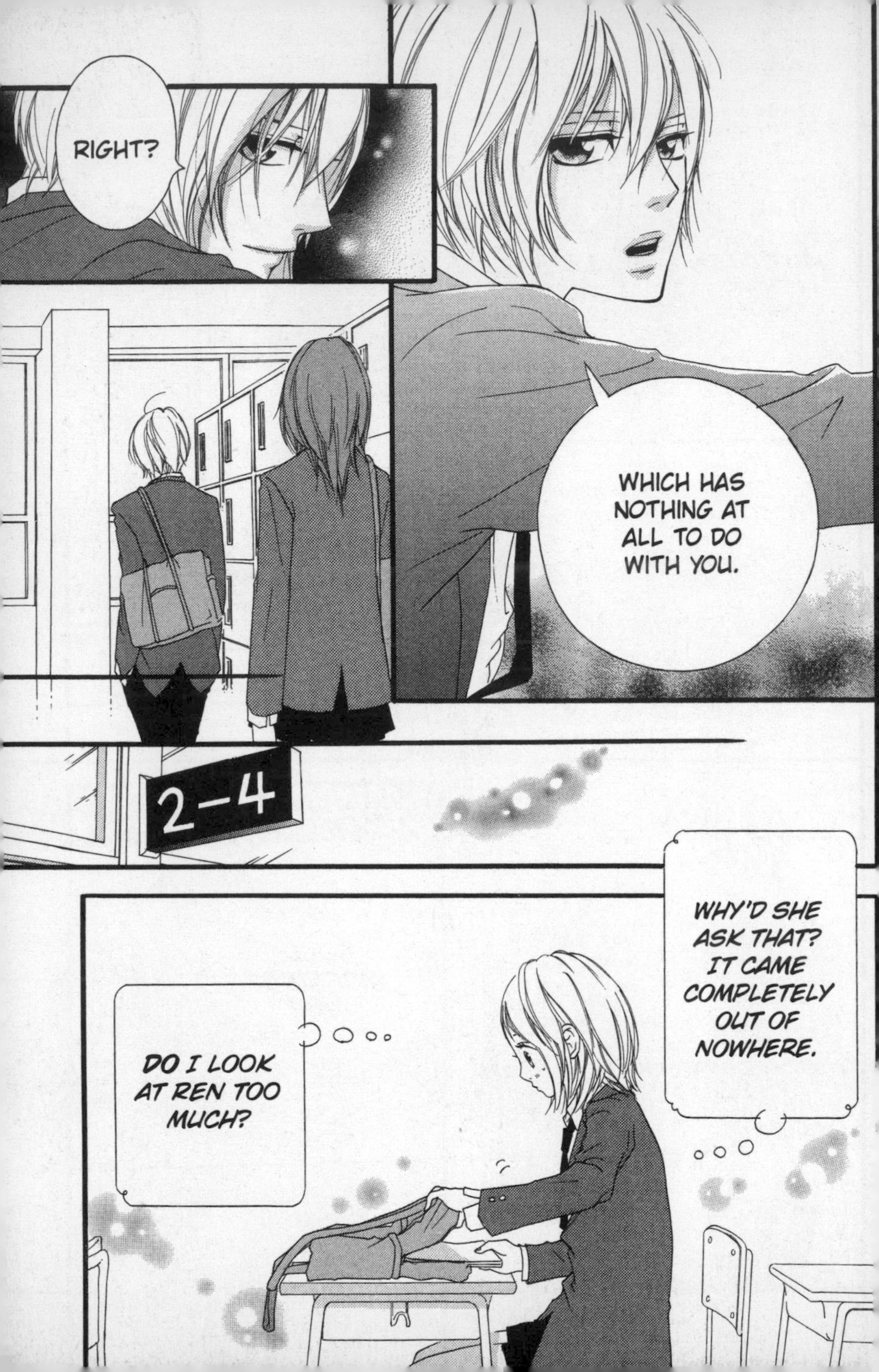
WHICH HAS NOTHING AT ALL TO DO WITH YOU.
RIGHT?
WHY'D SHE ASK THAT? IT CAME COMPLETELY OUT OF NOWHERE.
DO I LOOK AT REN TOO MUCH?

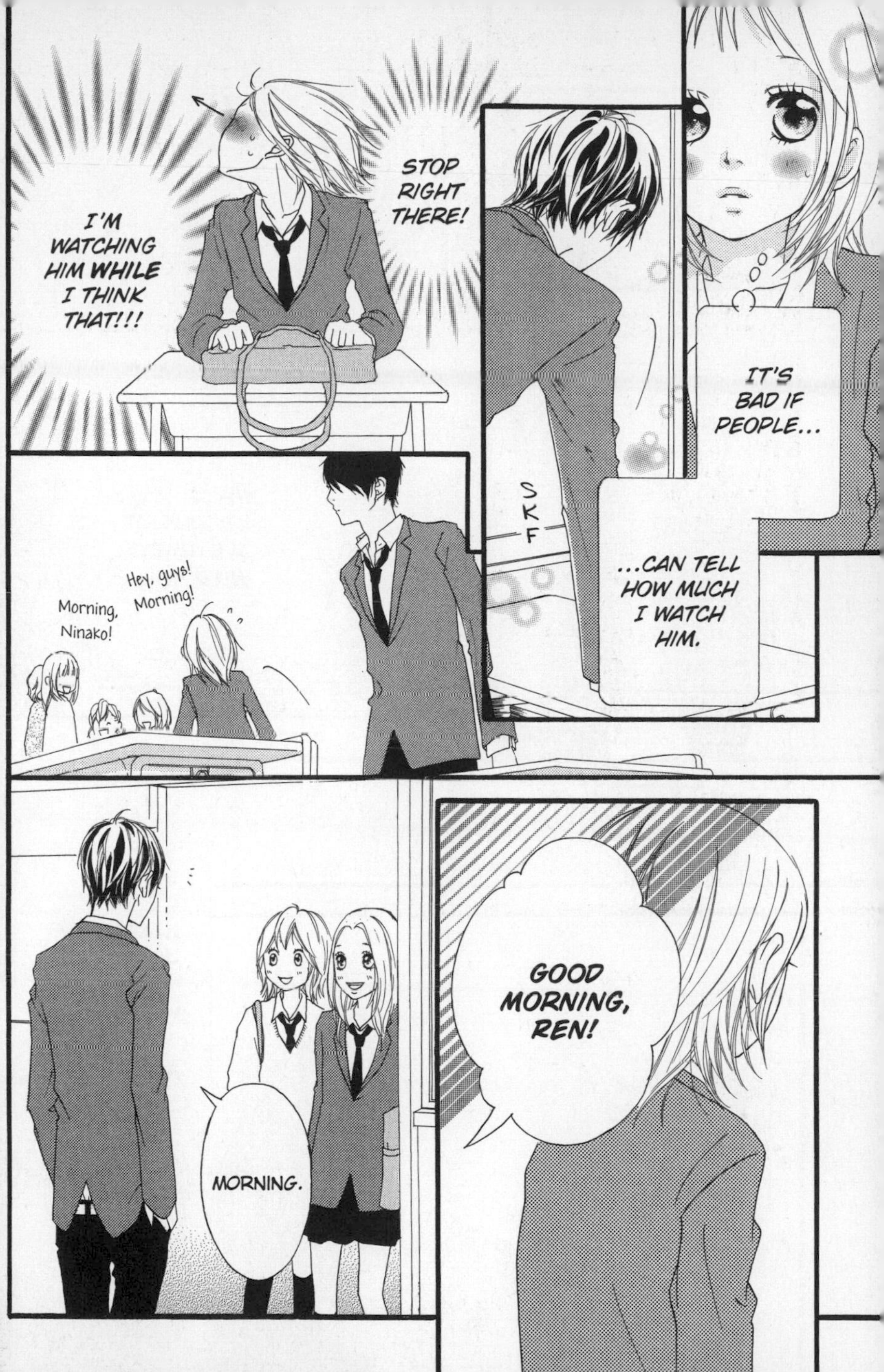
IT'S BAD IF PEOPLE...
SKF
...CAN TELL HOW MUCH I WATCH HIM.
STOP RIGHT THERE!
I'M WATCHING HIM WHILE I THINK THAT!!!
Hey, guys! Morning!
Morning, Ninako!
GOOD MORNING, REN!
MORNING.

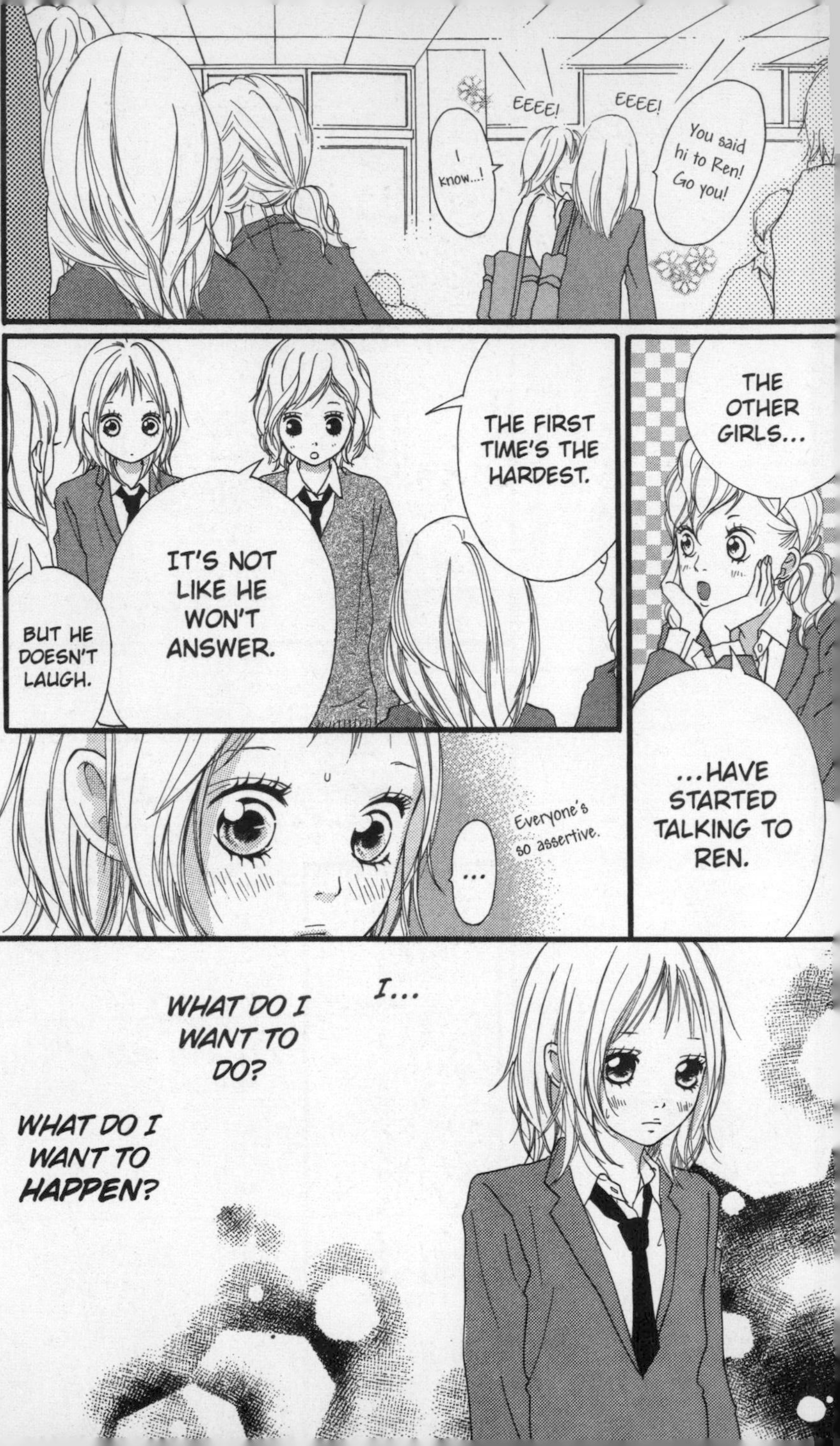
You said hi to Ren! Go you!
EEEE!
EEEE!
I know...!
THE OTHER GIRLS...
...HAVE STARTED TALKING TO REN.
THE FIRST TIME'S THE HARDEST.
IT'S NOT LIKE HE WON'T ANSWER.
BUT HE DOESN'T LAUGH.
Everyone's so assertive.
...
I...
WHAT DO I WANT TO DO?
WHAT DO I WANT TO HAPPEN?

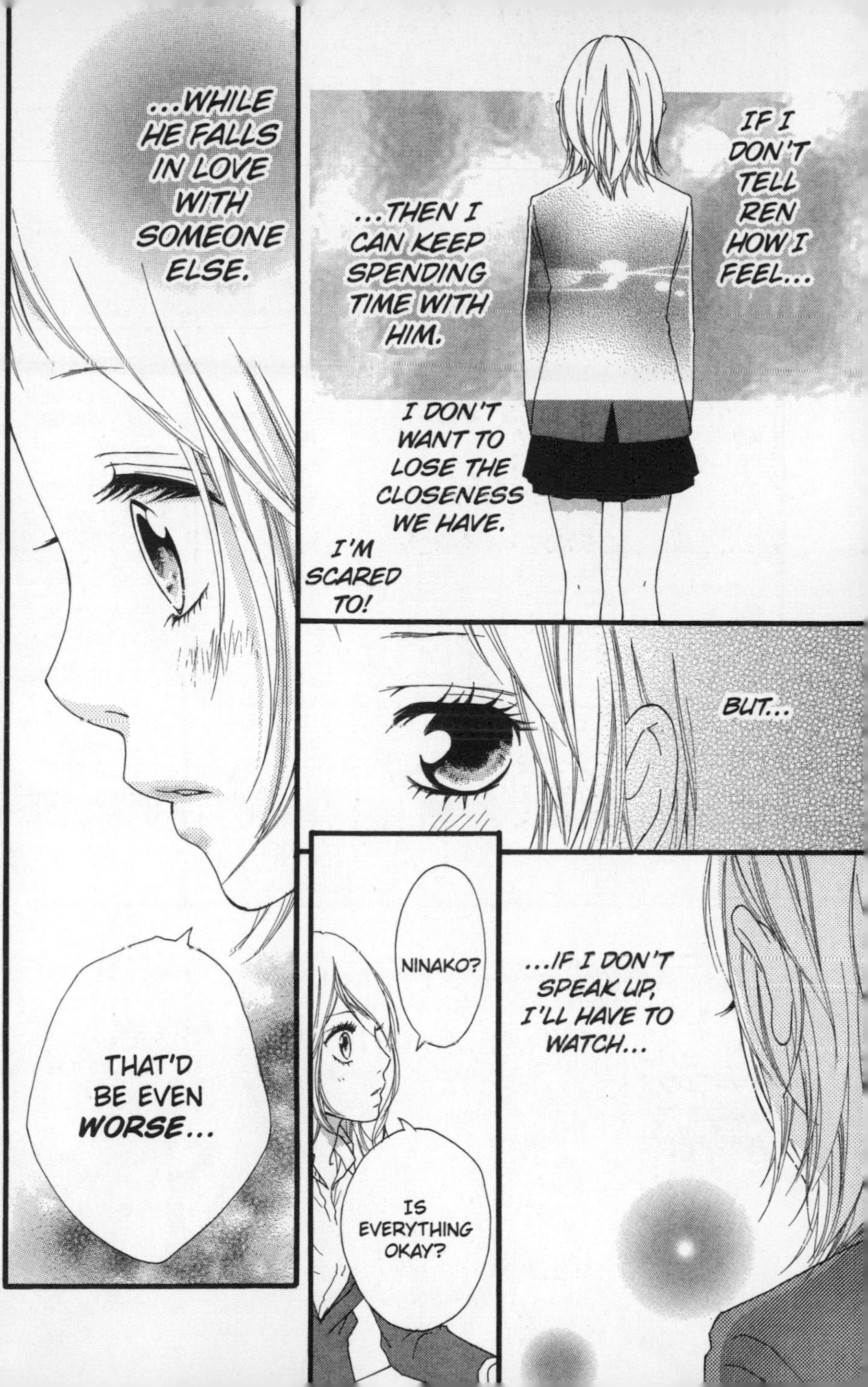
IF I DON'T TELL REN HOW I FEEL...
...THEN I CAN KEEP SPENDING TIME WITH HIM.
I DON'T WANT TO LOSE THE CLOSENESS WE HAVE.
I'M SCARED TO!
BUT...
...IF I DON'T SPEAK UP, I'LL HAVE TO WATCH...
...WHILE HE FALLS IN LOVE WITH SOMEONE ELSE.
THAT'D BE EVEN WORSE...
NINAKO?
IS EVERYTHING OKAY?

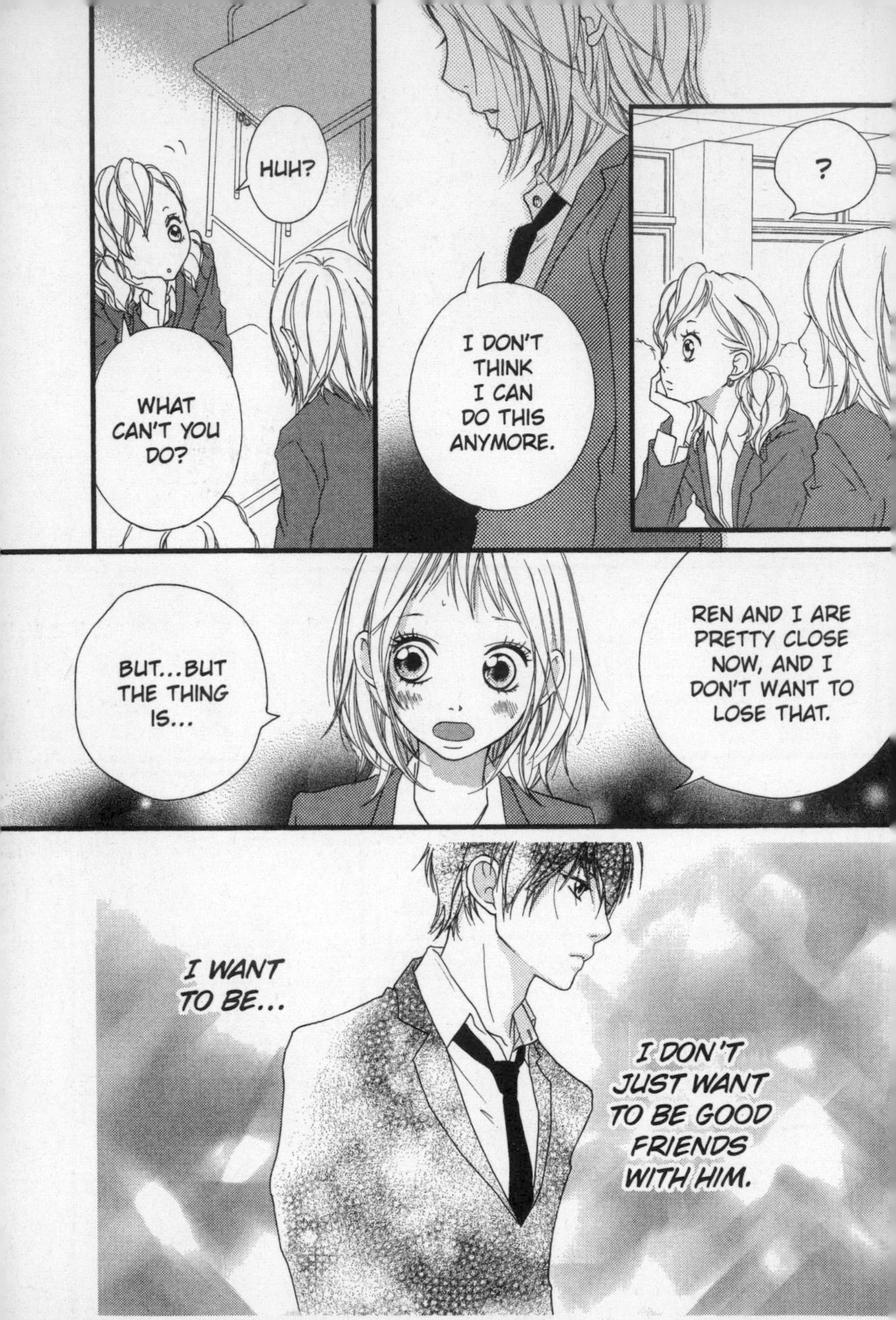
?
I DON'T THINK I CAN DO THIS ANYMORE.
HUH?
WHAT CAN'T YOU DO?
REN AND I ARE PRETTY CLOSE NOW, AND I DON'T WANT TO LOSE THAT.
BUT...BUT THE THING IS...
I DON'T JUST WANT TO BE GOOD FRIENDS WITH HIM.
I WANT TO BE...

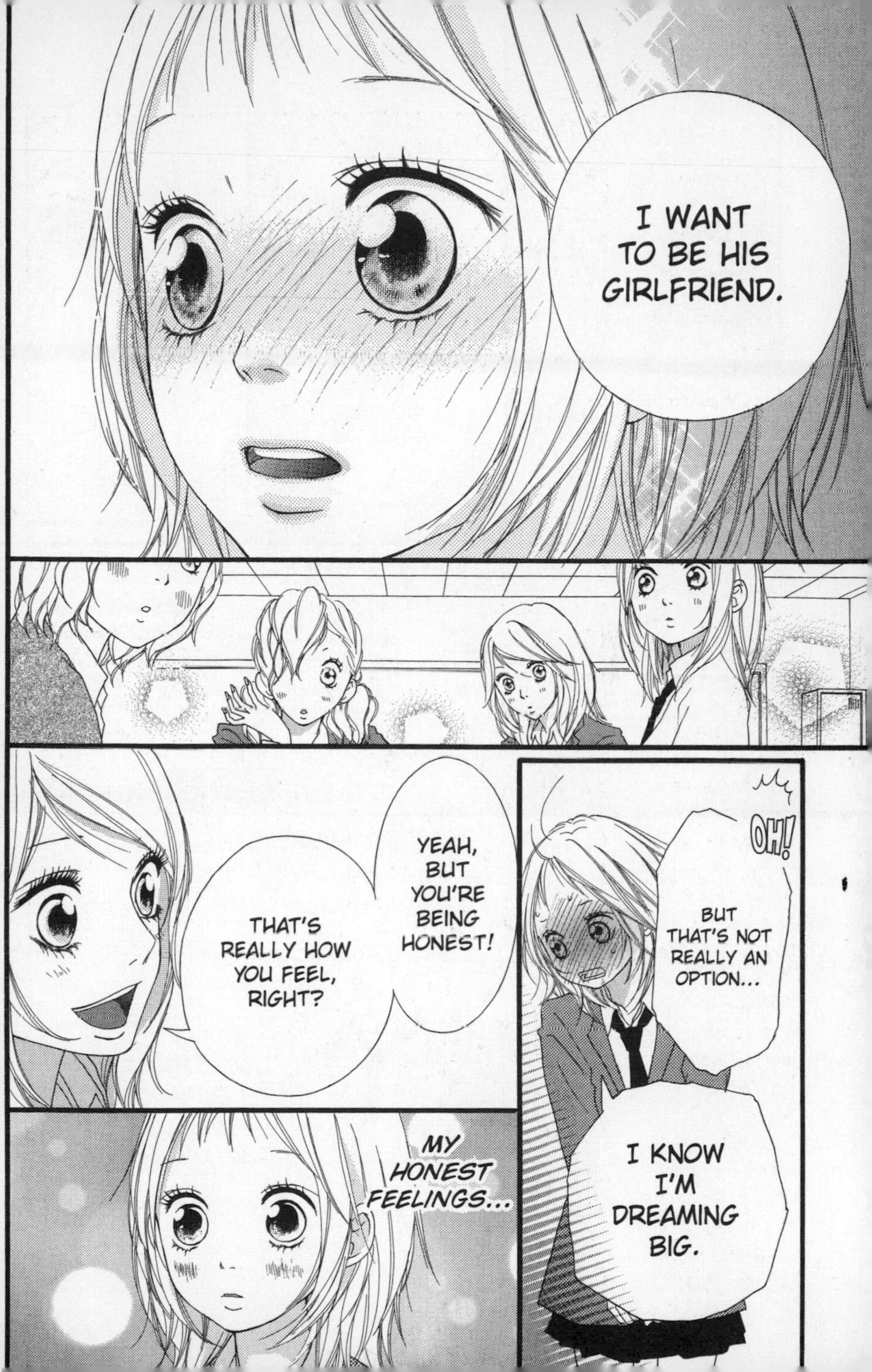
I WANT TO BE HIS GIRLFRIEND.
OH!
BUT THAT'S NOT REALLY AN OPTION...
I KNOW I'M DREAMING BIG.
YEAH, BUT YOU'RE BEING HONEST!
THAT'S REALLY HOW YOU FEEL, RIGHT?
MY HONEST FEELINGS...

When you guys write to me, a lot of you ask what *Strobe Edge's* title means, so I'm going to explain it now!

I started out looking for a word that would describe the sensation of being in love. What came to mind was that strong flash of light in photography—strobe light. It seemed like a good image of that powerful, bright, and sometimes stabbing sensation of being in love.

And then, for that "strobe" to pierce the heart, it has to be sharp, right? So I added the word "edge," with all of its meanings—blade, rim, end... I felt like it was perfect to describe that feeling of being cut into, as well as how instantaneously the feelings can strike you.

That's why I think it's the perfect title! It summons up an image of a bright, intense moment.

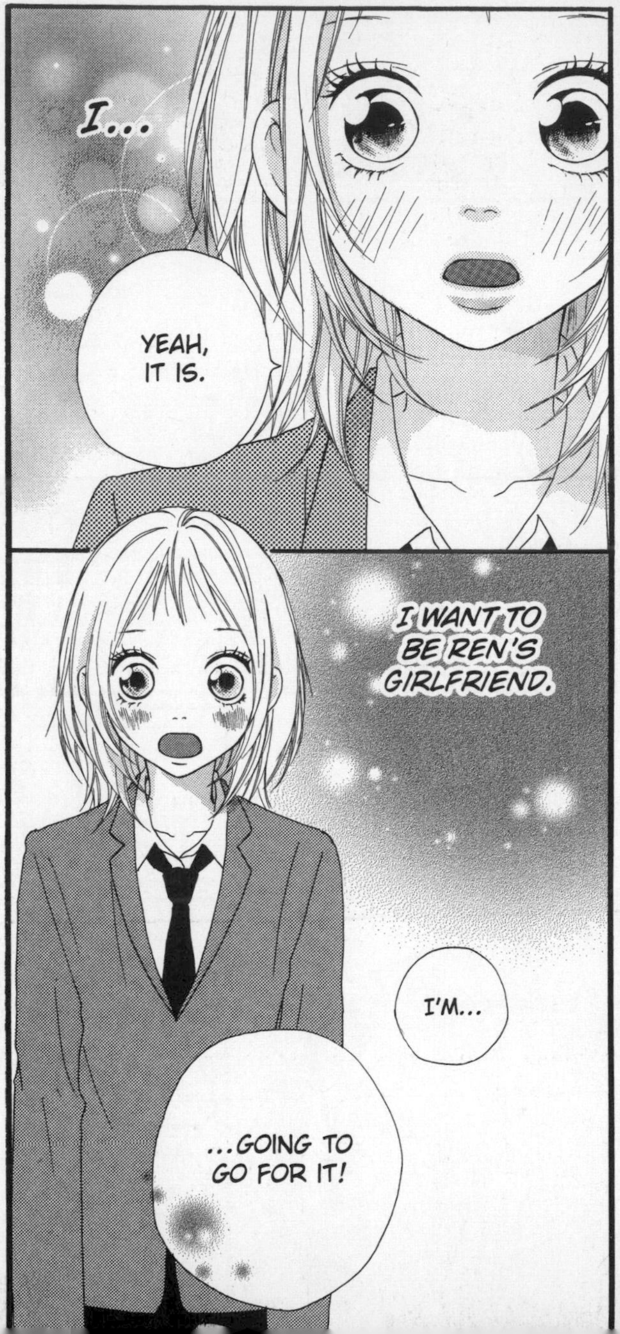
I...
YEAH, IT IS.
I WANT TO BE REN'S GIRLFRIEND.
I'M...
...GOING TO GO FOR IT!

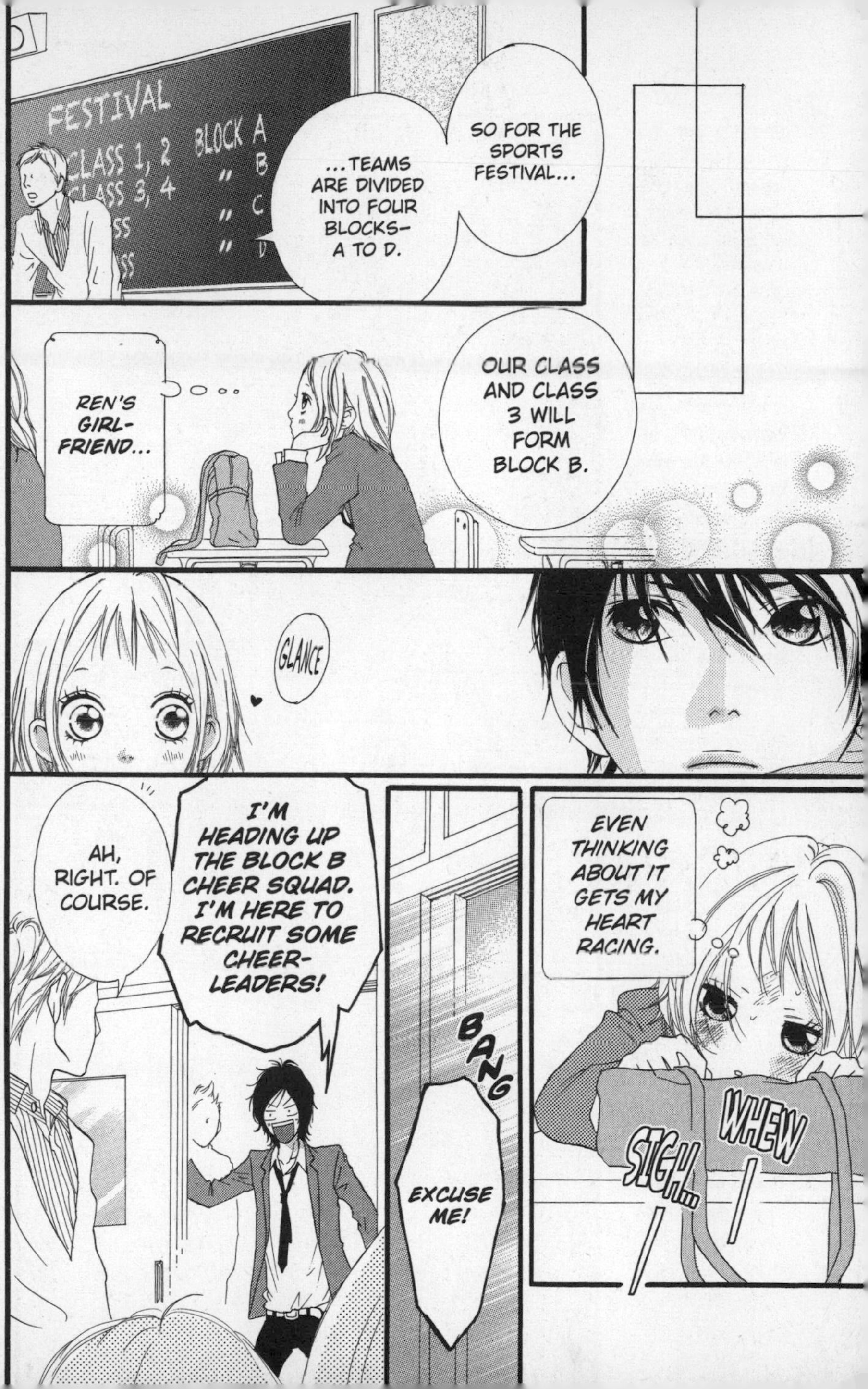
FESTIVAL
CLASS 1, 2 BLOCK A
CLASS 3, 4 " B
SO FOR THE SPORTS FESTIVAL...
...TEAMS ARE DIVIDED INTO FOUR BLOCKS– A TO D.
OUR CLASS AND CLASS 3 WILL FORM BLOCK B.
REN'S GIRL-FRIEND...
GLANCE
EVEN THINKING ABOUT IT GETS MY HEART RACING.
WHEW
SIGH...
BANG
EXCUSE ME!
I'M HEADING UP THE BLOCK B CHEER SQUAD. I'M HERE TO RECRUIT SOME CHEER-LEADERS!
AH, RIGHT. OF COURSE.

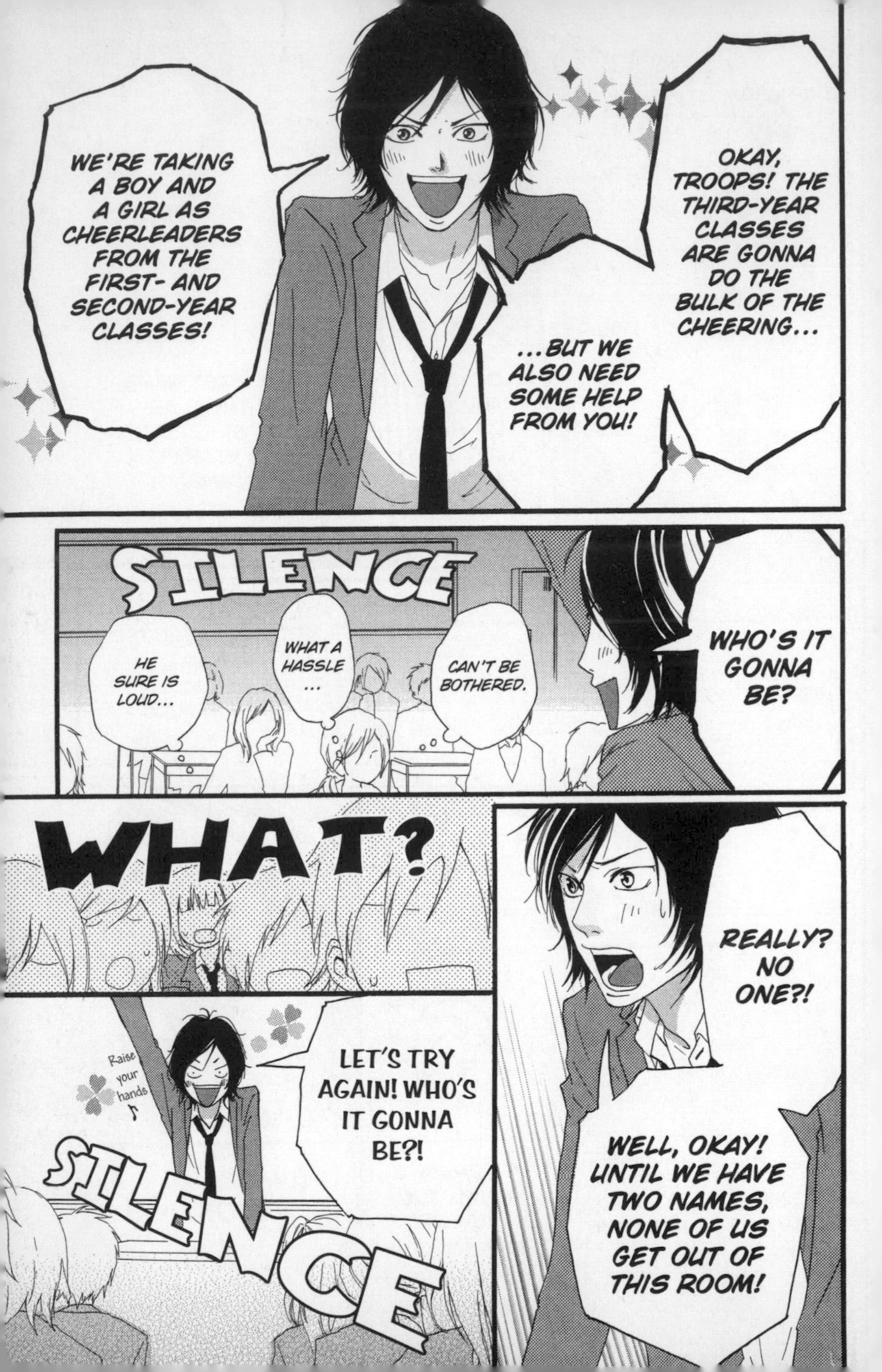
OKAY, TROOPS! THE THIRD-YEAR CLASSES ARE GONNA DO THE BULK OF THE CHEERING...
...BUT WE ALSO NEED SOME HELP FROM YOU!
WE'RE TAKING A BOY AND A GIRL AS CHEERLEADERS FROM THE FIRST- AND SECOND-YEAR CLASSES!
WHO'S IT GONNA BE?
SILENCE
CAN'T BE BOTHERED.
WHAT A HASSLE ...
HE SURE IS LOUD...
REALLY? NO ONE?!
WELL, OKAY! UNTIL WE HAVE TWO NAMES, NONE OF US GET OUT OF THIS ROOM!
WHAT?
LET'S TRY AGAIN! WHO'S IT GONNA BE?!
Raise your hands ♪
SILENCE

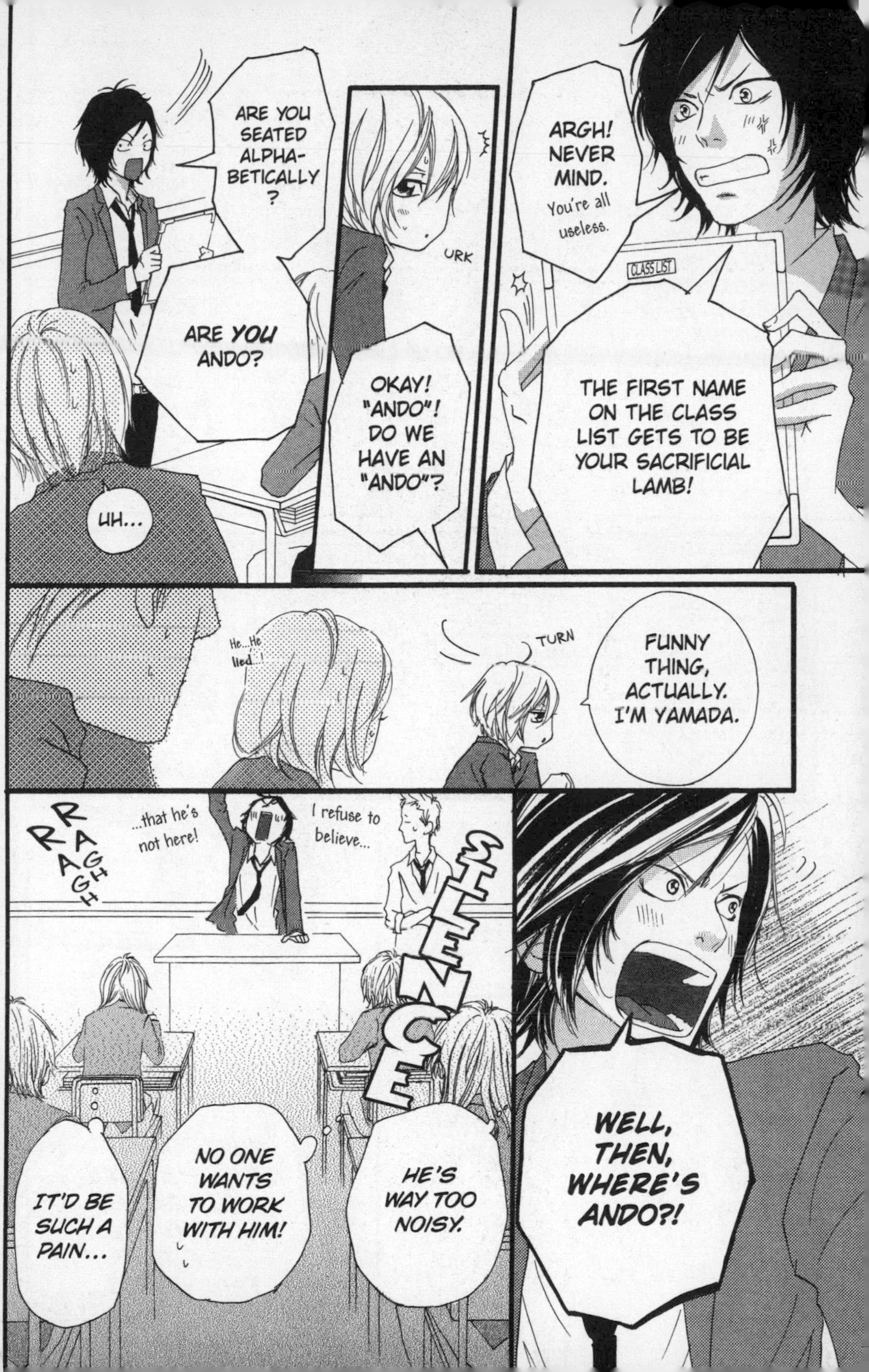
ARGH! NEVER MIND.
You're all useless.
CLASS LIST
THE FIRST NAME ON THE CLASS LIST GETS TO BE YOUR SACRIFICIAL LAMB!
URK
OKAY! "ANDO"! DO WE HAVE AN "ANDO"?
ARE YOU SEATED ALPHA-BETICALLY?
ARE YOU ANDO?
UH...
FUNNY THING, ACTUALLY. I'M YAMADA.
TURN
He...He lied...!
WELL, THEN, WHERE'S ANDO?!
SILENCE
I refuse to believe...
...that he's not here!
RRAAGH
HE'S WAY TOO NOISY.
NO ONE WANTS TO WORK WITH HIM!
IT'D BE SUCH A PAIN...

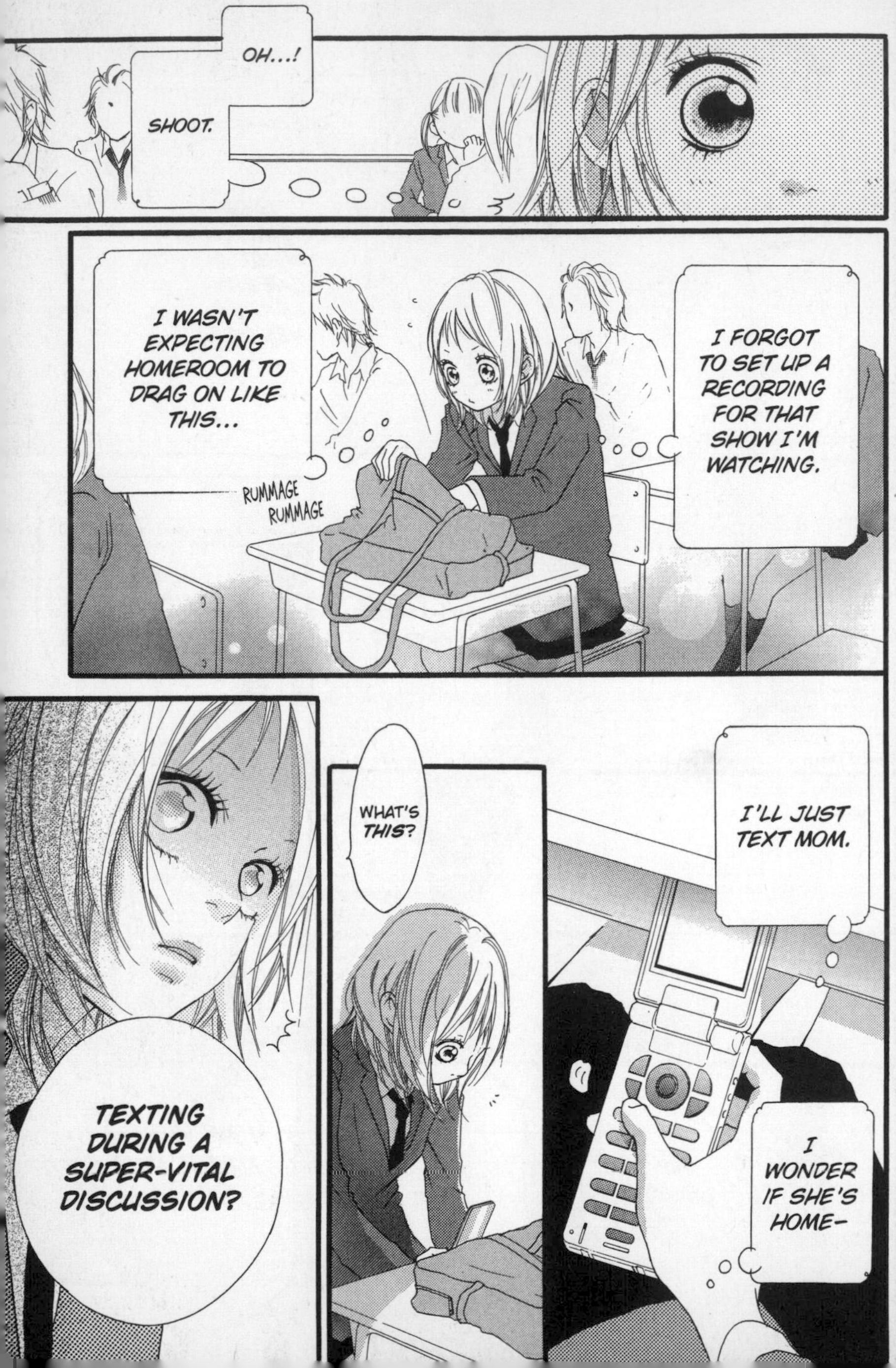
OH...!
SHOOT.
I FORGOT TO SET UP A RECORDING FOR THAT SHOW I'M WATCHING.
I WASN'T EXPECTING HOMEROOM TO DRAG ON LIKE THIS...
RUMMAGE RUMMAGE
I'LL JUST TEXT MOM.
I WONDER IF SHE'S HOME—
WHAT'S THIS?
TEXTING DURING A SUPER-VITAL DISCUSSION?

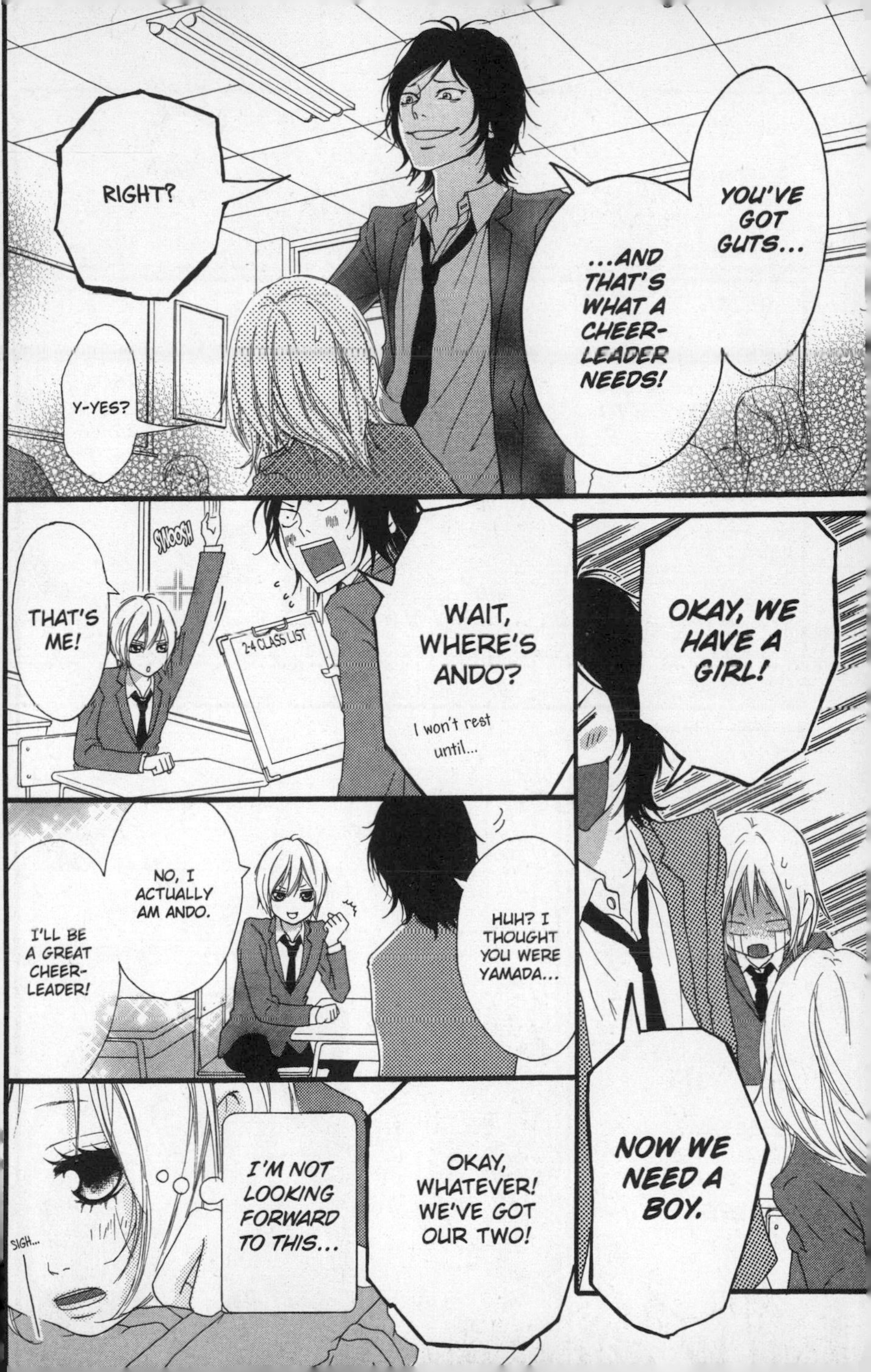
YOU'VE GOT GUTS...
...AND THAT'S WHAT A CHEER-LEADER NEEDS!
RIGHT?
Y-YES?
OKAY, WE HAVE A GIRL!
NOW WE NEED A BOY.
WAIT, WHERE'S ANDO?
I won't rest until...
2-4 CLASS LIST
SWOOSH
THAT'S ME!
HUH? I THOUGHT YOU WERE YAMADA...
NO, I ACTUALLY AM ANDO.
I'LL BE A GREAT CHEER-LEADER!
OKAY, WHATEVER! WE'VE GOT OUR TWO!
I'M NOT LOOKING FORWARD TO THIS...
SIGH...

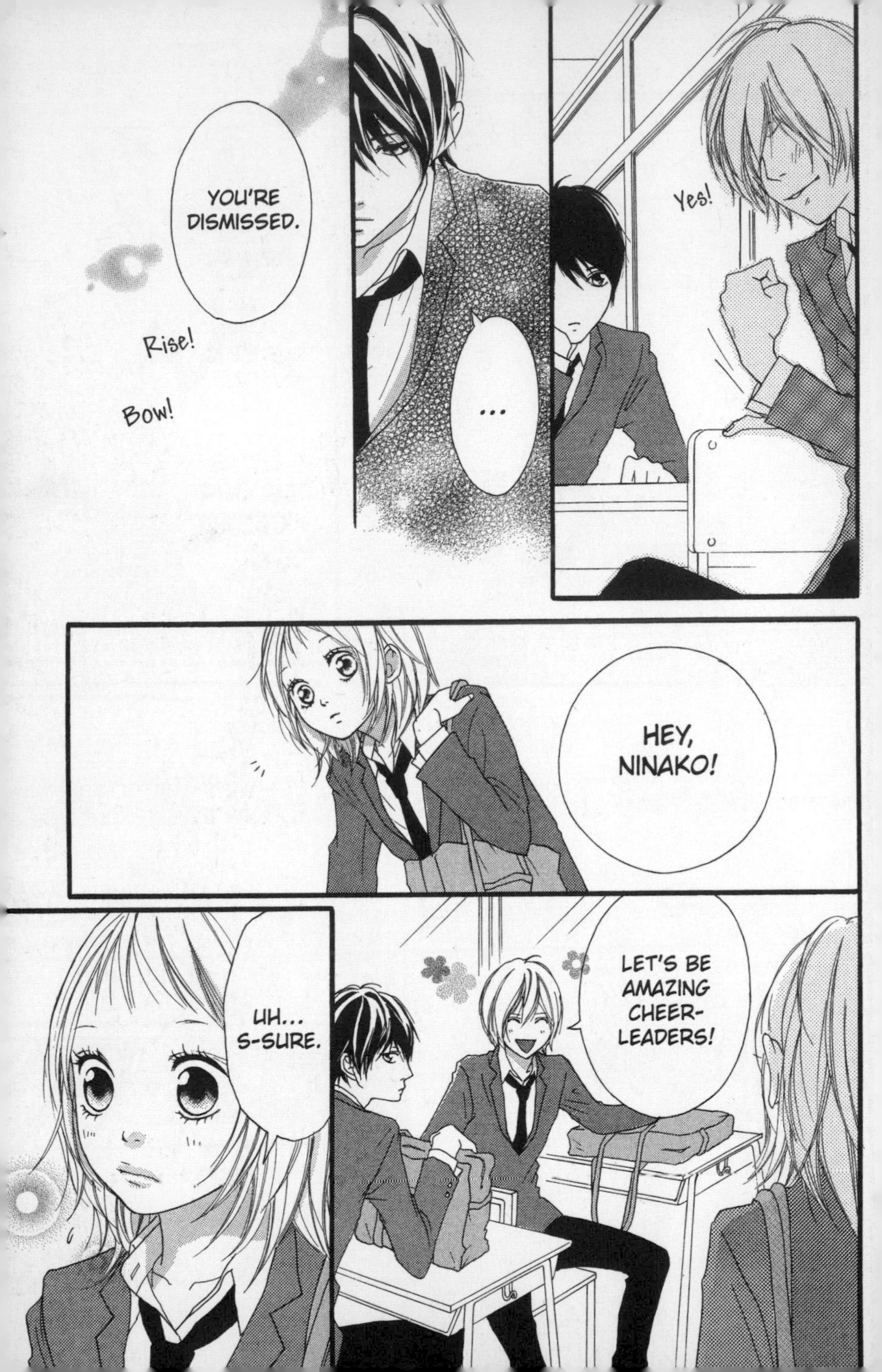
Yes!
...
YOU'RE DISMISSED.
Rise!
Bow!
HEY, NINAKO!
LET'S BE AMAZING CHEER-LEADERS!
UH... S-SURE.

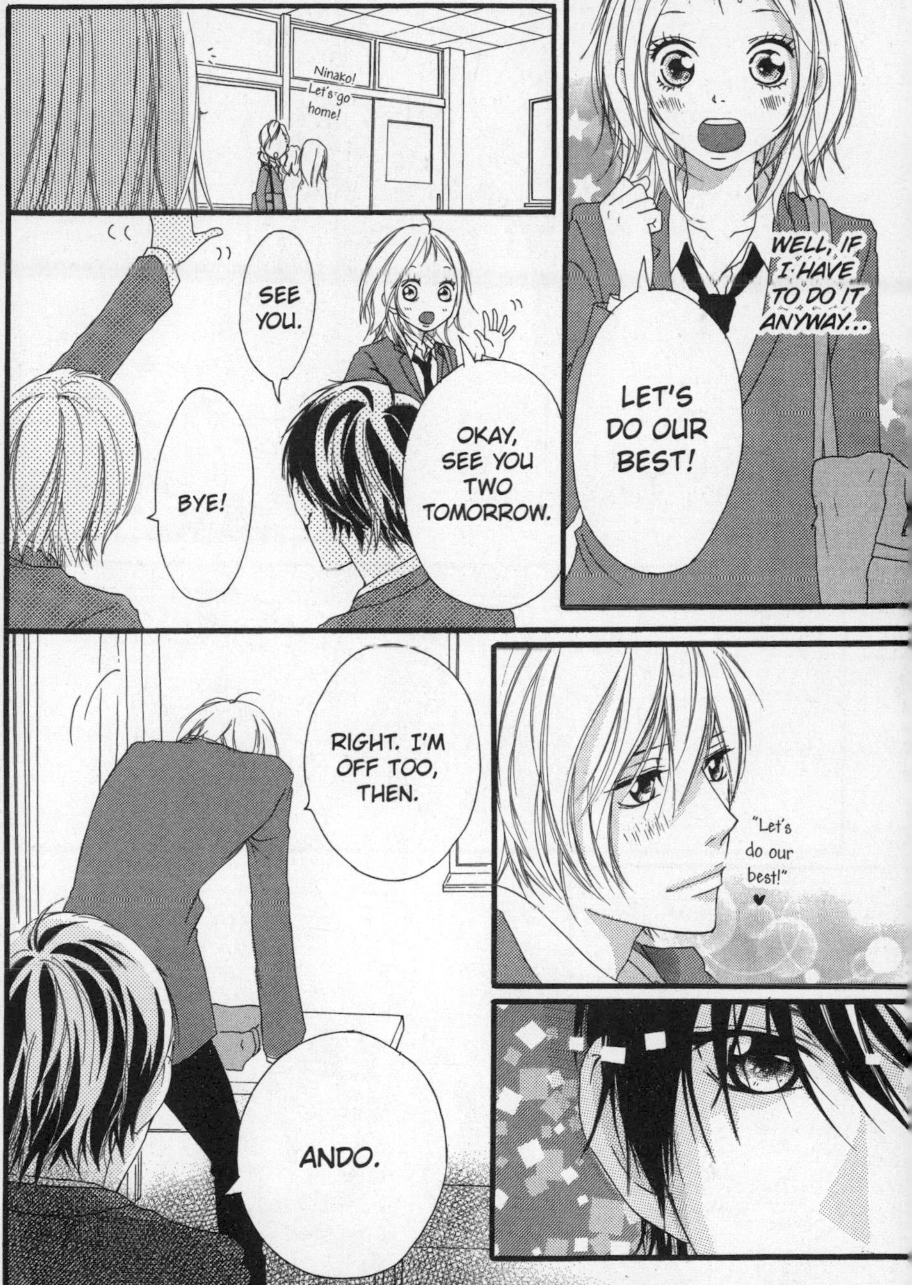
WELL, IF I HAVE TO DO IT ANYWAY...
LET'S DO OUR BEST!
Ninako! Let's go home!
OKAY, SEE YOU TWO TOMORROW.
SEE YOU.
BYE!
"Let's do our best!" ♥
RIGHT. I'M OFF TOO, THEN.
ANDO.

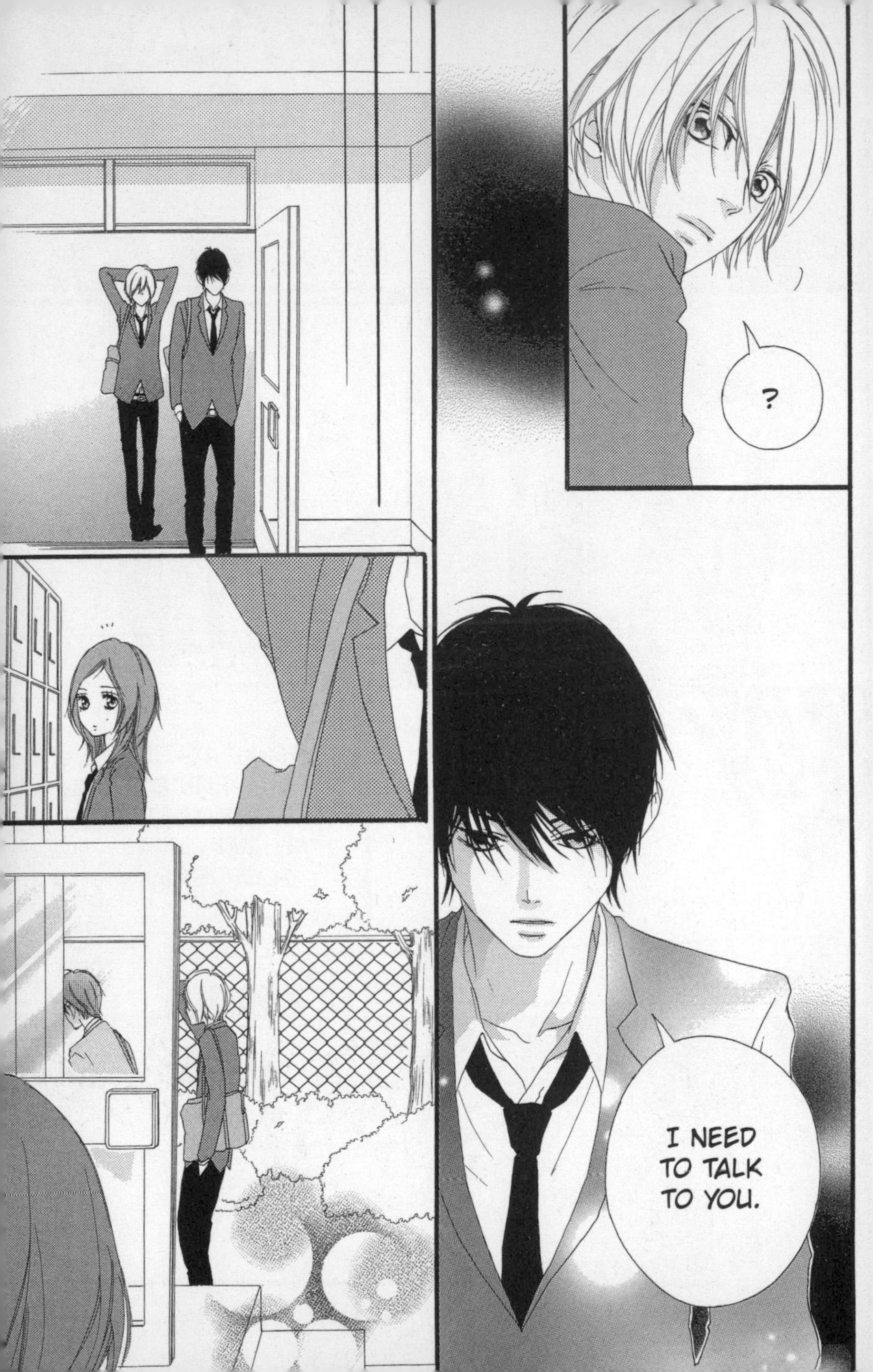
?
I NEED TO TALK TO YOU.

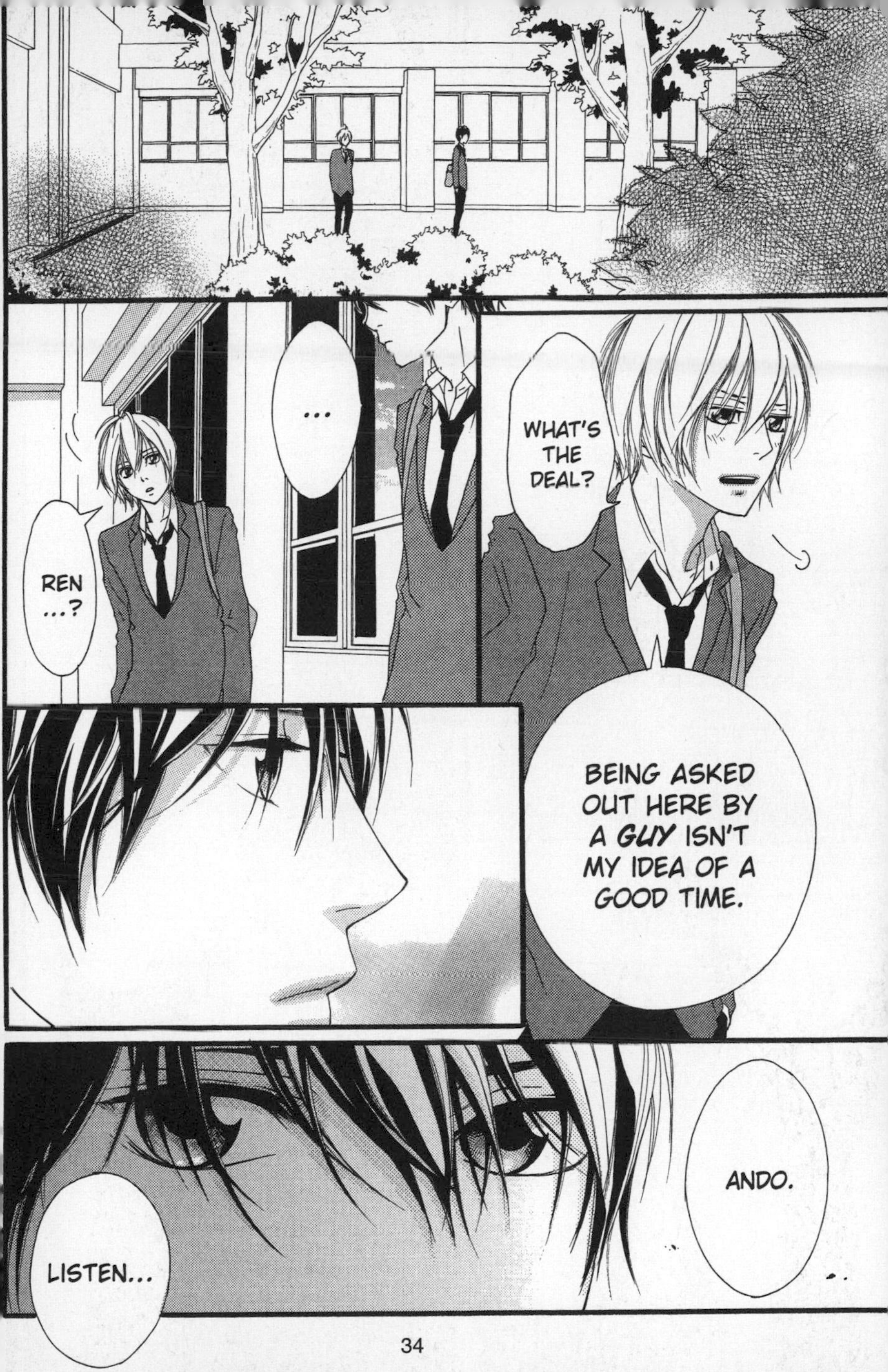
WHAT'S THE DEAL?
...
REN ...?
BEING ASKED OUT HERE BY A *GUY* ISN'T MY IDEA OF A GOOD TIME.
ANDO.
LISTEN...

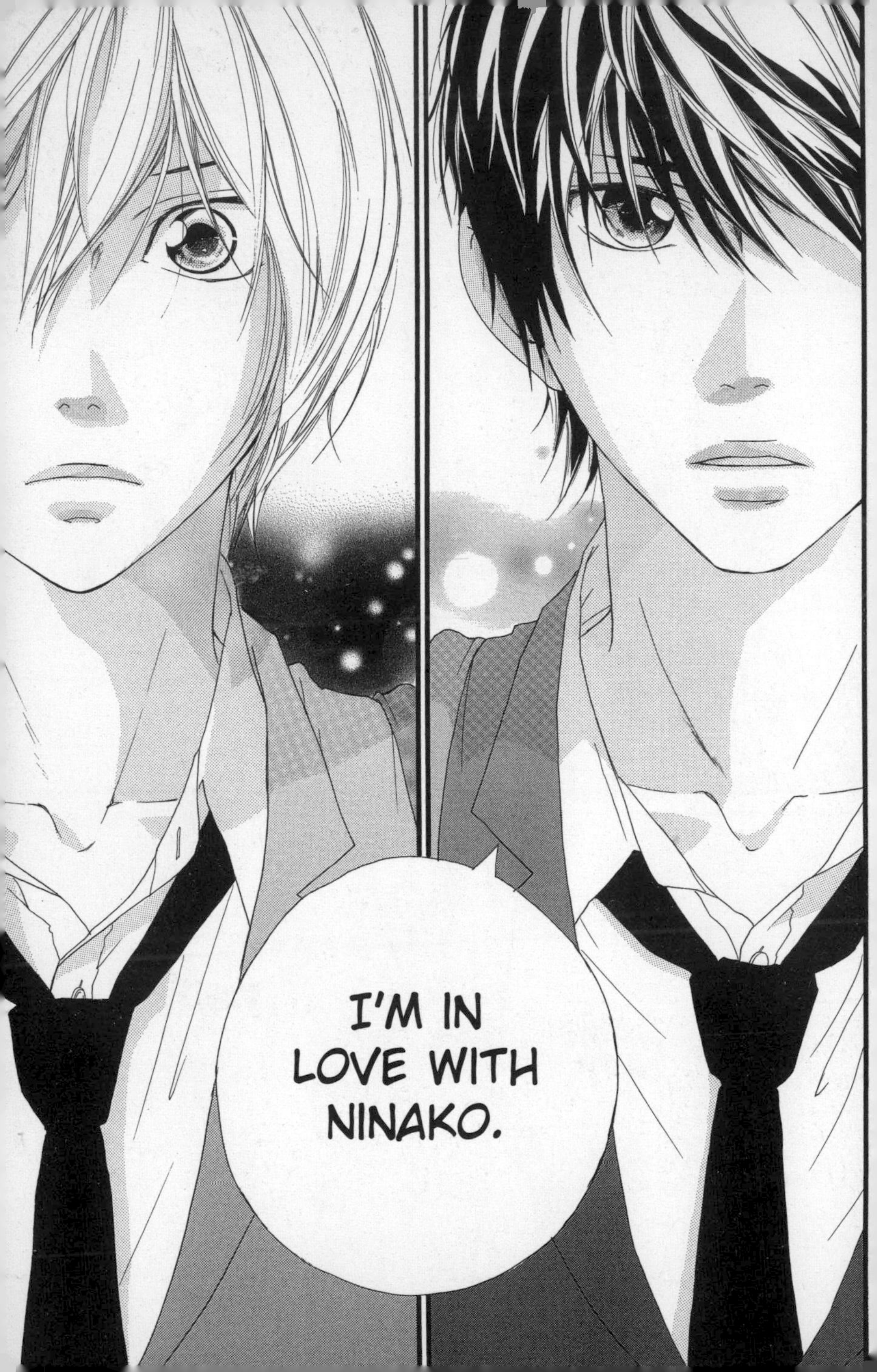
I'M IN LOVE WITH NINAKO.

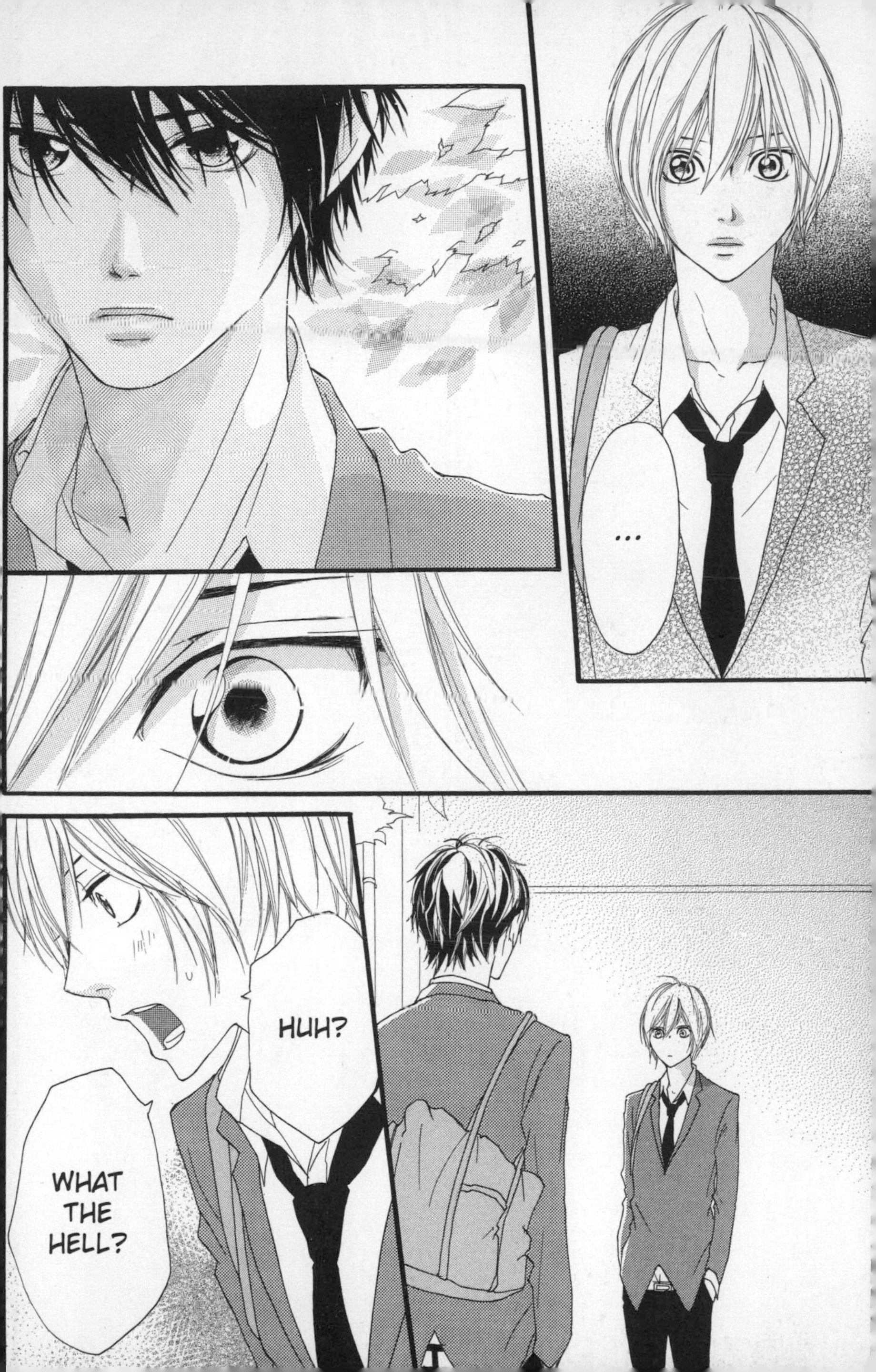
...
HUH?
WHAT THE HELL?

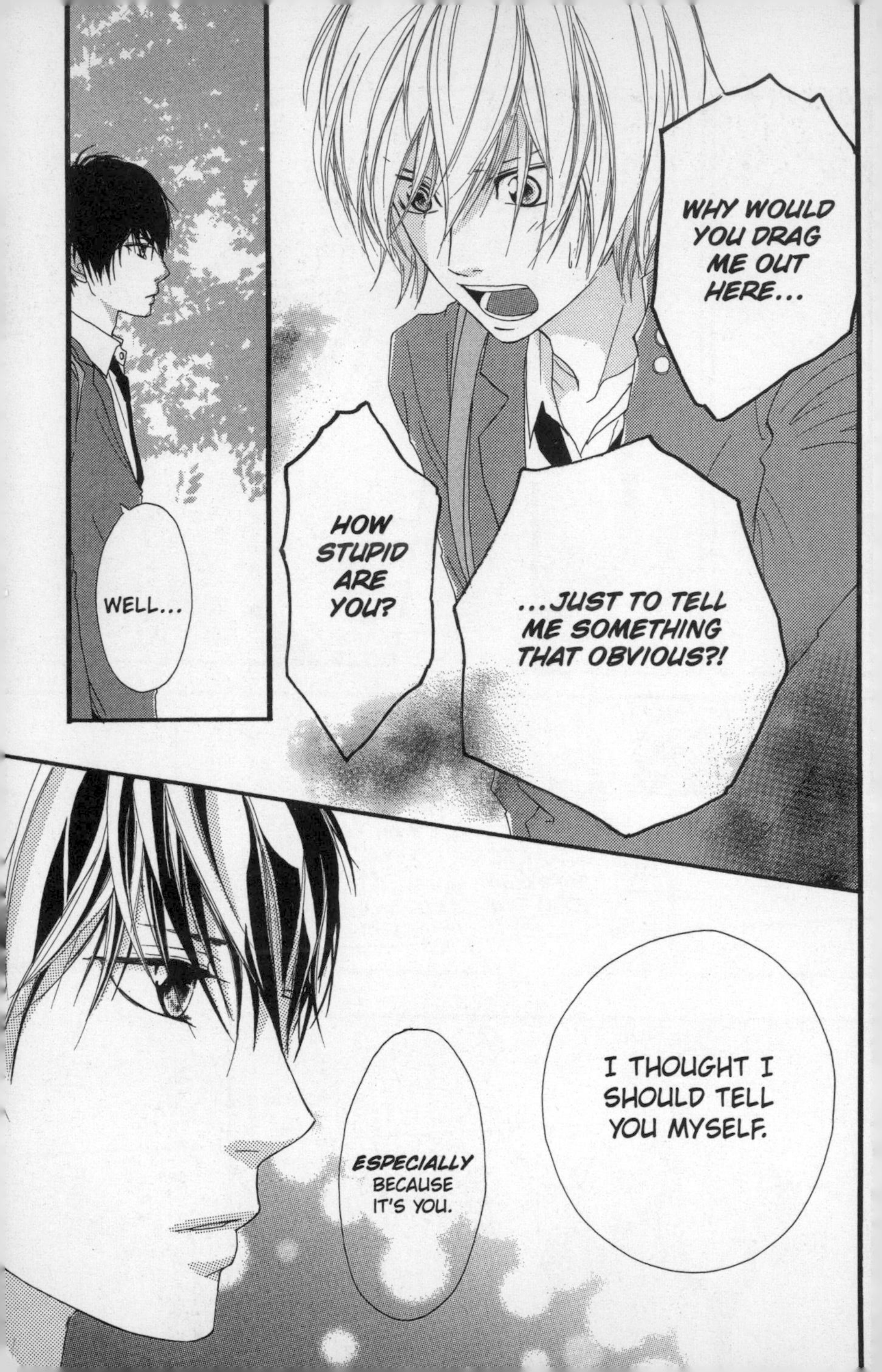
WHY WOULD YOU DRAG ME OUT HERE...
...JUST TO TELL ME SOMETHING THAT OBVIOUS?!
HOW STUPID ARE YOU?
WELL...
I THOUGHT I SHOULD TELL YOU MYSELF.
ESPECIALLY BECAUSE IT'S YOU.

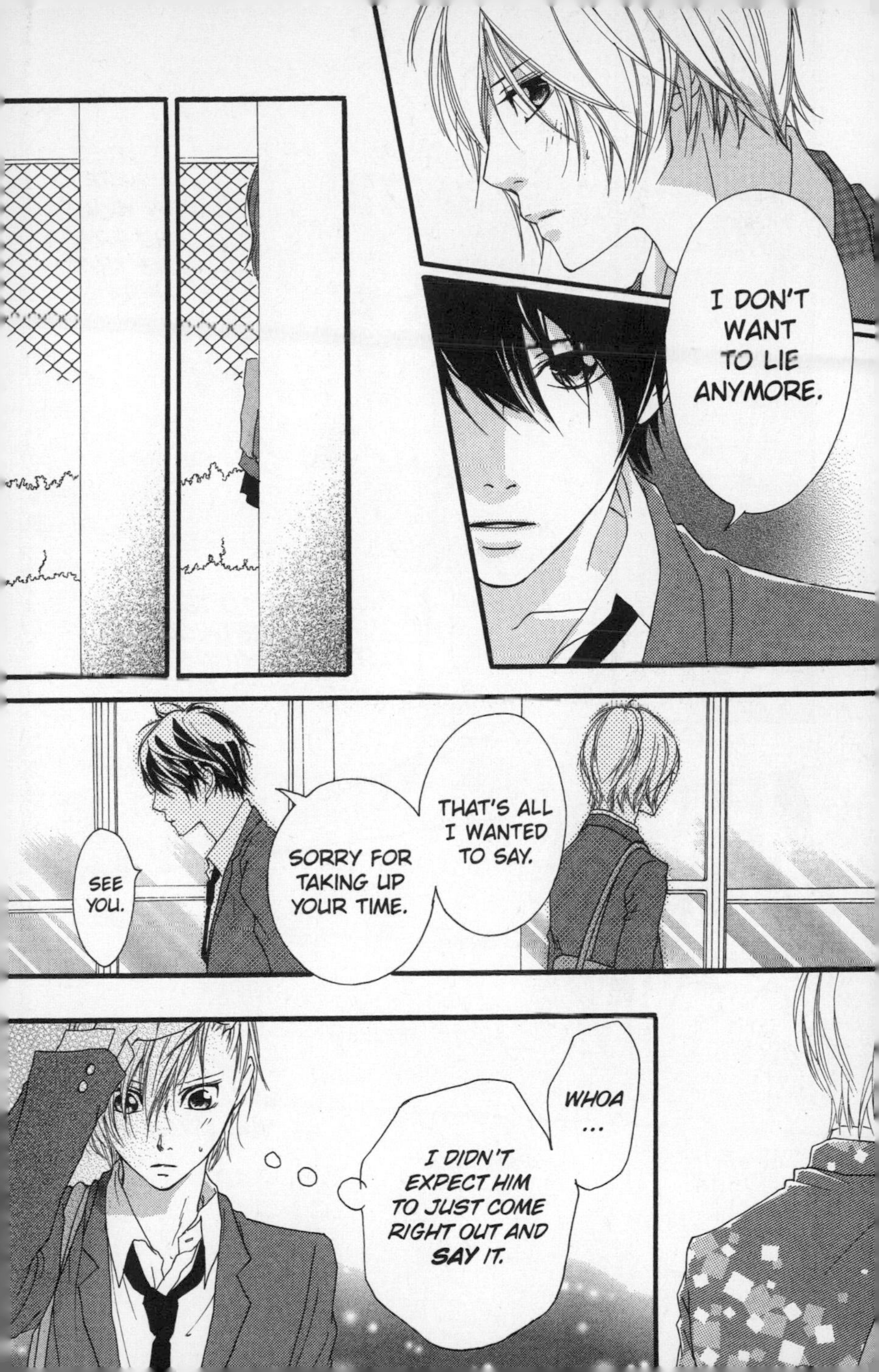
I DON'T WANT TO LIE ANYMORE.
THAT'S ALL I WANTED TO SAY.
SORRY FOR TAKING UP YOUR TIME.
SEE YOU.
WHOA ...
I DIDN'T EXPECT HIM TO JUST COME RIGHT OUT AND SAY IT.

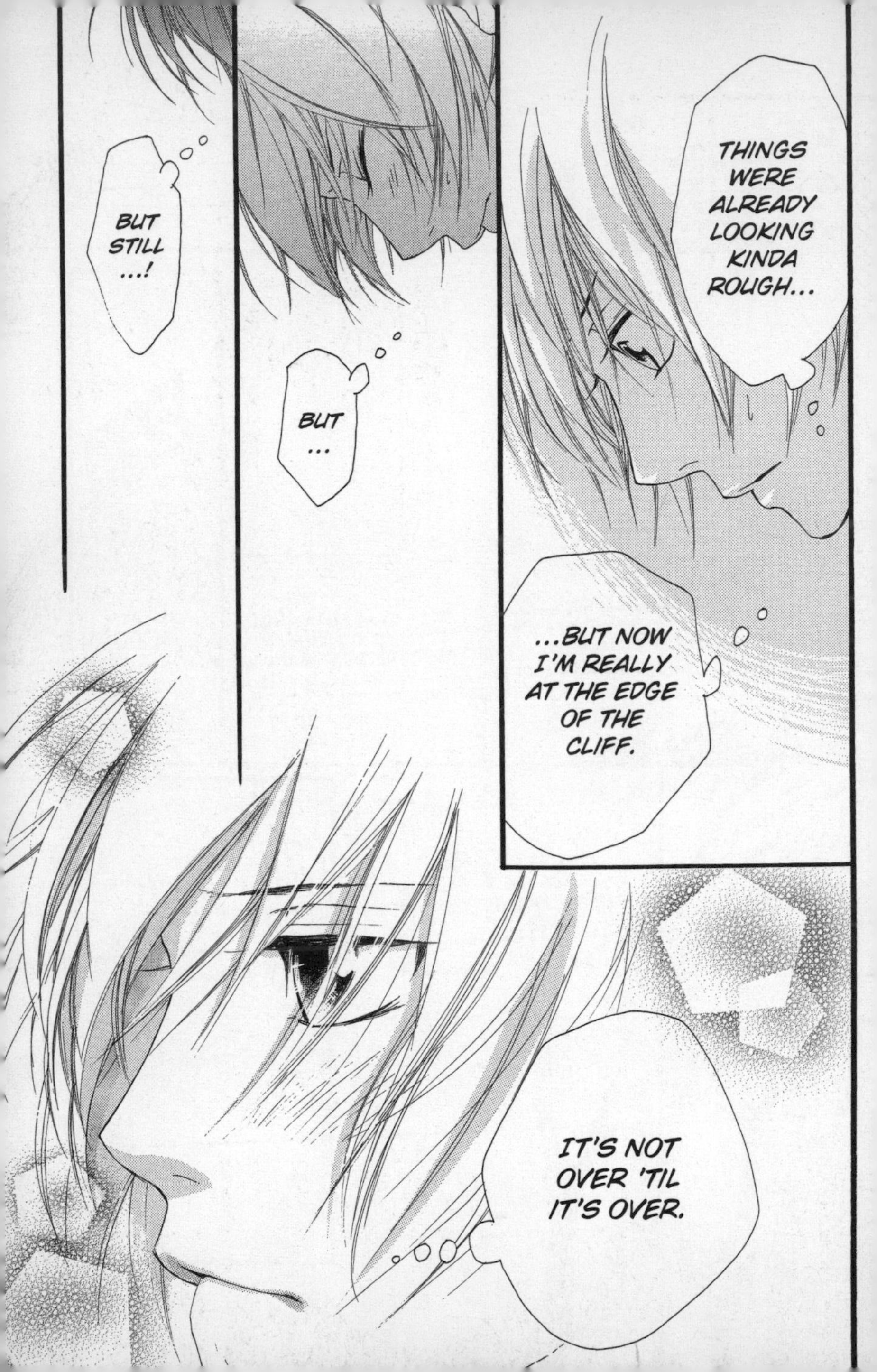
THINGS WERE ALREADY LOOKING KINDA ROUGH...
...BUT NOW I'M REALLY AT THE EDGE OF THE CLIFF.
BUT ...
BUT STILL ...!
IT'S NOT OVER 'TIL IT'S OVER.

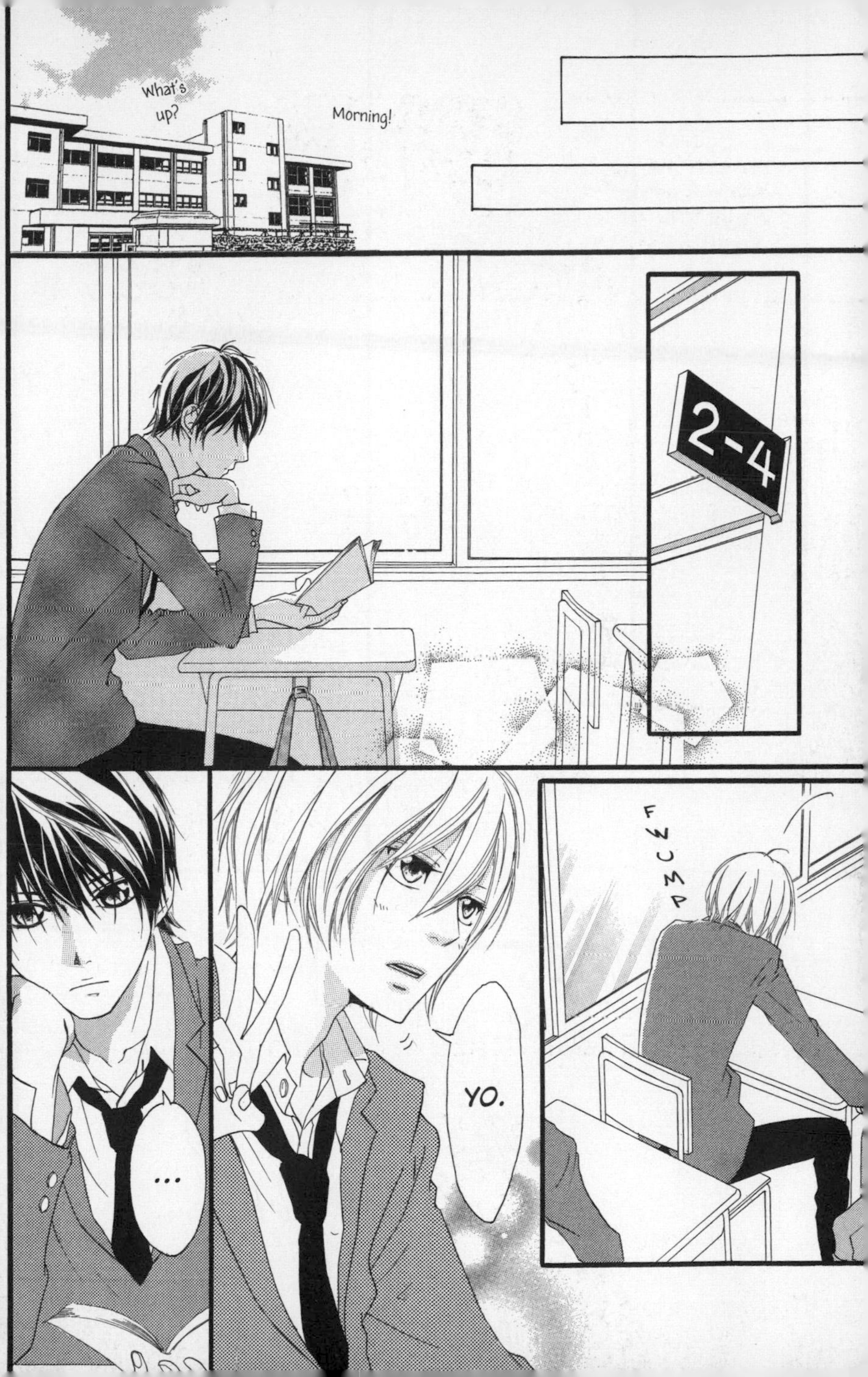
Morning!
What's up?
2-4
FWUMP
YO.
...

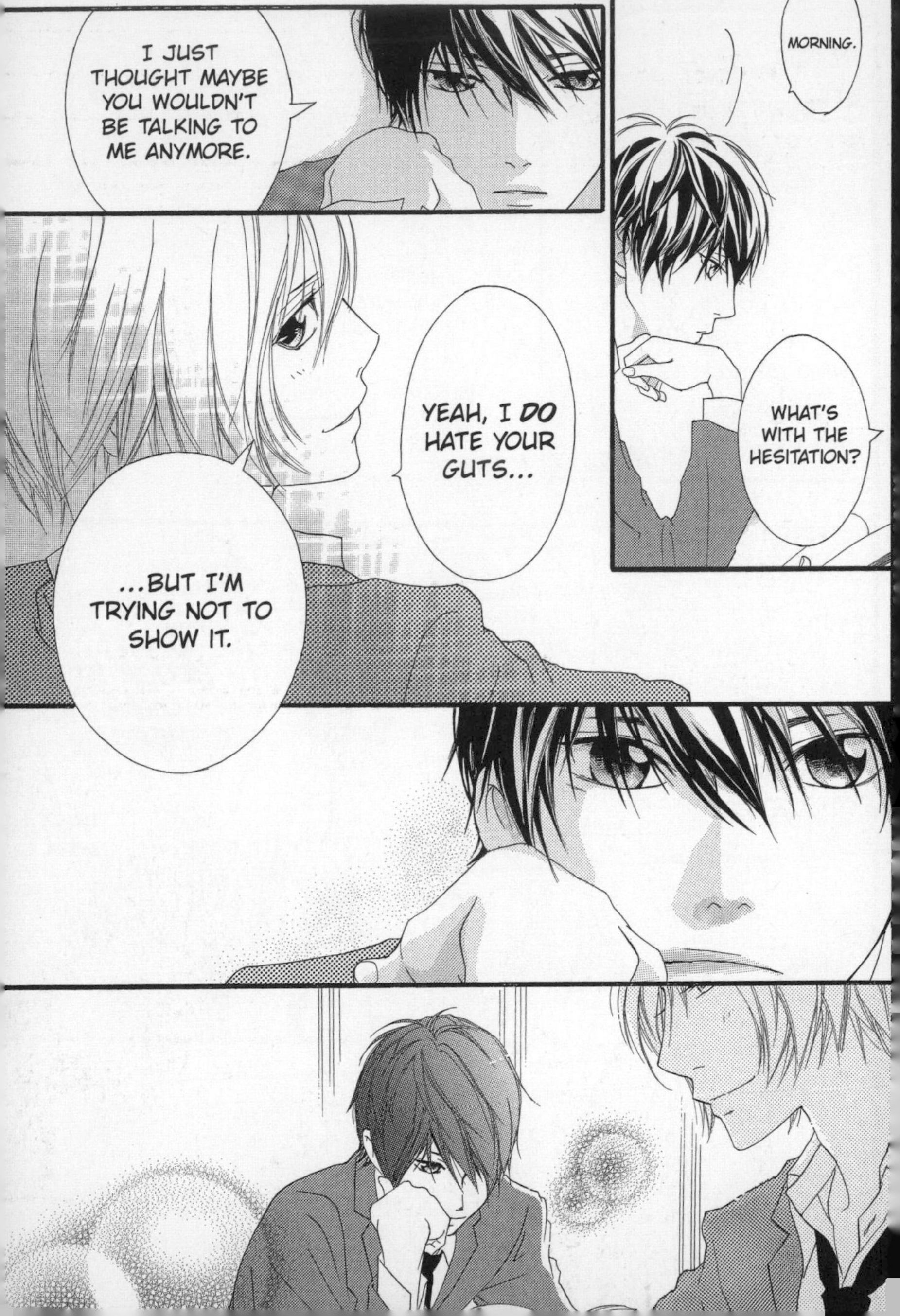
MORNING.
WHAT'S WITH THE HESITATION?
I JUST THOUGHT MAYBE YOU WOULDN'T BE TALKING TO ME ANYMORE.
YEAH, I *DO* HATE YOUR GUTS...
...BUT I'M TRYING NOT TO SHOW IT.

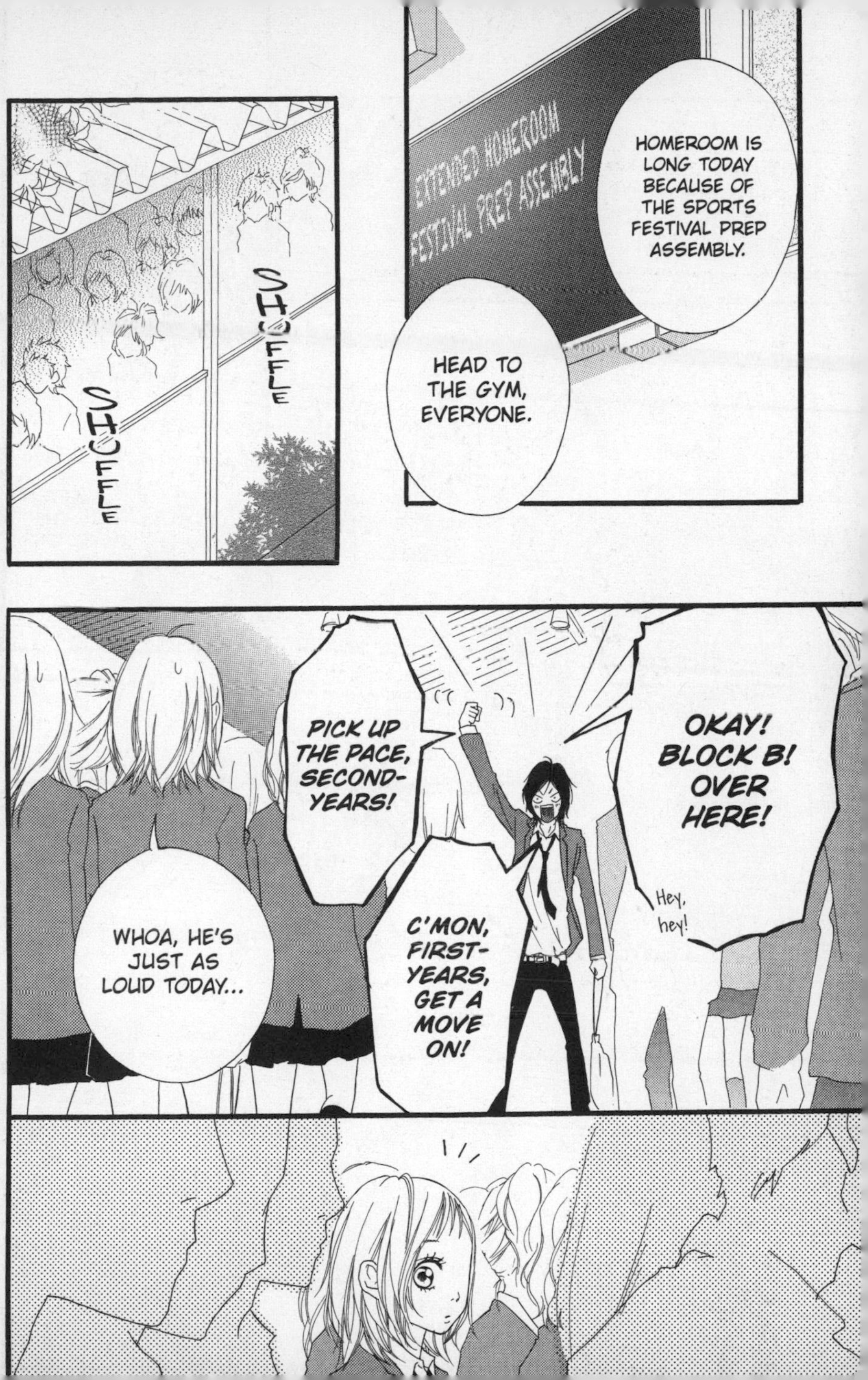
EXTENDED HOMEROOM
FESTIVAL PREP ASSEMBLY
HOMEROOM IS LONG TODAY BECAUSE OF THE SPORTS FESTIVAL PREP ASSEMBLY.
HEAD TO THE GYM, EVERYONE.
SHUFFLE
SHUFFLE
OKAY! BLOCK B! OVER HERE!
Hey, hey!
PICK UP THE PACE, SECOND-YEARS!
C'MON, FIRST-YEARS, GET A MOVE ON!
WHOA, HE'S JUST AS LOUD TODAY...

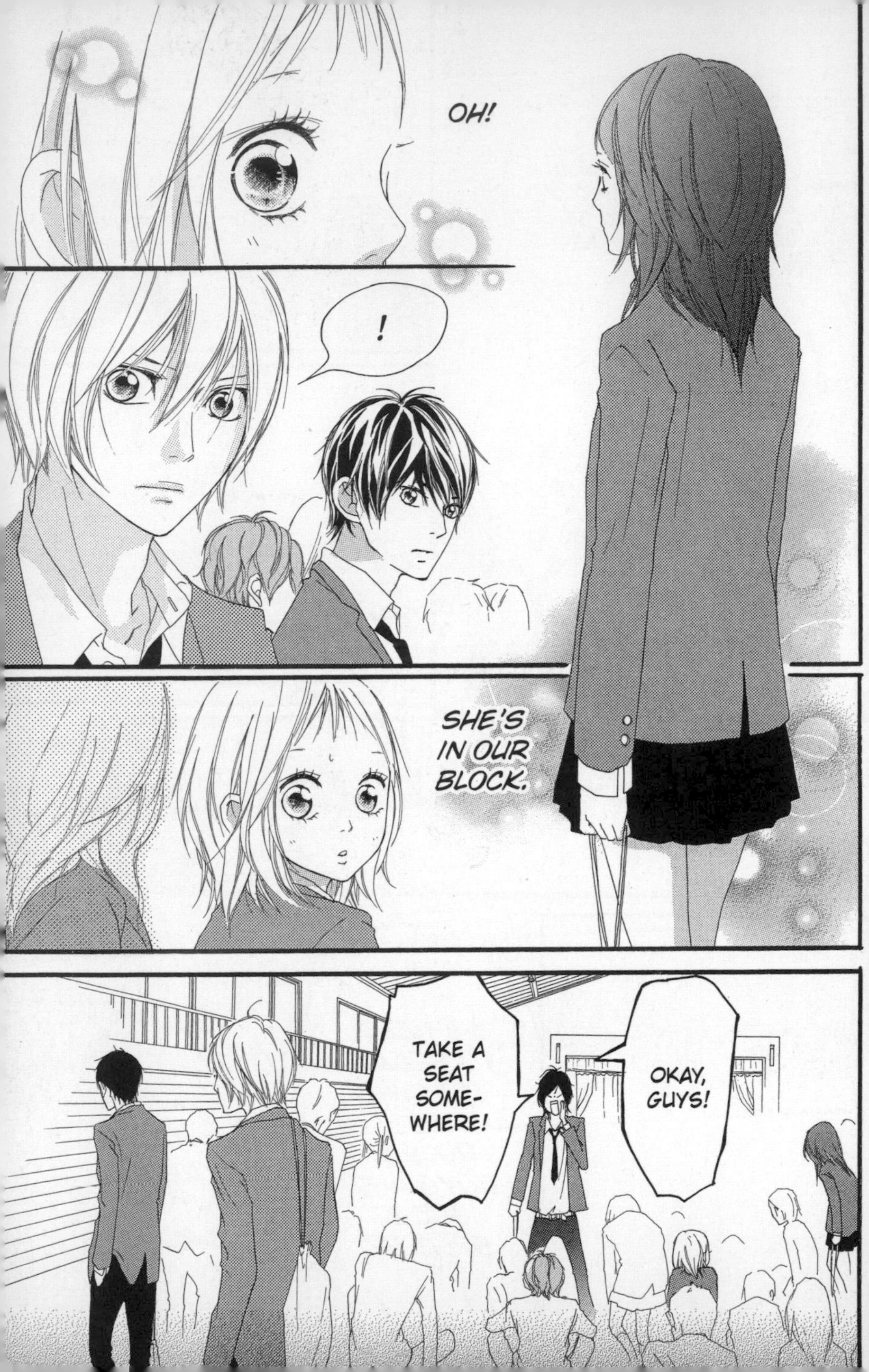
OH!
!
SHE'S IN OUR BLOCK.
OKAY, GUYS!
TAKE A SEAT SOME-WHERE!

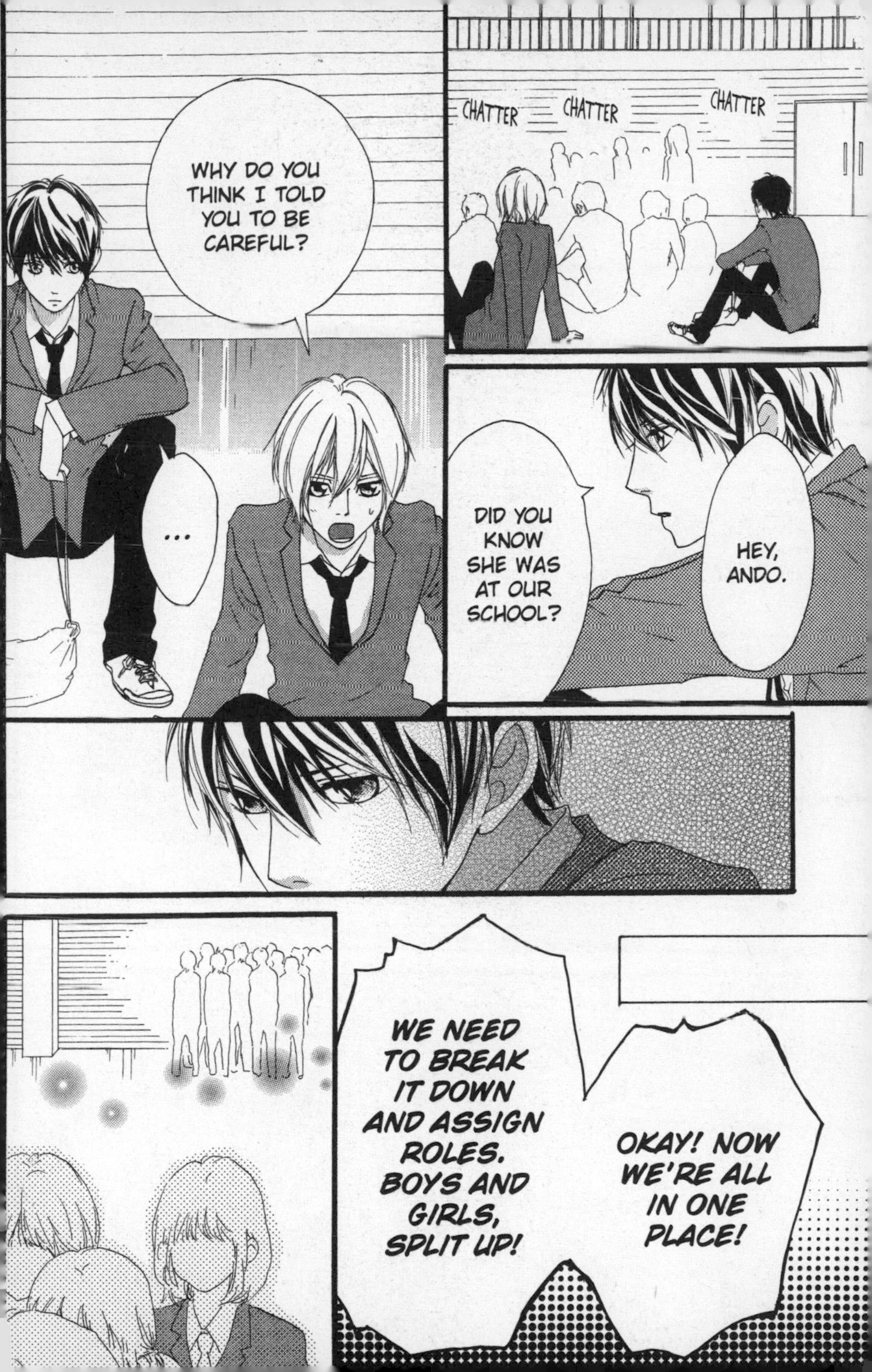
CHATTER
CHATTER
CHATTER
HEY, ANDO.
DID YOU KNOW SHE WAS AT OUR SCHOOL?
WHY DO YOU THINK I TOLD YOU TO BE CAREFUL?
...
OKAY! NOW WE'RE ALL IN ONE PLACE!
WE NEED TO BREAK IT DOWN AND ASSIGN ROLES. BOYS AND GIRLS, SPLIT UP!

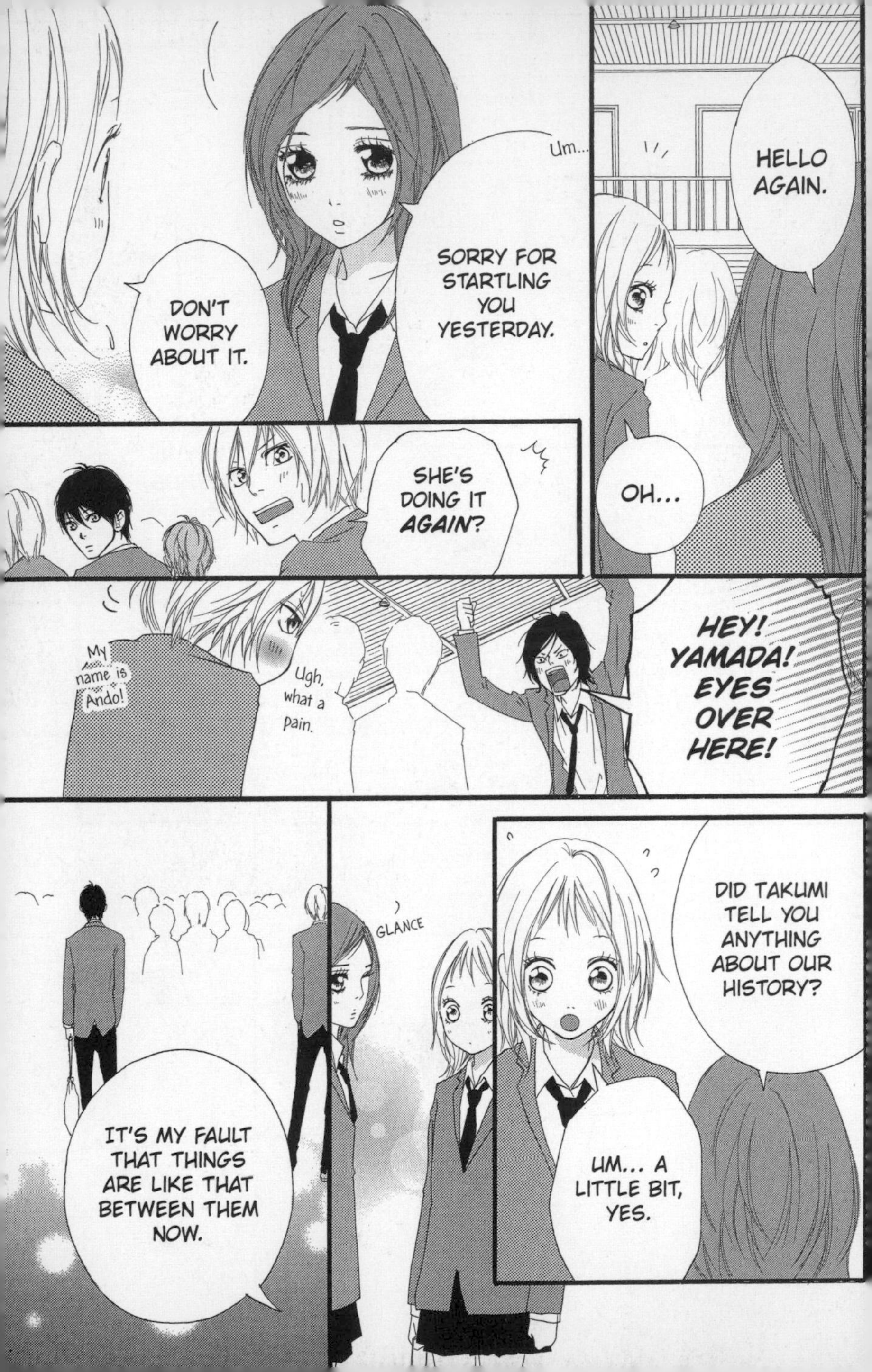
HELLO AGAIN.
OH...
Um...
SORRY FOR STARTLING YOU YESTERDAY.
DON'T WORRY ABOUT IT.
SHE'S DOING IT *AGAIN*?
HEY! YAMADA! EYES OVER HERE!
Ugh, what a pain.
My name is Ando!
DID TAKUMI TELL YOU ANYTHING ABOUT OUR HISTORY?
UM... A LITTLE BIT, YES.
GLANCE
IT'S MY FAULT THAT THINGS ARE LIKE THAT BETWEEN THEM NOW.

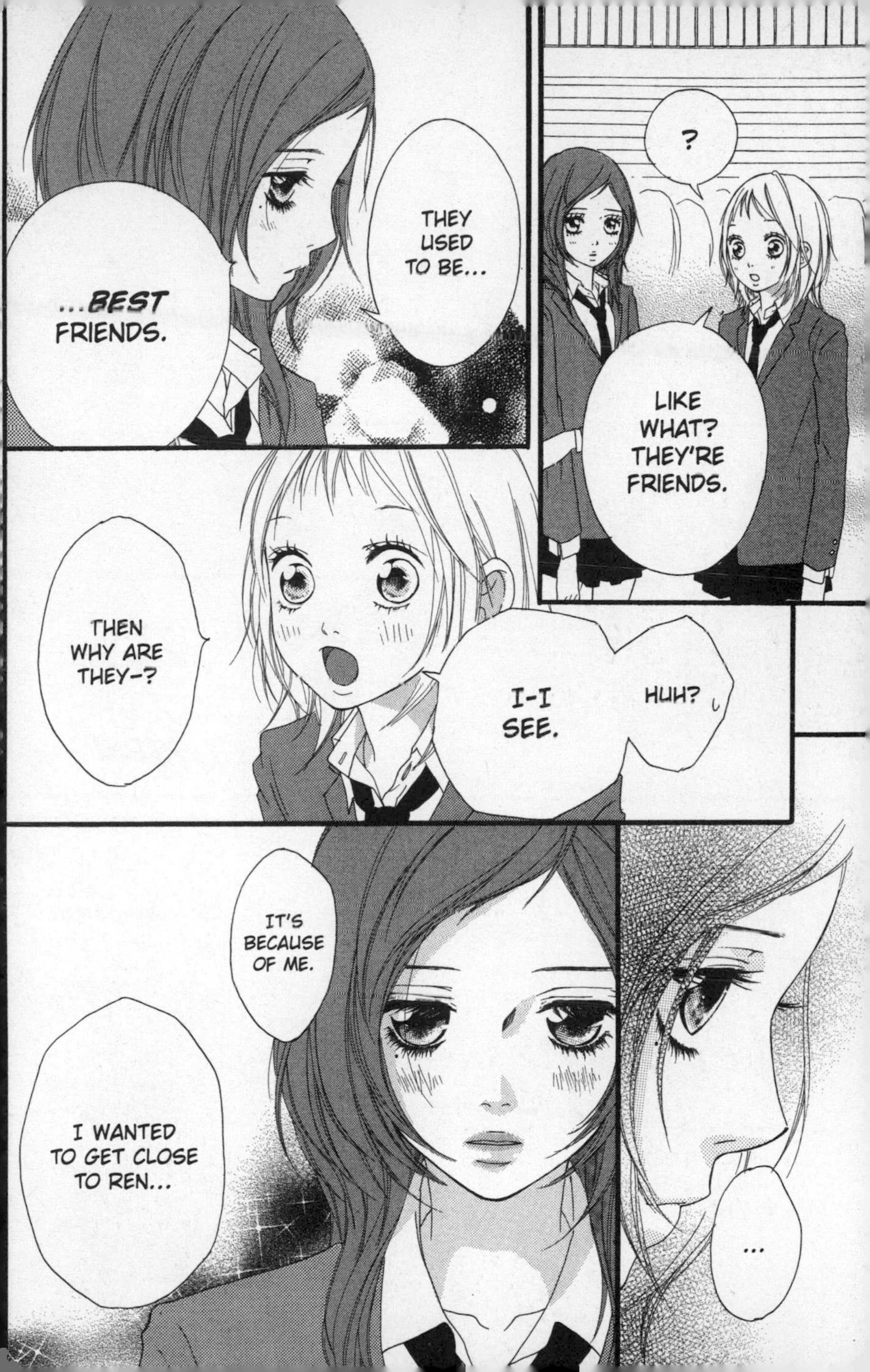
?
LIKE WHAT? THEY'RE FRIENDS.
THEY USED TO BE...
...BEST FRIENDS.
HUH?
I-I SEE.
THEN WHY ARE THEY-?
...
IT'S BECAUSE OF ME.
I WANTED TO GET CLOSE TO REN...

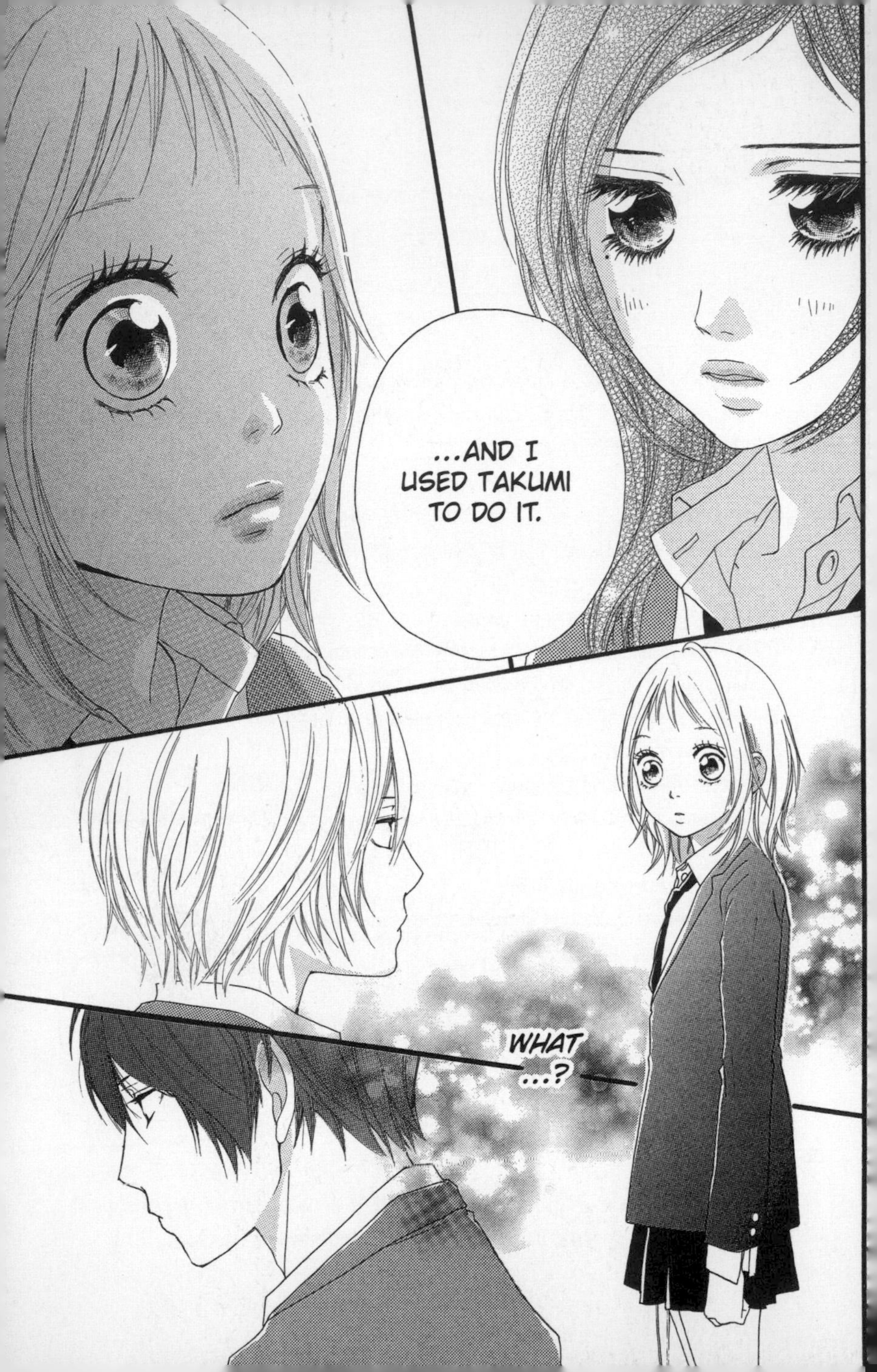
...AND I USED TAKUMI TO DO IT.
WHAT ...?

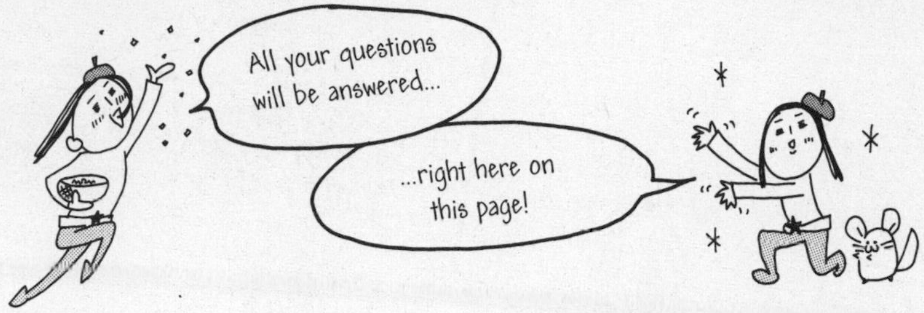
All your questions will be answered...
...right here on this page!

Different readers have asked me whether I'd take questions and answer them on these free pages. Since I already had some questions on hand from letters I'd received, I thought I'd start there!

Q: Which character is the easiest to draw in *Strobe Edge*?
A: Ando. He's a good boy in that he's easy to depict—both in terms of the actual drawing and of action.
Q: So far, which scene was your favorite to draw?
A: The school festival, and more recently, the school trip. I had such fun drawing all the kids having a good time. The incident with the Chihuahua is almost exactly what happened to a friend.
Q: Do you have a fetish?
A: Do I ever! The back of the neck. I'm convinced that it radiates pheromones, so I'm always looking at it. And that sounds kind of creepy. Sorry!
Q What kind of guys do you like?
A: Someone who is quiet but who sometimes does mysterious things.
Q: Share a memory of a past love?
A: I was supposed to go on a date, and I got stood up. I waited for three hours in the dead of winter, and as a result, I got sick and ended up with a 104 degree temperature. That was probably during my second year of high school.
Q: Are you in love?
A: Yes, I am—with all of you! ♡

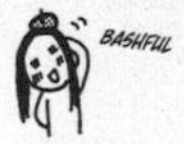
BASHFUL

If this Q & A makes me a little closer to you all, it would make me very happy. If there's anything else you'd like to know, please don't hesitate to ask! I'll be waiting!

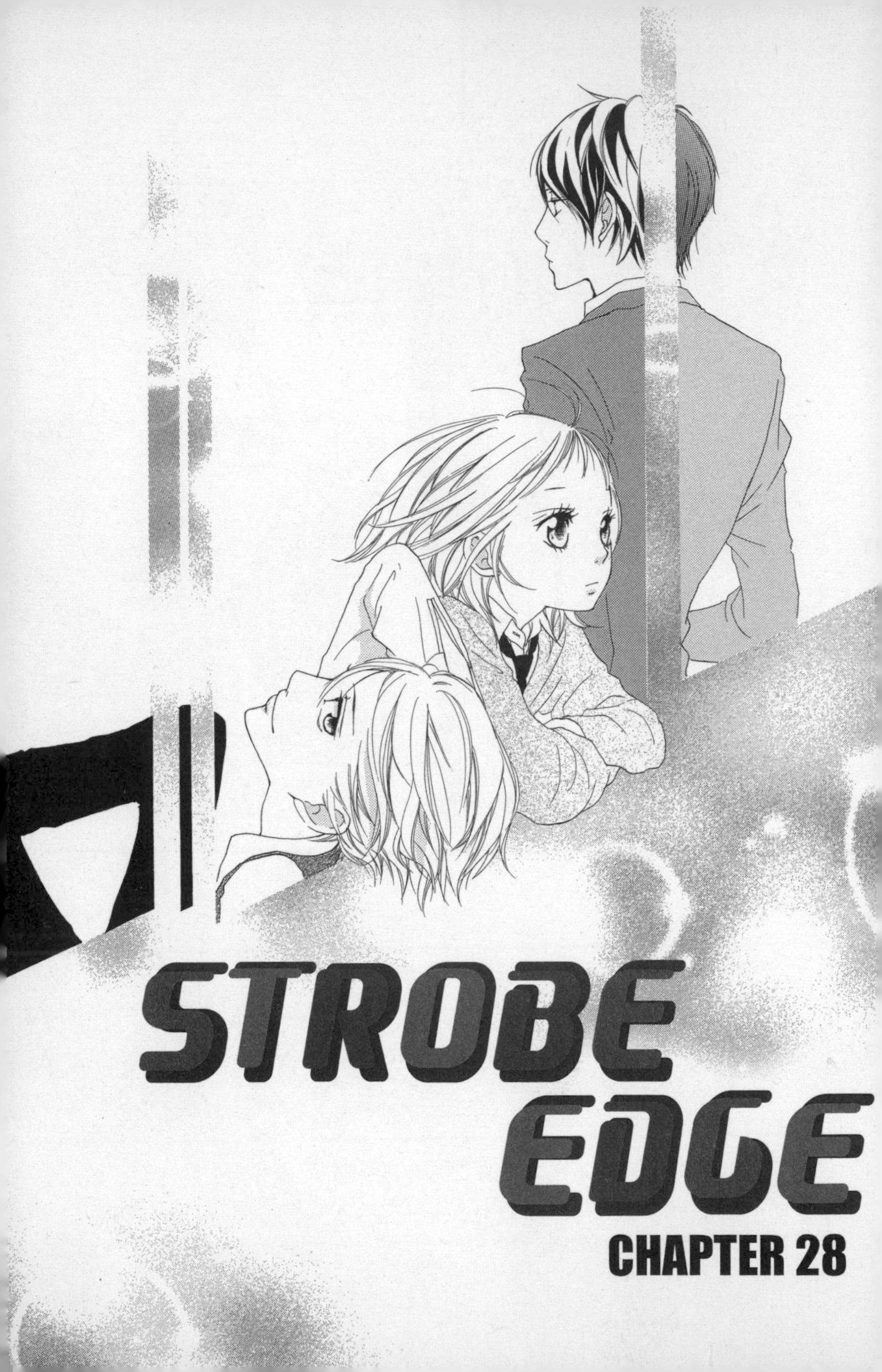
STROBE EDGE
CHAPTER 28

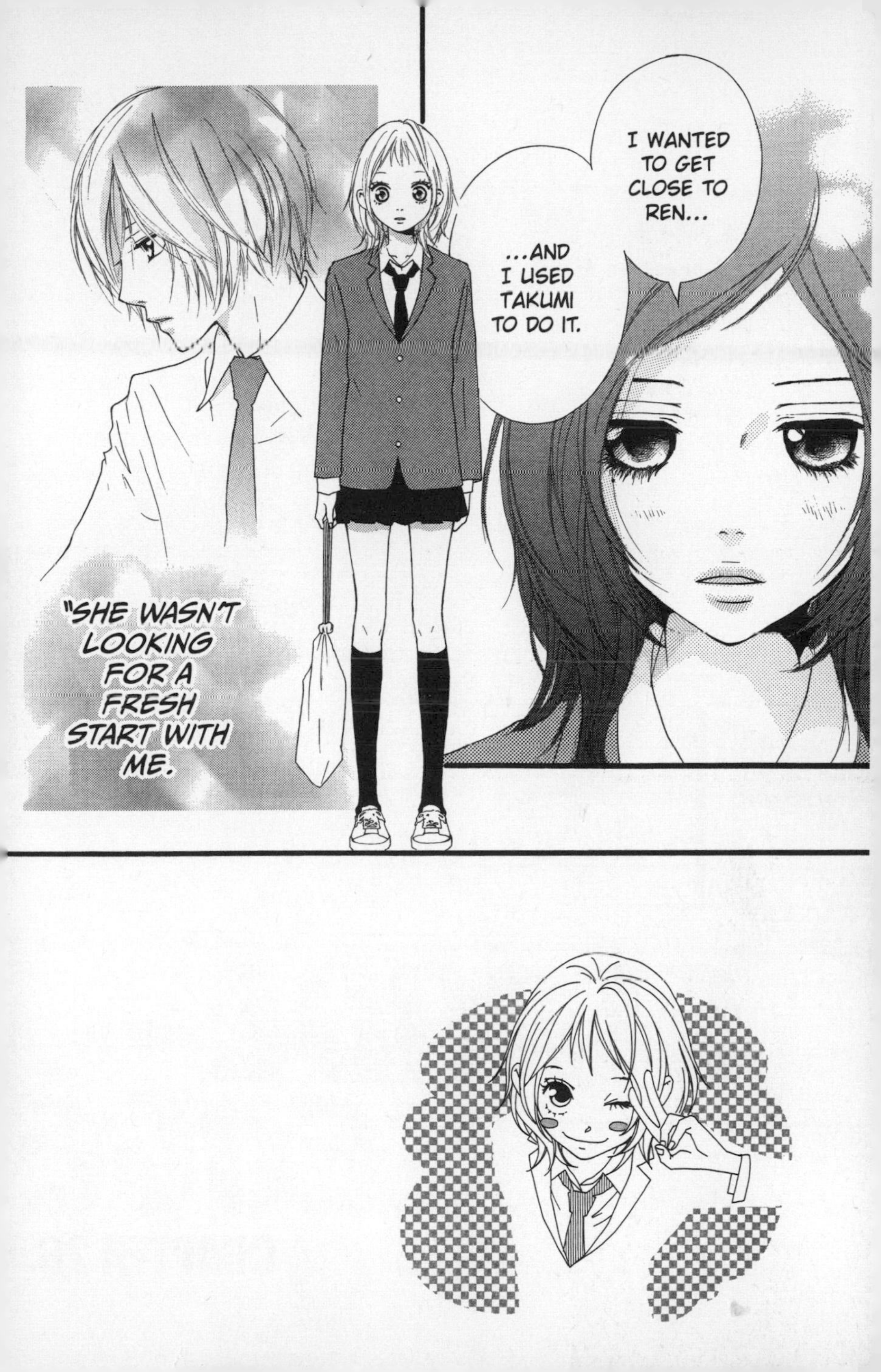
I WANTED TO GET CLOSE TO REN...
...AND I USED TAKUMI TO DO IT.
"SHE WASN'T LOOKING FOR A FRESH START WITH ME.

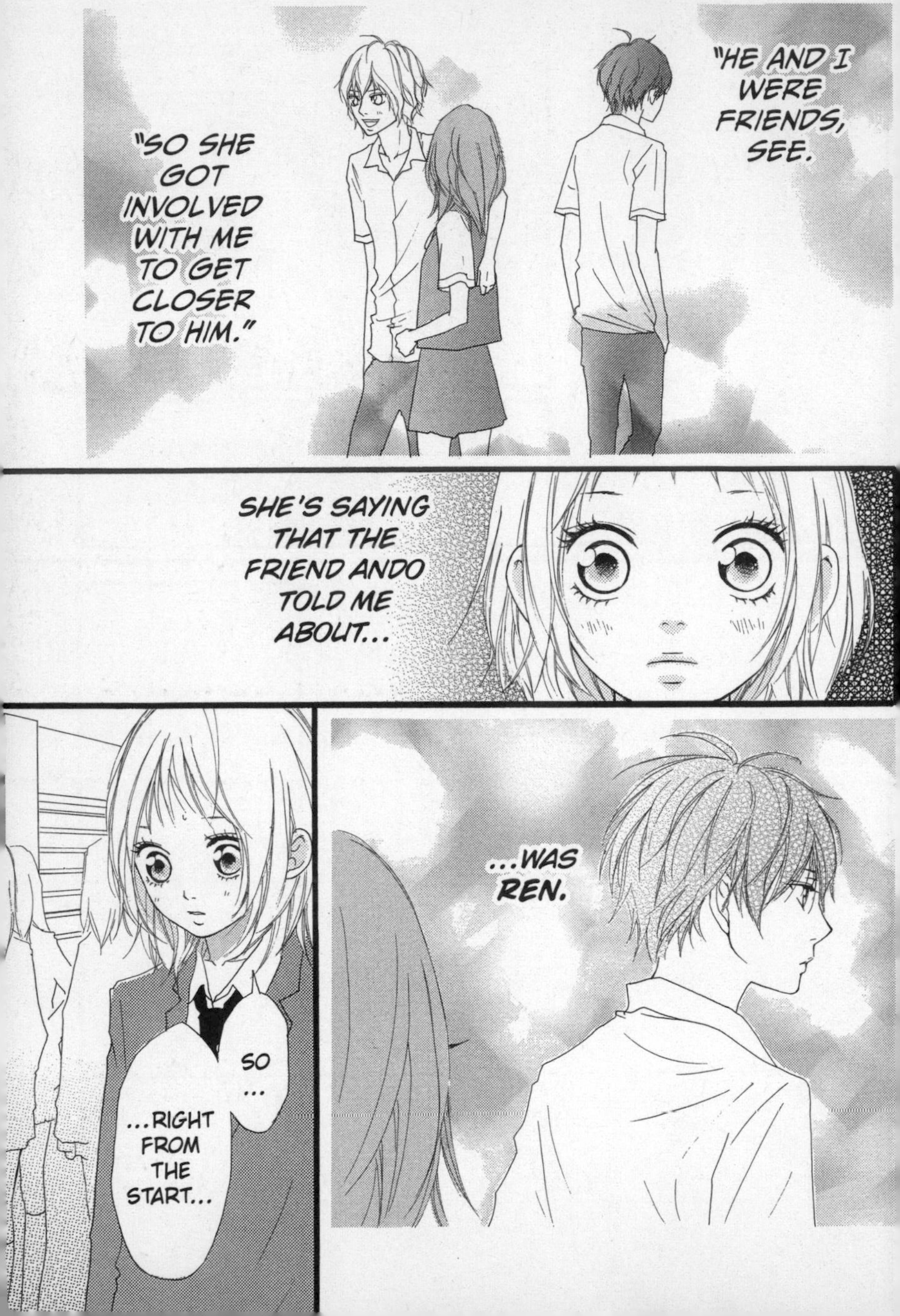
"HE AND I WERE FRIENDS, SEE.
"SO SHE GOT INVOLVED WITH ME TO GET CLOSER TO HIM."
SHE'S SAYING THAT THE FRIEND ANDO TOLD ME ABOUT...
...WAS REN.
SO...
...RIGHT FROM THE START...

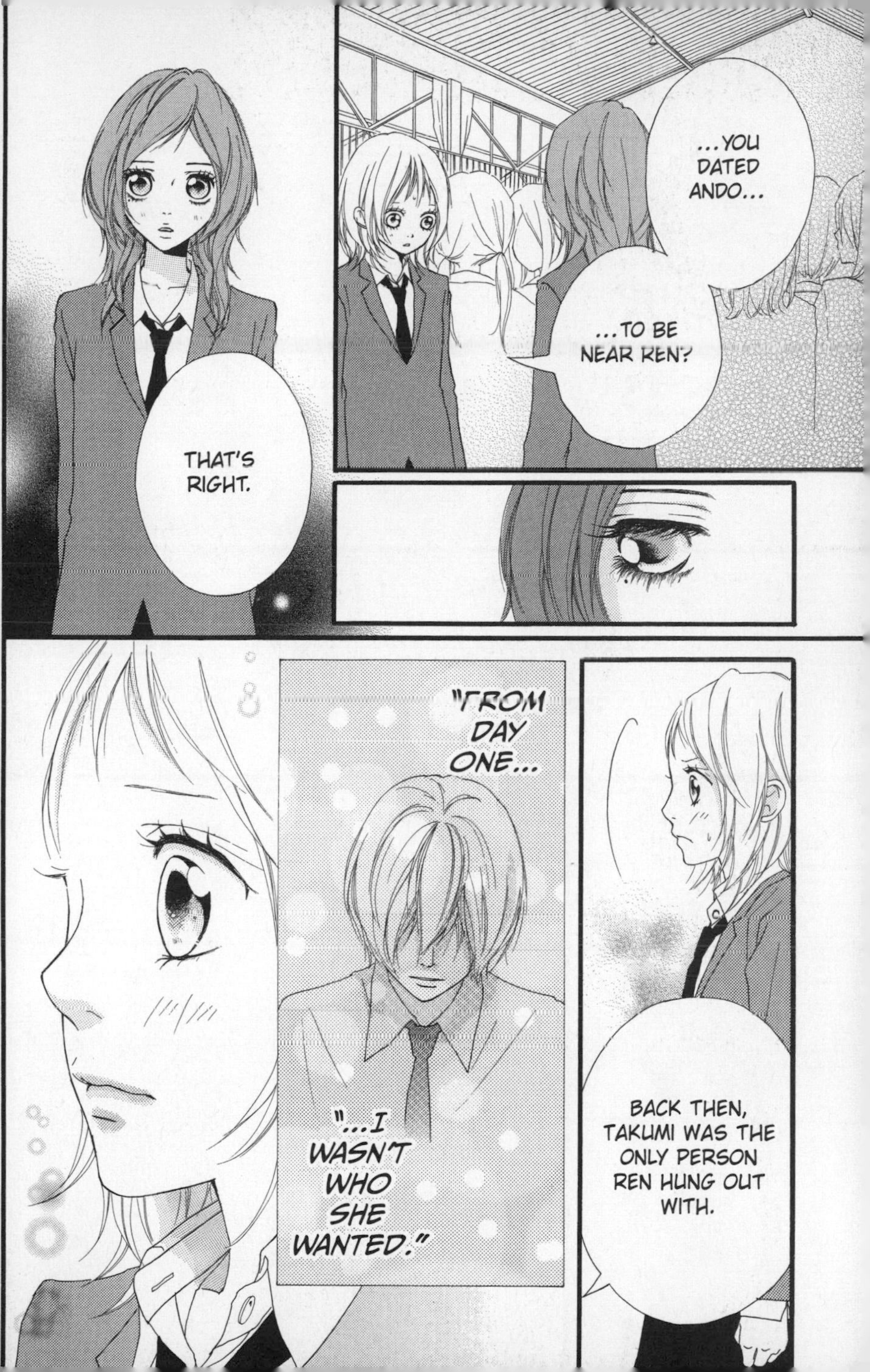
...YOU DATED ANDO...
...TO BE NEAR REN?
THAT'S RIGHT.
BACK THEN, TAKUMI WAS THE ONLY PERSON REN HUNG OUT WITH.
"FROM DAY ONE...
"...I WASN'T WHO SHE WANTED."

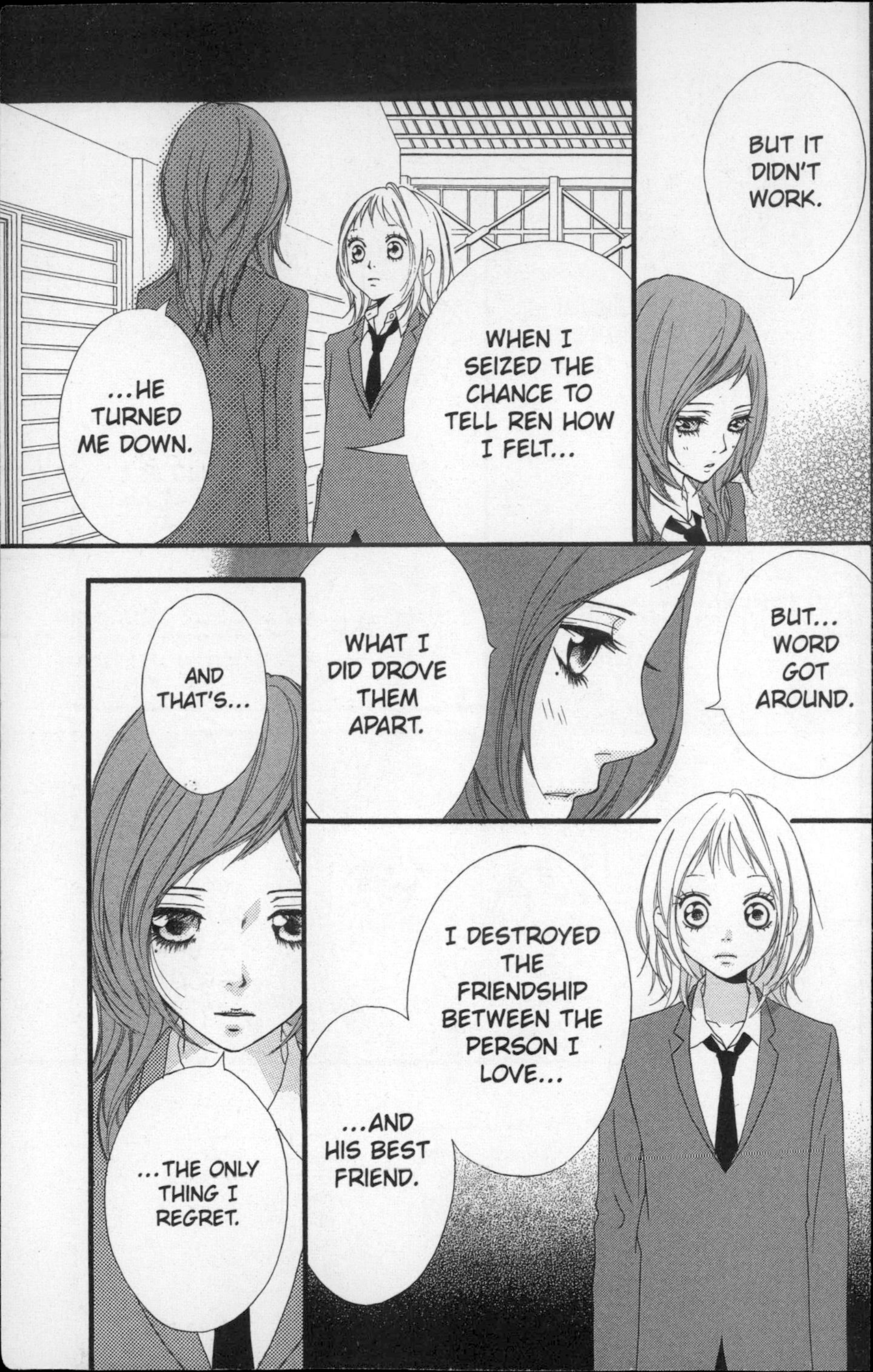
BUT IT DIDN'T WORK.
WHEN I SEIZED THE CHANCE TO TELL REN HOW I FELT...
...HE TURNED ME DOWN.
BUT... WORD GOT AROUND.
WHAT I DID DROVE THEM APART.
I DESTROYED THE FRIENDSHIP BETWEEN THE PERSON I LOVE...
...AND HIS BEST FRIEND.
AND THAT'S...
...THE ONLY THING I REGRET.

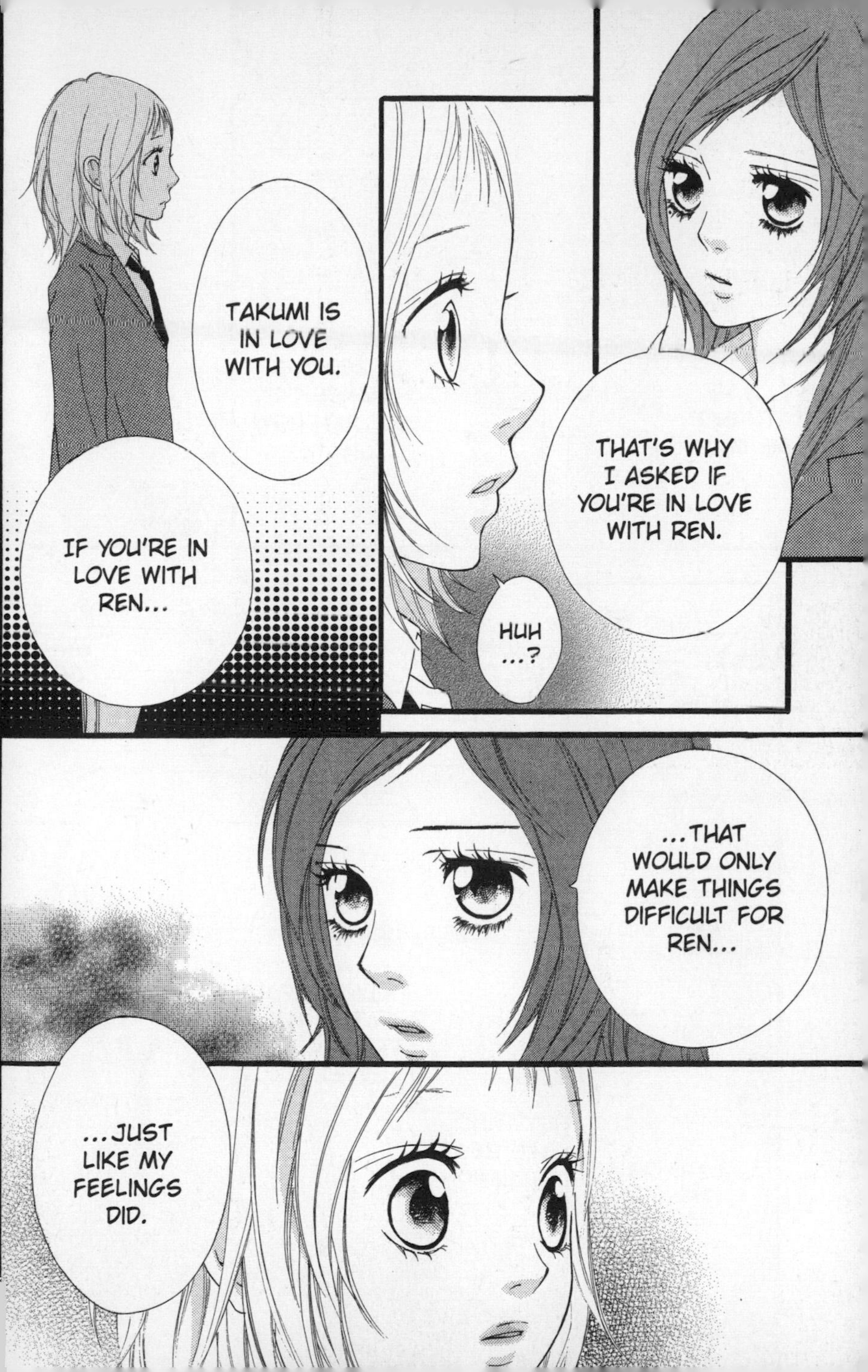
THAT'S WHY I ASKED IF YOU'RE IN LOVE WITH REN.
HUH ...?
TAKUMI IS IN LOVE WITH YOU.
IF YOU'RE IN LOVE WITH REN...
...THAT WOULD ONLY MAKE THINGS DIFFICULT FOR REN...
...JUST LIKE MY FEELINGS DID.

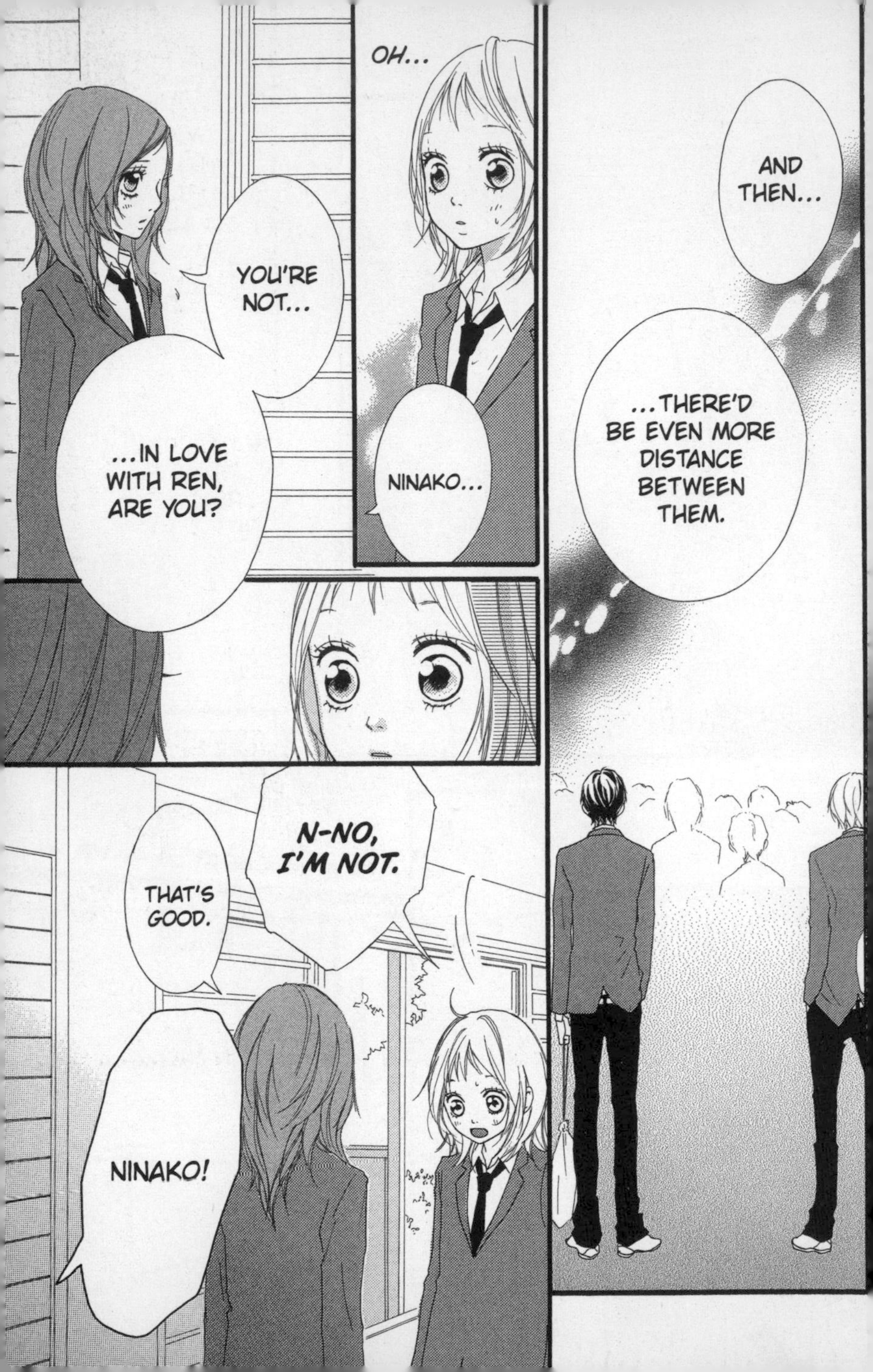
AND THEN...
...THERE'D BE EVEN MORE DISTANCE BETWEEN THEM.
OH...
NINAKO...
YOU'RE NOT...
...IN LOVE WITH REN, ARE YOU?
N-NO, I'M NOT.
THAT'S GOOD.
NINAKO!

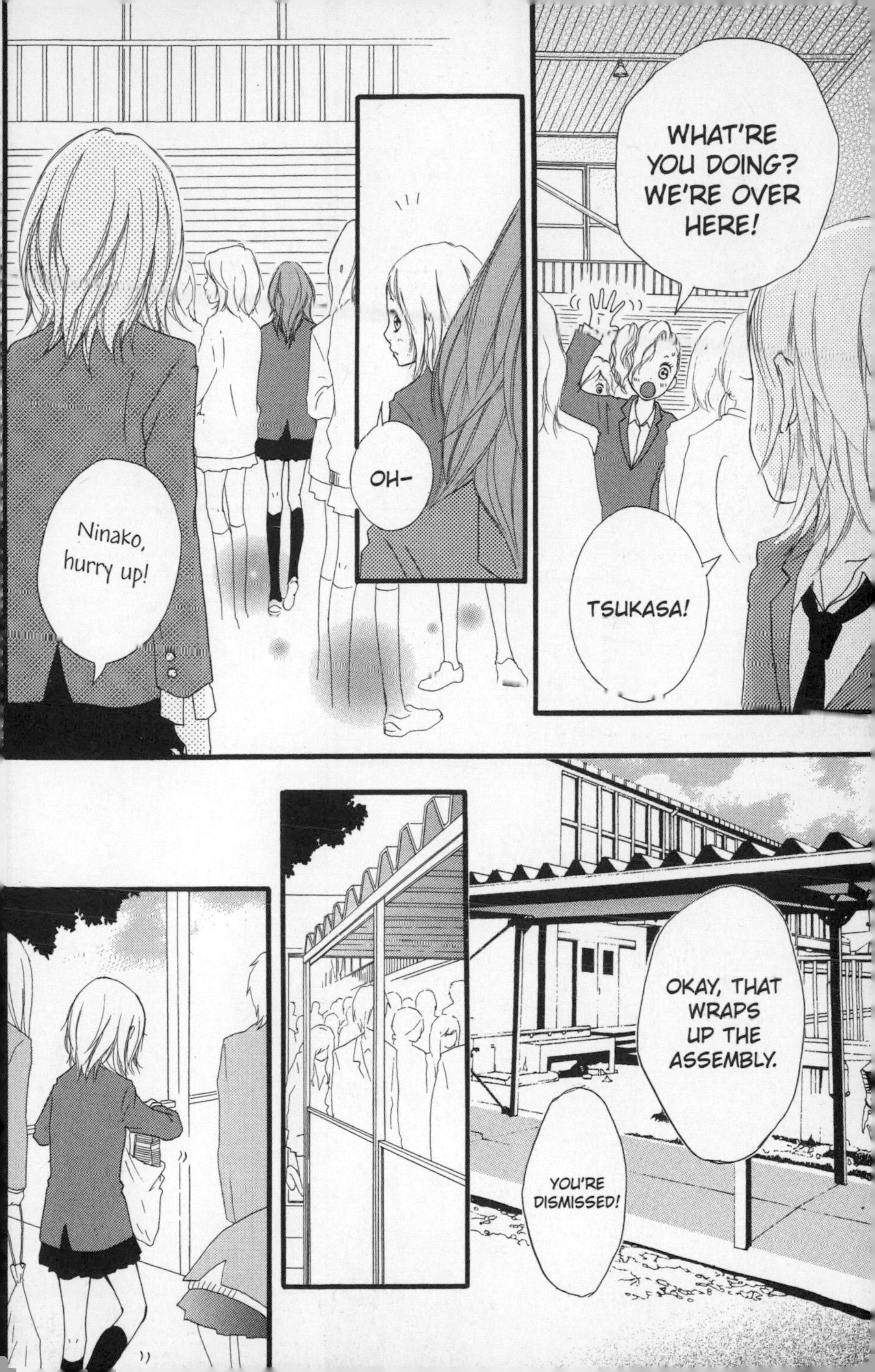
WHAT'RE YOU DOING? WE'RE OVER HERE!
TSUKASA!
OH-
Ninako, hurry up!
OKAY, THAT WRAPS UP THE ASSEMBLY.
YOU'RE DISMISSED!

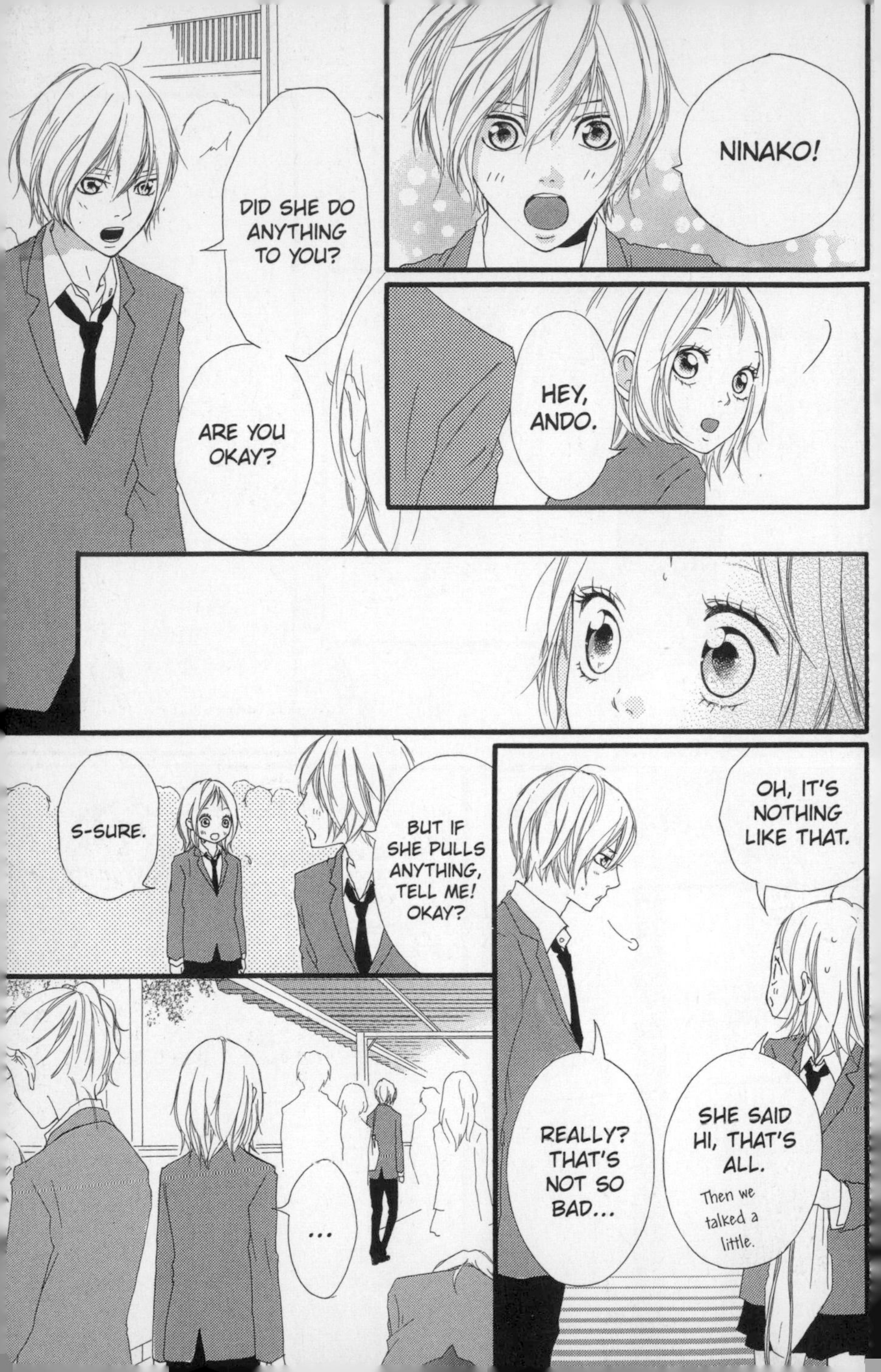
NINAKO!
HEY, ANDO.
DID SHE DO ANYTHING TO YOU?
ARE YOU OKAY?
OH, IT'S NOTHING LIKE THAT.
SHE SAID HI, THAT'S ALL. Then we talked a little.
REALLY? THAT'S NOT SO BAD...
BUT IF SHE PULLS ANYTHING, TELL ME! OKAY?
S-SURE.
...

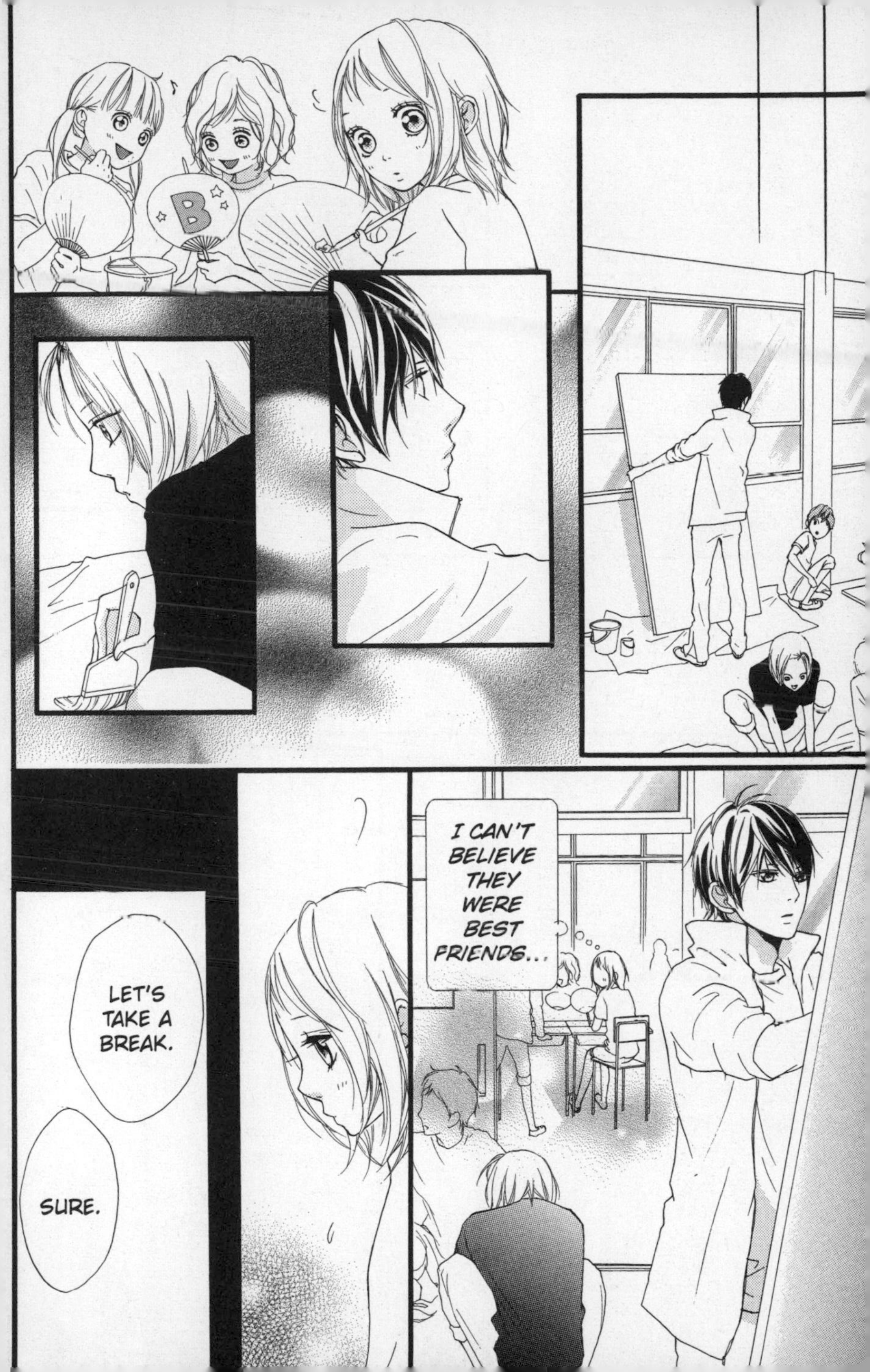
I CAN'T BELIEVE THEY WERE BEST FRIENDS...
LET'S TAKE A BREAK.
SURE.

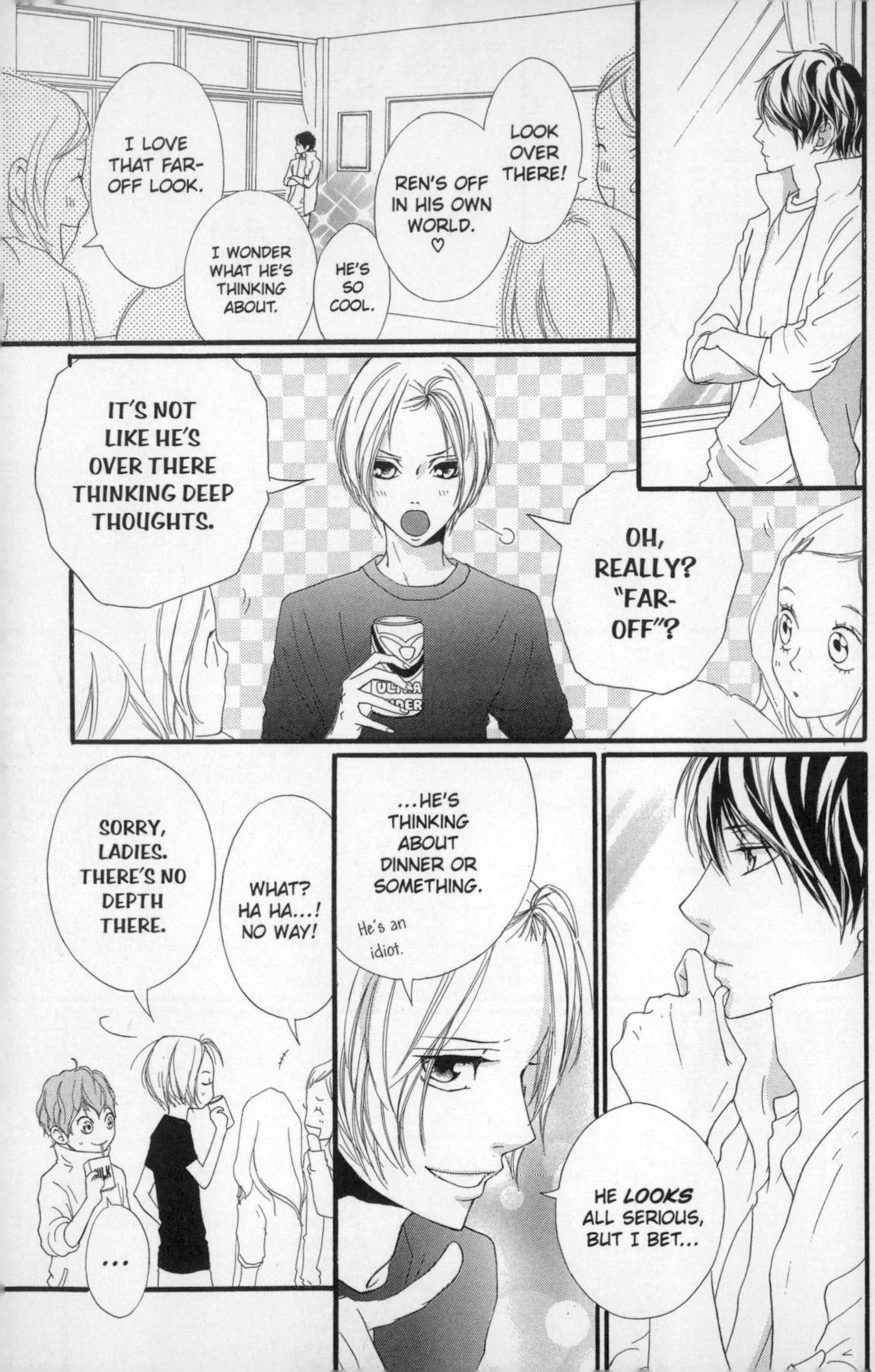
LOOK OVER THERE!
REN'S OFF IN HIS OWN WORLD. ♡
HE'S SO COOL.
I WONDER WHAT HE'S THINKING ABOUT.
I LOVE THAT FAR-OFF LOOK.
OH, REALLY? "FAR-OFF"?
IT'S NOT LIKE HE'S OVER THERE THINKING DEEP THOUGHTS.
HE *LOOKS* ALL SERIOUS, BUT I BET...
...HE'S THINKING ABOUT DINNER OR SOMETHING.
He's an idiot.
WHAT? HA HA...! NO WAY!
SORRY, LADIES. THERE'S NO DEPTH THERE.
...

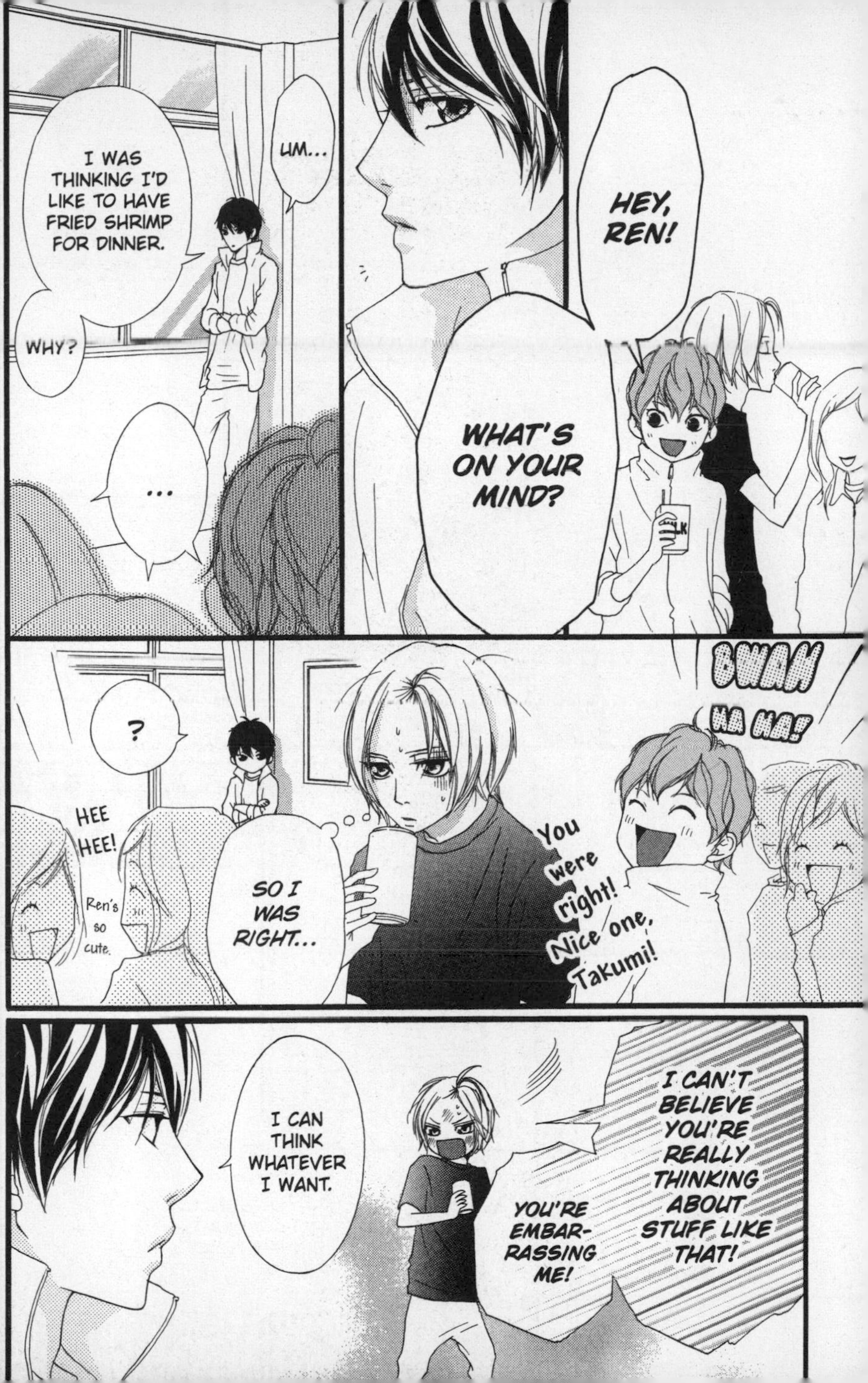
HEY, REN!
WHAT'S ON YOUR MIND?
UM...
I WAS THINKING I'D LIKE TO HAVE FRIED SHRIMP FOR DINNER.
WHY?
...
BWAH HA HA!
You were right! Nice one, Takumi!
SO I WAS RIGHT...
?
HEE HEE!
Ren's so cute.
I CAN'T BELIEVE YOU'RE REALLY THINKING ABOUT STUFF LIKE THAT!
YOU'RE EMBARRASSING ME!
I CAN THINK WHATEVER I WANT.

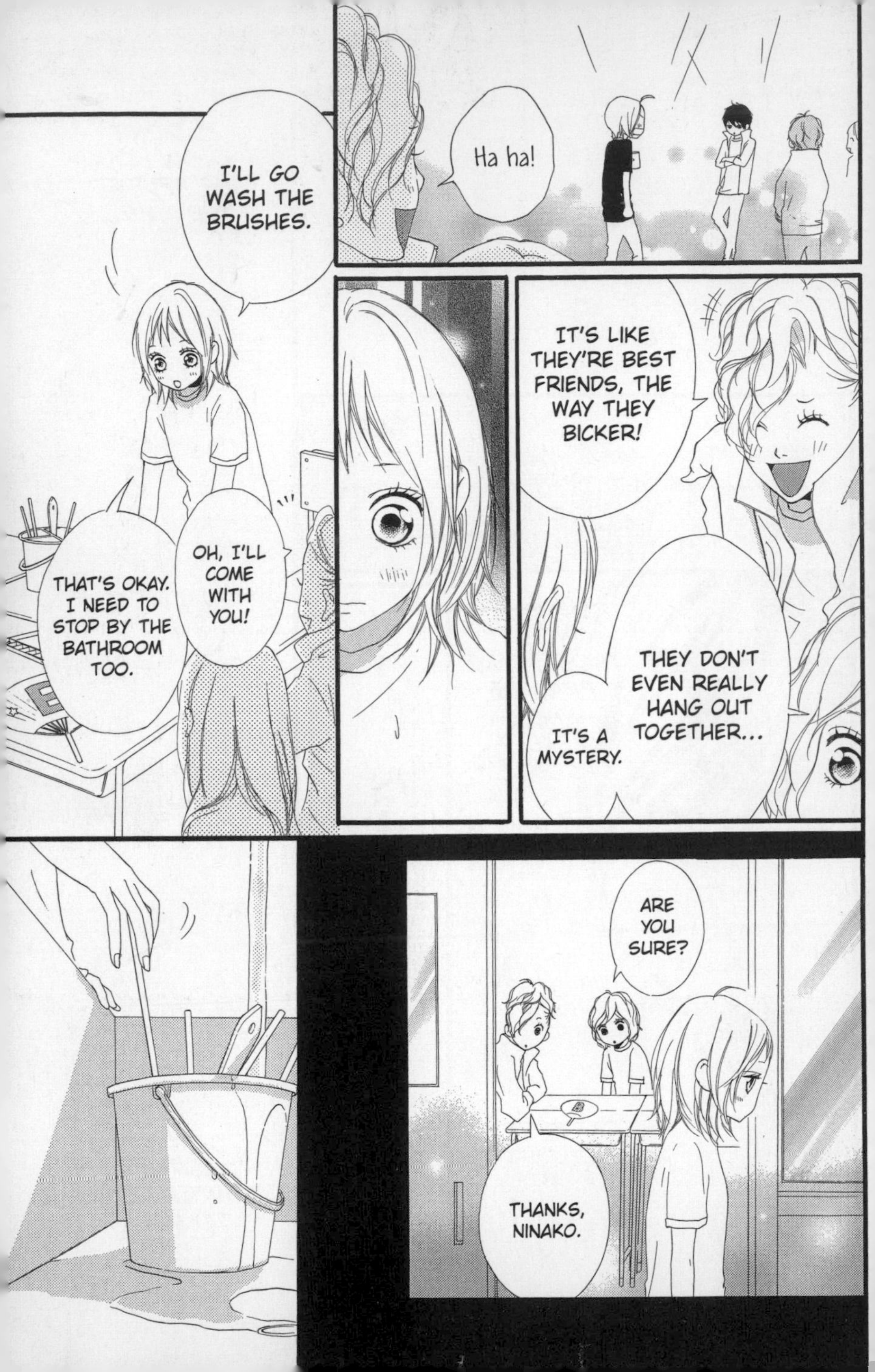
Ha ha!
IT'S LIKE THEY'RE BEST FRIENDS, THE WAY THEY BICKER!
THEY DON'T EVEN REALLY HANG OUT TOGETHER...
IT'S A MYSTERY.
I'LL GO WASH THE BRUSHES.
OH, I'LL COME WITH YOU!
THAT'S OKAY. I NEED TO STOP BY THE BATHROOM TOO.
ARE YOU SURE?
THANKS, NINAKO.

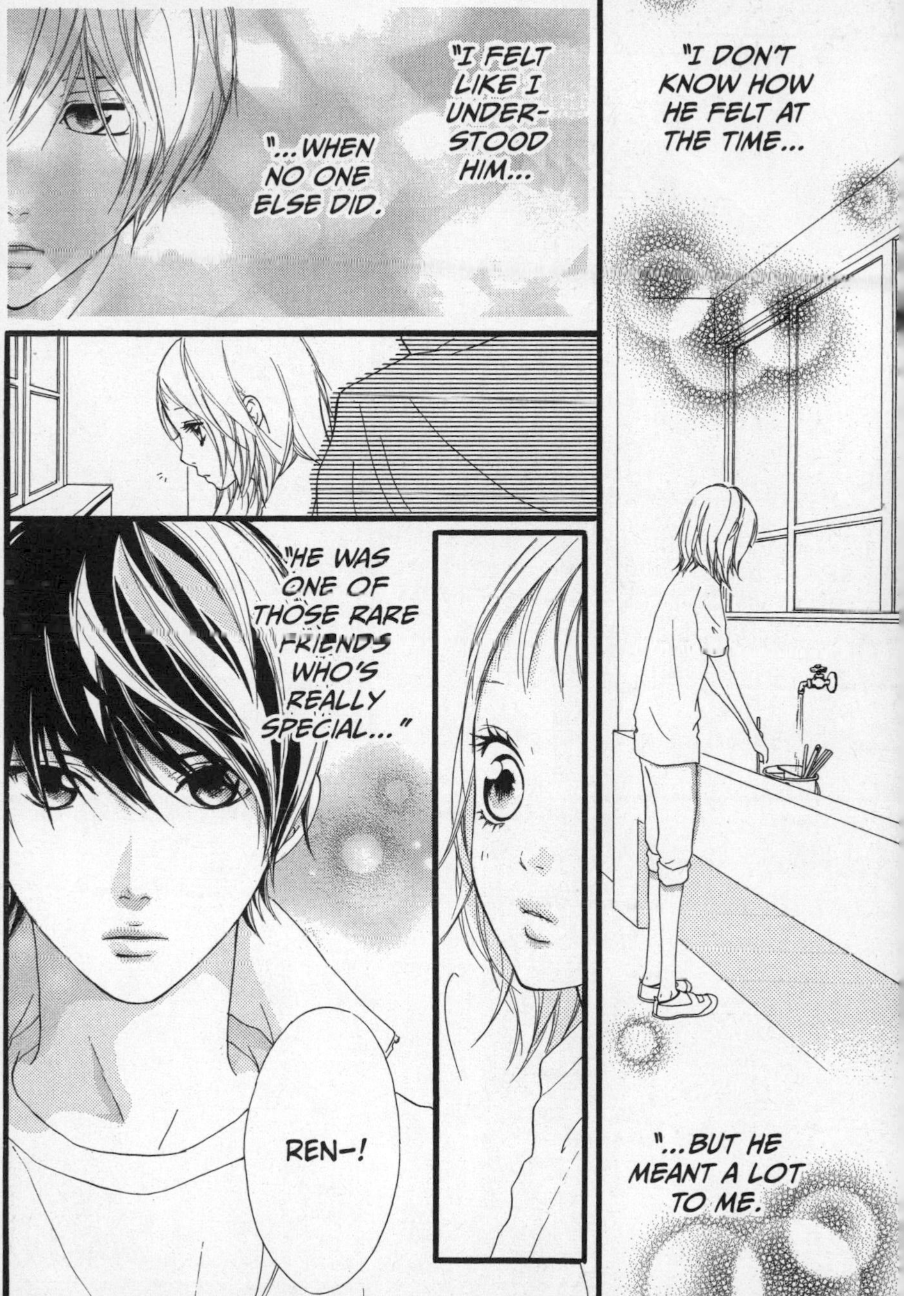
"I DON'T KNOW HOW HE FELT AT THE TIME...
"...BUT HE MEANT A LOT TO ME.
"I FELT LIKE I UNDER-STOOD HIM...
"...WHEN NO ONE ELSE DID.
"HE WAS ONE OF THOSE RARE FRIENDS WHO'S REALLY SPECIAL..."
REN-!

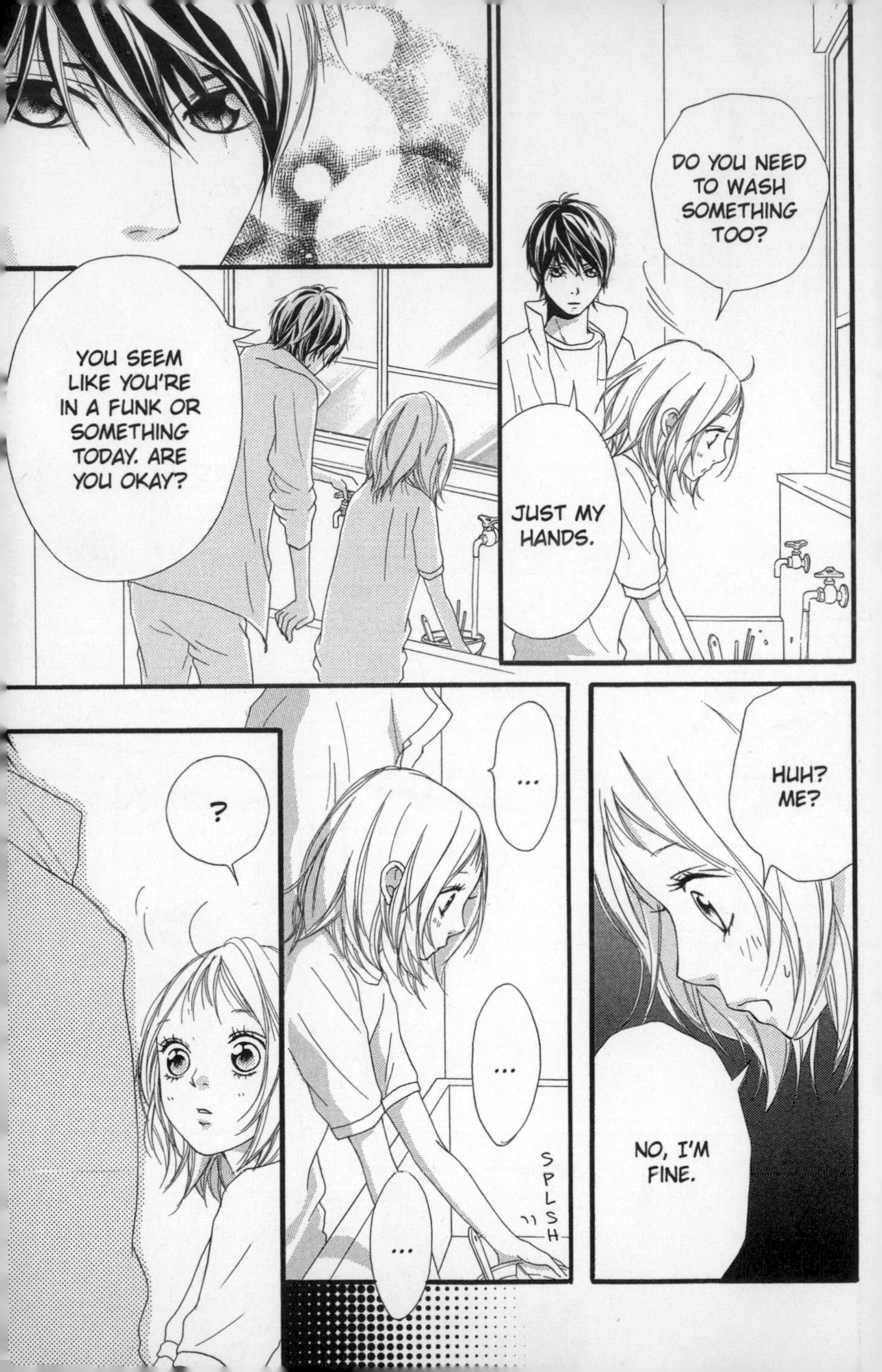
DO YOU NEED TO WASH SOMETHING TOO?
JUST MY HANDS.
YOU SEEM LIKE YOU'RE IN A FUNK OR SOMETHING TODAY. ARE YOU OKAY?
HUH? ME?
NO, I'M FINE.
...
...
SPLSH
...
?

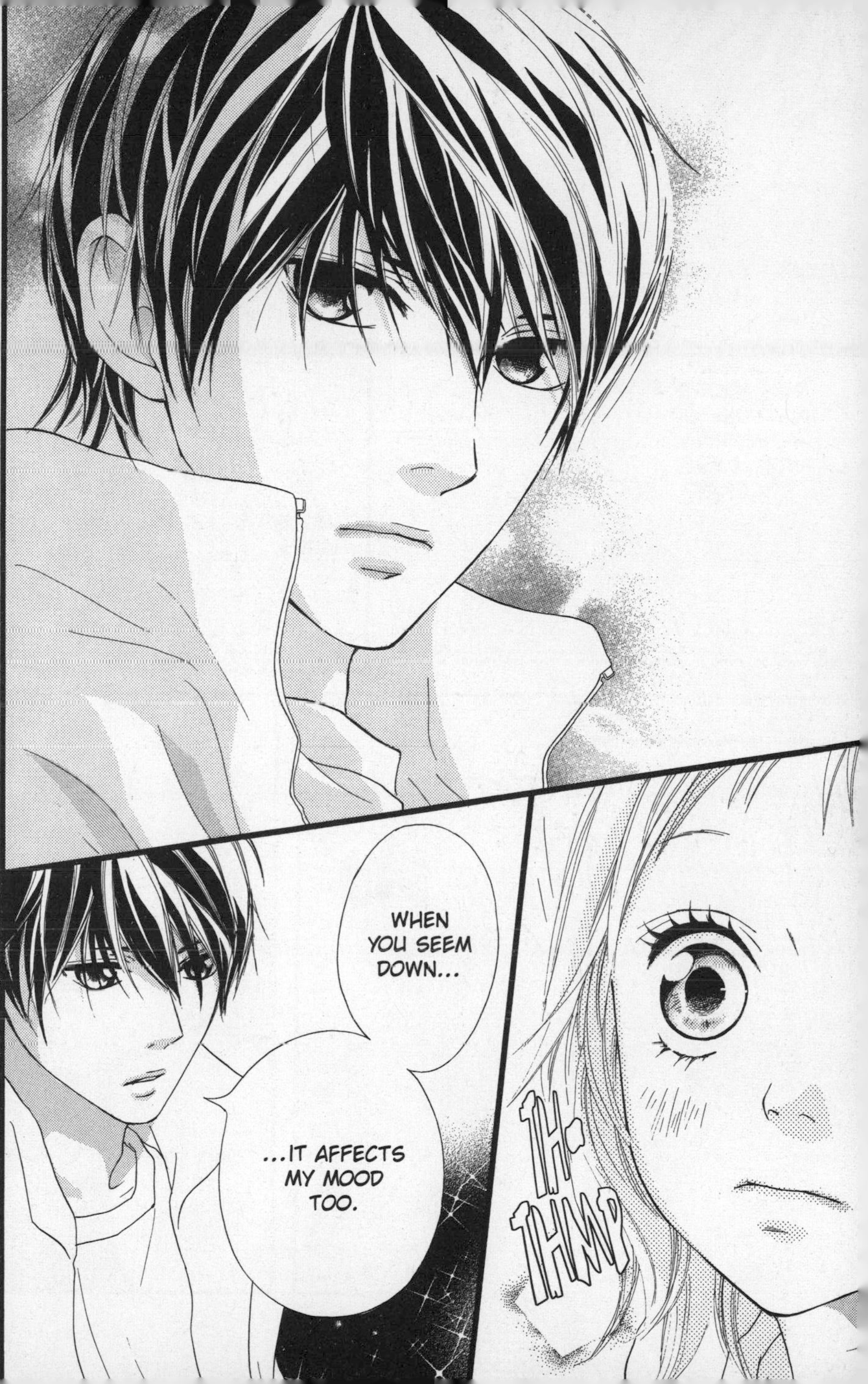
TH-THMP
WHEN YOU SEEM DOWN...
...IT AFFECTS MY MOOD TOO.

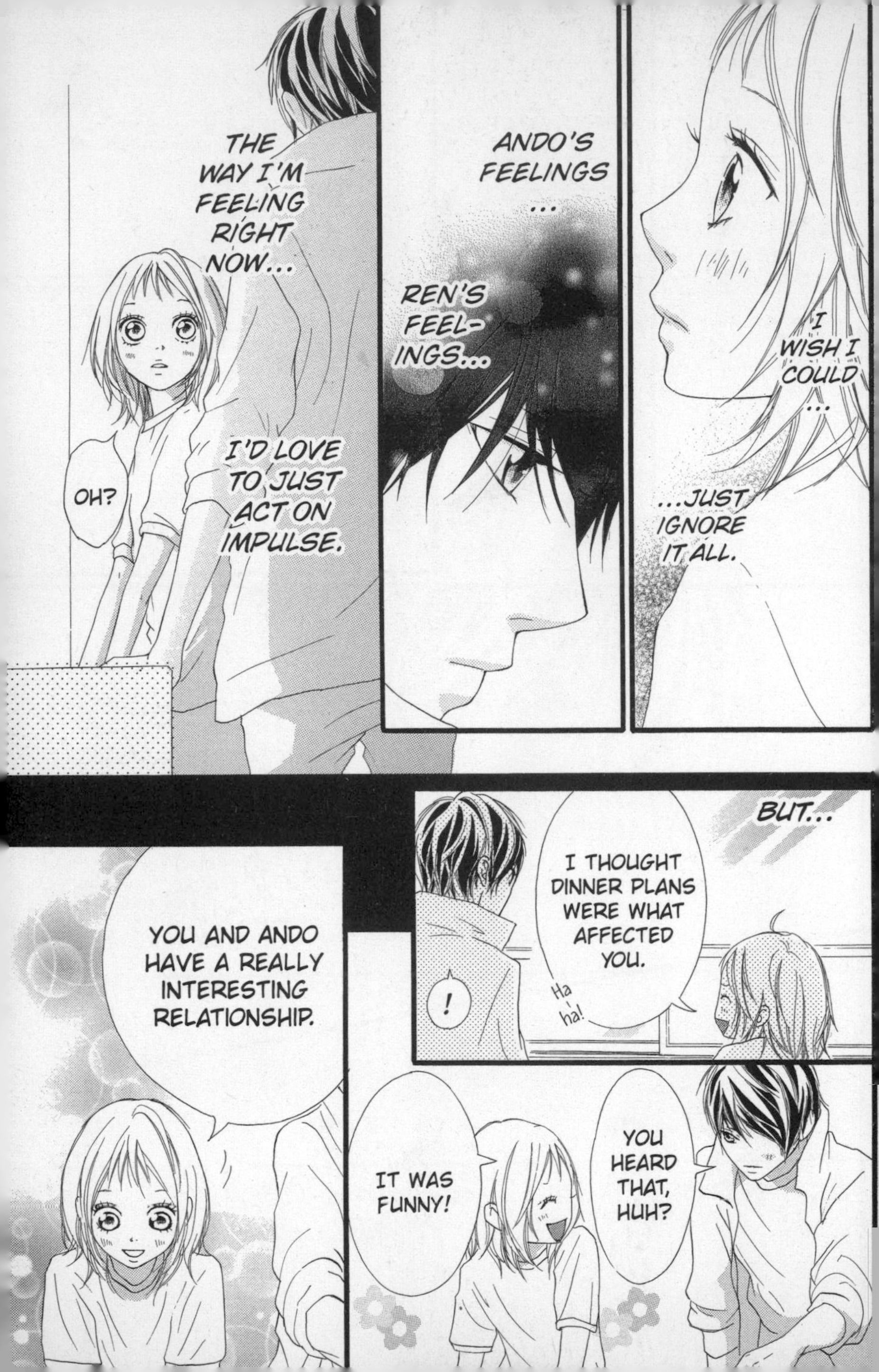
I WISH I COULD...
...JUST IGNORE IT ALL.
ANDO'S FEELINGS...
REN'S FEELINGS...
THE WAY I'M FEELING RIGHT NOW...
I'D LOVE TO JUST ACT ON IMPULSE.
OH?
BUT...
I THOUGHT DINNER PLANS WERE WHAT AFFECTED YOU.
Ha ha!
!
YOU HEARD THAT, HUH?
IT WAS FUNNY!
YOU AND ANDO HAVE A REALLY INTERESTING RELATIONSHIP.

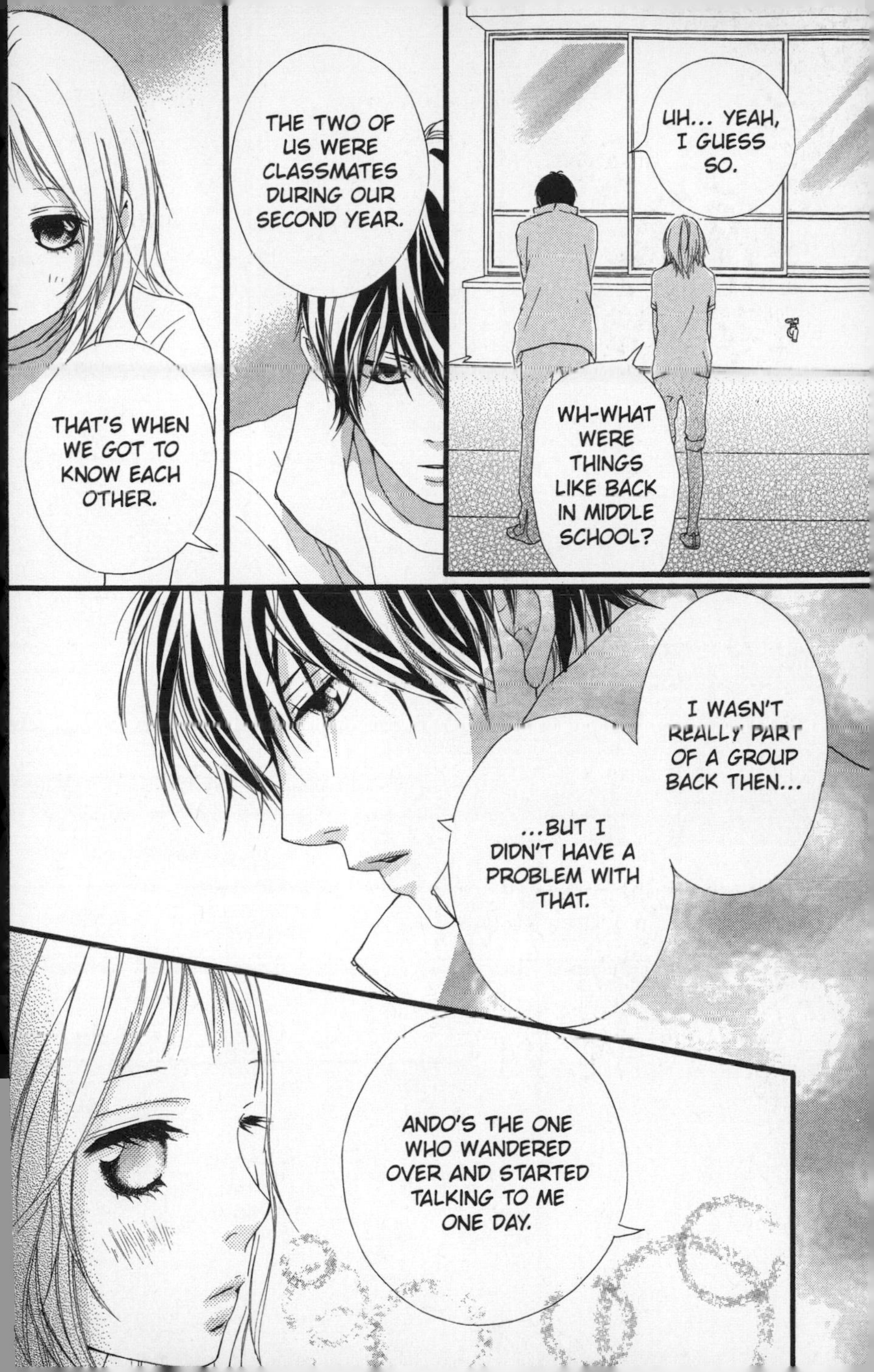
UH... YEAH, I GUESS SO.
WH-WHAT WERE THINGS LIKE BACK IN MIDDLE SCHOOL?
THE TWO OF US WERE CLASSMATES DURING OUR SECOND YEAR.
THAT'S WHEN WE GOT TO KNOW EACH OTHER.
I WASN'T REALLY PART OF A GROUP BACK THEN...
...BUT I DIDN'T HAVE A PROBLEM WITH THAT.
ANDO'S THE ONE WHO WANDERED OVER AND STARTED TALKING TO ME ONE DAY.

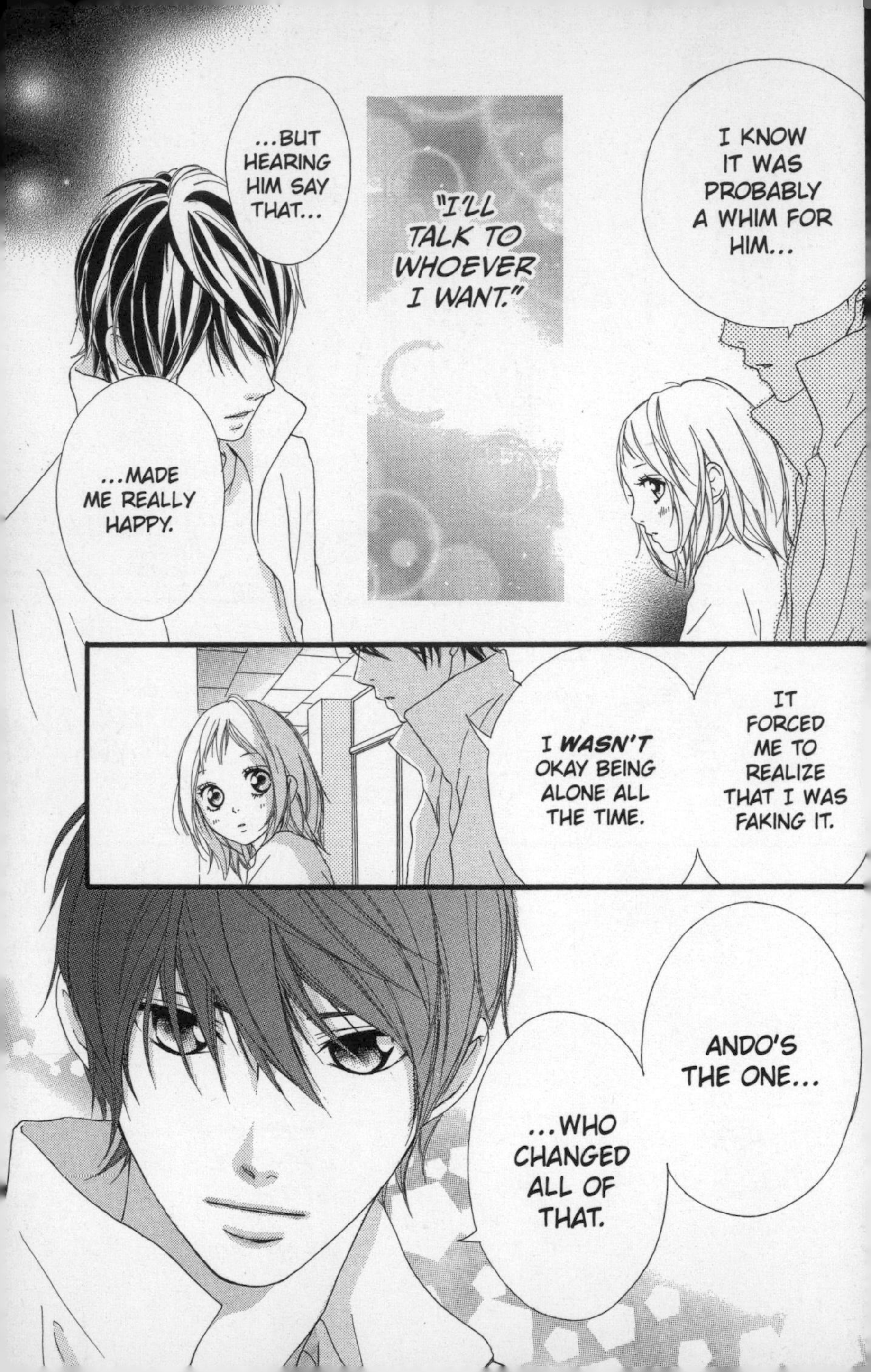
I KNOW IT WAS PROBABLY A WHIM FOR HIM...
"I'LL TALK TO WHOEVER I WANT."
...BUT HEARING HIM SAY THAT...
...MADE ME REALLY HAPPY.
IT FORCED ME TO REALIZE THAT I WAS FAKING IT.
I **WASN'T** OKAY BEING ALONE ALL THE TIME.
ANDO'S THE ONE...
...WHO CHANGED ALL OF THAT.

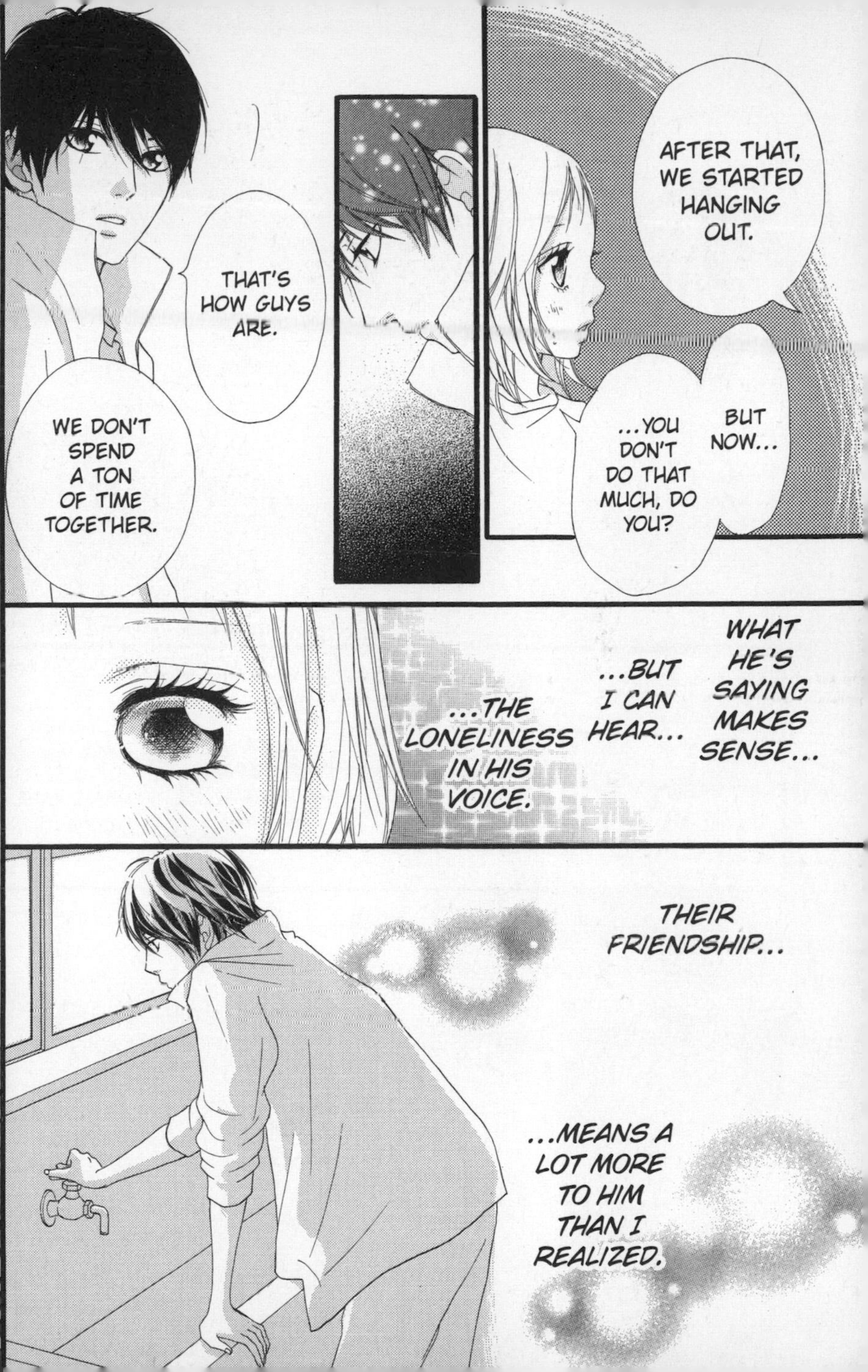
AFTER THAT, WE STARTED HANGING OUT.
BUT NOW...
...YOU DON'T DO THAT MUCH, DO YOU?
THAT'S HOW GUYS ARE.
WE DON'T SPEND A TON OF TIME TOGETHER.
WHAT HE'S SAYING MAKES SENSE...
...BUT I CAN HEAR...
...THE LONELINESS IN HIS VOICE.
THEIR FRIENDSHIP...
...MEANS A LOT MORE TO HIM THAN I REALIZED.

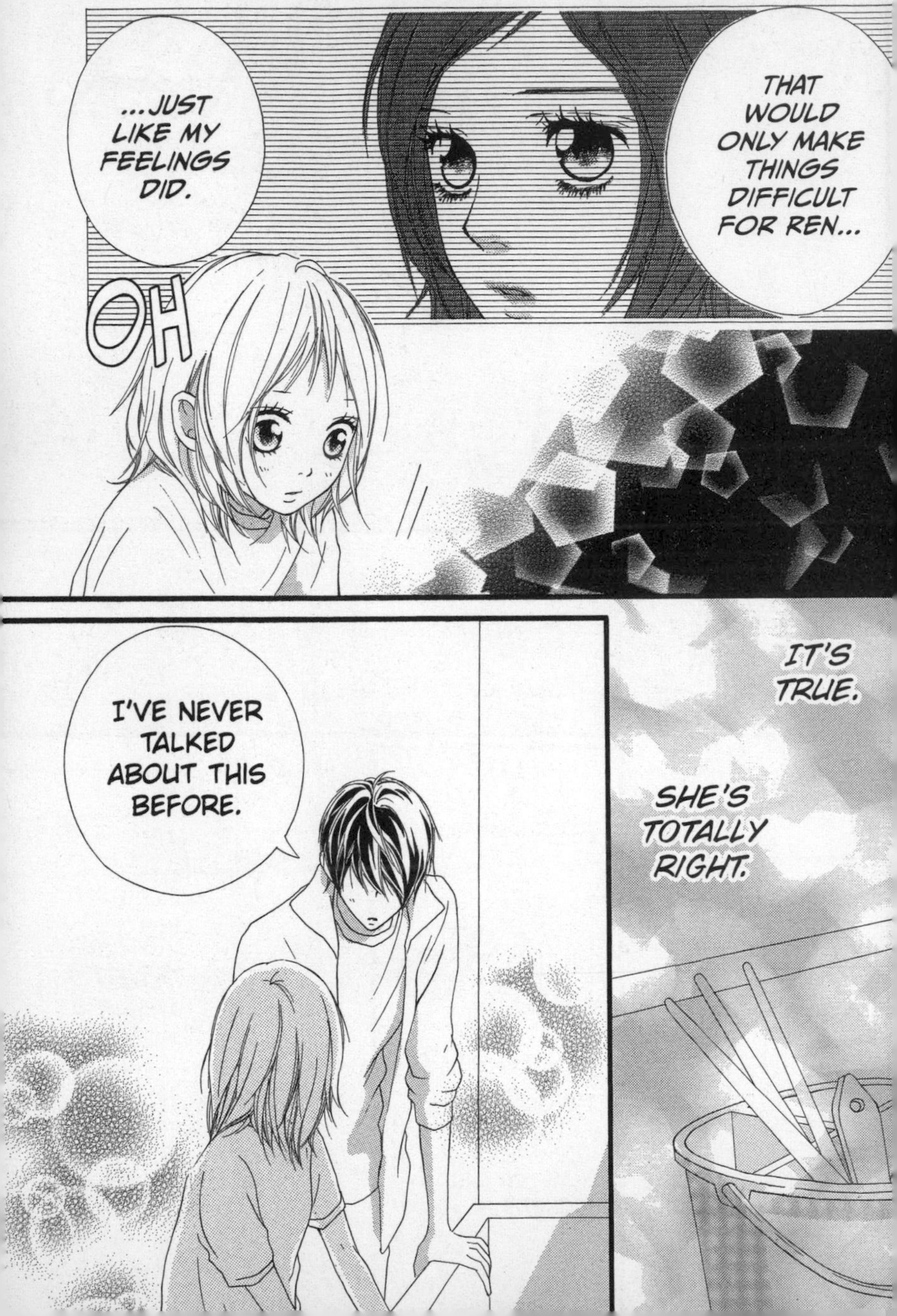
THAT WOULD ONLY MAKE THINGS DIFFICULT FOR REN...
...JUST LIKE MY FEELINGS DID.
OH
IT'S TRUE.
SHE'S TOTALLY RIGHT.
I'VE NEVER TALKED ABOUT THIS BEFORE.

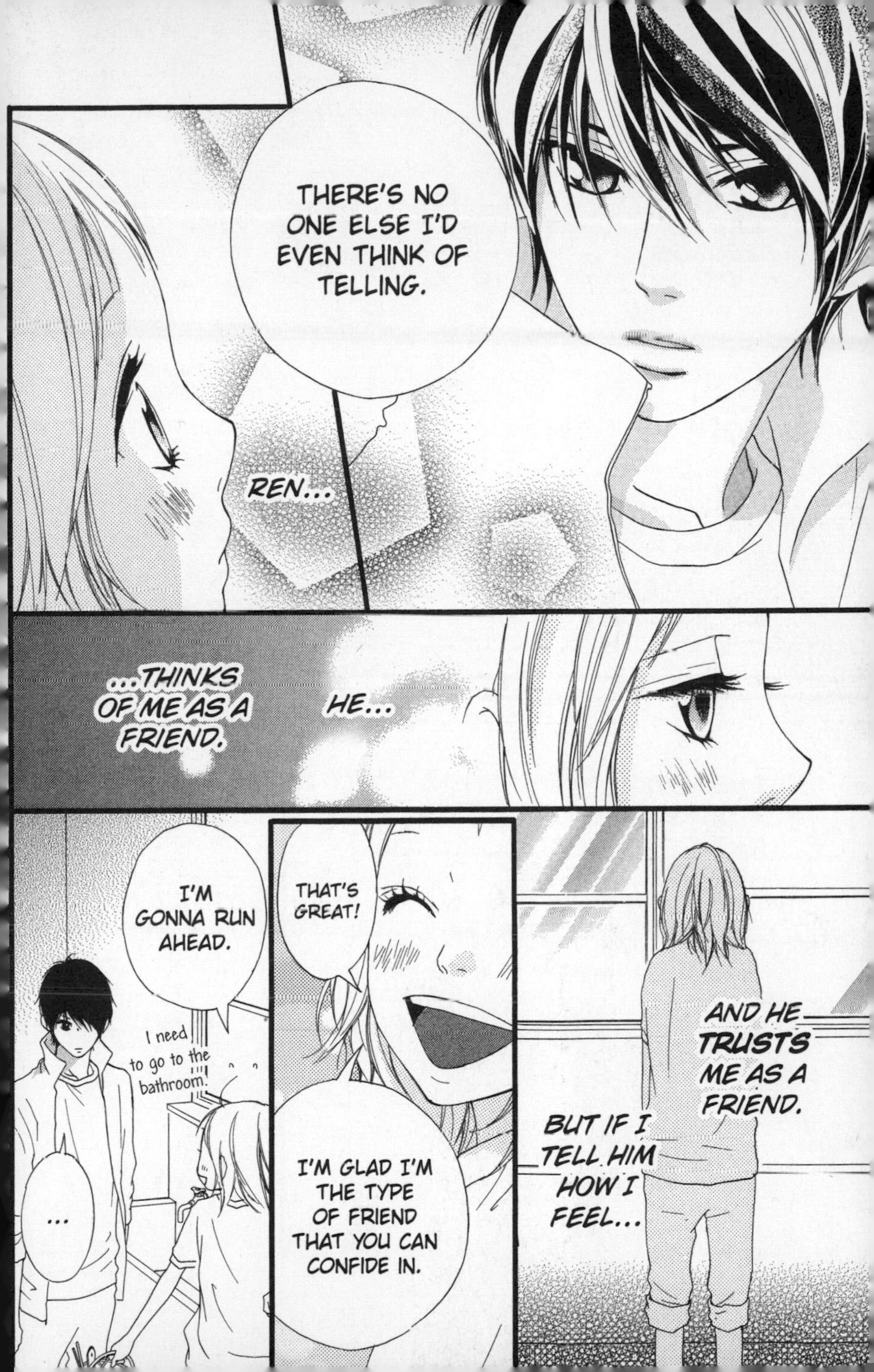
THERE'S NO ONE ELSE I'D EVEN THINK OF TELLING.
REN...
HE...
...THINKS OF ME AS A FRIEND.
AND HE TRUSTS ME AS A FRIEND.
BUT IF I TELL HIM HOW I FEEL...
THAT'S GREAT!
I'M GLAD I'M THE TYPE OF FRIEND THAT YOU CAN CONFIDE IN.
I'M GONNA RUN AHEAD.
I need to go to the bathroom.
...

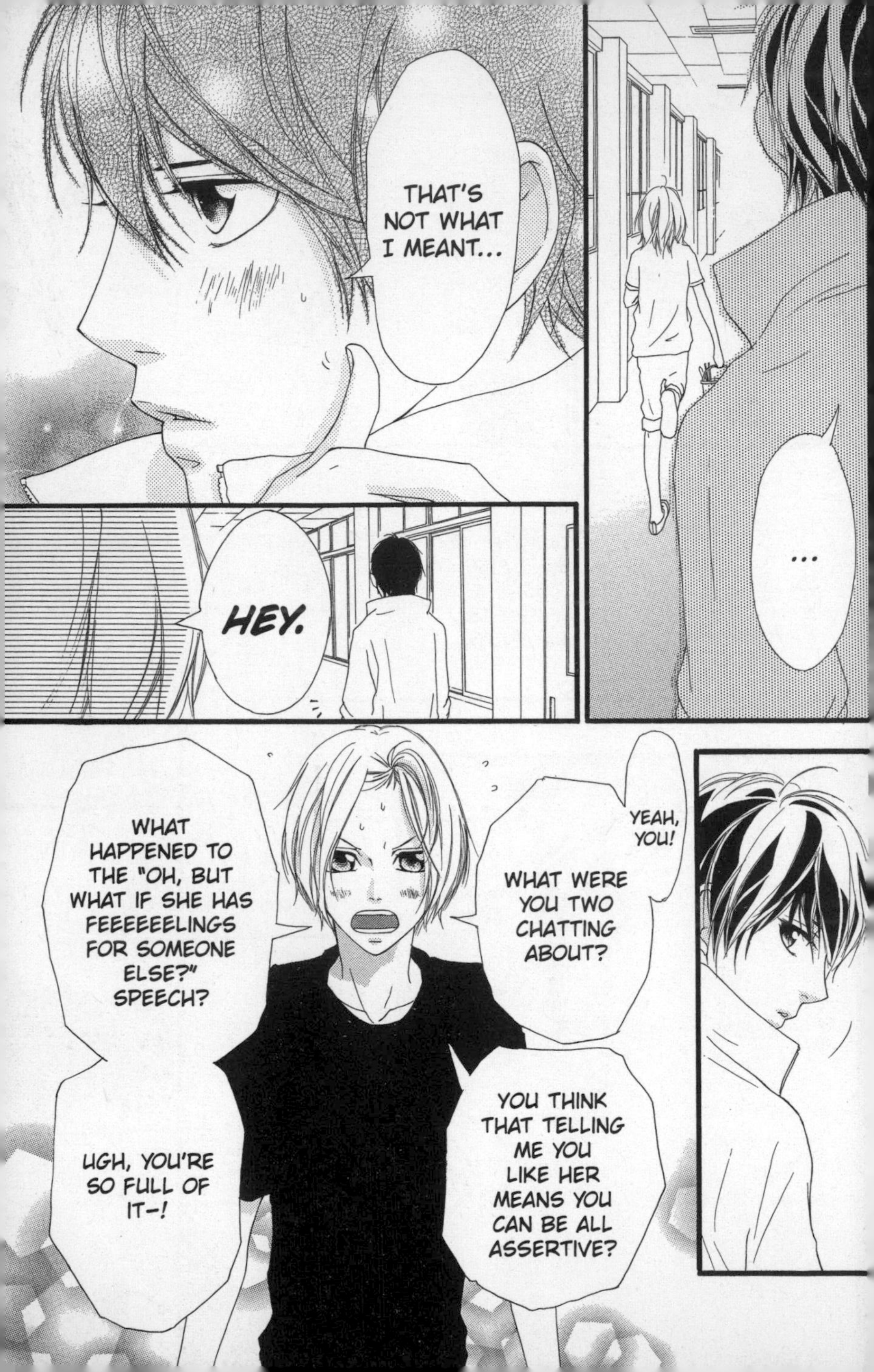
...
THAT'S NOT WHAT I MEANT...
HEY.
YEAH, YOU!
WHAT WERE YOU TWO CHATTING ABOUT?
WHAT HAPPENED TO THE "OH, BUT WHAT IF SHE HAS FEEEEEELINGS FOR SOMEONE ELSE?" SPEECH?
YOU THINK THAT TELLING ME YOU LIKE HER MEANS YOU CAN BE ALL ASSERTIVE?
UGH, YOU'RE SO FULL OF IT-!

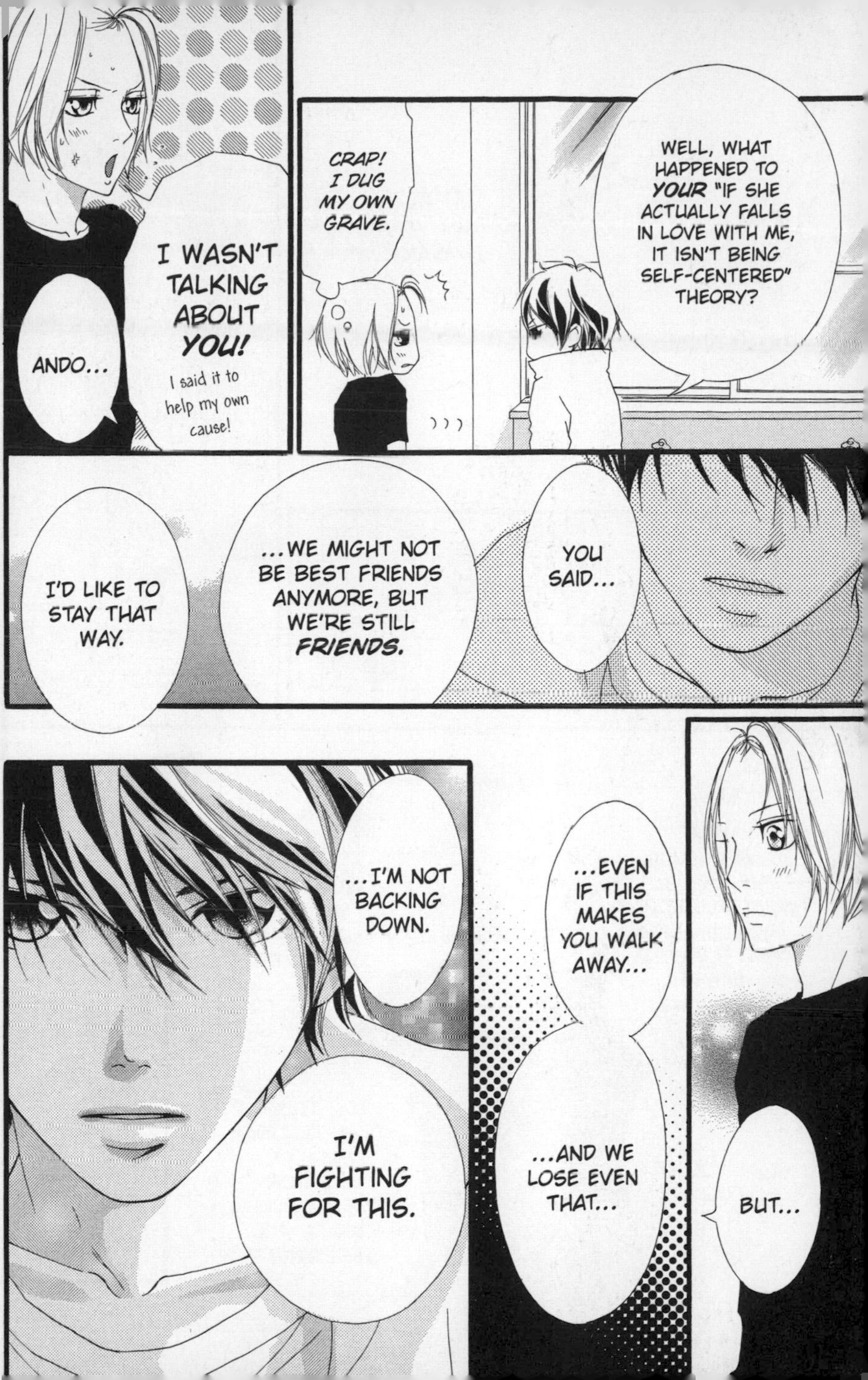
WELL, WHAT HAPPENED TO YOUR "IF SHE ACTUALLY FALLS IN LOVE WITH ME, IT ISN'T BEING SELF-CENTERED" THEORY?
CRAP! I DUG MY OWN GRAVE.
I WASN'T TALKING ABOUT YOU!
I said it to help my own cause!
ANDO...
YOU SAID...
...WE MIGHT NOT BE BEST FRIENDS ANYMORE, BUT WE'RE STILL FRIENDS.
I'D LIKE TO STAY THAT WAY.
BUT...
...EVEN IF THIS MAKES YOU WALK AWAY...
...AND WE LOSE EVEN THAT...
...I'M NOT BACKING DOWN.
I'M FIGHTING FOR THIS.

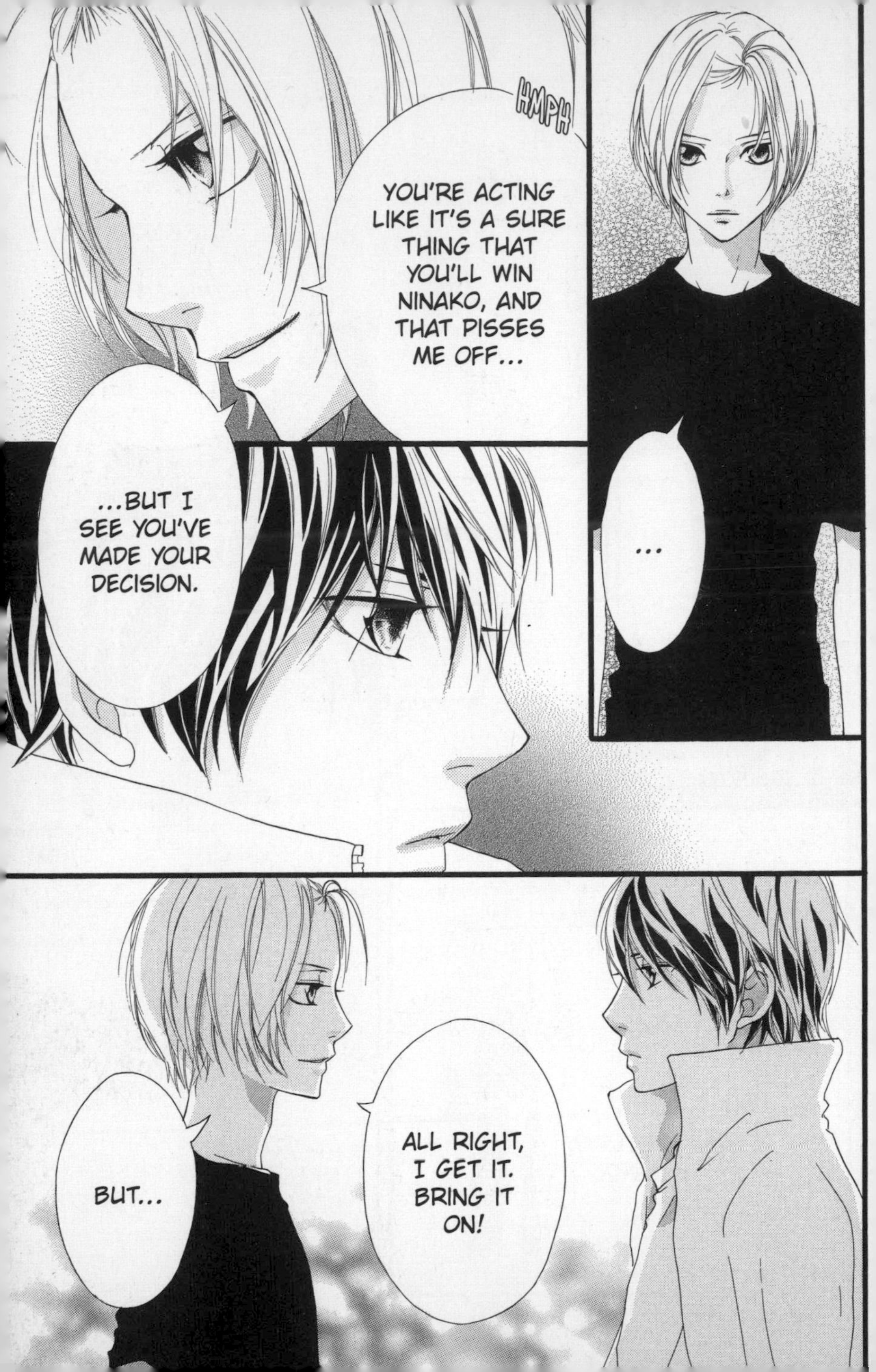
...
HMPH
YOU'RE ACTING LIKE IT'S A SURE THING THAT YOU'LL WIN NINAKO, AND THAT PISSES ME OFF...
...BUT I SEE YOU'VE MADE YOUR DECISION.
ALL RIGHT, I GET IT. BRING IT ON!
BUT...

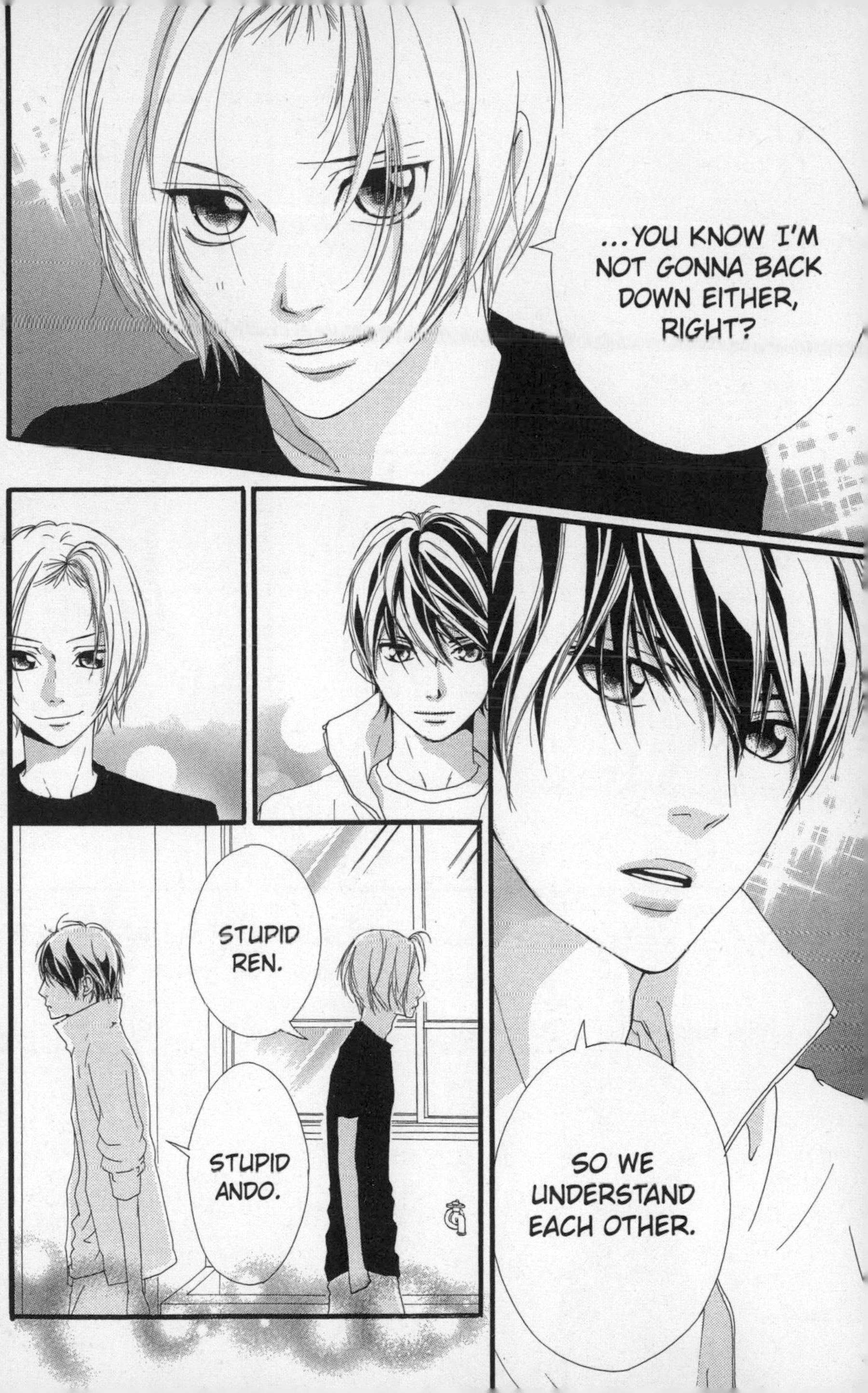
...YOU KNOW I'M NOT GONNA BACK DOWN EITHER, RIGHT?
SO WE UNDERSTAND EACH OTHER.
STUPID REN.
STUPID ANDO.

MY RANDOM GOALS ✚

- Eat chocolate and waffles in Belgium
- Become more feminine
- Have longer arms and legs
- Get smarter
- Learn to draw manga faster
- Fly
- Build up my walking muscles
- Get fillings for my cavities
- Have a physical exam
- Become enthralled with something
- Be frivolous
- Be silly
- Jump headlong into my future
- Replace my broken living-room clock
  When I brought the new one home, the old one was fine.
  What am I supposed to do now?
- Go on a picnic
- Take an overnight train
- Go back to high school
  But I don't want to study. Especially math.
- Have a cup of coffee
- I want a copy machine
- I want to hook up with a cute guy who could be a model for my drawings.
  But I won't.
- I want to draw fun manga.

Here I go!!!

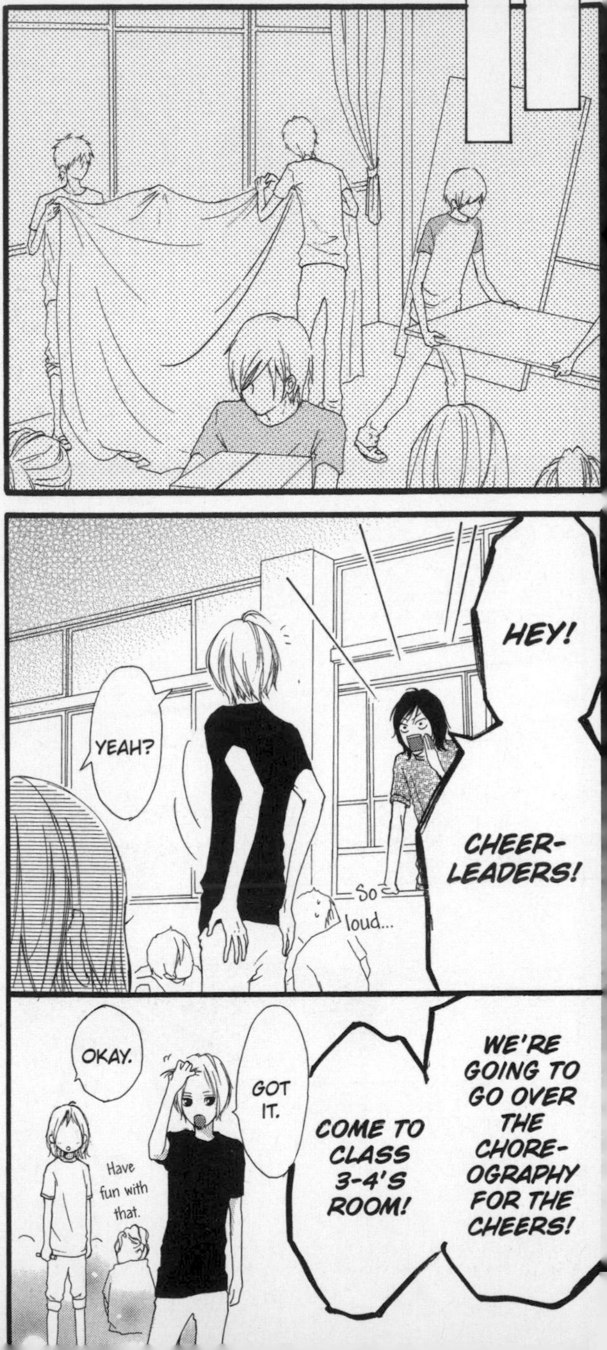
HEY!
CHEER-LEADERS!
YEAH?
So loud...
WE'RE GOING TO GO OVER THE CHOREOGRAPHY FOR THE CHEERS!
COME TO CLASS 3-4'S ROOM!
GOT IT.
OKAY.
Have fun with that.

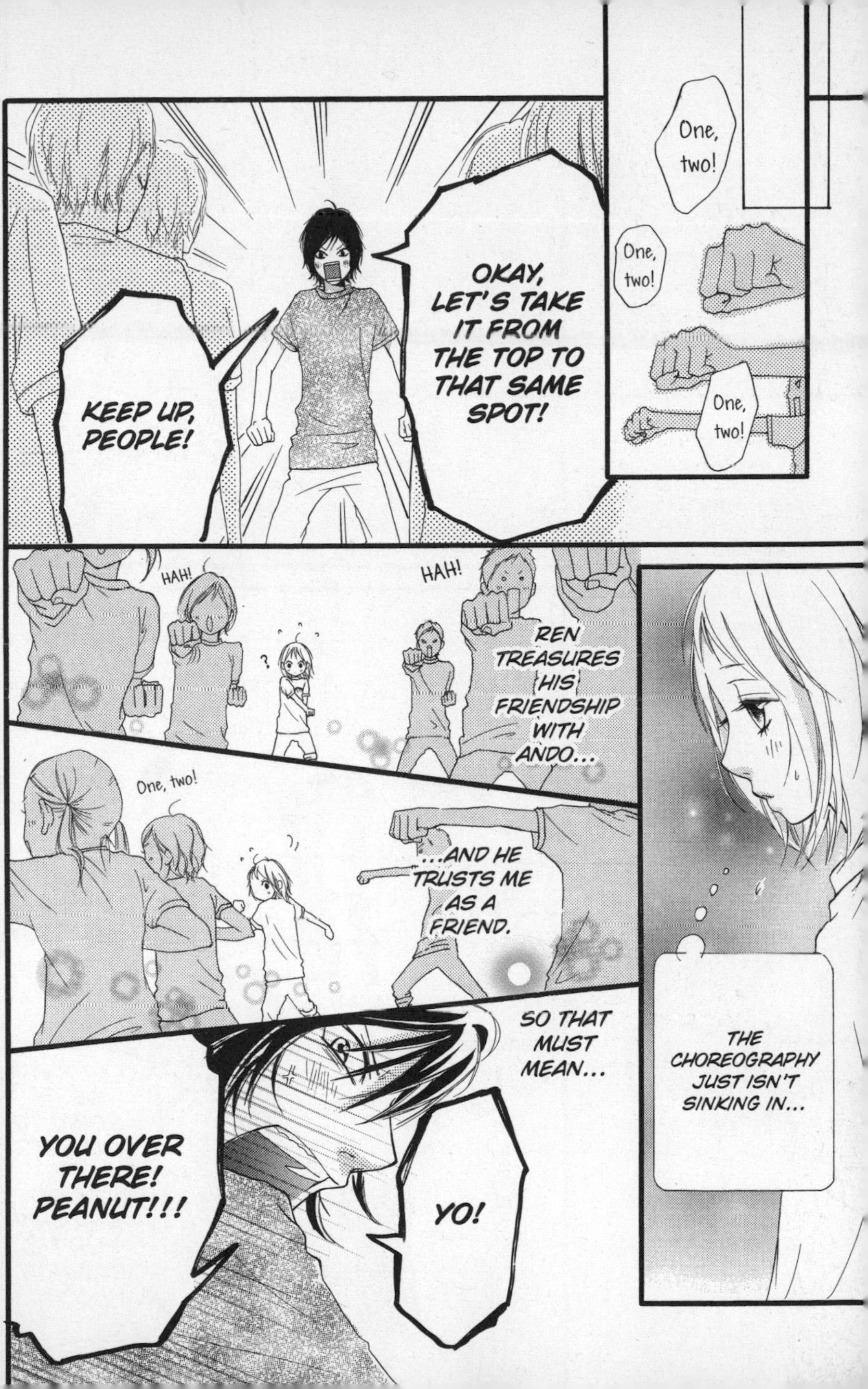
One, two!
One, two!
One, two!
OKAY, LET'S TAKE IT FROM THE TOP TO THAT SAME SPOT!
KEEP UP, PEOPLE!
THE CHOREOGRAPHY JUST ISN'T SINKING IN...
HAH!
REN TREASURES HIS FRIENDSHIP WITH ANDO...
HAH!
One, two!
...AND HE TRUSTS ME AS A FRIEND.
SO THAT MUST MEAN...
YO!
YOU OVER THERE! PEANUT!!!

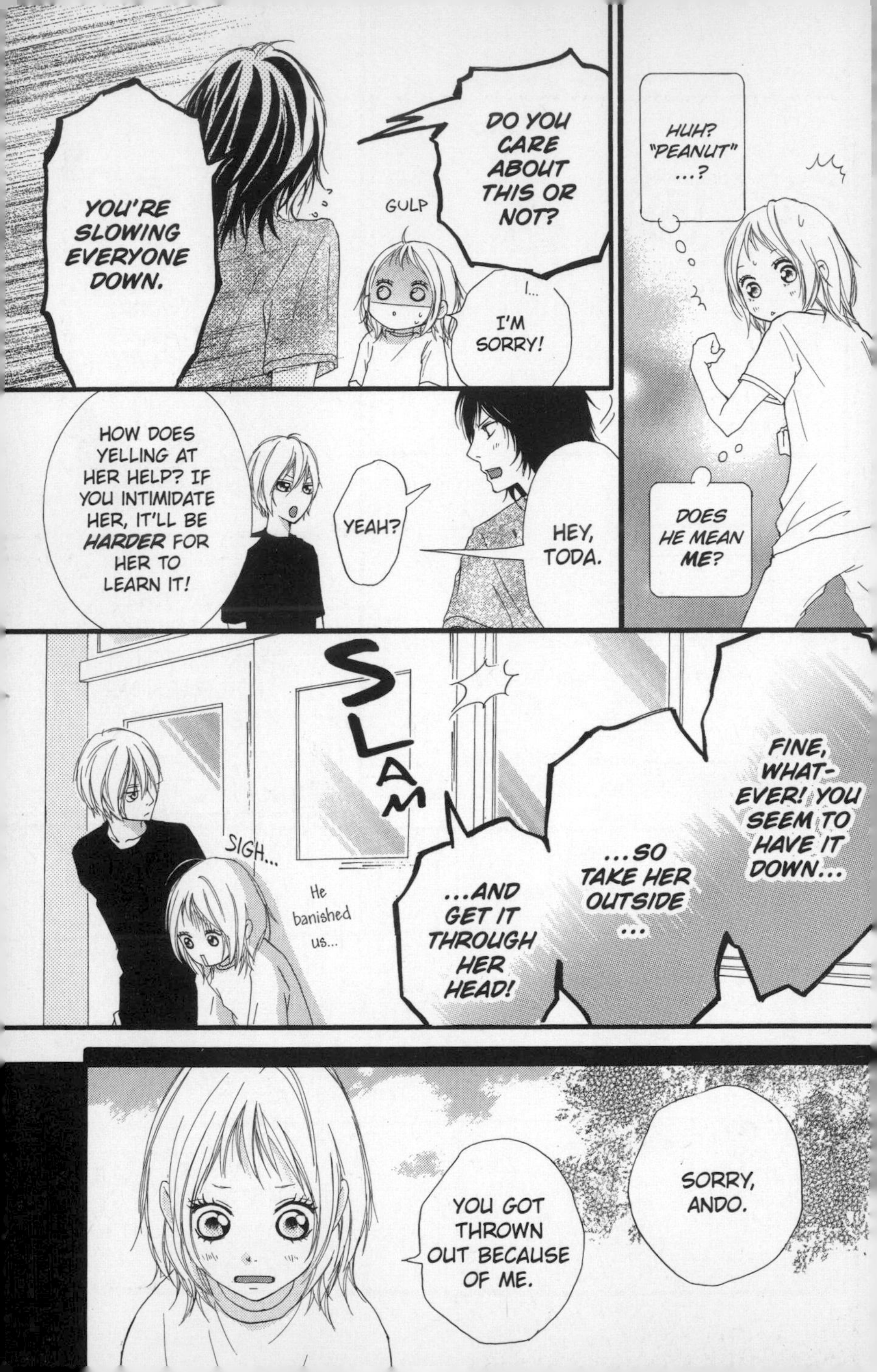
HUH? "PEANUT" ...?
DOES HE MEAN ME?
DO YOU CARE ABOUT THIS OR NOT?
YOU'RE SLOWING EVERYONE DOWN.
GULP
I... I'M SORRY!
HEY, TODA.
YEAH?
HOW DOES YELLING AT HER HELP? IF YOU INTIMIDATE HER, IT'LL BE HARDER FOR HER TO LEARN IT!
FINE, WHAT-EVER! YOU SEEM TO HAVE IT DOWN...
...SO TAKE HER OUTSIDE...
...AND GET IT THROUGH HER HEAD!
SLAM
SIGH...
He banished us...
SORRY, ANDO.
YOU GOT THROWN OUT BECAUSE OF ME.

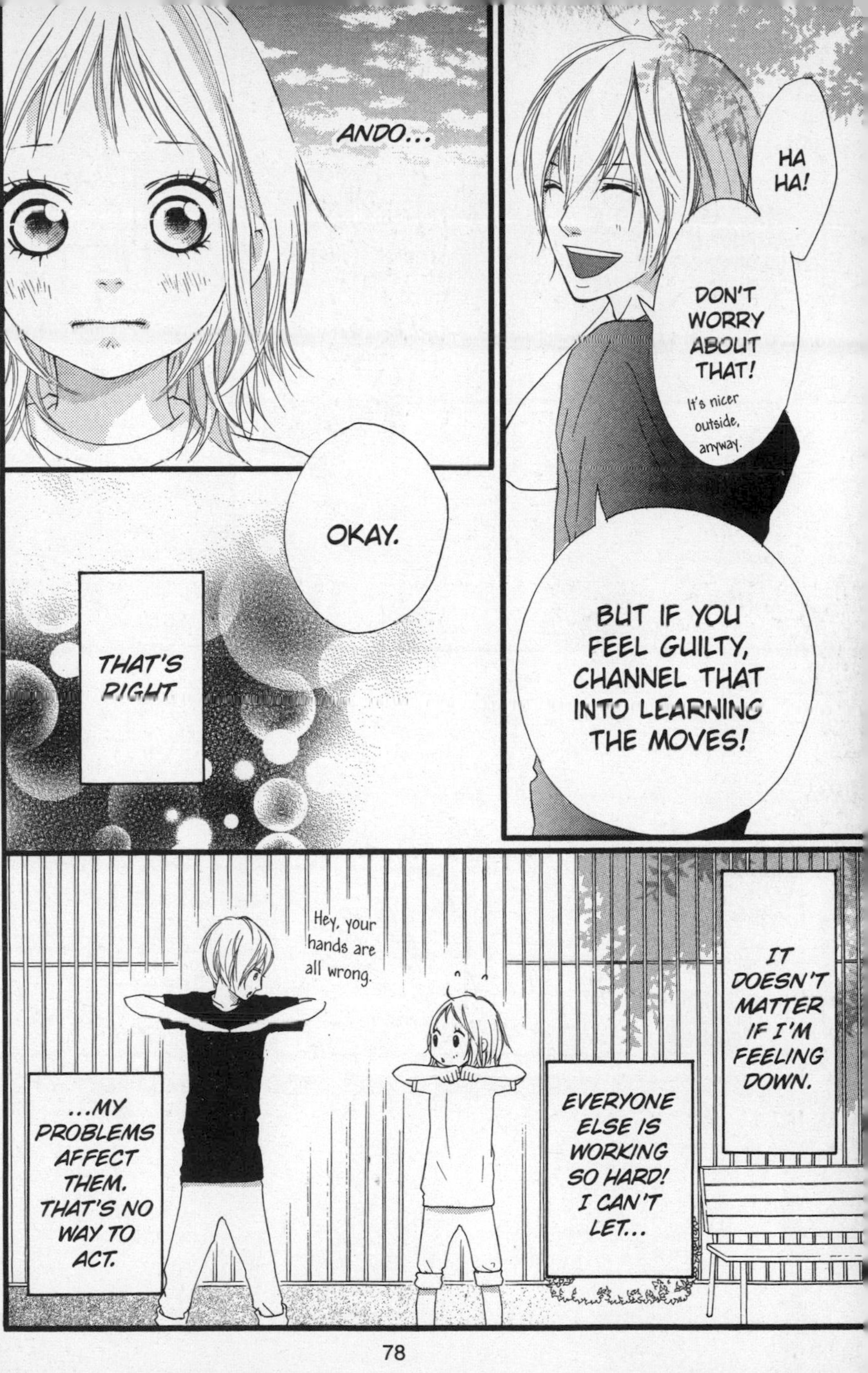
HA HA!
DON'T WORRY ABOUT THAT!
It's nicer outside, anyway.
BUT IF YOU FEEL GUILTY, CHANNEL THAT INTO LEARNING THE MOVES!
ANDO...
OKAY.
THAT'S RIGHT
IT DOESN'T MATTER IF I'M FEELING DOWN.
EVERYONE ELSE IS WORKING SO HARD! I CAN'T LET...
Hey, your hands are all wrong.
...MY PROBLEMS AFFECT THEM. THAT'S NO WAY TO ACT.

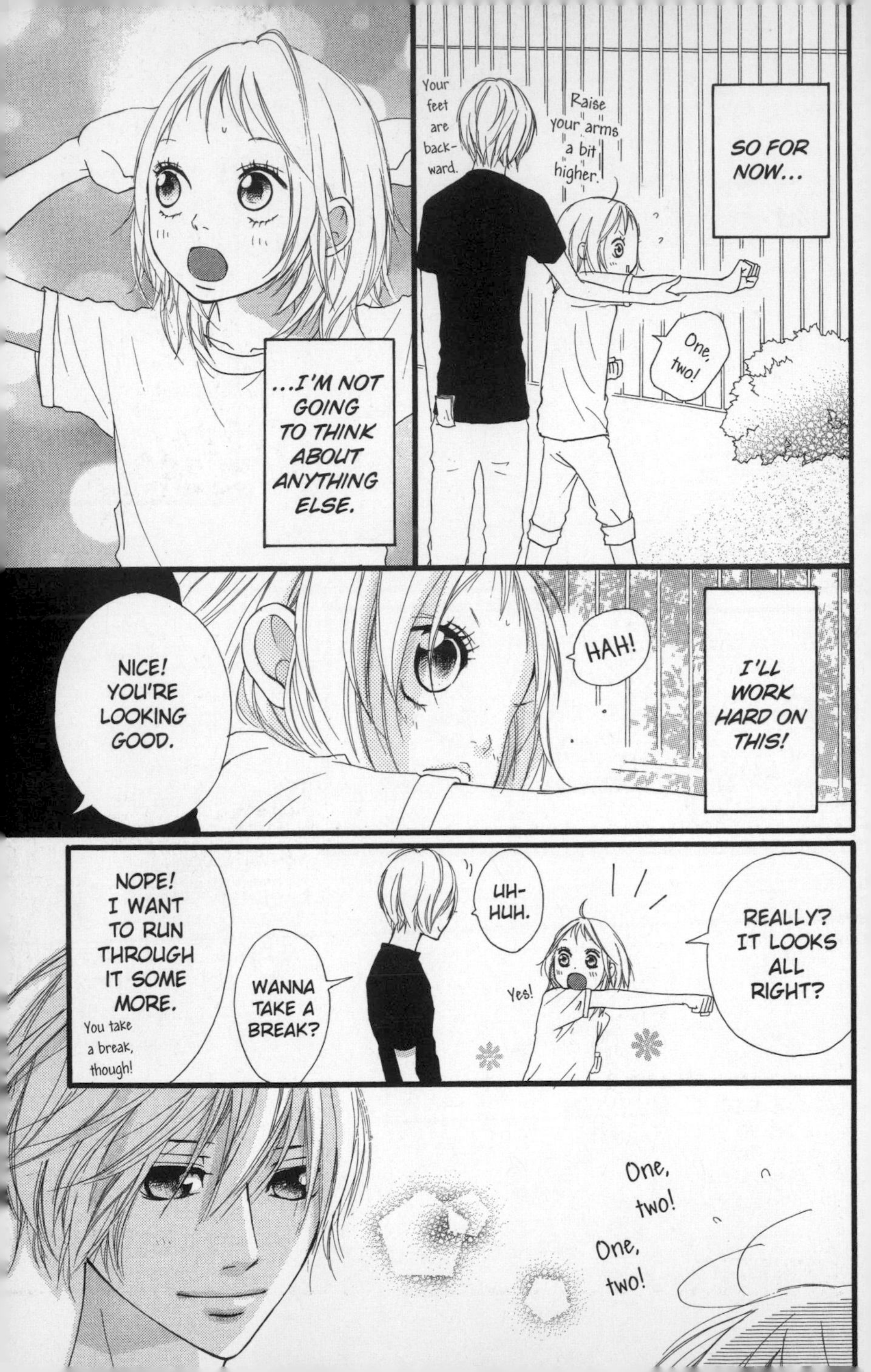
SO FOR NOW...
Raise your arms a bit higher.
Your feet are backward.
One, two!
...I'M NOT GOING TO THINK ABOUT ANYTHING ELSE.
I'LL WORK HARD ON THIS!
HAH!
NICE! YOU'RE LOOKING GOOD.
REALLY? IT LOOKS ALL RIGHT?
Yes!
UH-HUH.
WANNA TAKE A BREAK?
NOPE! I WANT TO RUN THROUGH IT SOME MORE.
You take a break, though!
One, two!
One, two!

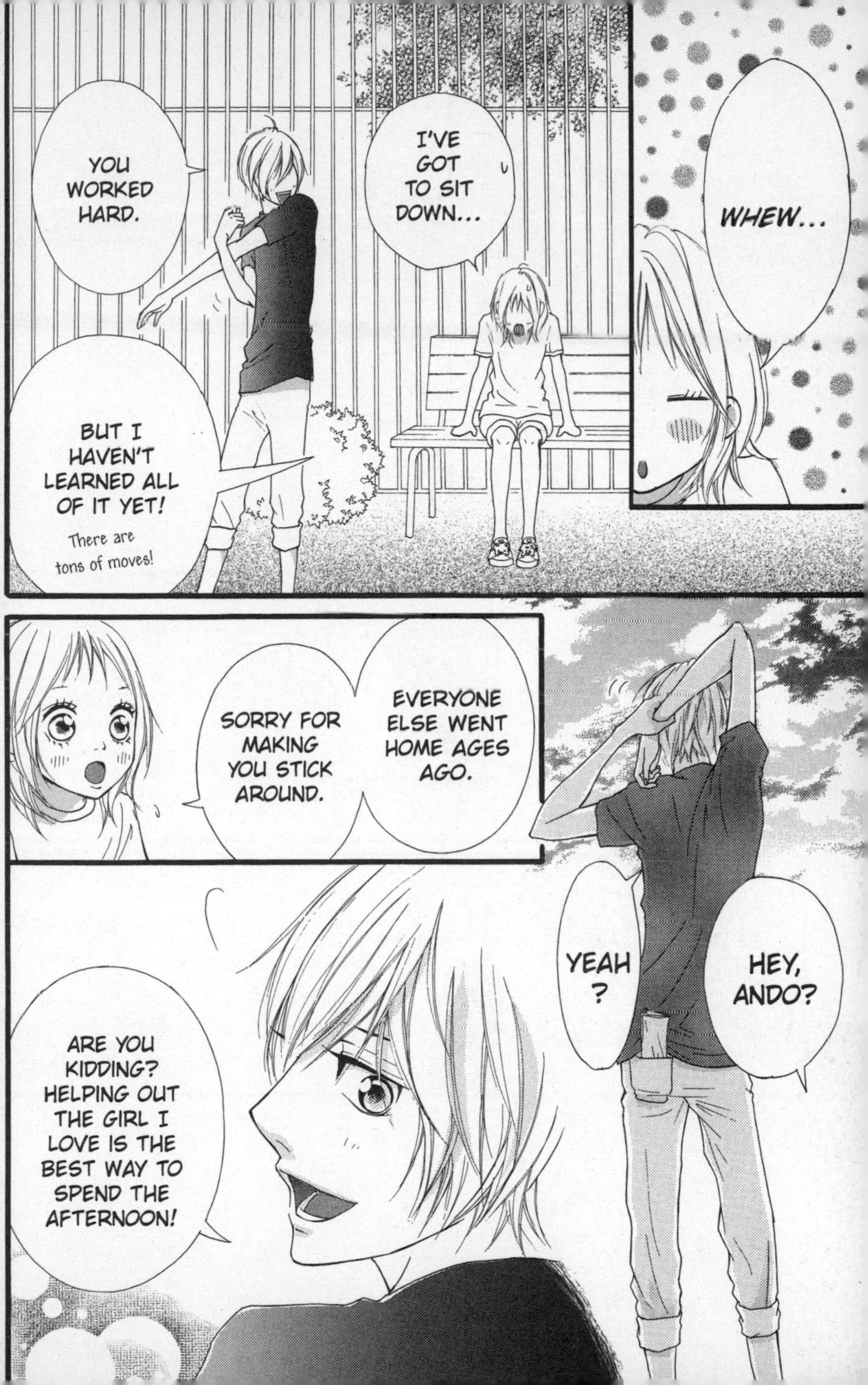
WHEW...
I'VE GOT TO SIT DOWN...
YOU WORKED HARD.
BUT I HAVEN'T LEARNED ALL OF IT YET!
There are tons of moves!
HEY, ANDO?
YEAH?
EVERYONE ELSE WENT HOME AGES AGO.
SORRY FOR MAKING YOU STICK AROUND.
ARE YOU KIDDING? HELPING OUT THE GIRL I LOVE IS THE BEST WAY TO SPEND THE AFTERNOON!

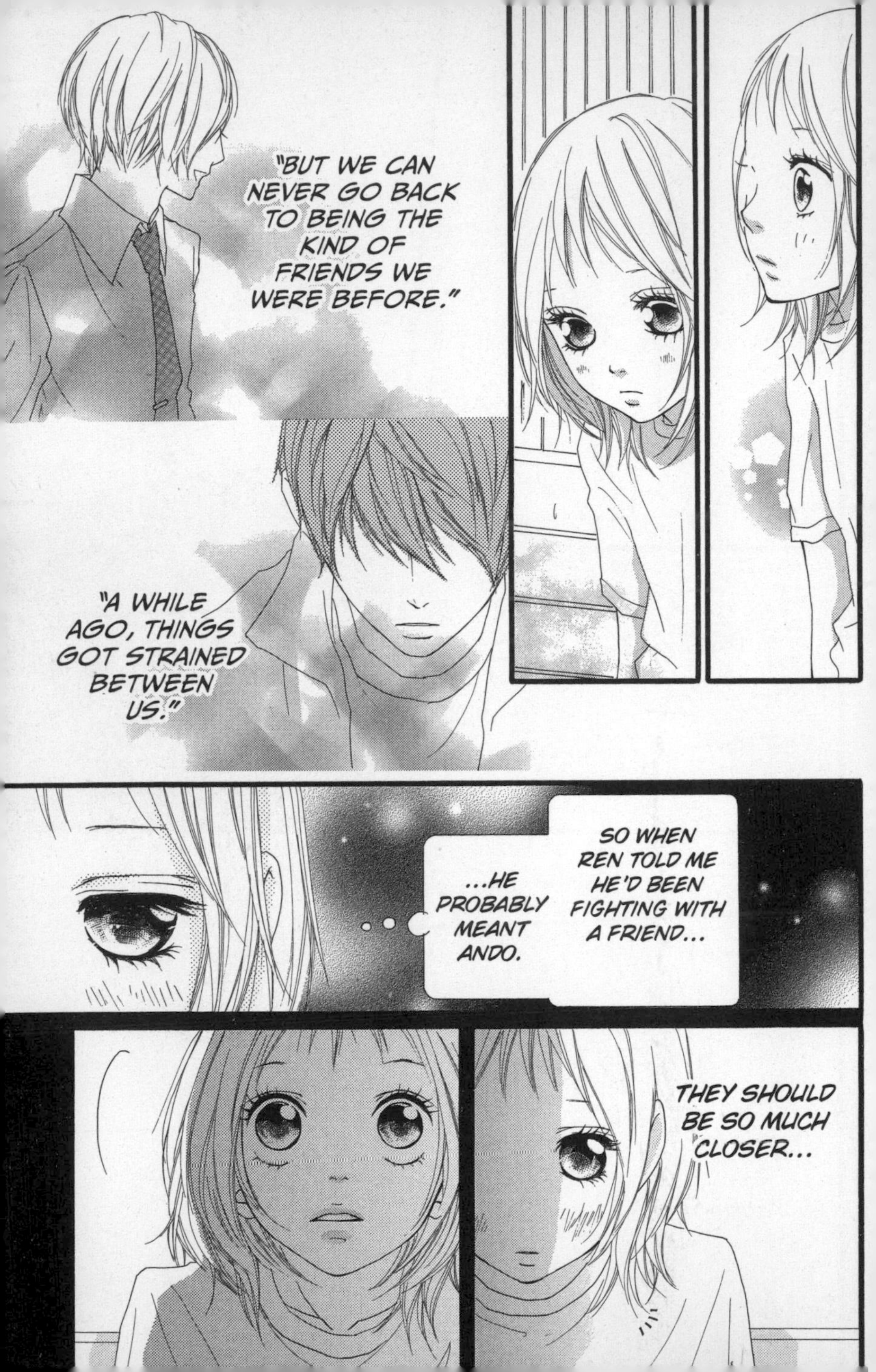
"BUT WE CAN NEVER GO BACK TO BEING THE KIND OF FRIENDS WE WERE BEFORE."
"A WHILE AGO, THINGS GOT STRAINED BETWEEN US."
SO WHEN REN TOLD ME HE'D BEEN FIGHTING WITH A FRIEND...
...HE PROBABLY MEANT ANDO.
THEY SHOULD BE SO MUCH CLOSER...

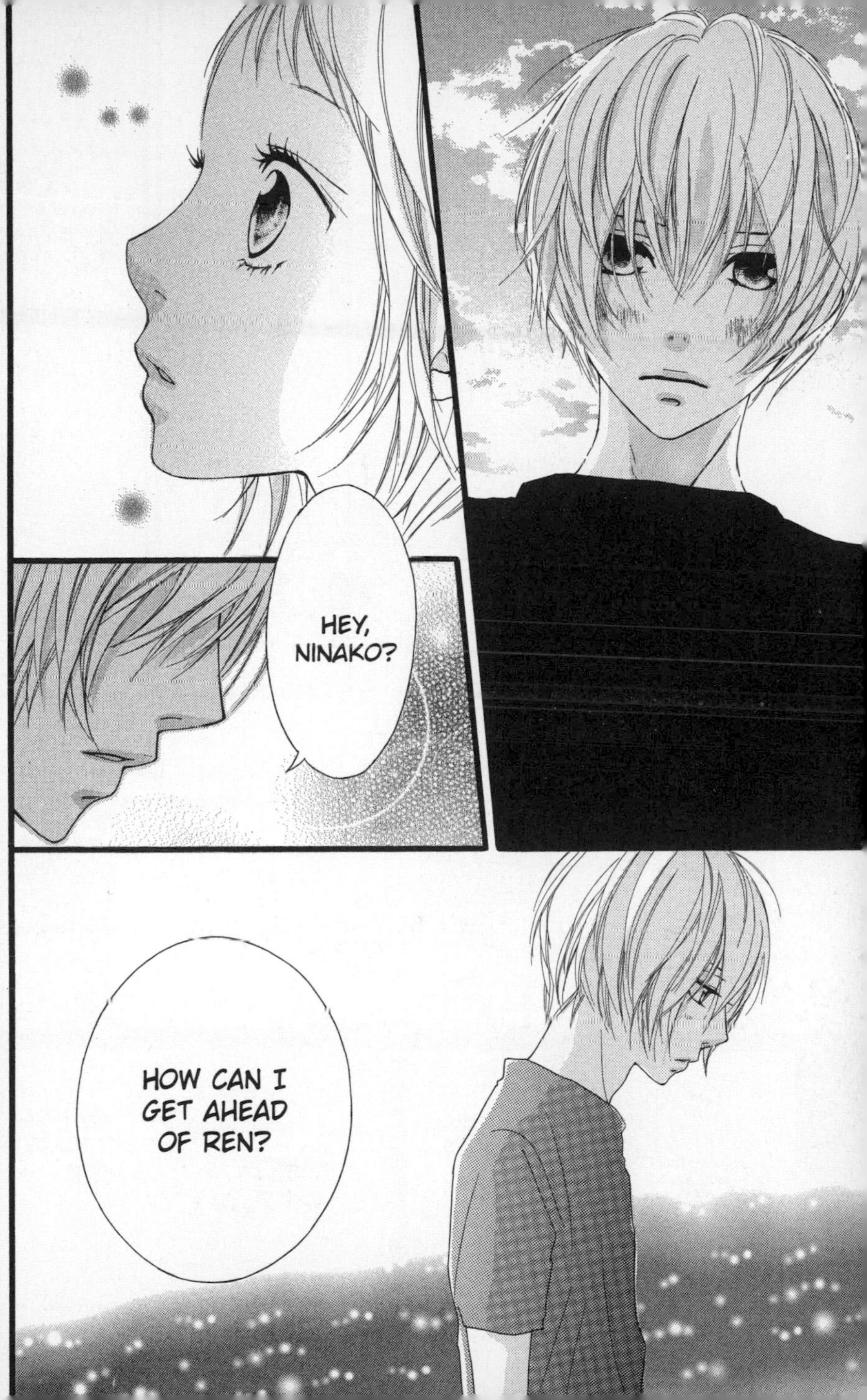
HEY, NINAKO?
HOW CAN I GET AHEAD OF REN?

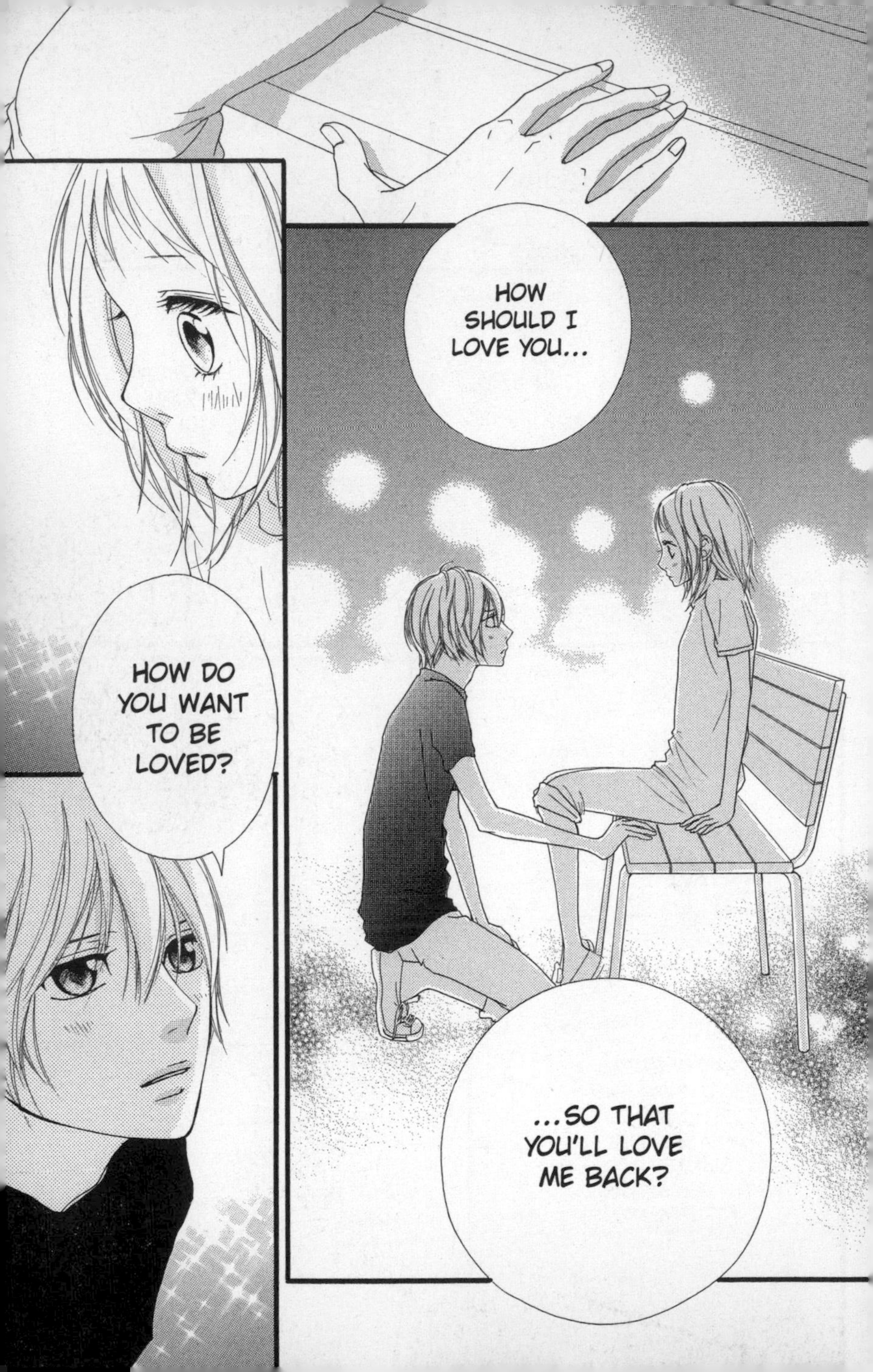
HOW SHOULD I LOVE YOU...
...SO THAT YOU'LL LOVE ME BACK?
HOW DO YOU WANT TO BE LOVED?

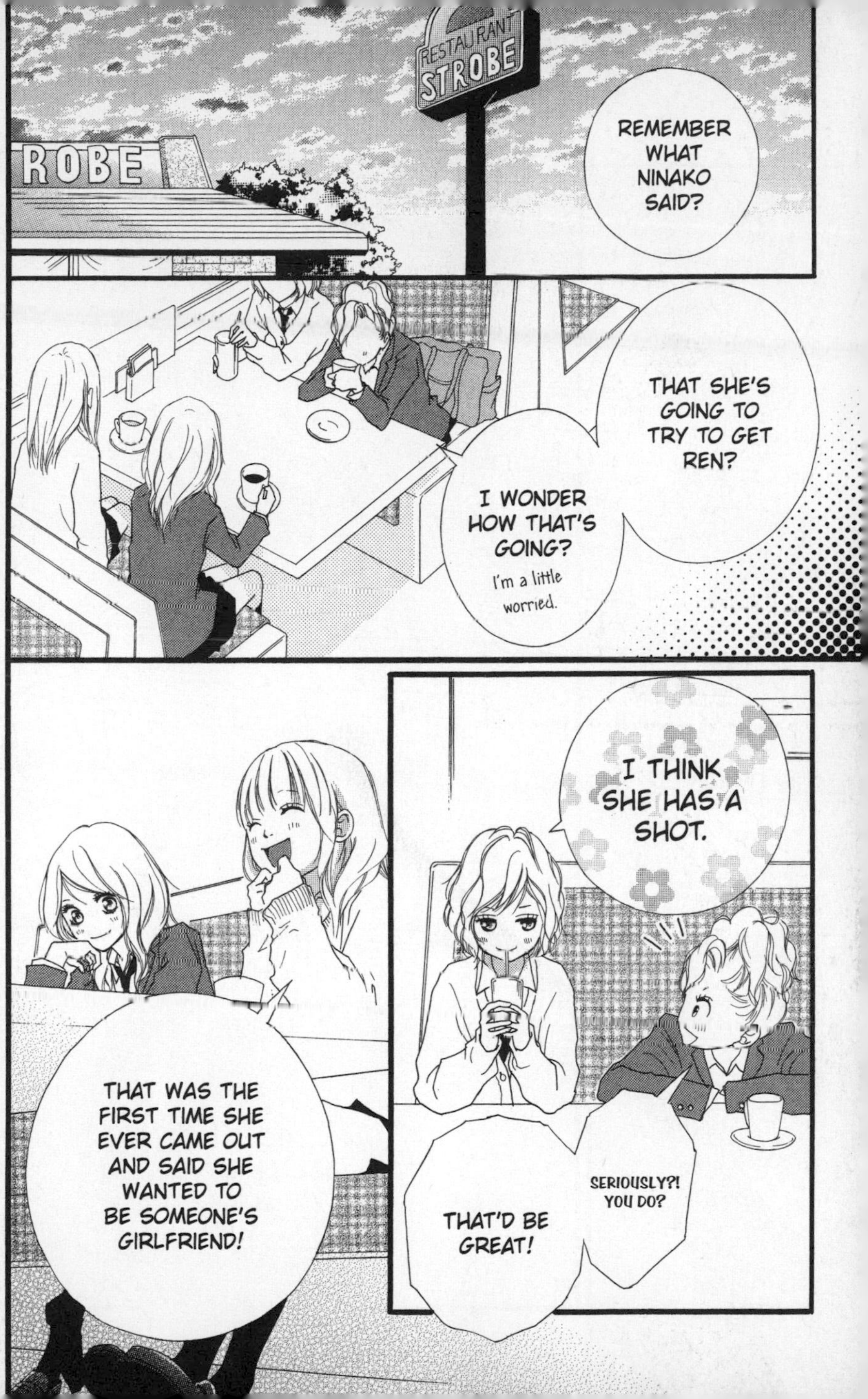
RESTAURANT STROBE
ROBE
REMEMBER WHAT NINAKO SAID?
THAT SHE'S GOING TO TRY TO GET REN?
I WONDER HOW THAT'S GOING?
I'm a little worried.
I THINK SHE HAS A SHOT.
SERIOUSLY?! YOU DO?
THAT'D BE GREAT!
THAT WAS THE FIRST TIME SHE EVER CAME OUT AND SAID SHE WANTED TO BE SOMEONE'S GIRLFRIEND!

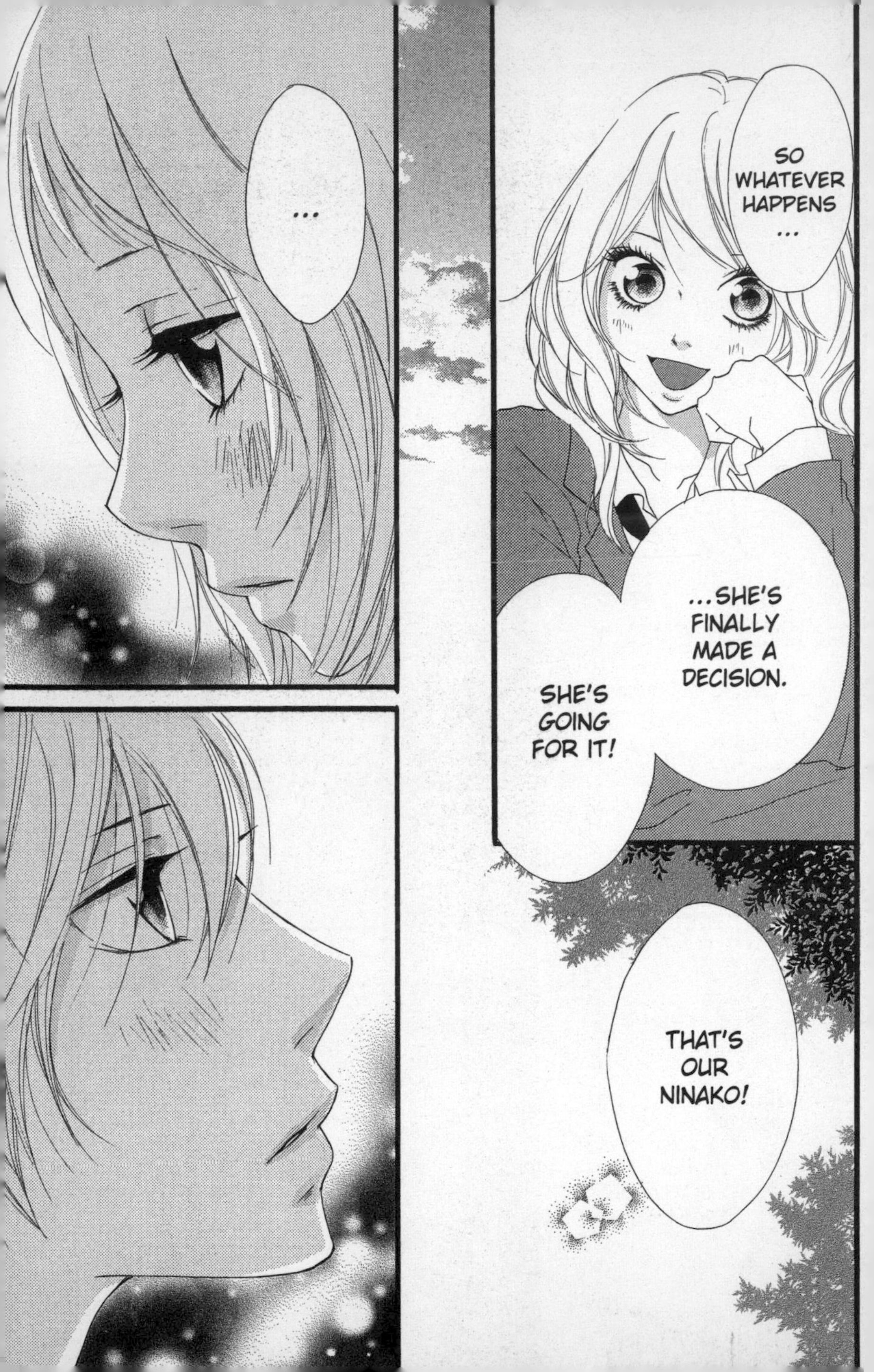
SO WHATEVER HAPPENS ...
...SHE'S FINALLY MADE A DECISION.
SHE'S GOING FOR IT!
THAT'S OUR NINAKO!
...

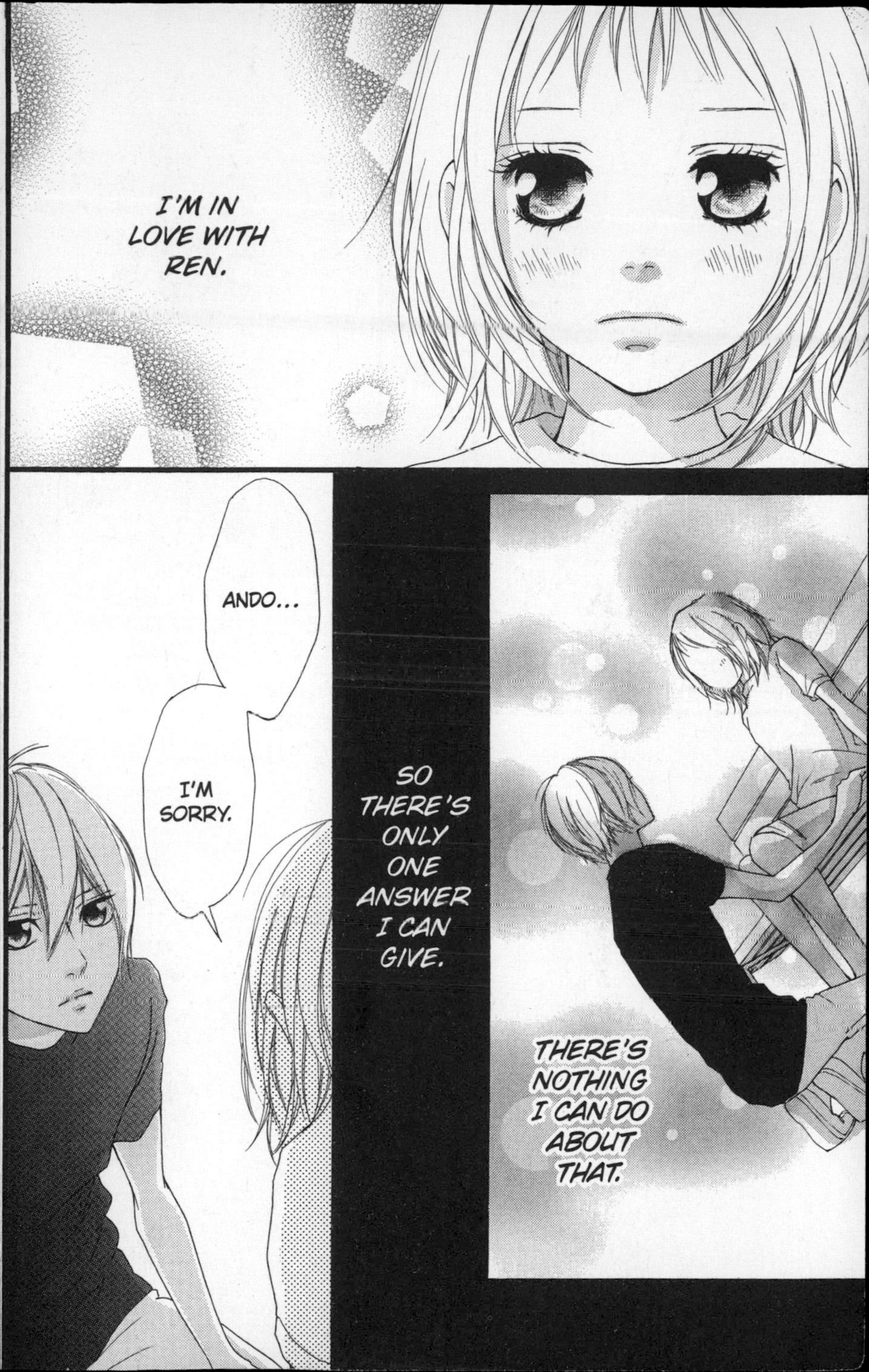
I'M IN LOVE WITH REN.
THERE'S NOTHING I CAN DO ABOUT THAT.
SO THERE'S ONLY ONE ANSWER I CAN GIVE.
ANDO...
I'M SORRY.

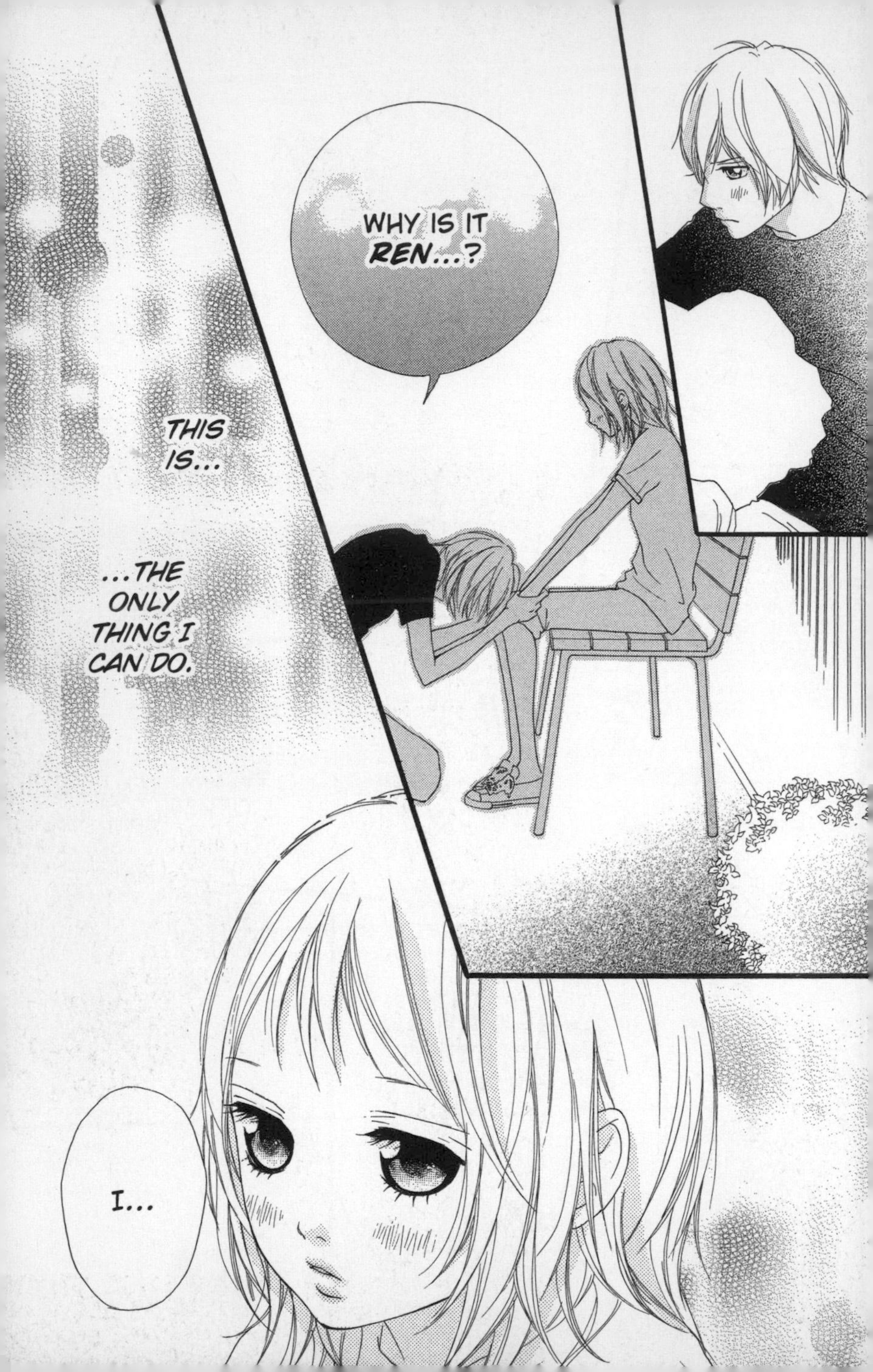
WHY IS IT REN...?
THIS IS...
...THE ONLY THING I CAN DO.
I...

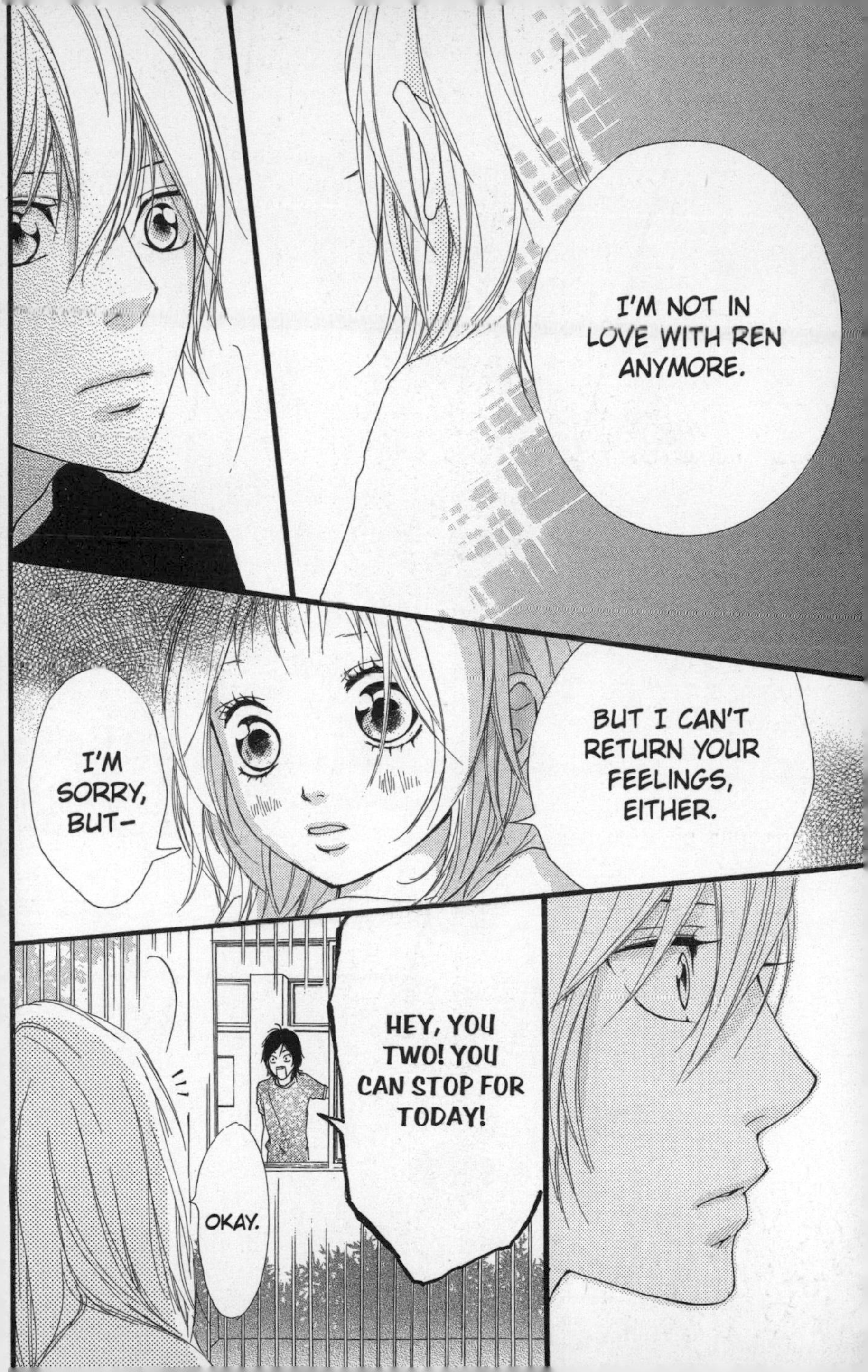
I'M NOT IN LOVE WITH REN ANYMORE.
BUT I CAN'T RETURN YOUR FEELINGS, EITHER.
I'M SORRY, BUT-
HEY, YOU TWO! YOU CAN STOP FOR TODAY!
OKAY.

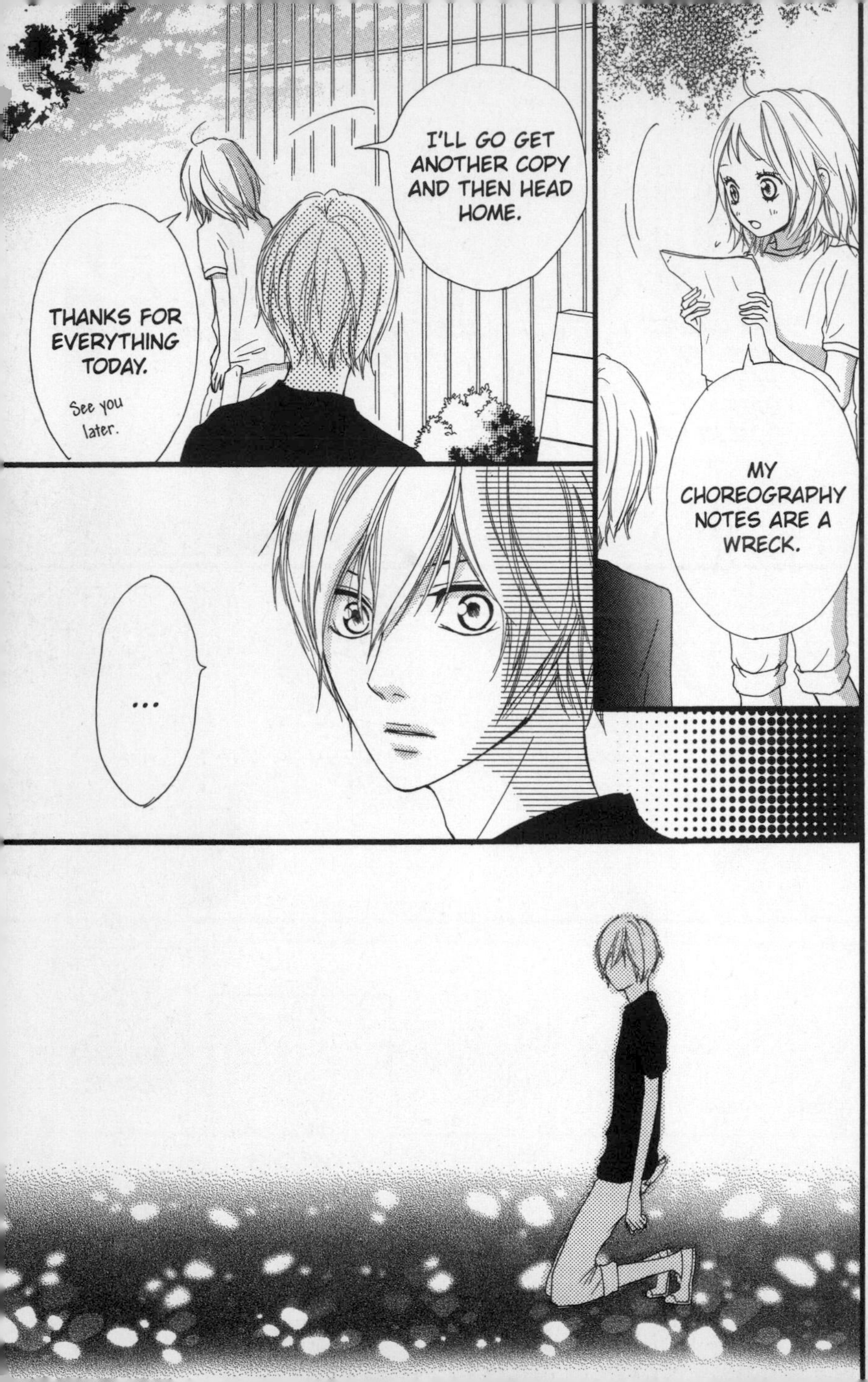
MY CHOREOGRAPHY NOTES ARE A WRECK.
I'LL GO GET ANOTHER COPY AND THEN HEAD HOME.
THANKS FOR EVERYTHING TODAY.
See you later.
...

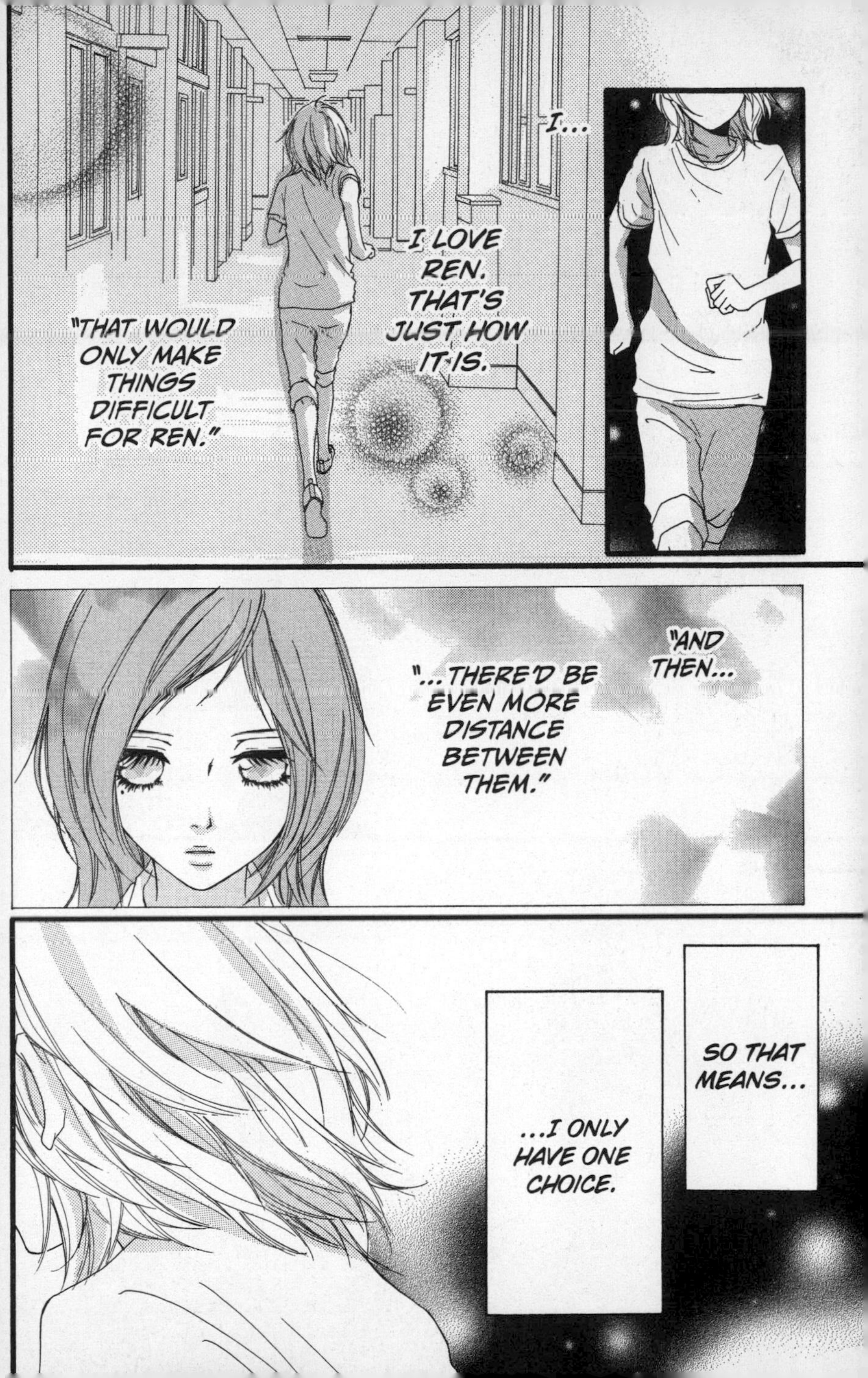
I...
I LOVE REN. THAT'S JUST HOW IT IS.
"THAT WOULD ONLY MAKE THINGS DIFFICULT FOR REN."
"AND THEN...
"...THERE'D BE EVEN MORE DISTANCE BETWEEN THEM."
SO THAT MEANS...
...I ONLY HAVE ONE CHOICE.

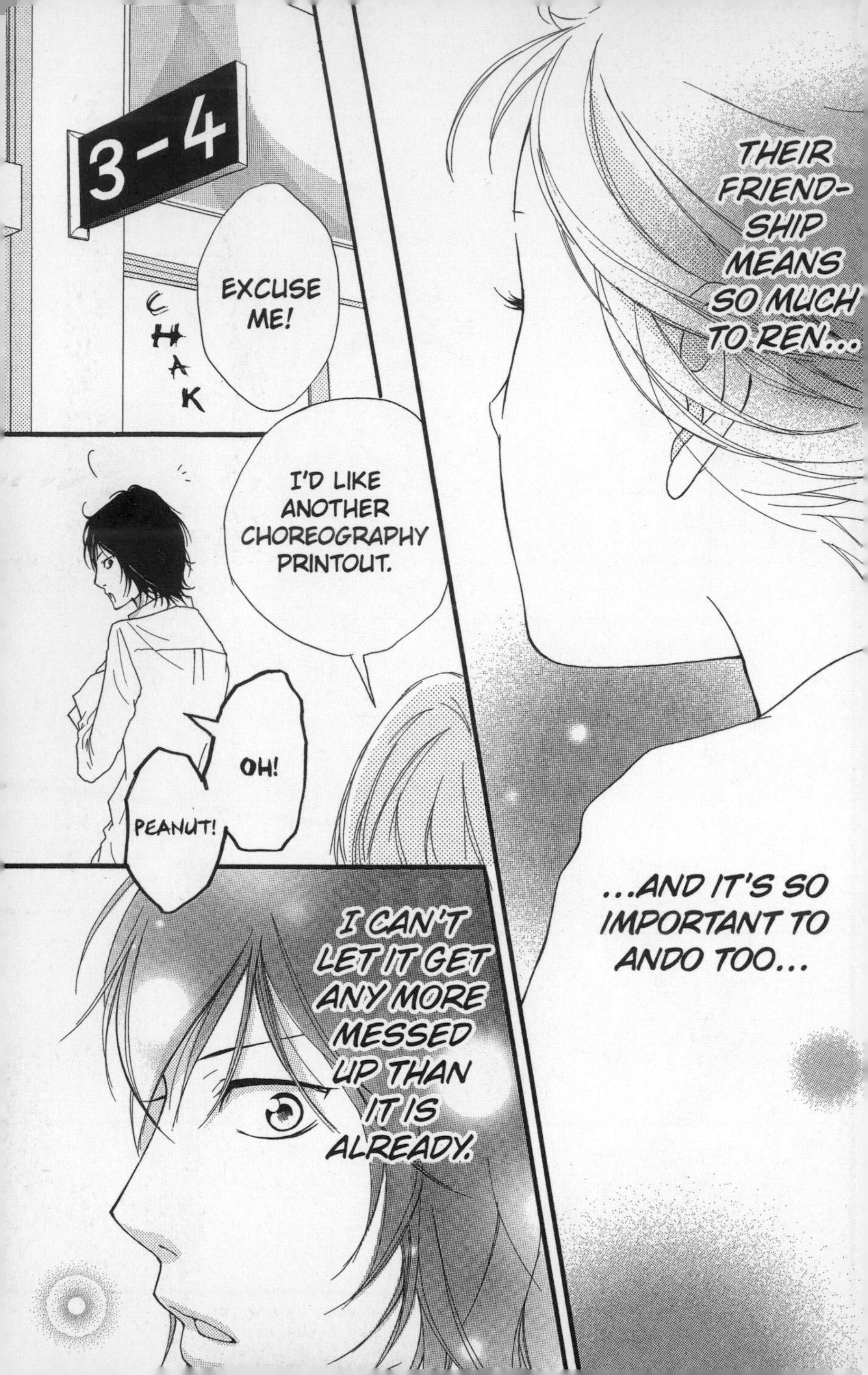
THEIR FRIEND-SHIP MEANS SO MUCH TO REN...
...AND IT'S SO IMPORTANT TO ANDO TOO...
3-4
EXCUSE ME!
CHAK
I'D LIKE ANOTHER CHOREOGRAPHY PRINTOUT.
OH!
PEANUT!
I CAN'T LET IT GET ANY MORE MESSED UP THAN IT IS ALREADY.

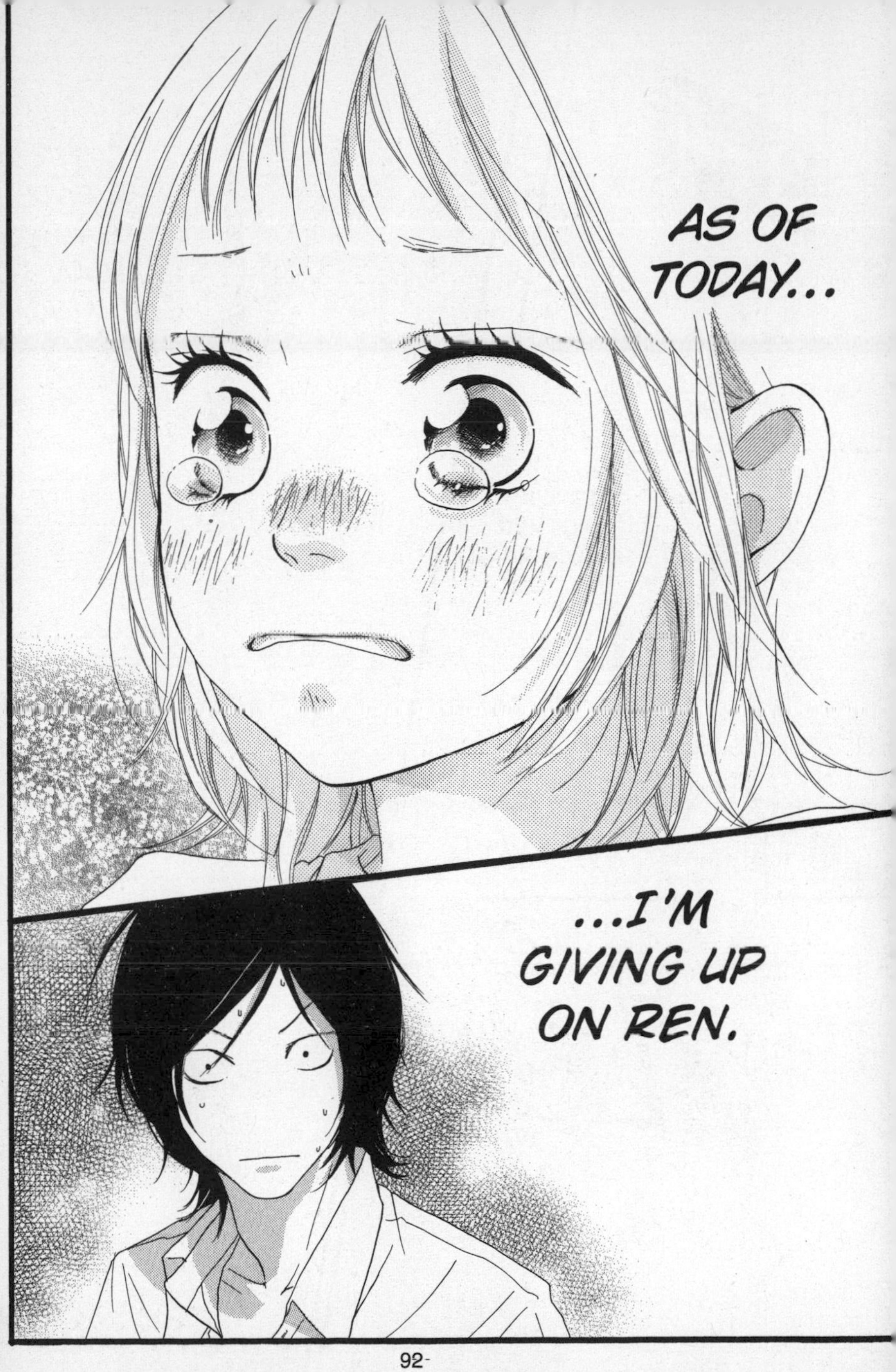
AS OF TODAY...
...I'M GIVING UP ON REN.

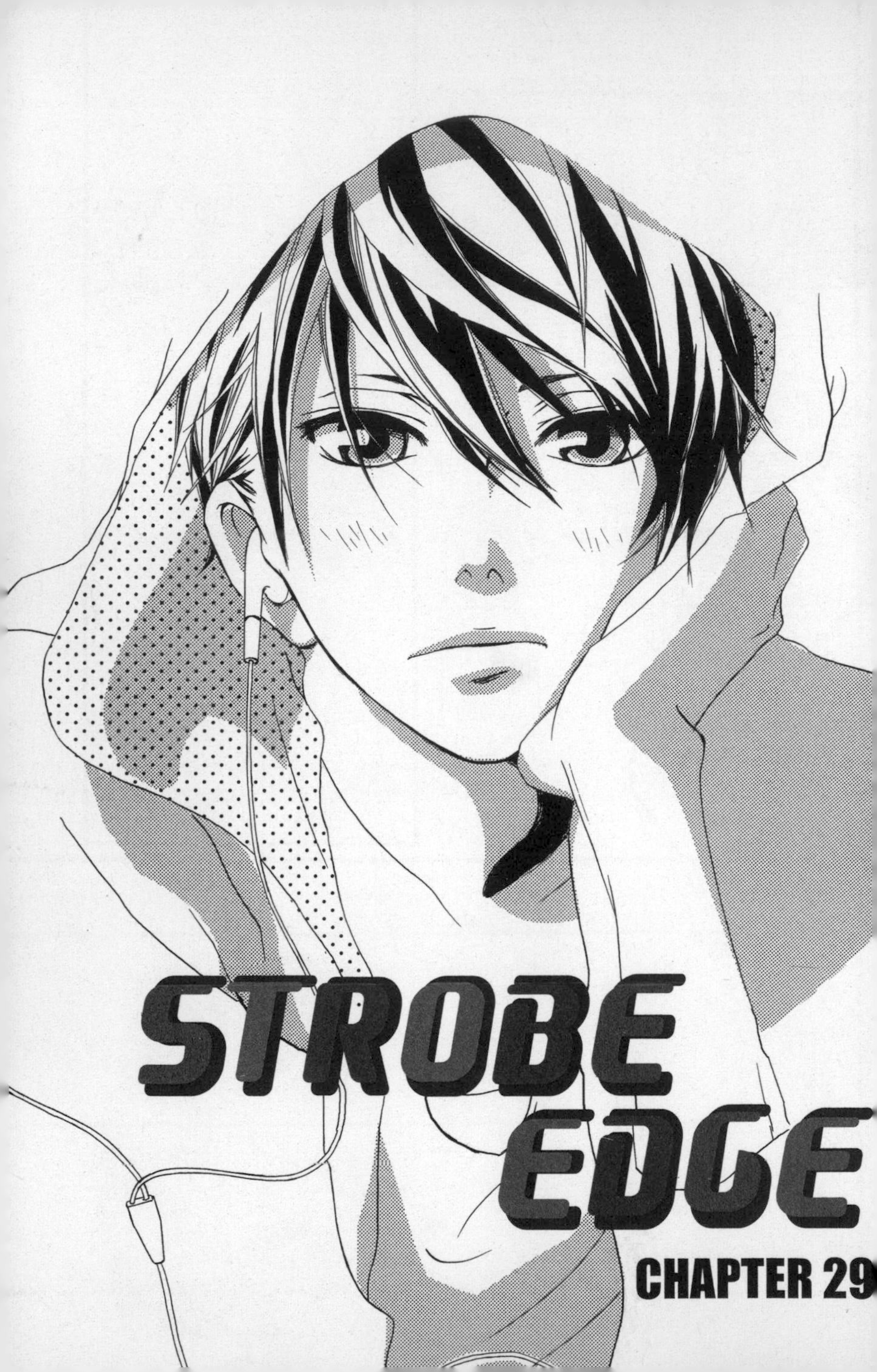
STROBE EDGE
CHAPTER 29

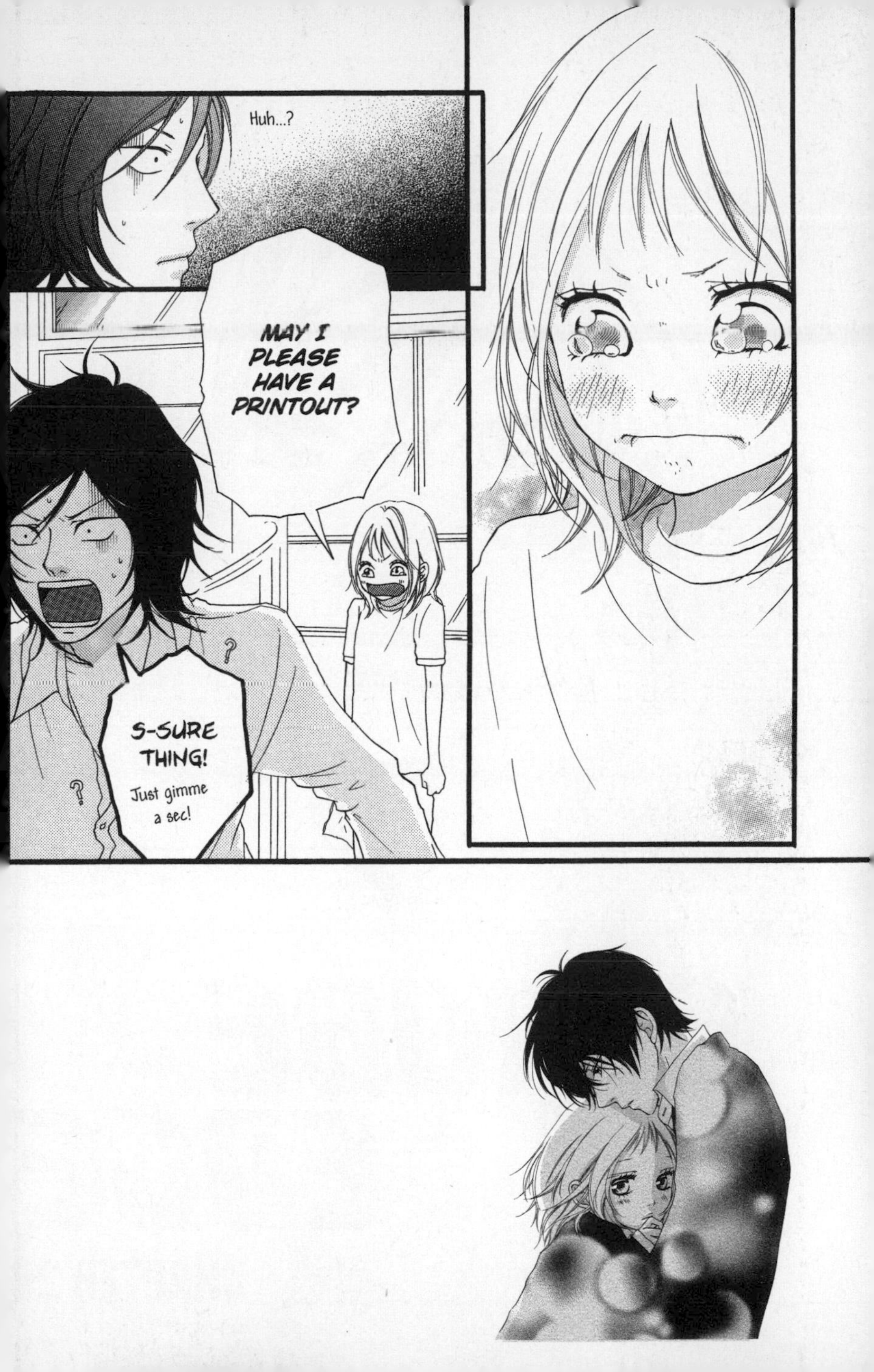
Huh...?
MAY I PLEASE HAVE A PRINTOUT?
S-SURE THING!
Just gimme a sec!

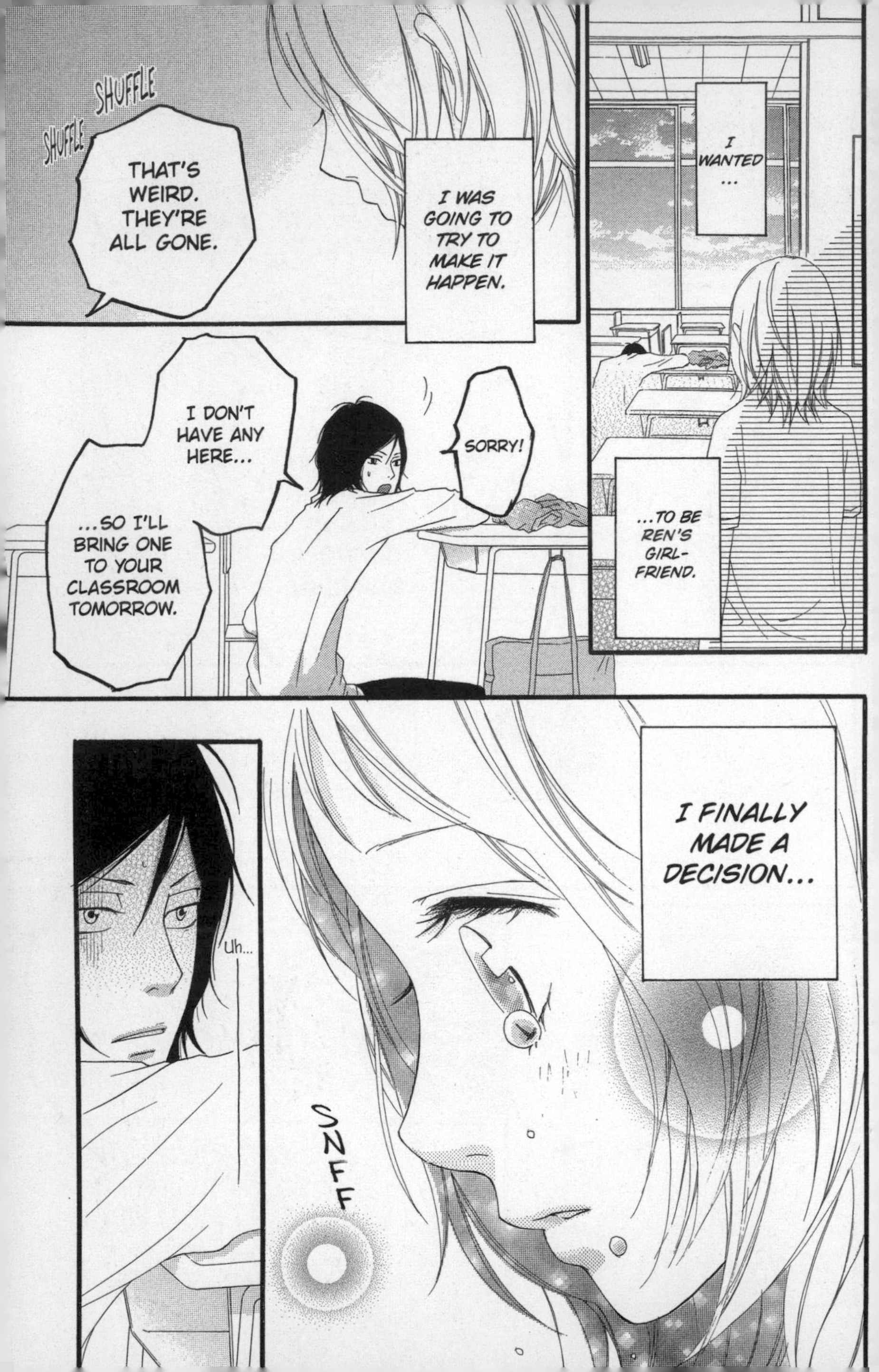
I WANTED ...
...TO BE REN'S GIRL-FRIEND.
I WAS GOING TO TRY TO MAKE IT HAPPEN.
SHUFFLE
SHUFFLE
THAT'S WEIRD. THEY'RE ALL GONE.
SORRY!
I DON'T HAVE ANY HERE...
...SO I'LL BRING ONE TO YOUR CLASSROOM TOMORROW.
I FINALLY MADE A DECISION...
SNFF
Uh...

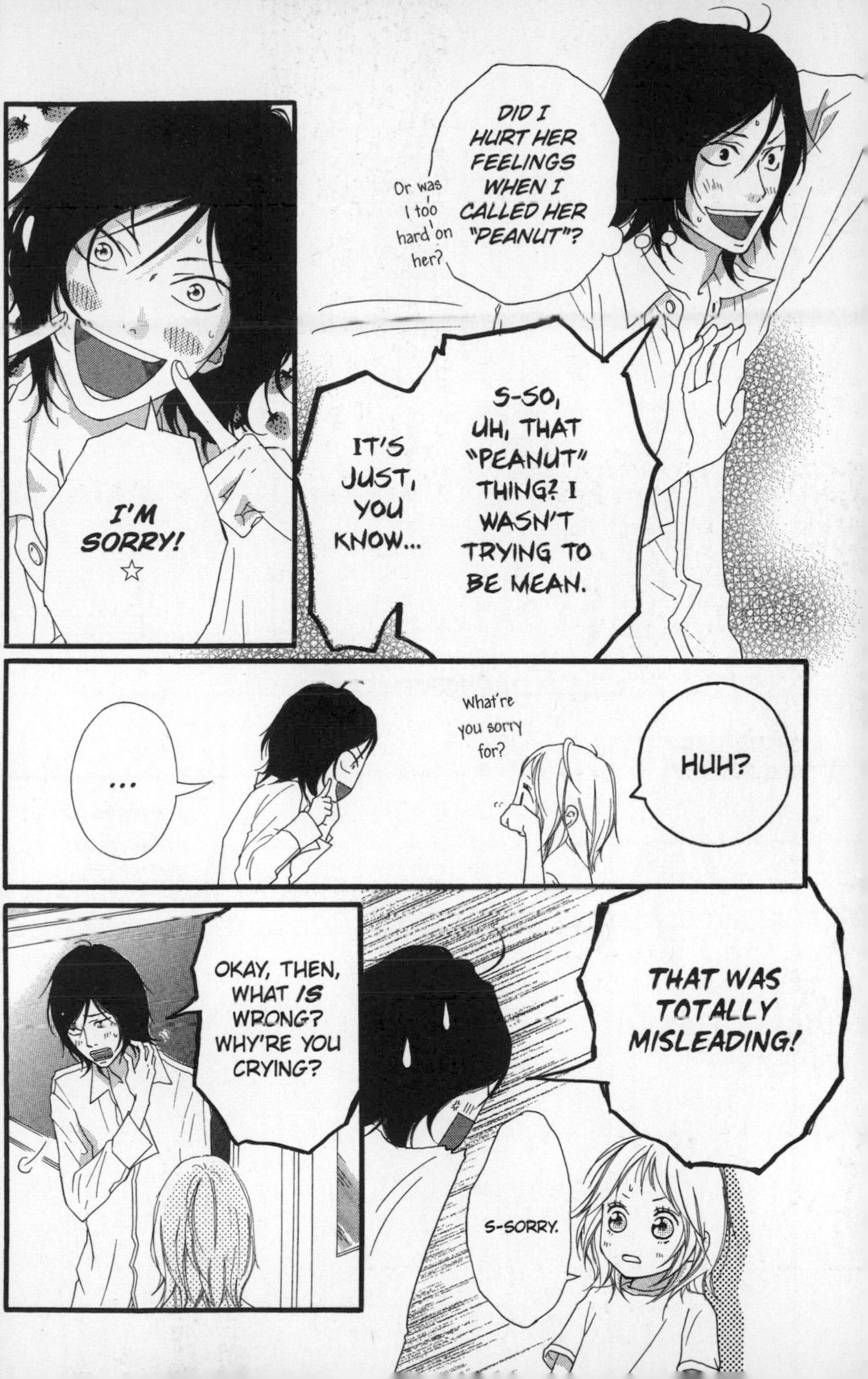
DID I HURT HER FEELINGS WHEN I CALLED HER "PEANUT"?
Or was I too hard on her?
S-SO, UH, THAT "PEANUT" THING? I WASN'T TRYING TO BE MEAN.
IT'S JUST, YOU KNOW...
I'M SORRY! ☆
HUH?
What're you sorry for?
...
THAT WAS TOTALLY MISLEADING!
S-SORRY.
OKAY, THEN, WHAT IS WRONG? WHY'RE YOU CRYING?

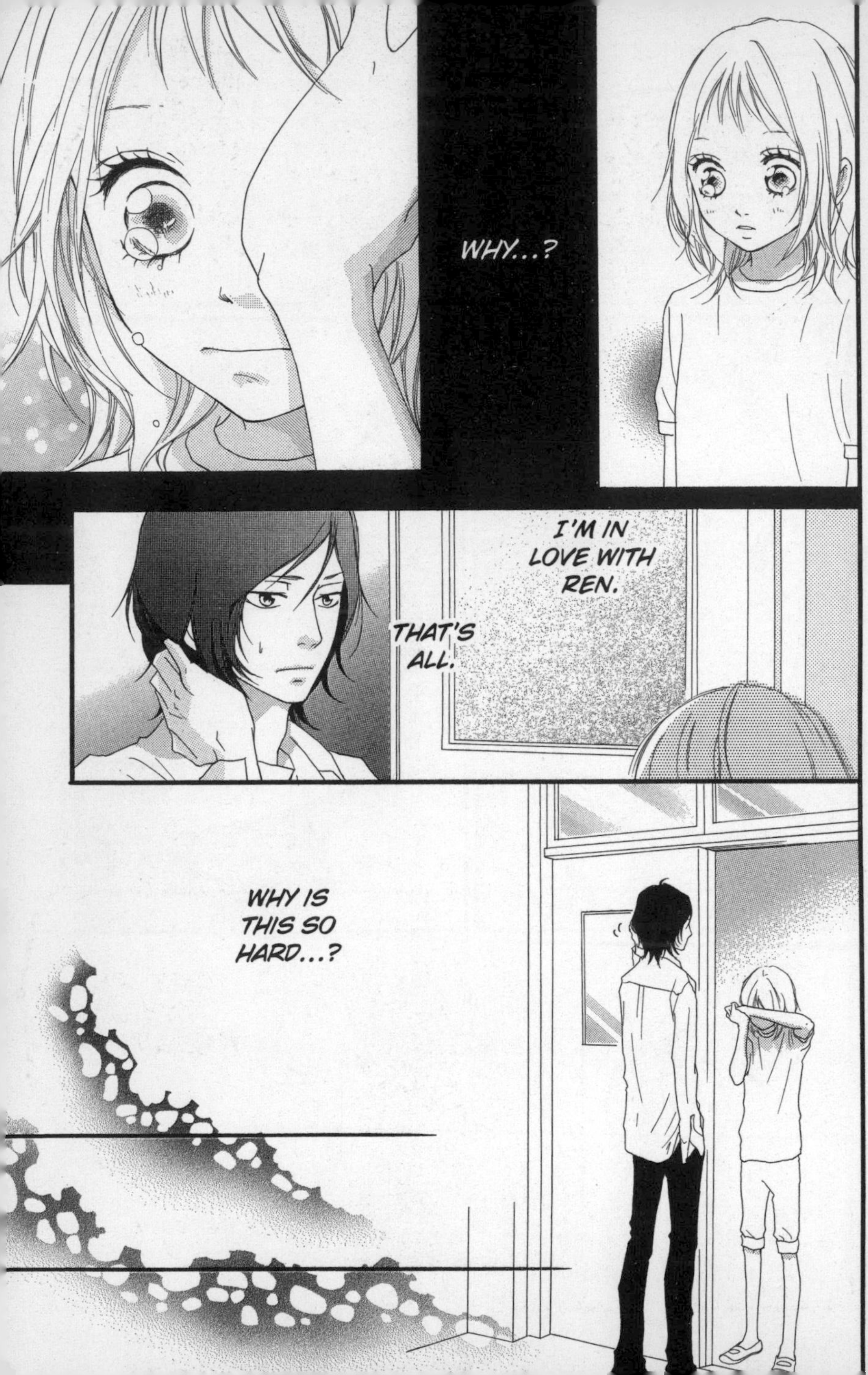
WHY...?
I'M IN LOVE WITH REN.
THAT'S ALL.
WHY IS THIS SO HARD...?

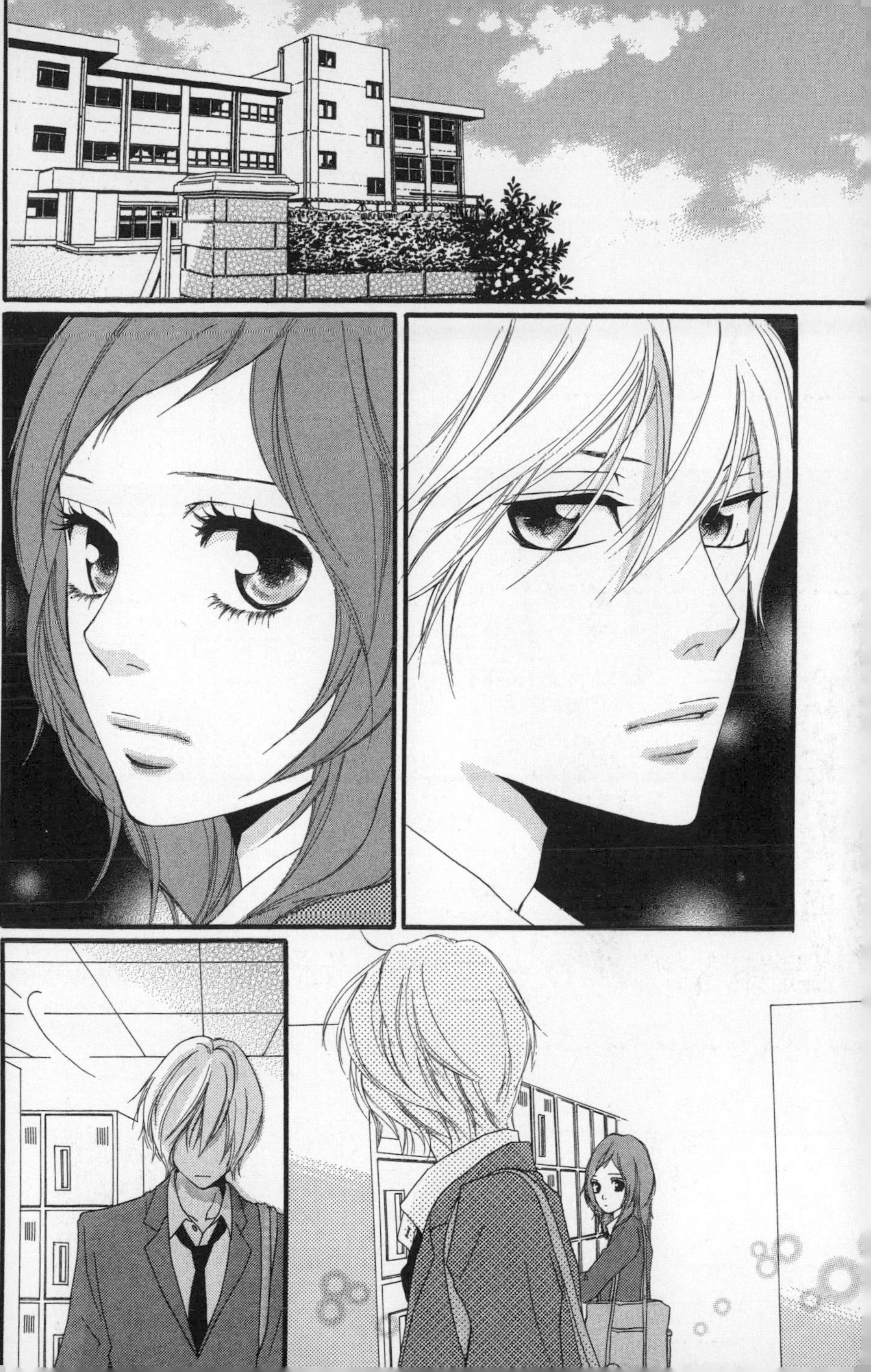

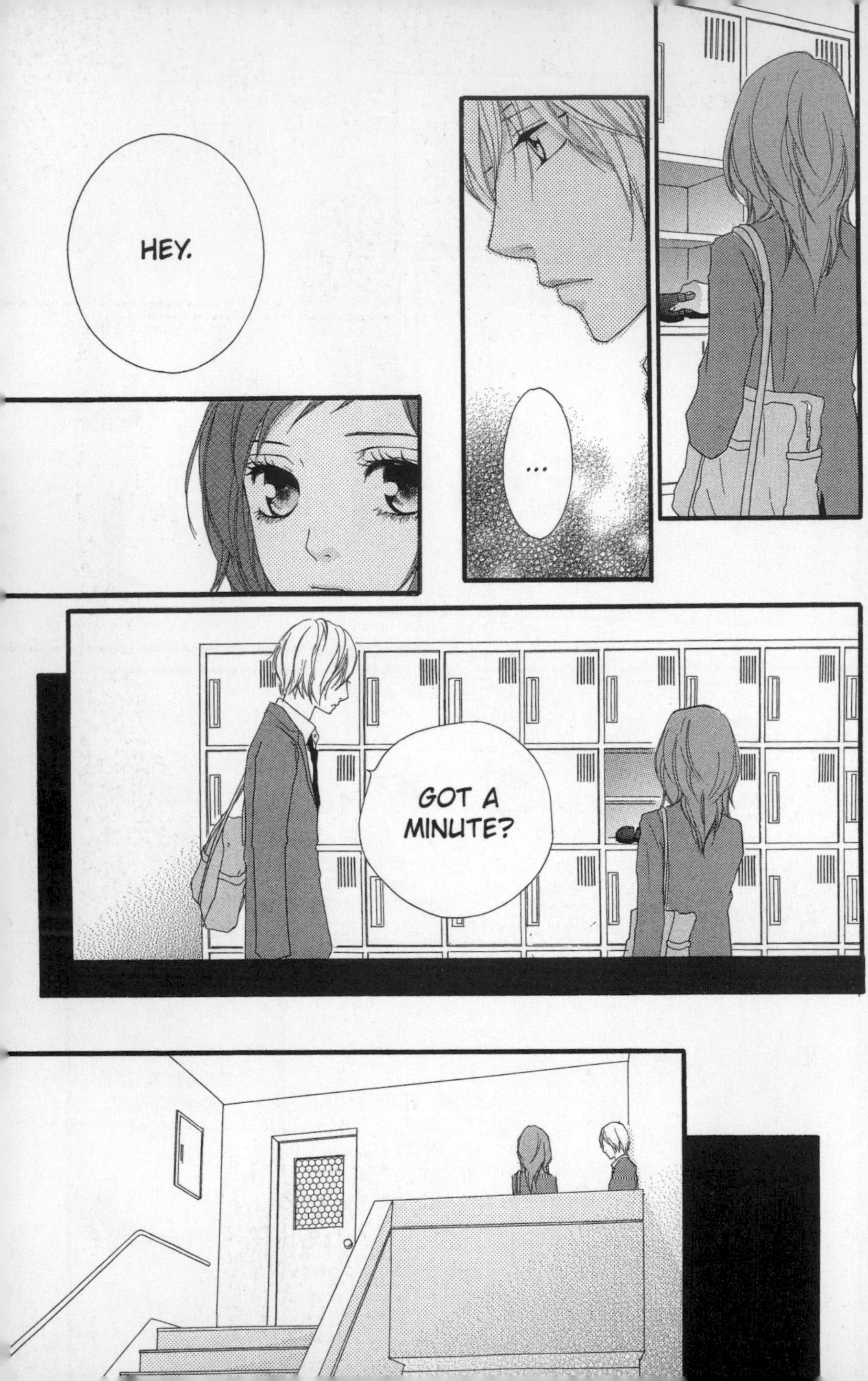
...
HEY.
GOT A MINUTE?

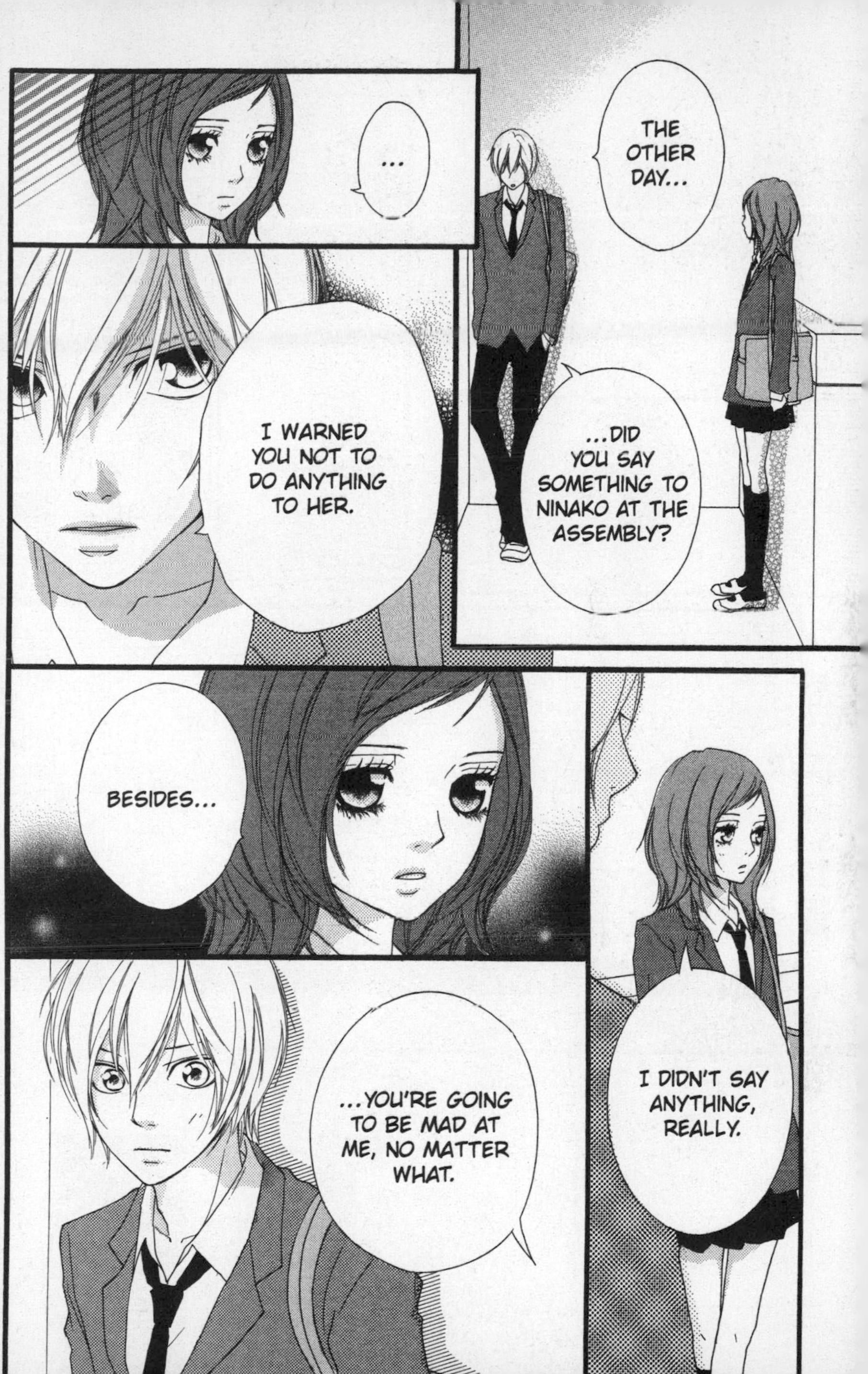
THE OTHER DAY...
...DID YOU SAY SOMETHING TO NINAKO AT THE ASSEMBLY?
...
I WARNED YOU NOT TO DO ANYTHING TO HER.
I DIDN'T SAY ANYTHING, REALLY.
BESIDES...
...YOU'RE GOING TO BE MAD AT ME, NO MATTER WHAT.

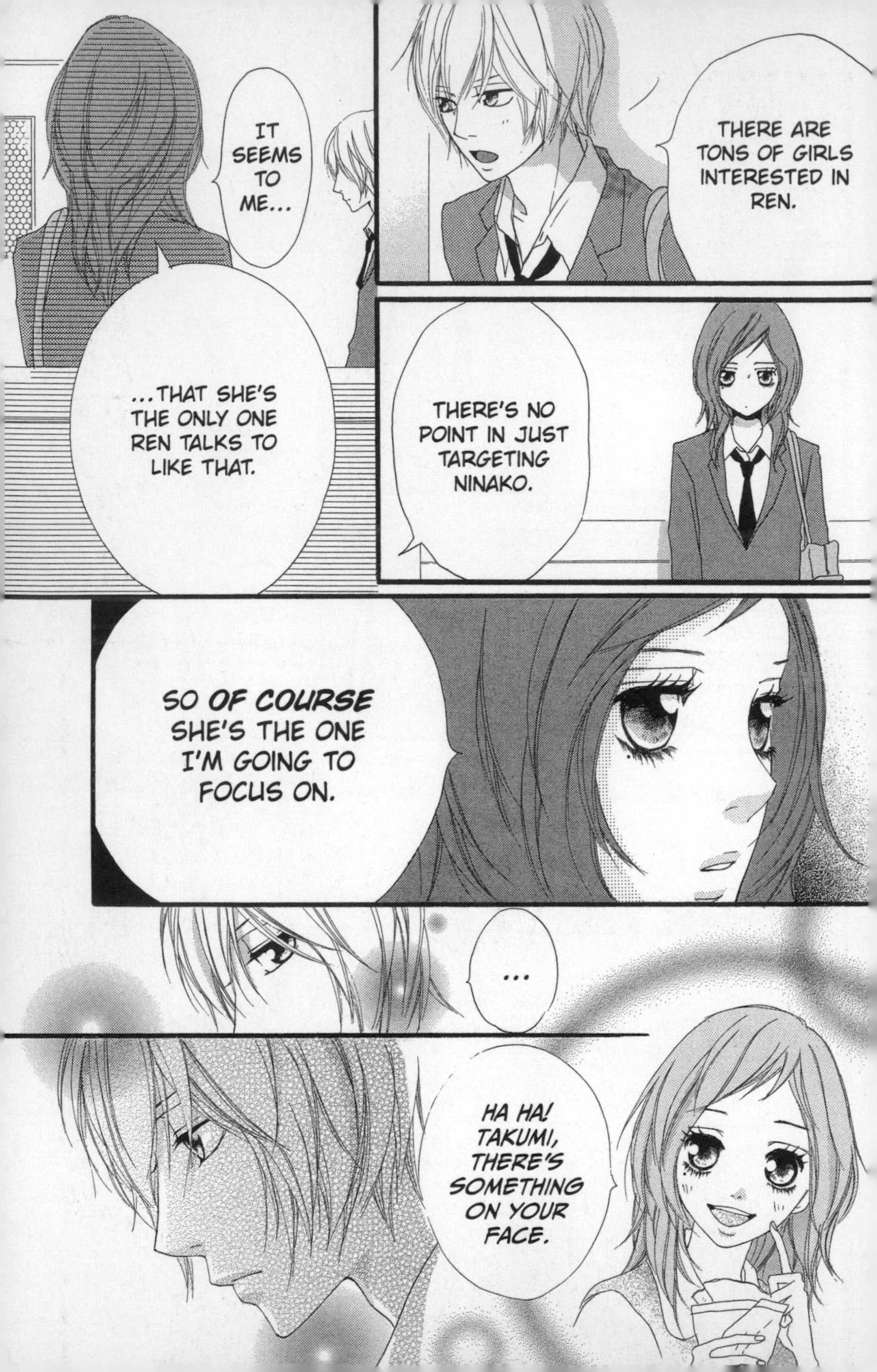
THERE ARE TONS OF GIRLS INTERESTED IN REN.
THERE'S NO POINT IN JUST TARGETING NINAKO.
IT SEEMS TO ME...
...THAT SHE'S THE ONLY ONE REN TALKS TO LIKE THAT.
SO *OF COURSE* SHE'S THE ONE I'M GOING TO FOCUS ON.
...
HA HA! TAKUMI, THERE'S SOMETHING ON YOUR FACE.

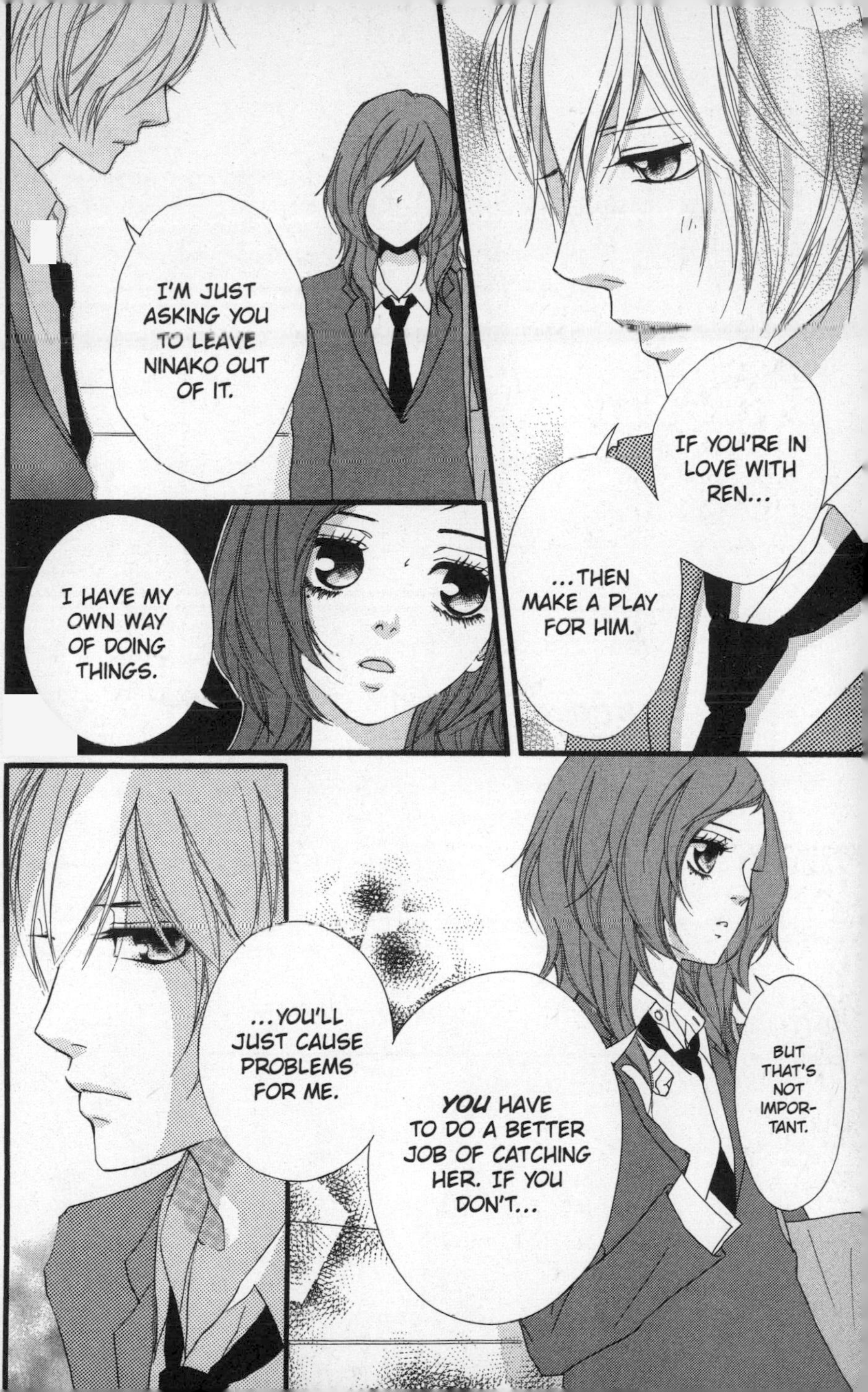
IF YOU'RE IN LOVE WITH REN...
...THEN MAKE A PLAY FOR HIM.
I'M JUST ASKING YOU TO LEAVE NINAKO OUT OF IT.
I HAVE MY OWN WAY OF DOING THINGS.
BUT THAT'S NOT IMPOR-TANT.
YOU HAVE TO DO A BETTER JOB OF CATCHING HER. IF YOU DON'T...
...YOU'LL JUST CAUSE PROBLEMS FOR ME.

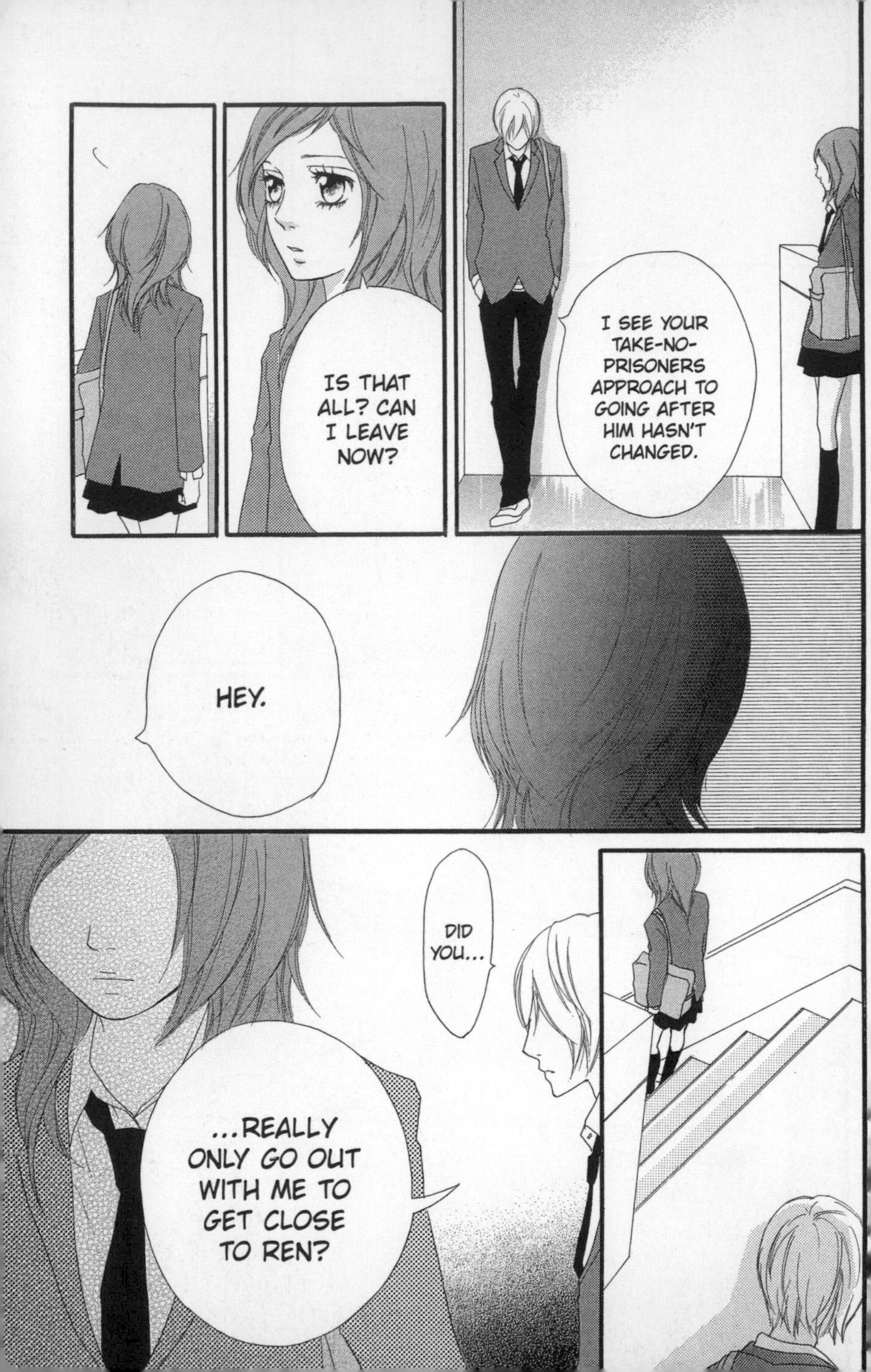
I SEE YOUR TAKE-NO-PRISONERS APPROACH TO GOING AFTER HIM HASN'T CHANGED.
IS THAT ALL? CAN I LEAVE NOW?
HEY.
DID YOU...
...REALLY ONLY GO OUT WITH ME TO GET CLOSE TO REN?

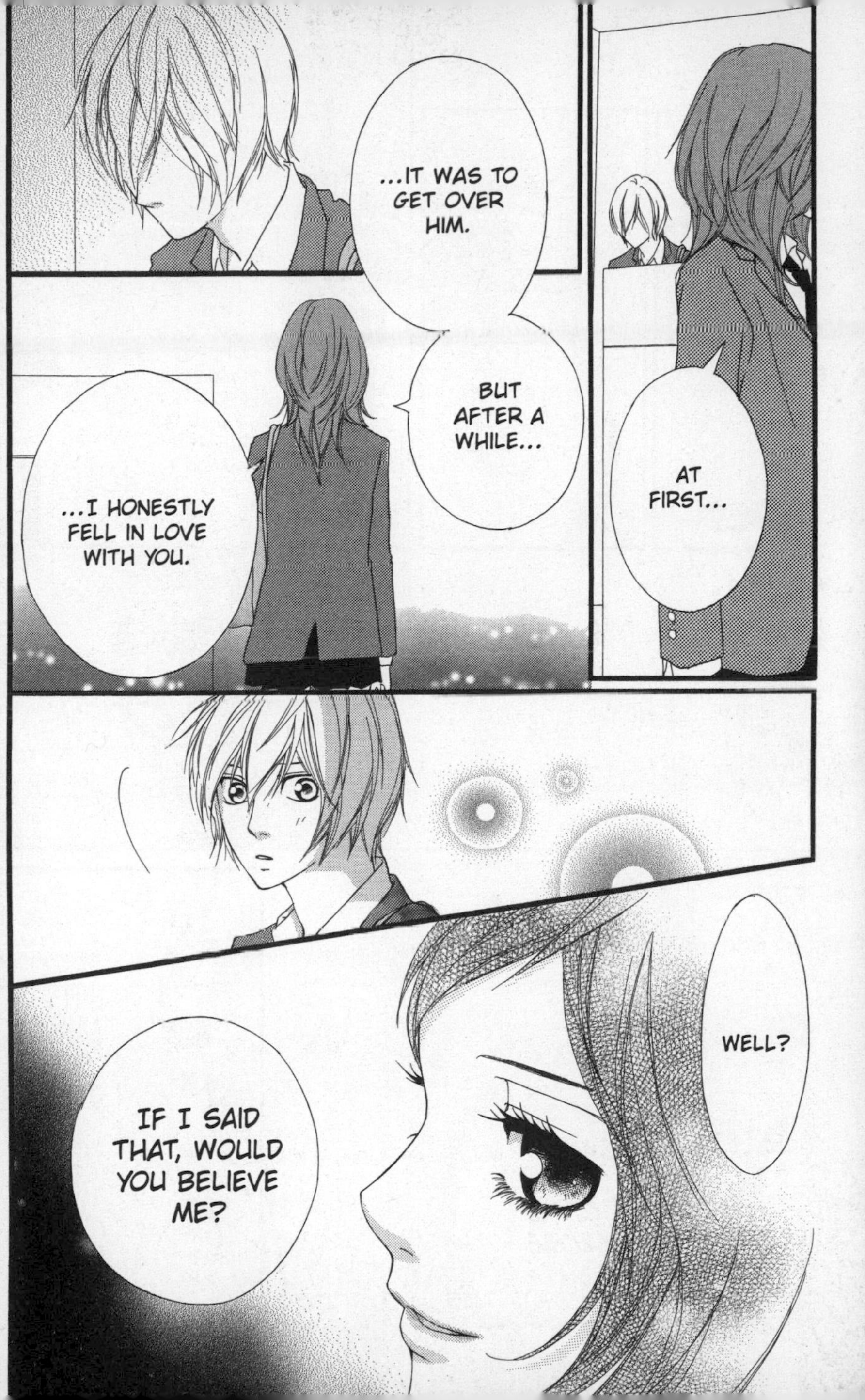
AT FIRST...
...IT WAS TO GET OVER HIM.
BUT AFTER A WHILE...
...I HONESTLY FELL IN LOVE WITH YOU.
WELL?
IF I SAID THAT, WOULD YOU BELIEVE ME?

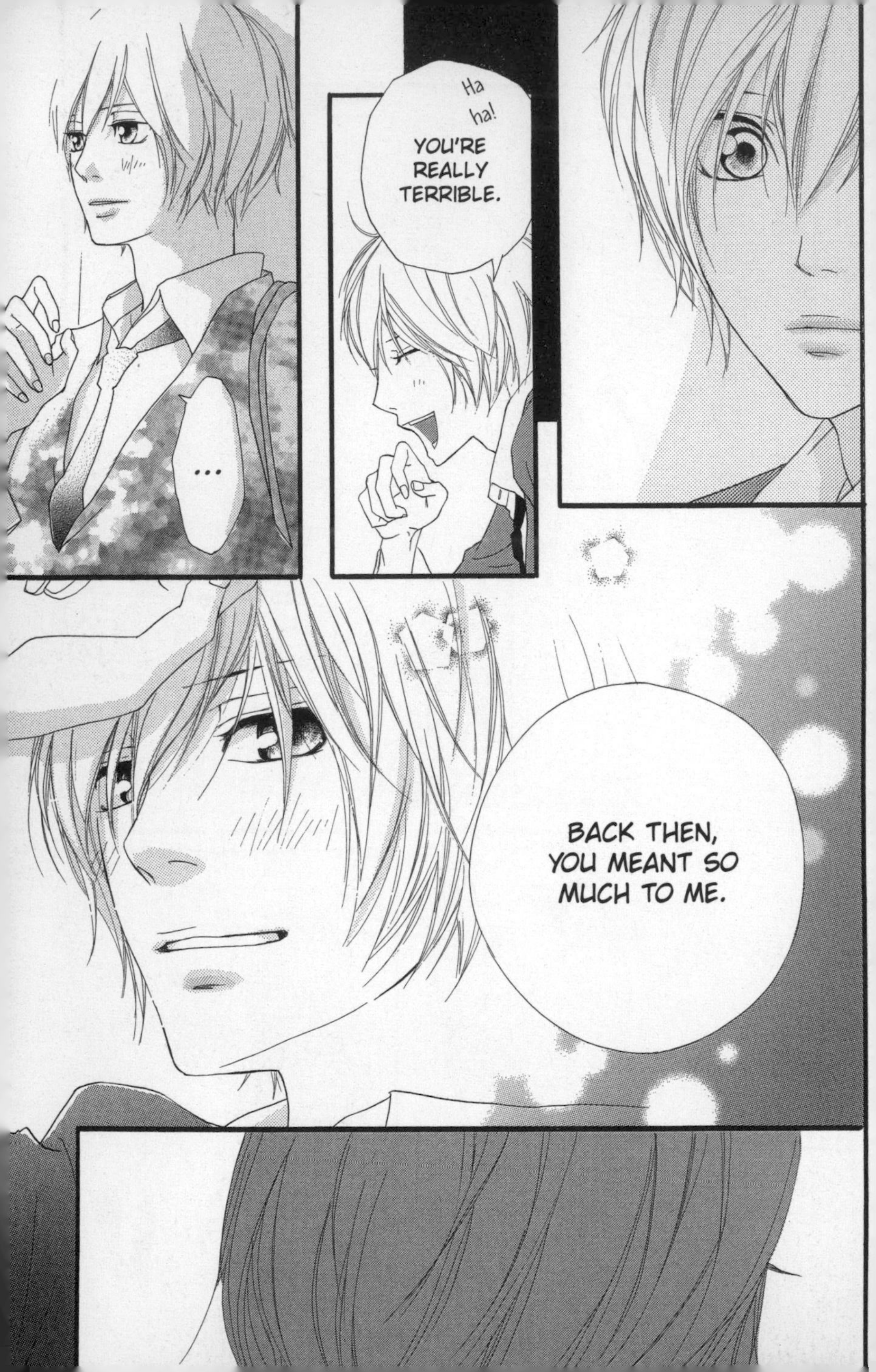
Ha ha!
YOU'RE REALLY TERRIBLE.
...
BACK THEN, YOU MEANT SO MUCH TO ME.

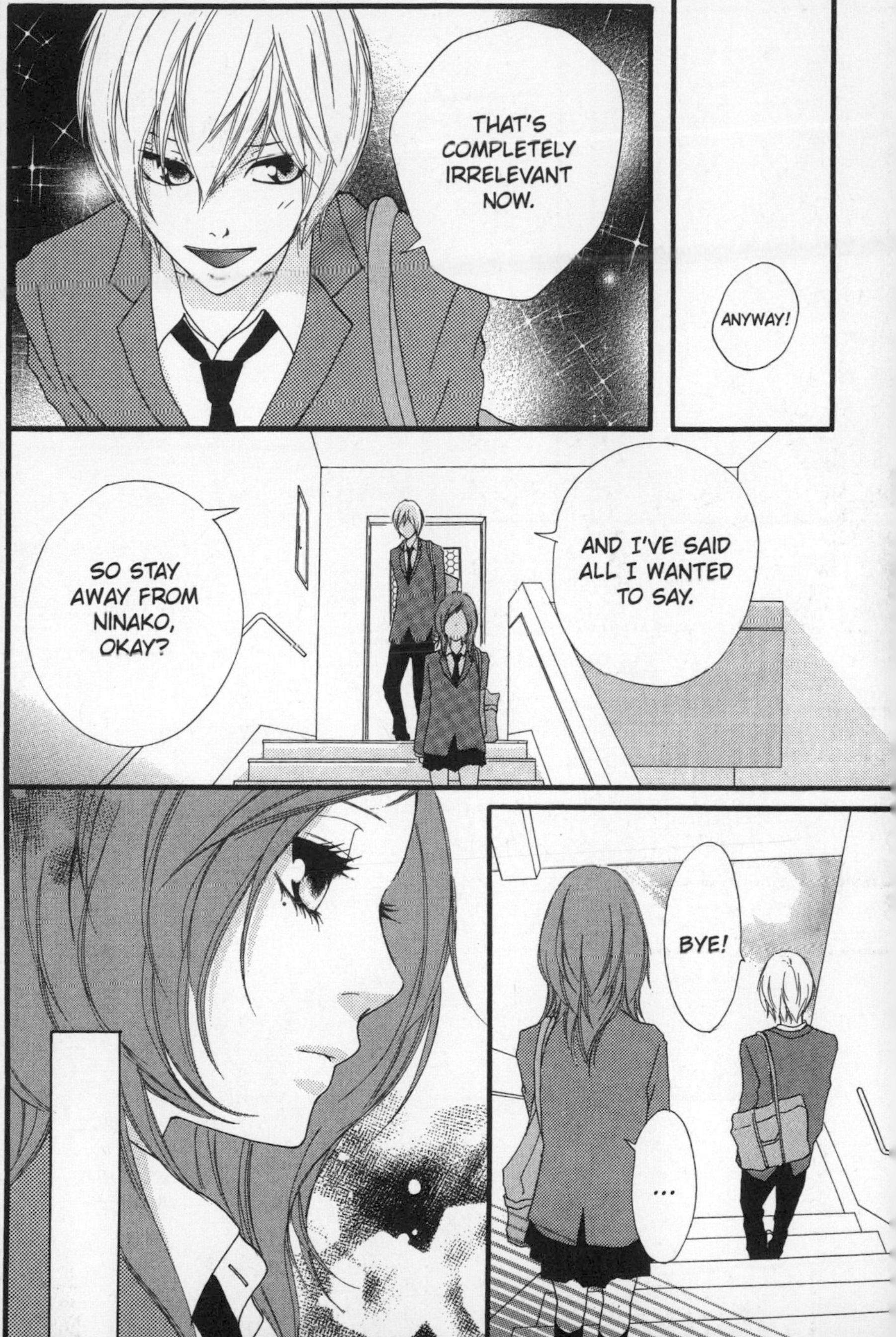
ANYWAY!
THAT'S COMPLETELY IRRELEVANT NOW.
AND I'VE SAID ALL I WANTED TO SAY.
SO STAY AWAY FROM NINAKO, OKAY?
BYE!
...

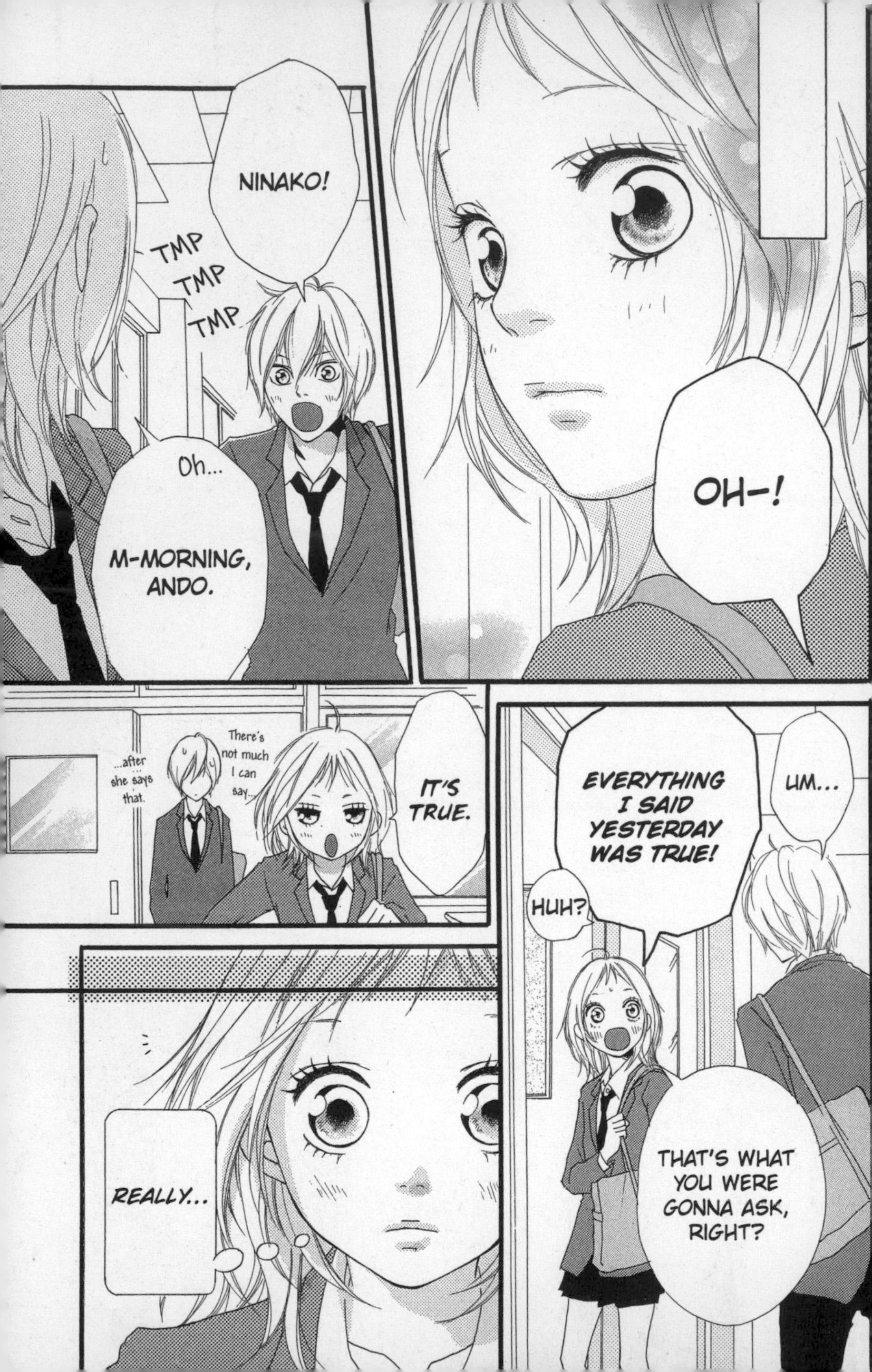
OH-!
NINAKO!
TMP
TMP
TMP
Oh...
M-MORNING, ANDO.
UM...
EVERYTHING I SAID YESTERDAY WAS TRUE!
HUH?
THAT'S WHAT YOU WERE GONNA ASK, RIGHT?
IT'S TRUE.
There's not much I can say...
...after she says that.
REALLY...

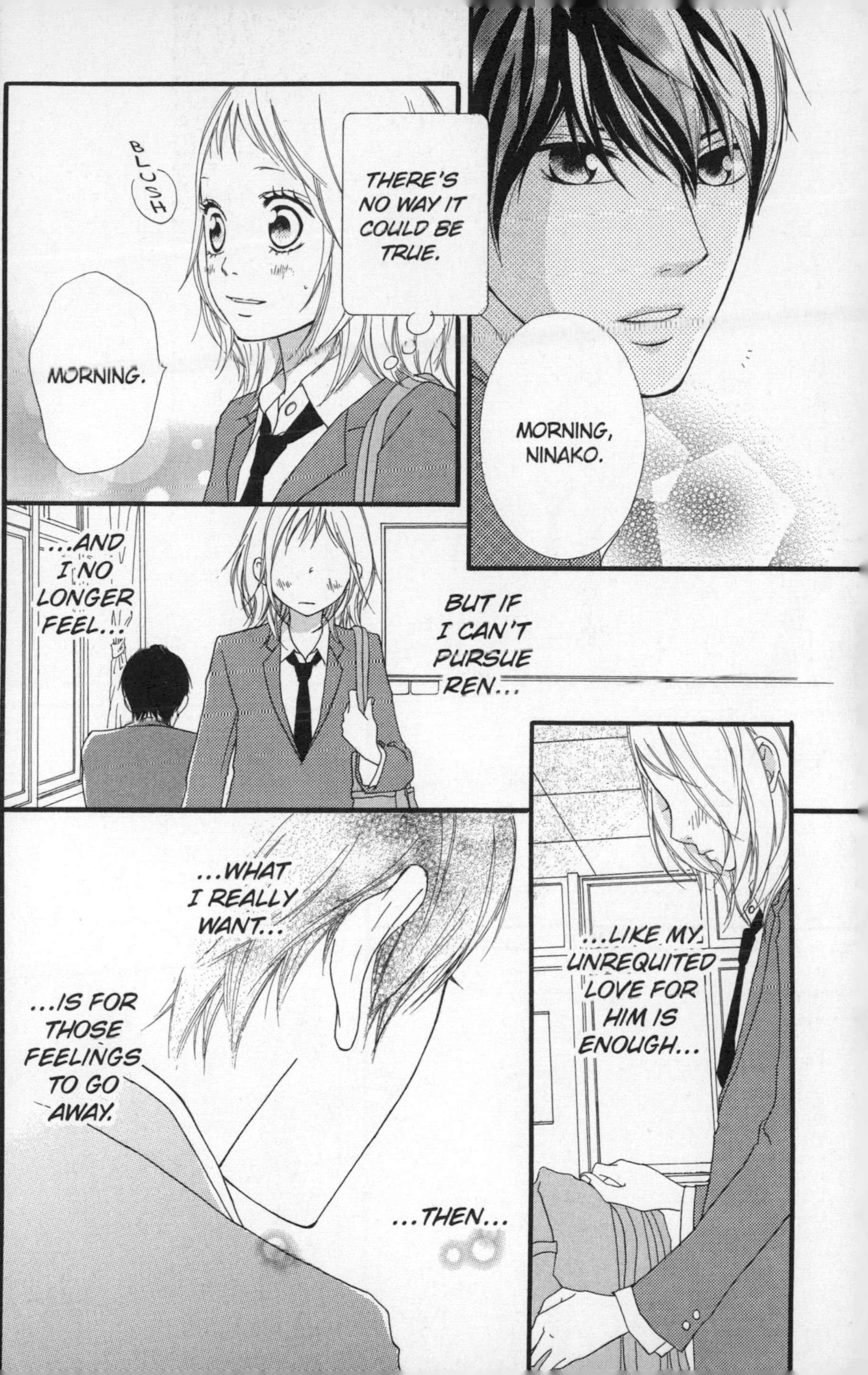

MORNING, NINAKO.
THERE'S NO WAY IT COULD BE TRUE.
BLUSH
MORNING.
BUT IF I CAN'T PURSUE REN...
...AND I NO LONGER FEEL...
...LIKE MY UNREQUITED LOVE FOR HIM IS ENOUGH...
...THEN...
...WHAT I REALLY WANT...
...IS FOR THOSE FEELINGS TO GO AWAY.

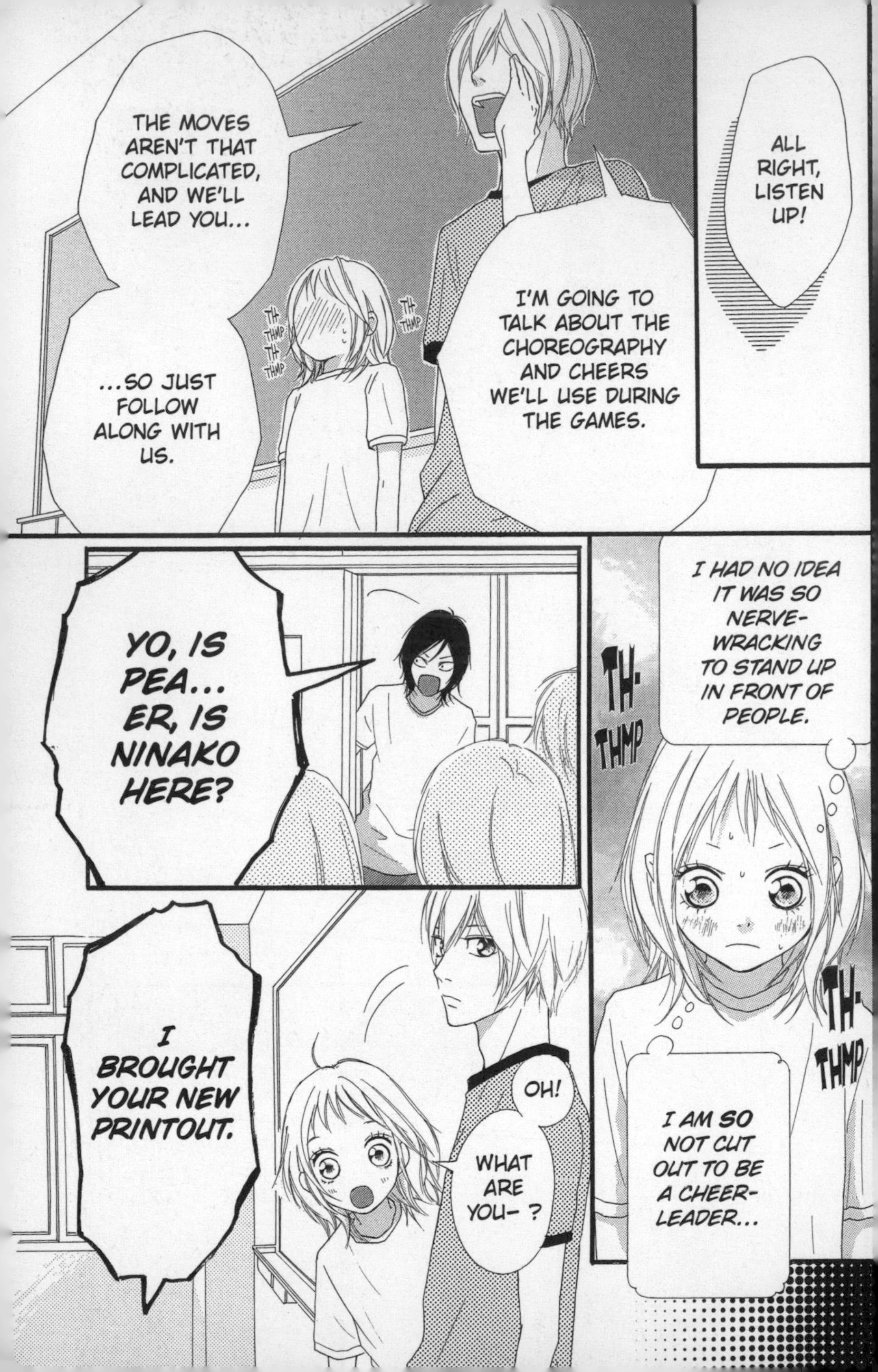

ALL RIGHT, LISTEN UP!
I'M GOING TO TALK ABOUT THE CHOREOGRAPHY AND CHEERS WE'LL USE DURING THE GAMES.
THE MOVES AREN'T THAT COMPLICATED, AND WE'LL LEAD YOU...
TH-THMP TH-THMP
TH-THMP
...SO JUST FOLLOW ALONG WITH US.
I HAD NO IDEA IT WAS SO NERVE-WRACKING TO STAND UP IN FRONT OF PEOPLE.
TH-THMP
TH-THMP
I AM SO NOT CUT OUT TO BE A CHEER-LEADER...
YO, IS PEA... ER, IS NINAKO HERE?
OH!
WHAT ARE YOU- ?
I BROUGHT YOUR NEW PRINTOUT.

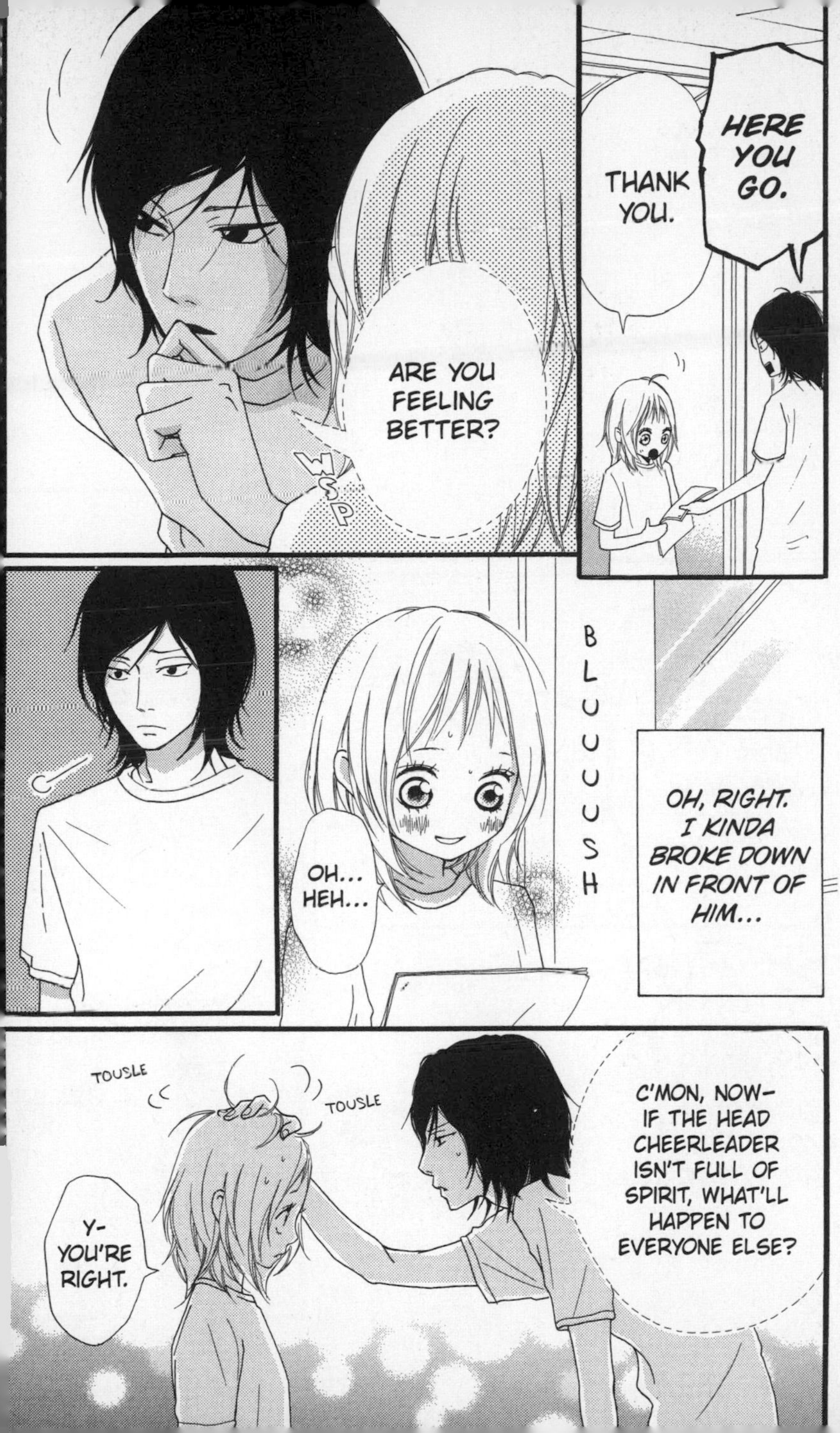
HERE YOU GO.
THANK YOU.
ARE YOU FEELING BETTER?
WSP
OH, RIGHT. I KINDA BROKE DOWN IN FRONT OF HIM...
BLUUUUSH
OH... HEH...
C'MON, NOW- IF THE HEAD CHEERLEADER ISN'T FULL OF SPIRIT, WHAT'LL HAPPEN TO EVERYONE ELSE?
TOUSLE
TOUSLE
Y- YOU'RE RIGHT.

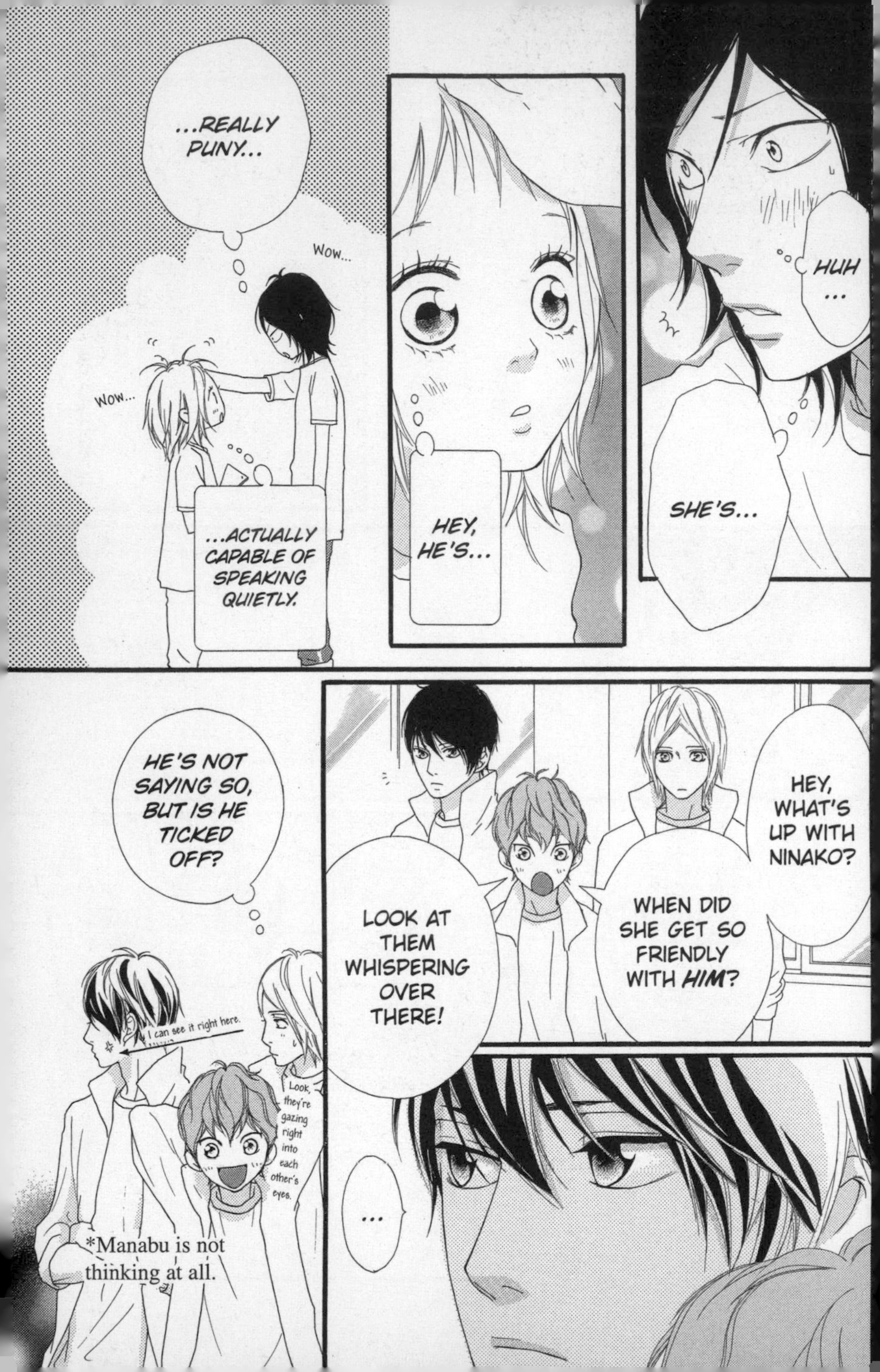
HUH ...
SHE'S...
HEY, HE'S...
...REALLY PUNY...
WOW...
WOW...
...ACTUALLY CAPABLE OF SPEAKING QUIETLY.
HEY, WHAT'S UP WITH NINAKO?
WHEN DID SHE GET SO FRIENDLY WITH HIM?
LOOK AT THEM WHISPERING OVER THERE!
...
HE'S NOT SAYING SO, BUT IS HE TICKED OFF?
I can see it right here.
Look, they're gazing right into each other's eyes.
*Manabu is not thinking at all.

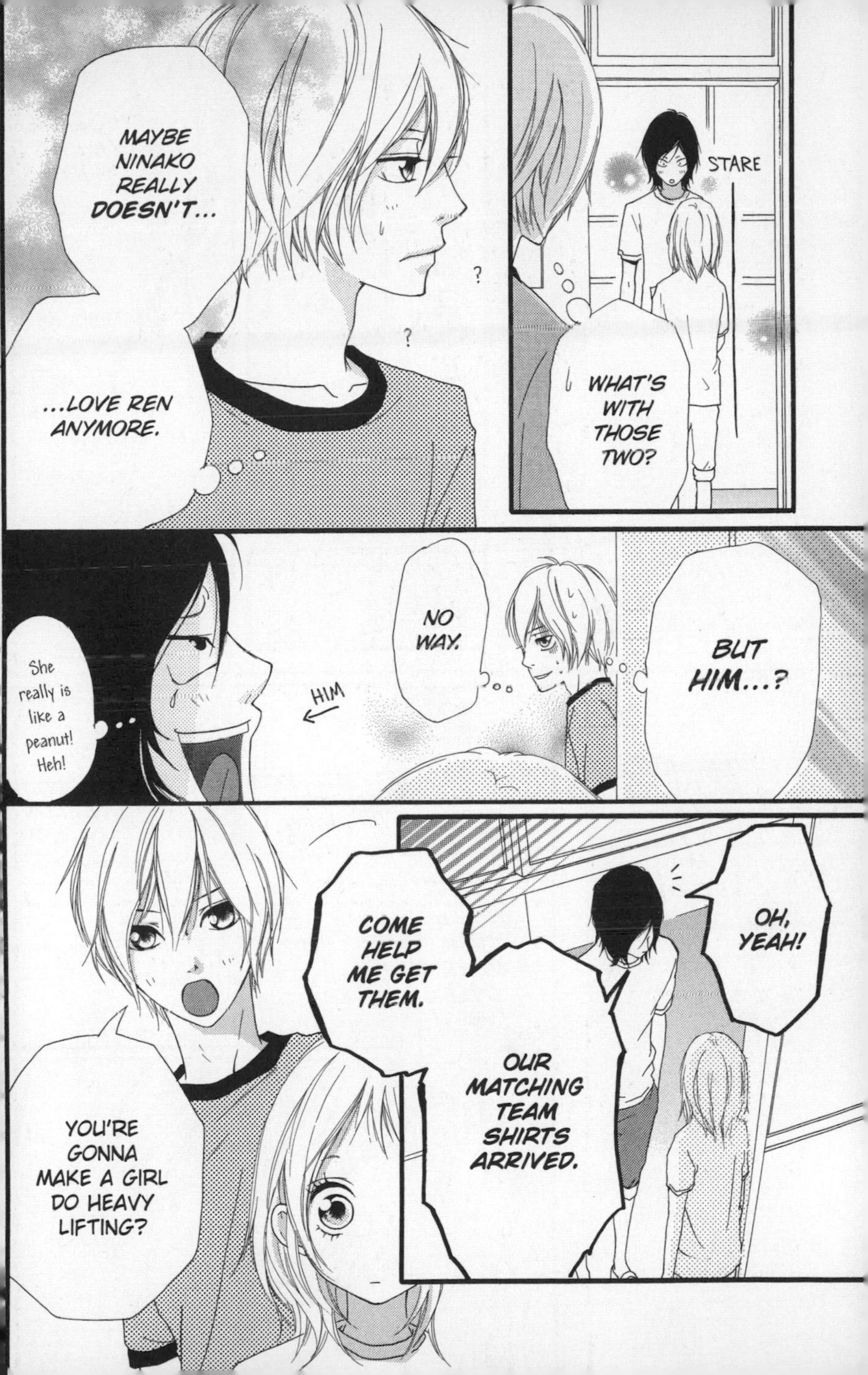
STARE
WHAT'S WITH THOSE TWO?
MAYBE NINAKO REALLY DOESN'T...
...LOVE REN ANYMORE.
BUT HIM...?
NO WAY.
HIM
She really is like a peanut! Heh!
OH, YEAH!
COME HELP ME GET THEM.
OUR MATCHING TEAM SHIRTS ARRIVED.
YOU'RE GONNA MAKE A GIRL DO HEAVY LIFTING?

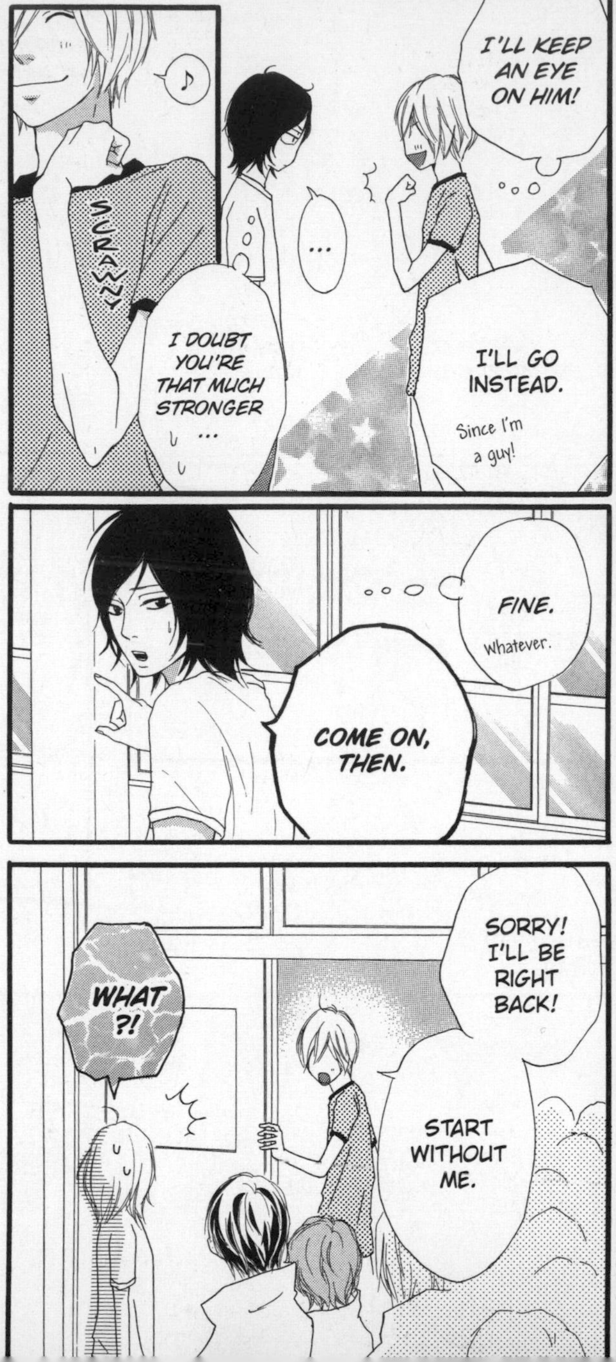
I'LL KEEP AN EYE ON HIM!
I'LL GO INSTEAD.
Since I'm a guy!
...
♪
SCRAWNY
I DOUBT YOU'RE THAT MUCH STRONGER ...
FINE.
Whatever.
COME ON, THEN.
SORRY! I'LL BE RIGHT BACK!
START WITHOUT ME.
WHAT?!

In the last volume, I asked you to tell me what song you think Ninako was humming. It was a silly question, but I got a huge response! Thank you so much! I'm going through your answers now, and I'll announce a winner soon.

The Towel Blanket and Fantasy Clubs continue to add members. Since they're individual activities, it's not like we get together to do anything, but the club ranks are definitely swelling!

I received a letter from the director of a nursery school that said they have a three-year-old who is just like Ando. I can't imagine!

The lovely ladies who helped me out for this volume:

- ♥ Hanemi Ayase
- ♥ Chidan Mizuguchi
- ♥ Runchi Koyama
- ♥ Natsumi Ozaki
- ♥ Satomi Sera

Thank you very, very much!!!

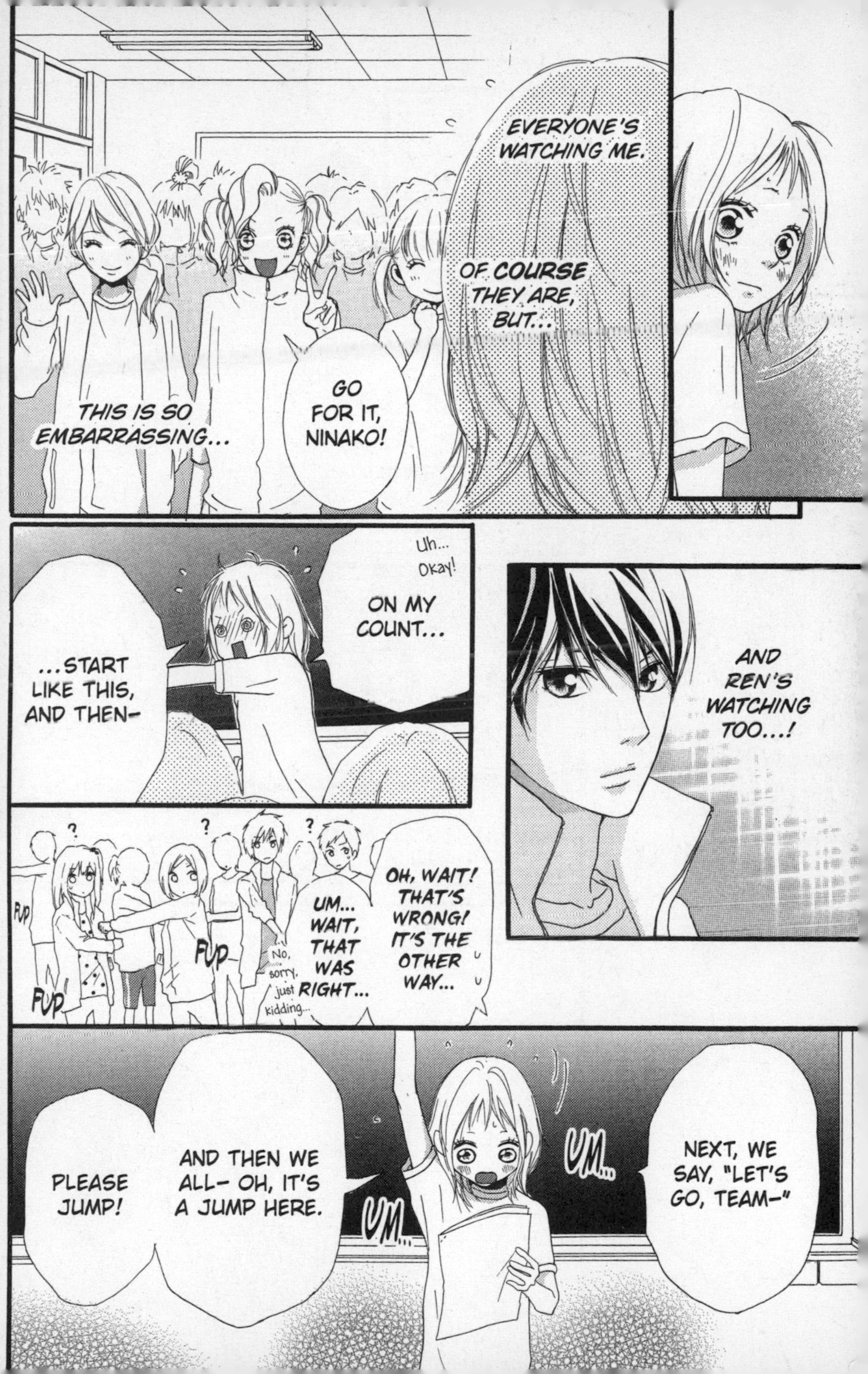
EVERYONE'S WATCHING ME.
OF COURSE THEY ARE, BUT...
GO FOR IT, NINAKO!
THIS IS SO EMBARRASSING...
AND REN'S WATCHING TOO...!
Uh... Okay!
ON MY COUNT...
...START LIKE THIS, AND THEN-
OH, WAIT! THAT'S WRONG! IT'S THE OTHER WAY...
UM... WAIT, THAT WAS RIGHT...
No, sorry, just kidding...
FUP
FUP
FUP
NEXT, WE SAY, "LET'S GO, TEAM-"
UM...
UM...
AND THEN WE ALL- OH, IT'S A JUMP HERE.
PLEASE JUMP!

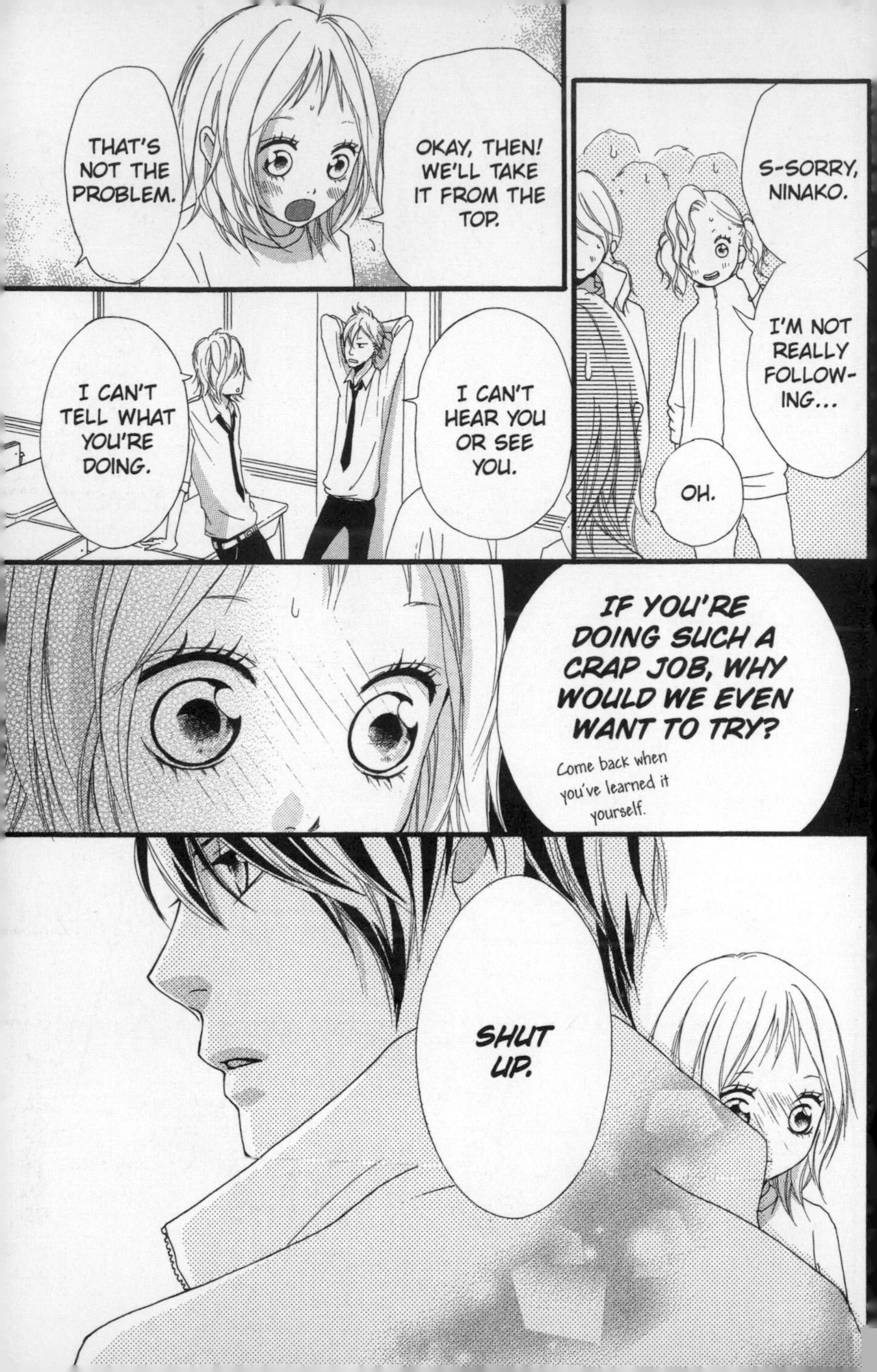
S-SORRY, NINAKO.
I'M NOT REALLY FOLLOW-ING...
OH.
OKAY, THEN! WE'LL TAKE IT FROM THE TOP.
THAT'S NOT THE PROBLEM.
I CAN'T HEAR YOU OR SEE YOU.
I CAN'T TELL WHAT YOU'RE DOING.
IF YOU'RE DOING SUCH A CRAP JOB, WHY WOULD WE EVEN WANT TO TRY?
Come back when you've learned it yourself.
SHUT UP.

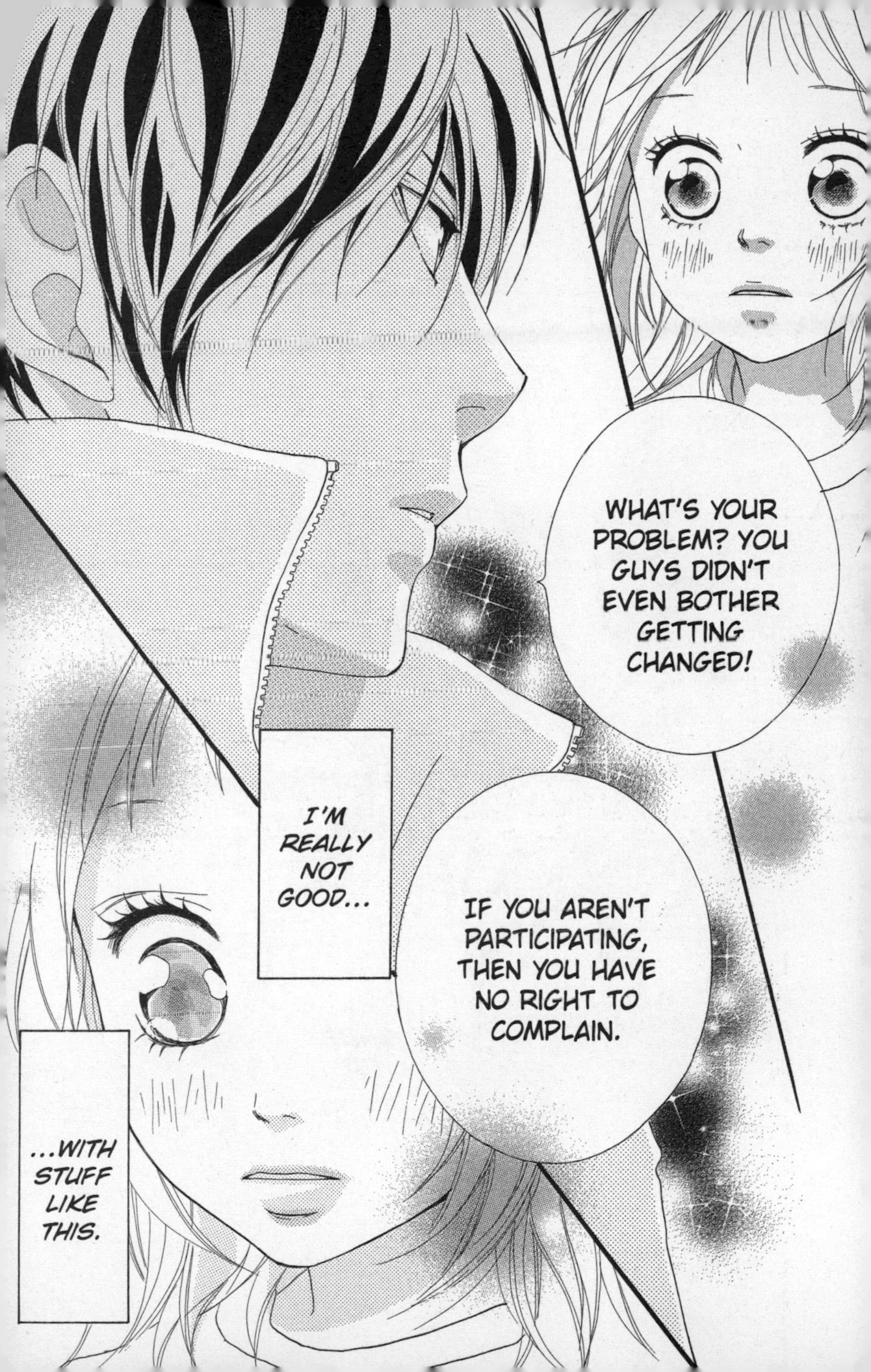
WHAT'S YOUR PROBLEM? YOU GUYS DIDN'T EVEN BOTHER GETTING CHANGED!
IF YOU AREN'T PARTICIPATING, THEN YOU HAVE NO RIGHT TO COMPLAIN.
I'M REALLY NOT GOOD...
...WITH STUFF LIKE THIS.

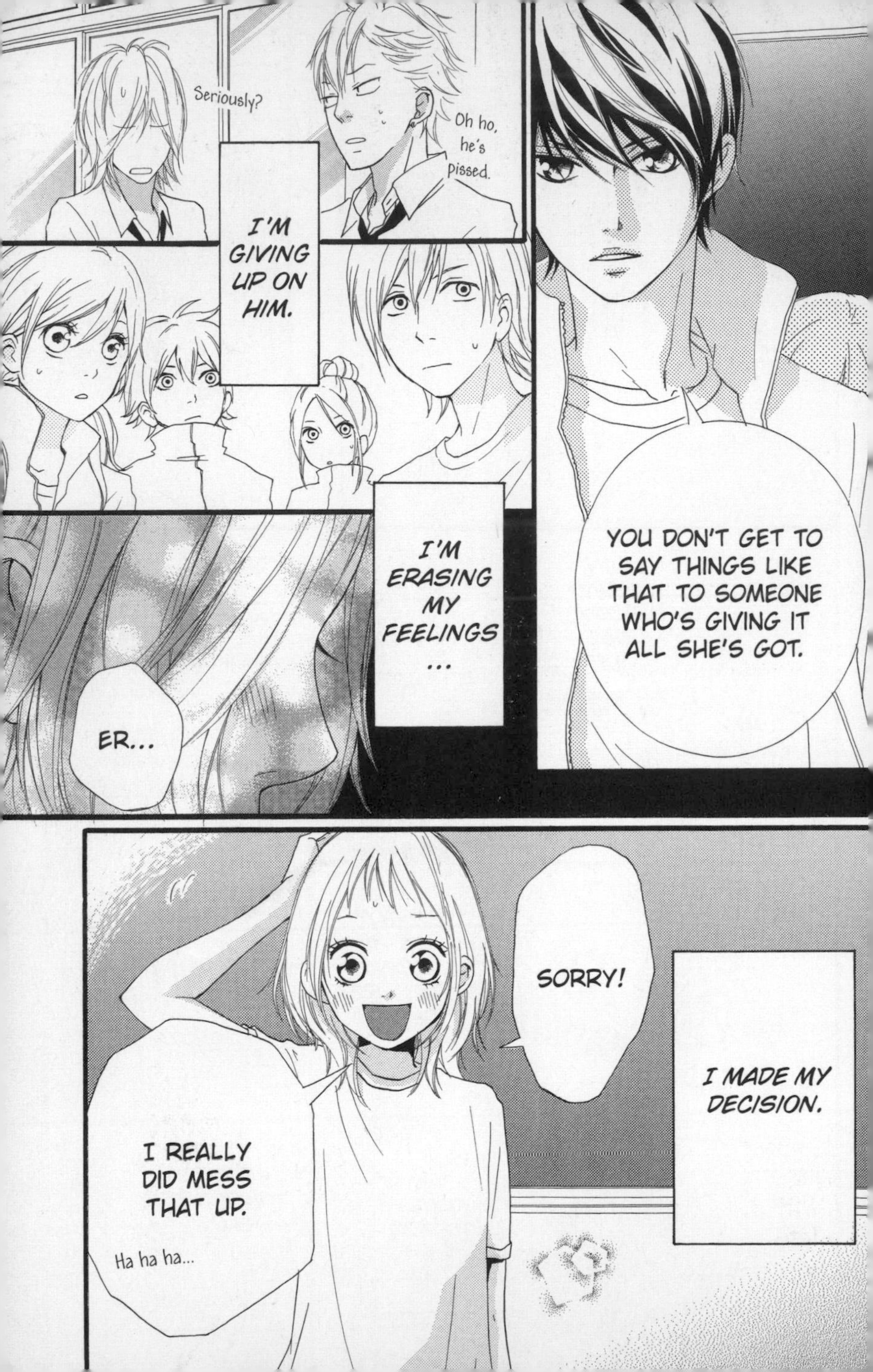
YOU DON'T GET TO SAY THINGS LIKE THAT TO SOMEONE WHO'S GIVING IT ALL SHE'S GOT.
Oh ho, he's pissed.
Seriously?
I'M GIVING UP ON HIM.
I'M ERASING MY FEELINGS ...
ER...
I MADE MY DECISION.
SORRY!
I REALLY DID MESS THAT UP.
Ha ha ha...

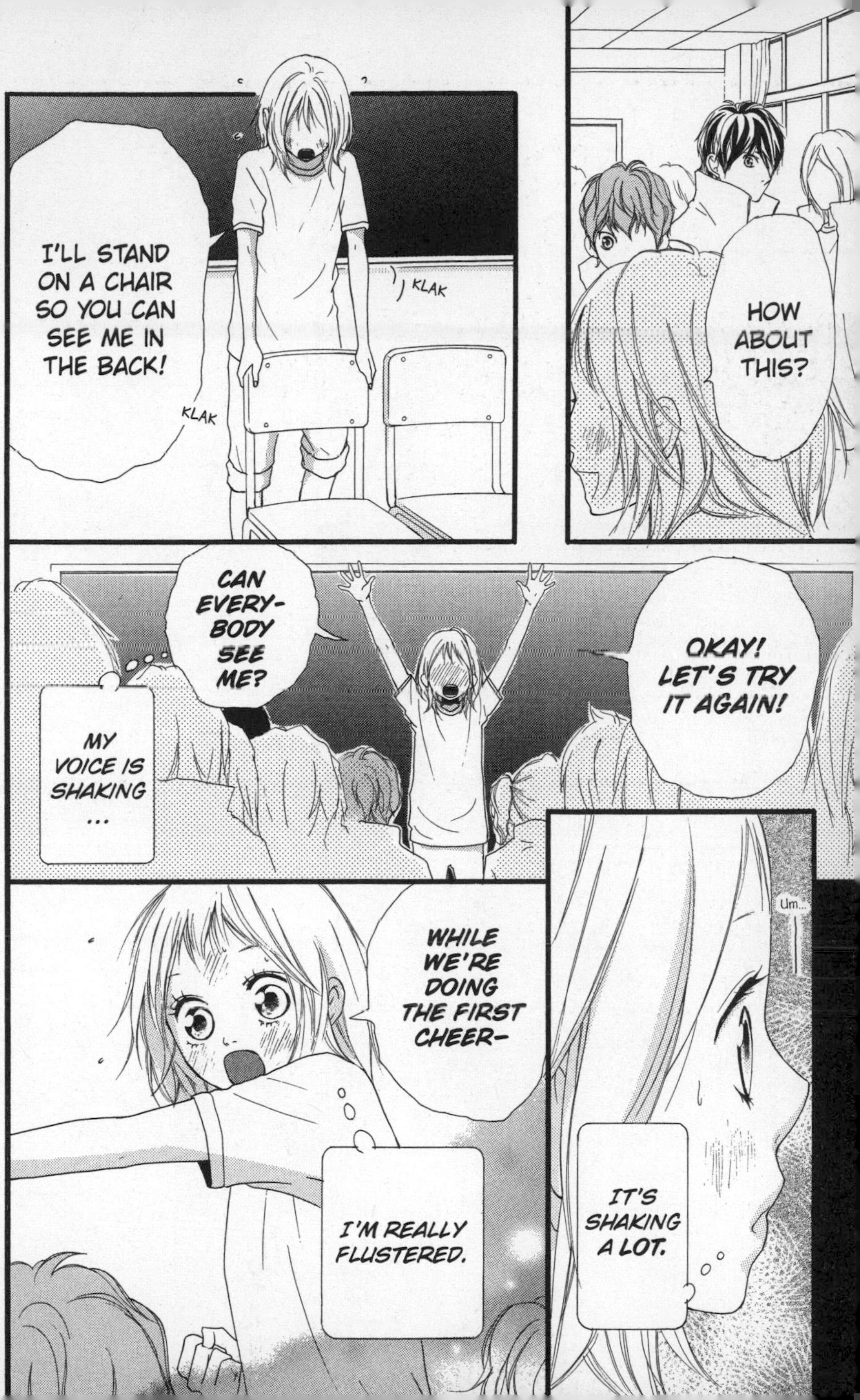
HOW ABOUT THIS?
I'LL STAND ON A CHAIR SO YOU CAN SEE ME IN THE BACK!
KLAK
KLAK
OKAY! LET'S TRY IT AGAIN!
CAN EVERY-BODY SEE ME?
MY VOICE IS SHAKING ...
Um...
IT'S SHAKING A LOT.
WHILE WE'RE DOING THE FIRST CHEER-
I'M REALLY FLUSTERED.

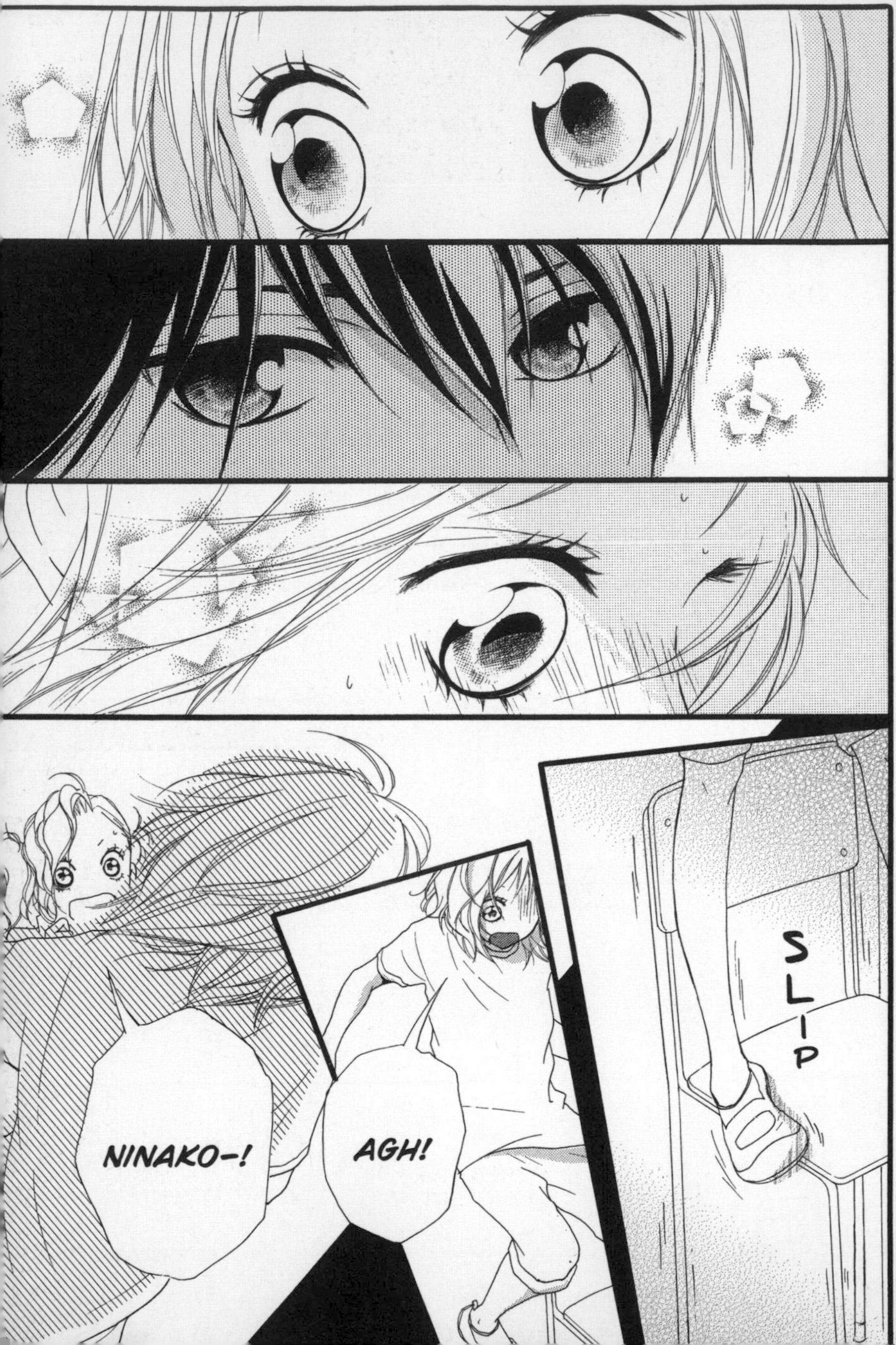
SLIP
AGH!
NINAKO-!

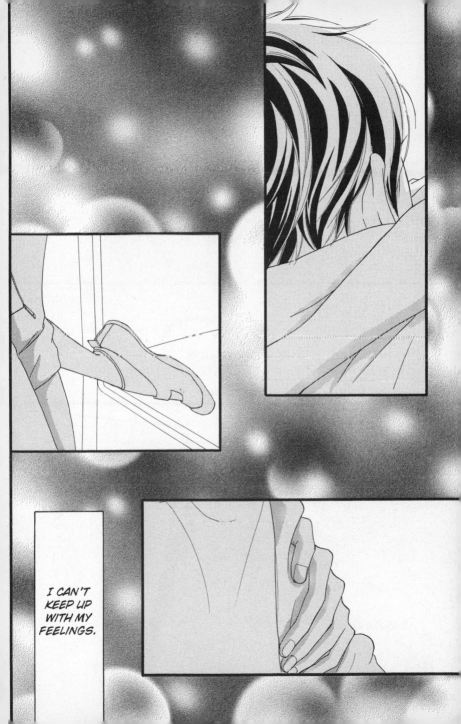

I CAN'T
KEEP UP
WITH MY
FEELINGS.

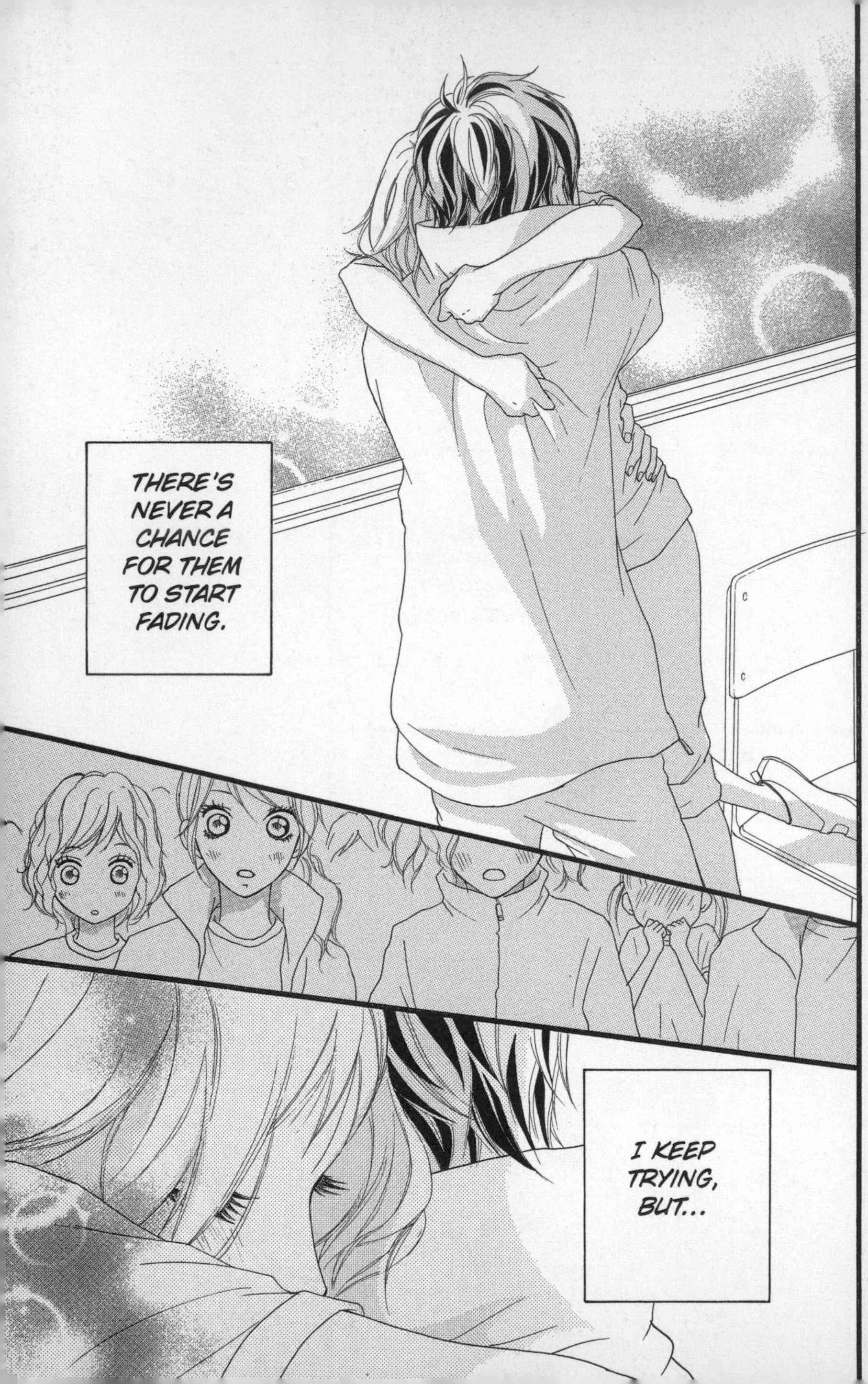
THERE'S NEVER A CHANCE FOR THEM TO START FADING.
I KEEP TRYING, BUT...

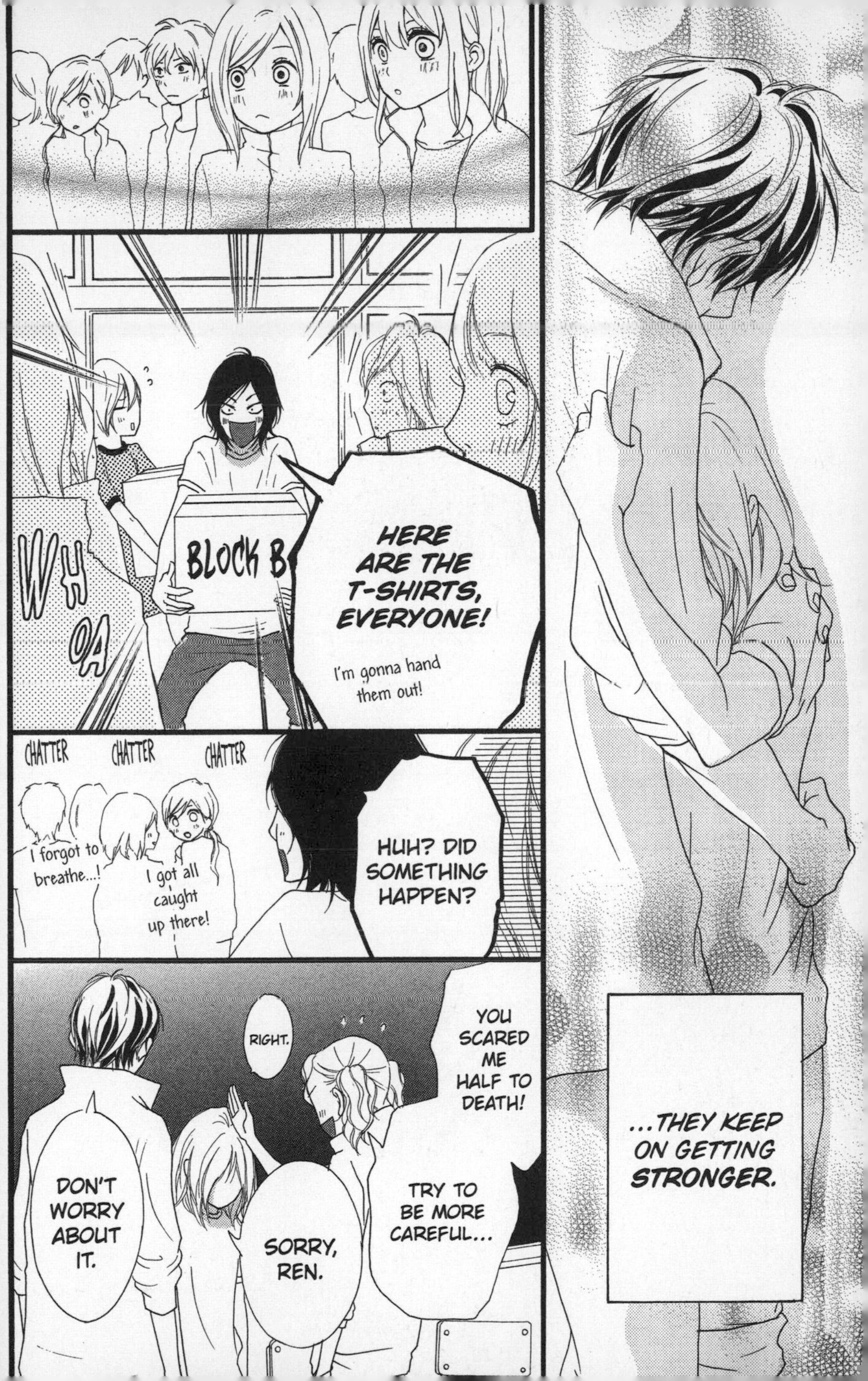
...THEY KEEP ON GETTING STRONGER.
HERE ARE THE T-SHIRTS, EVERYONE!
I'm gonna hand them out!
BLOCK B
WHOA
CHATTER
CHATTER
CHATTER
HUH? DID SOMETHING HAPPEN?
I got all caught up there!
I forgot to breathe...!
YOU SCARED ME HALF TO DEATH!
RIGHT.
TRY TO BE MORE CAREFUL...
SORRY, REN.
DON'T WORRY ABOUT IT.

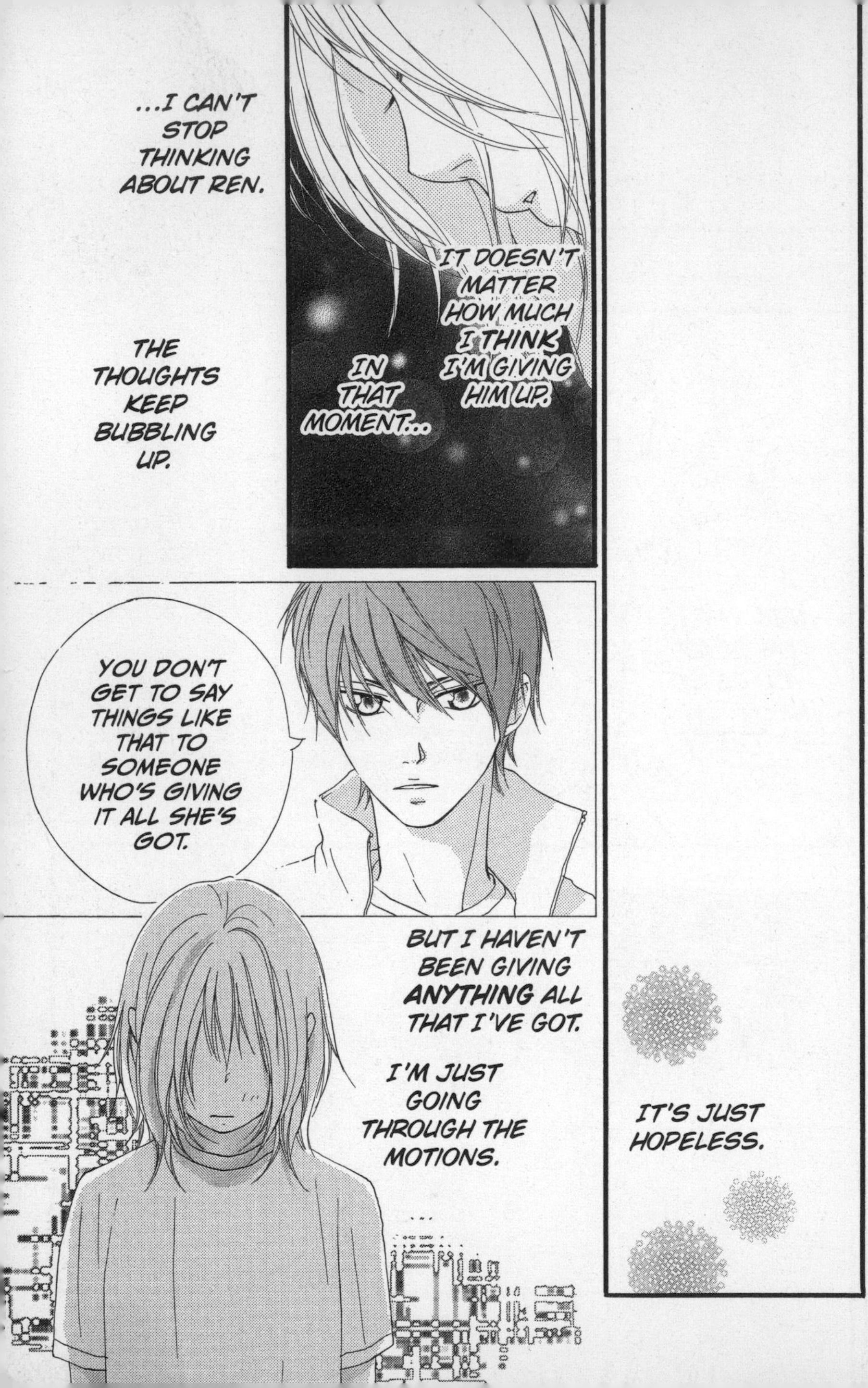
IT'S JUST HOPELESS.
IT DOESN'T MATTER HOW MUCH I THINK I'M GIVING HIM UP.
IN THAT MOMENT...
...I CAN'T STOP THINKING ABOUT REN.
THE THOUGHTS KEEP BUBBLING UP.
YOU DON'T GET TO SAY THINGS LIKE THAT TO SOMEONE WHO'S GIVING IT ALL SHE'S GOT.
BUT I HAVEN'T BEEN GIVING ANYTHING ALL THAT I'VE GOT.
I'M JUST GOING THROUGH THE MOTIONS.
...

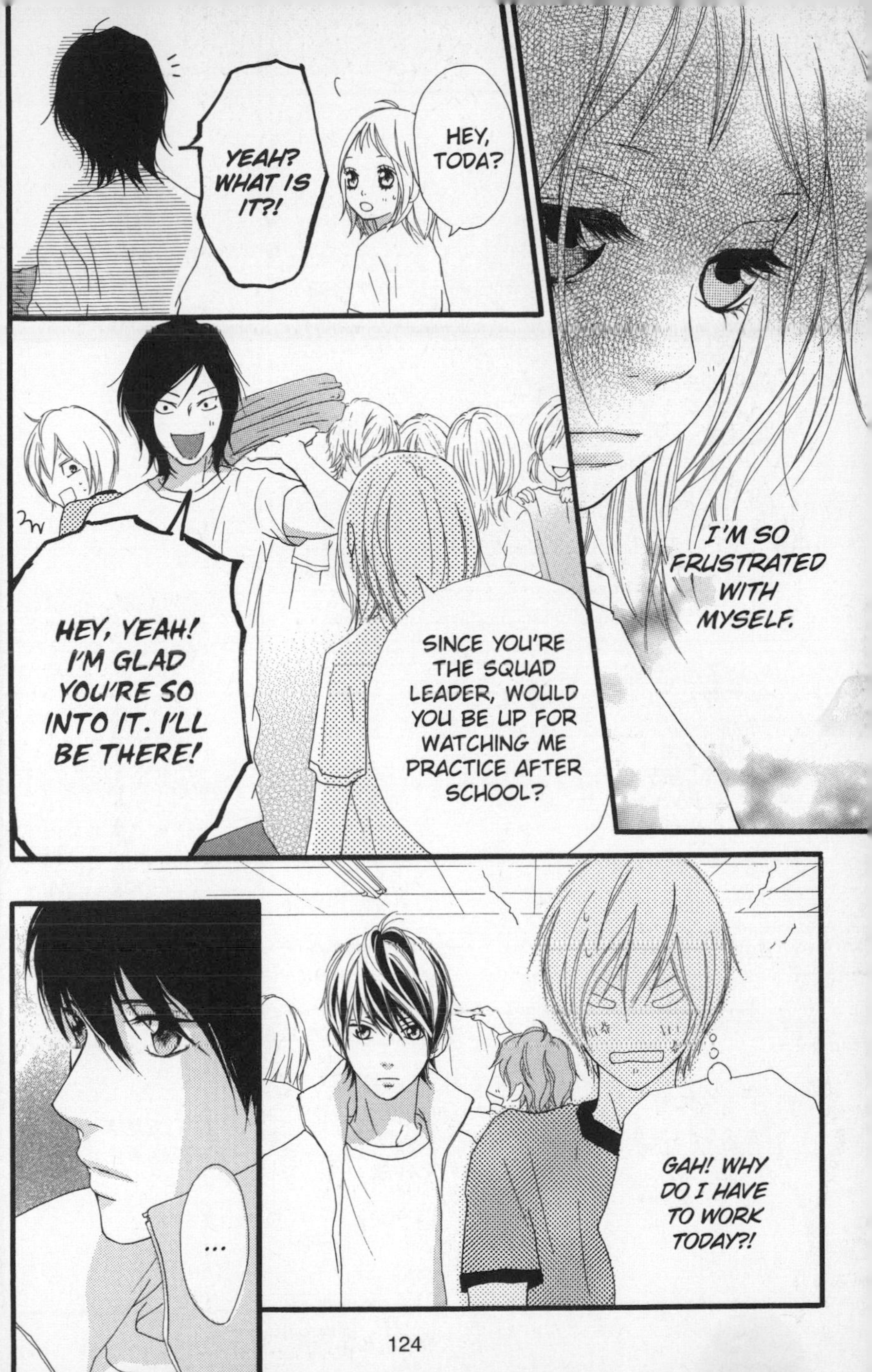
I'M SO FRUSTRATED WITH MYSELF.
HEY, TODA?
YEAH? WHAT IS IT?!
SINCE YOU'RE THE SQUAD LEADER, WOULD YOU BE UP FOR WATCHING ME PRACTICE AFTER SCHOOL?
HEY, YEAH! I'M GLAD YOU'RE SO INTO IT. I'LL BE THERE!
GAH! WHY DO I HAVE TO WORK TODAY?!
...

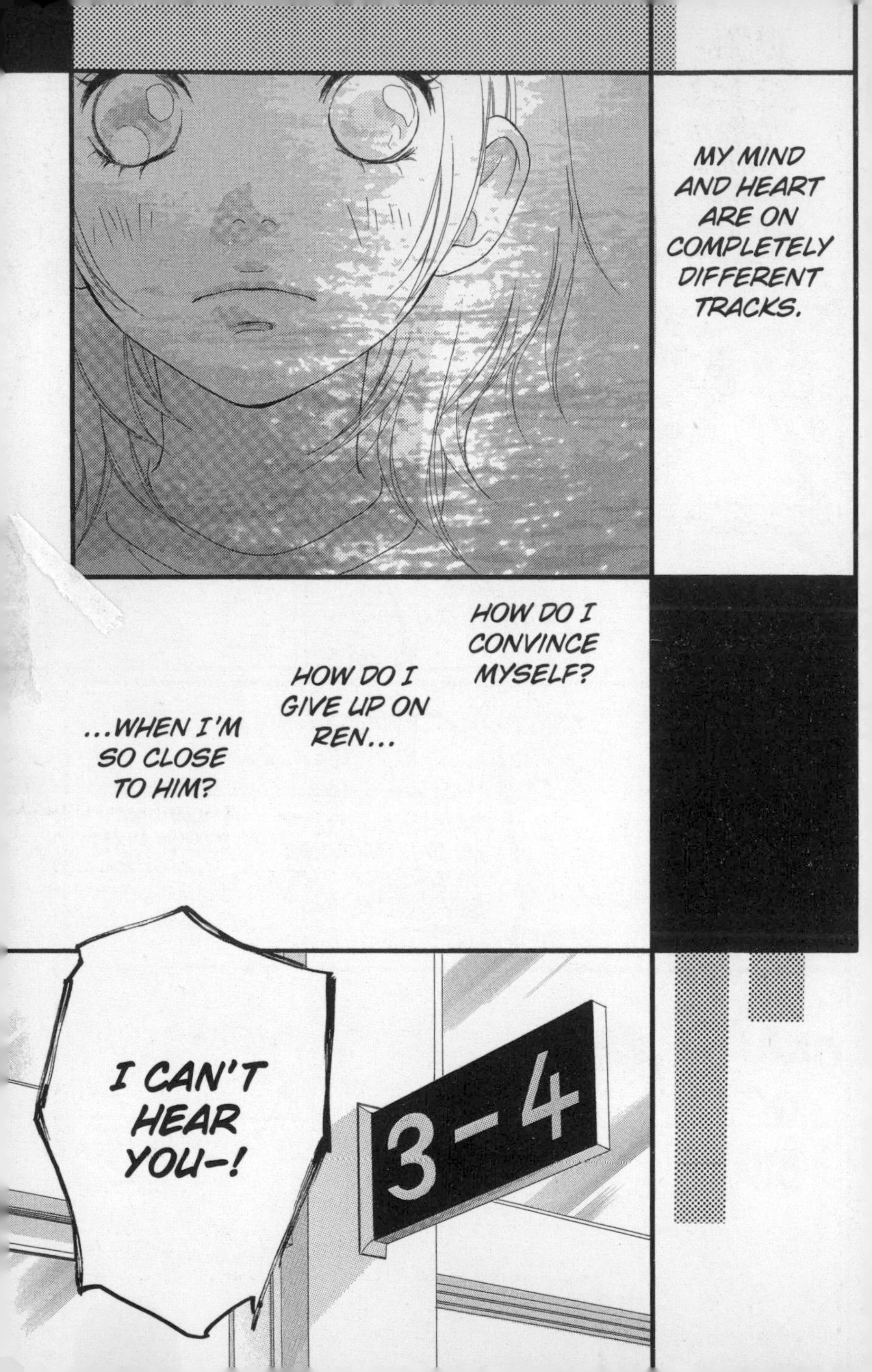
MY MIND AND HEART ARE ON COMPLETELY DIFFERENT TRACKS.
HOW DO I CONVINCE MYSELF?
HOW DO I GIVE UP ON REN...
...WHEN I'M SO CLOSE TO HIM?
I CAN'T HEAR YOU-!
3-4

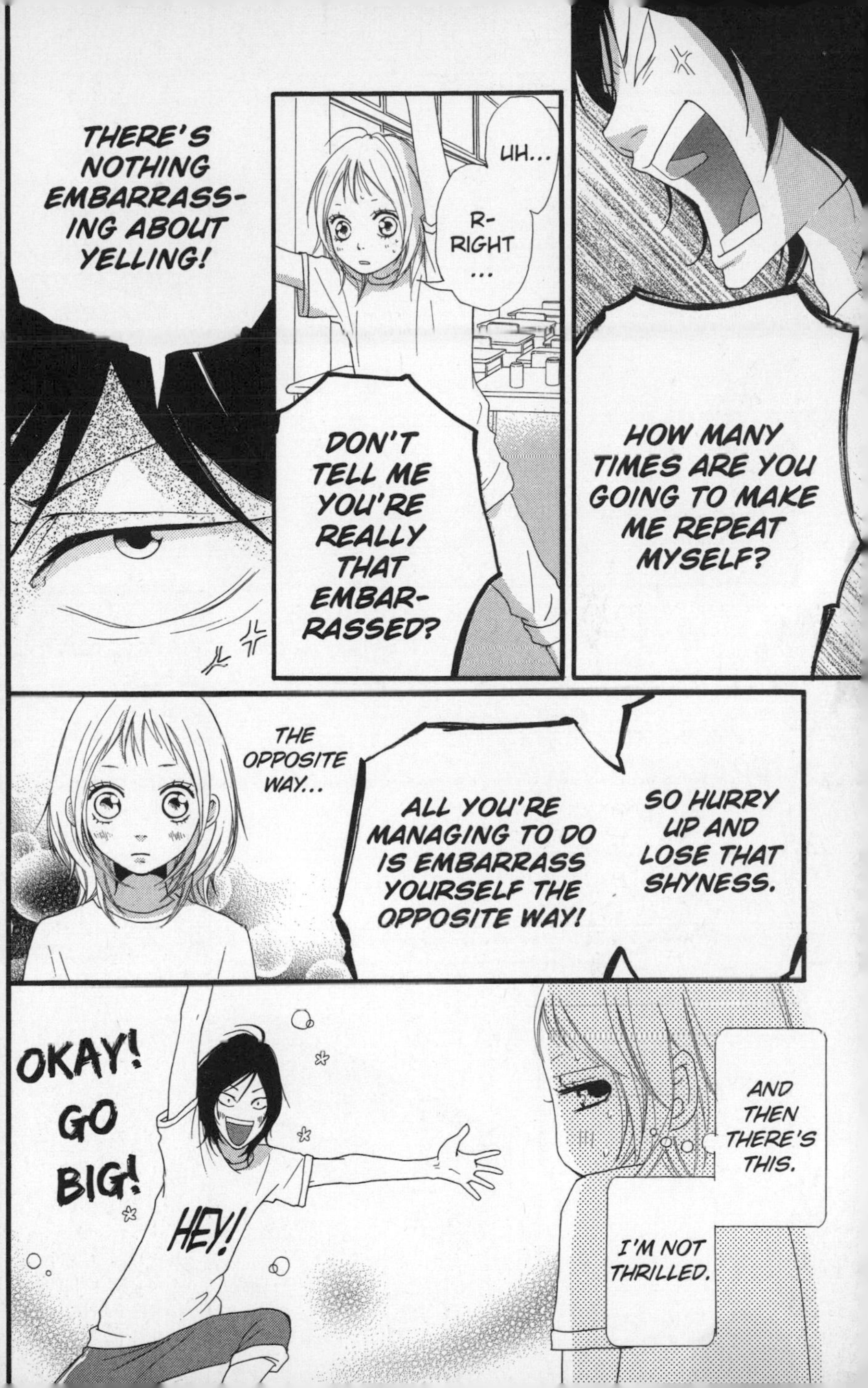
HOW MANY TIMES ARE YOU GOING TO MAKE ME REPEAT MYSELF?
UH...
R-RIGHT...
THERE'S NOTHING EMBARRASSING ABOUT YELLING!
DON'T TELL ME YOU'RE REALLY THAT EMBARRASSED?
SO HURRY UP AND LOSE THAT SHYNESS.
ALL YOU'RE MANAGING TO DO IS EMBARRASS YOURSELF THE OPPOSITE WAY!
THE OPPOSITE WAY...
AND THEN THERE'S THIS.
I'M NOT THRILLED.
OKAY! GO BIG!
HEY!

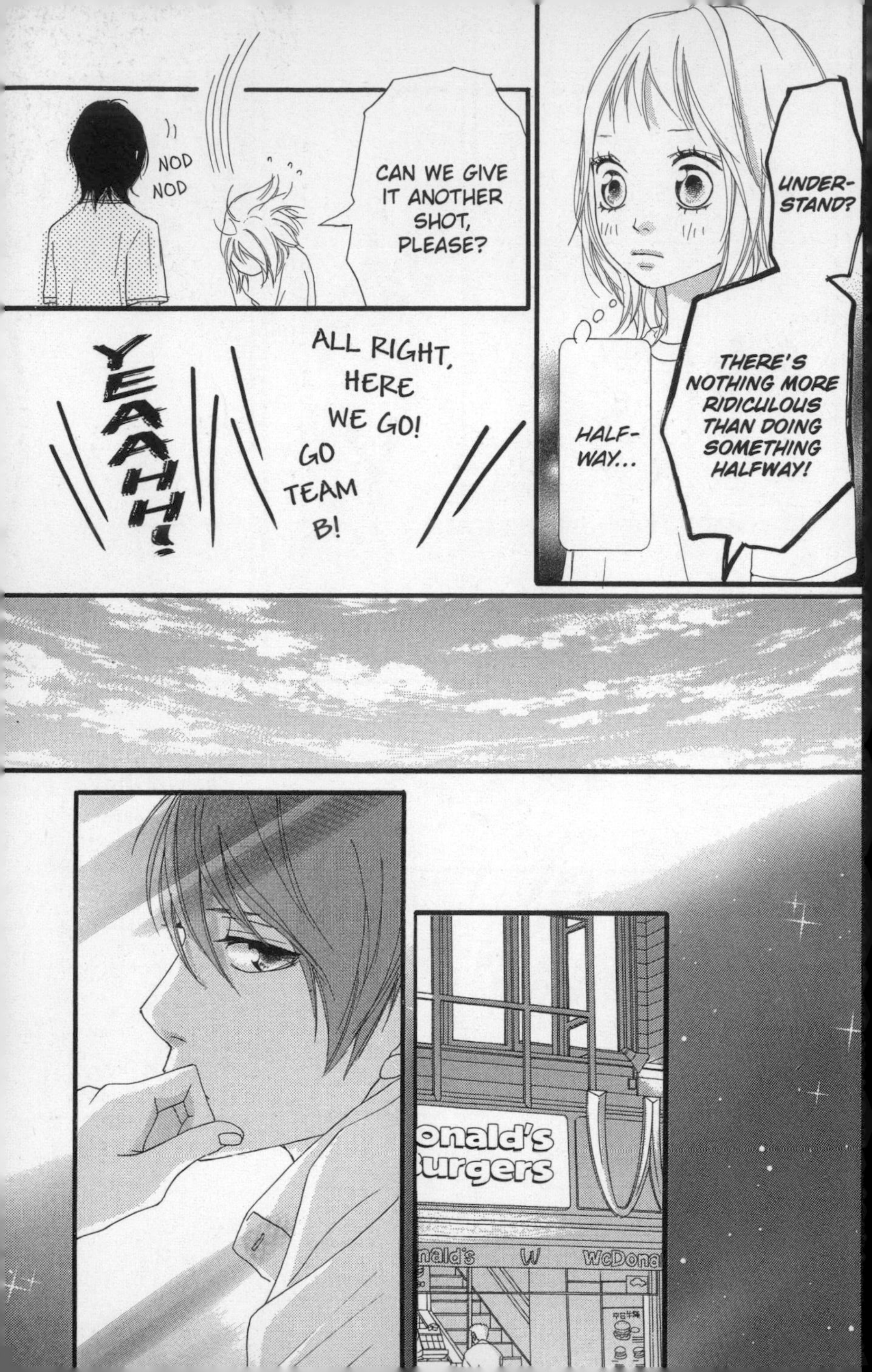
UNDER-STAND?
THERE'S NOTHING MORE RIDICULOUS THAN DOING SOMETHING HALFWAY!
HALF-WAY...
CAN WE GIVE IT ANOTHER SHOT, PLEASE?
NOD NOD
ALL RIGHT, HERE WE GO!
GO TEAM B!
YEAAHH!
onald's
urgers
nald's
W
WcDona

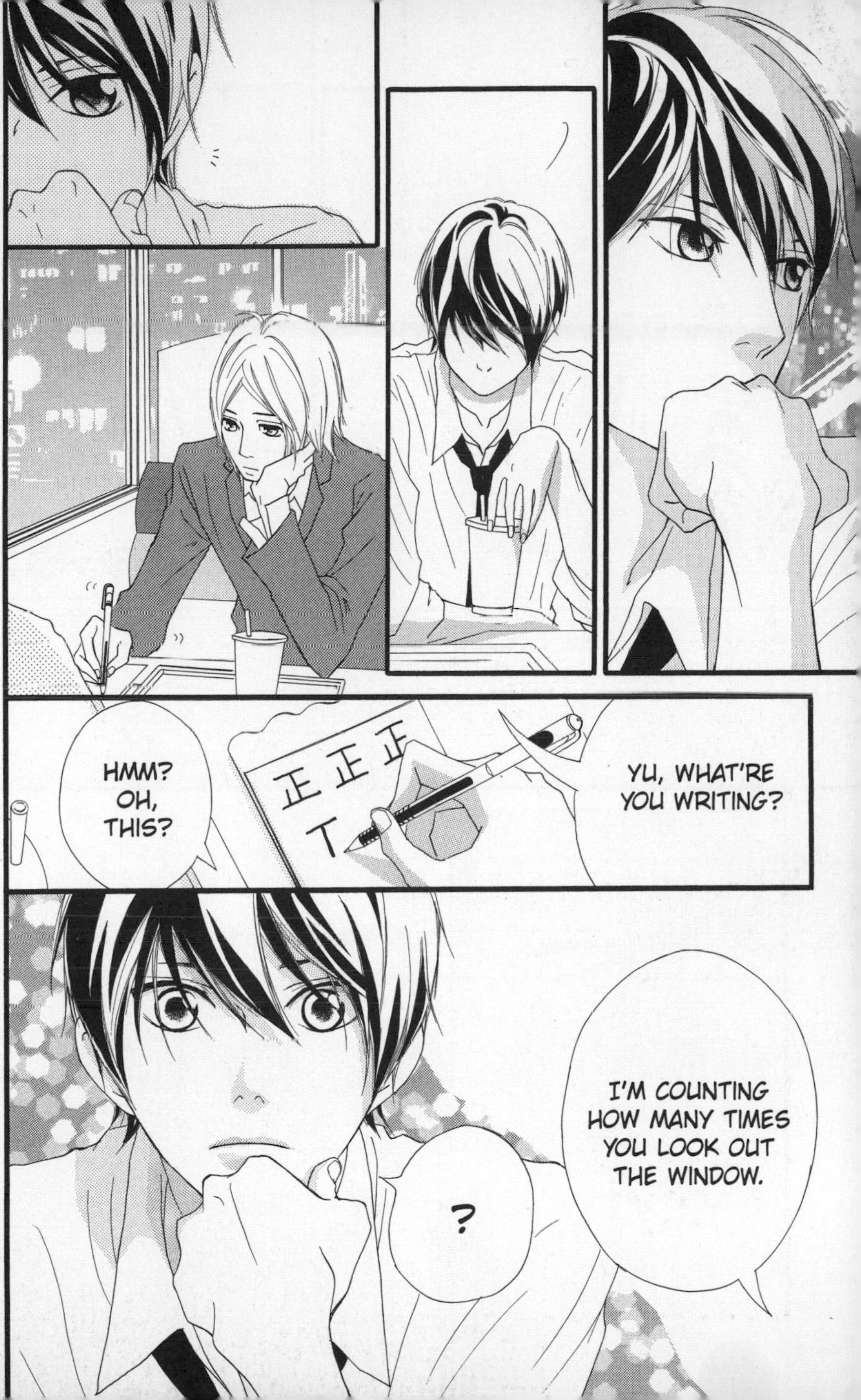
YU, WHAT'RE YOU WRITING?
HMM? OH, THIS?
I'M COUNTING HOW MANY TIMES YOU LOOK OUT THE WINDOW.
?

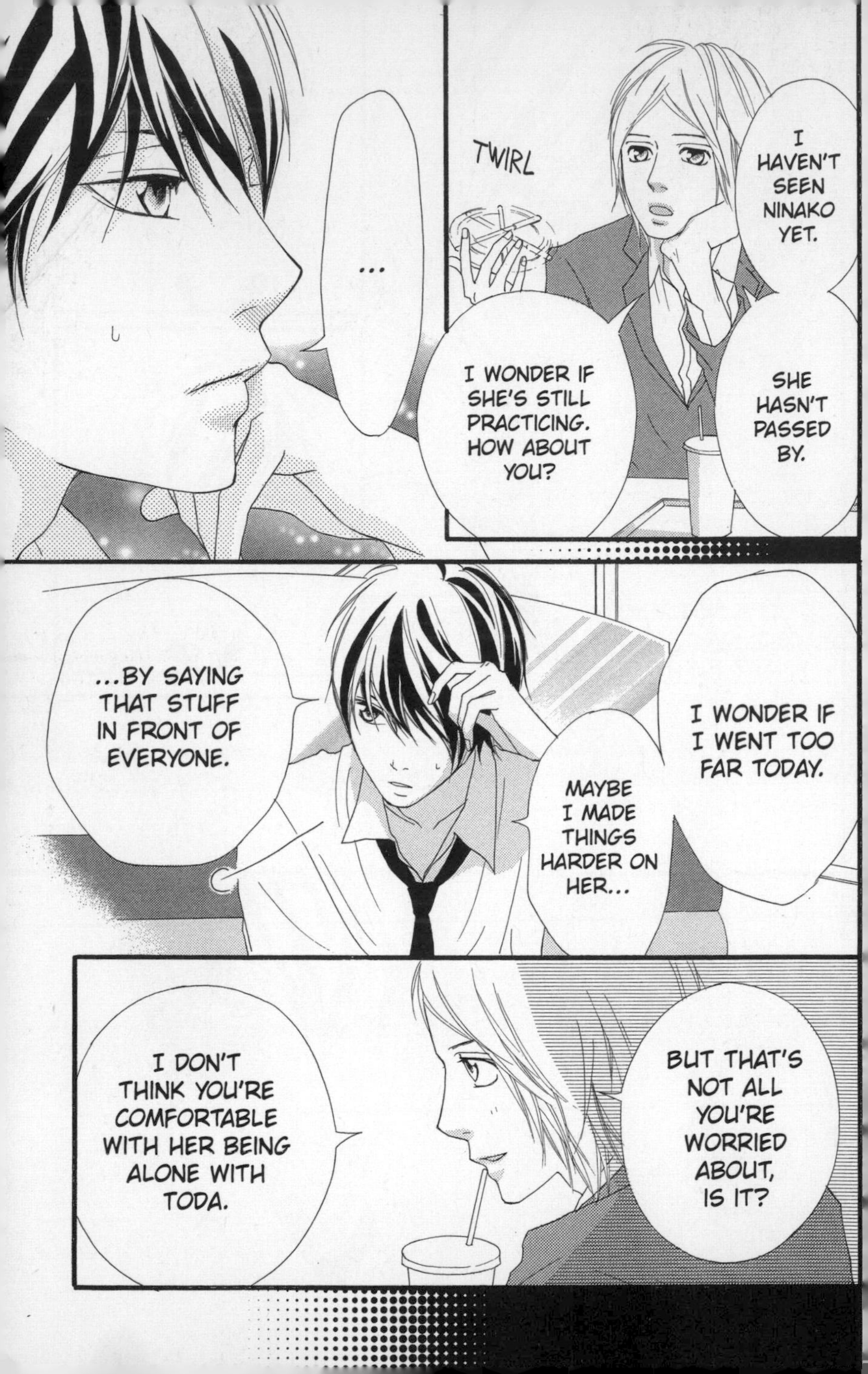
I HAVEN'T SEEN NINAKO YET.
SHE HASN'T PASSED BY.
TWIRL
I WONDER IF SHE'S STILL PRACTICING. HOW ABOUT YOU?
...
I WONDER IF I WENT TOO FAR TODAY.
MAYBE I MADE THINGS HARDER ON HER...
...BY SAYING THAT STUFF IN FRONT OF EVERYONE.
BUT THAT'S NOT ALL YOU'RE WORRIED ABOUT, IS IT?
I DON'T THINK YOU'RE COMFORTABLE WITH HER BEING ALONE WITH TODA.

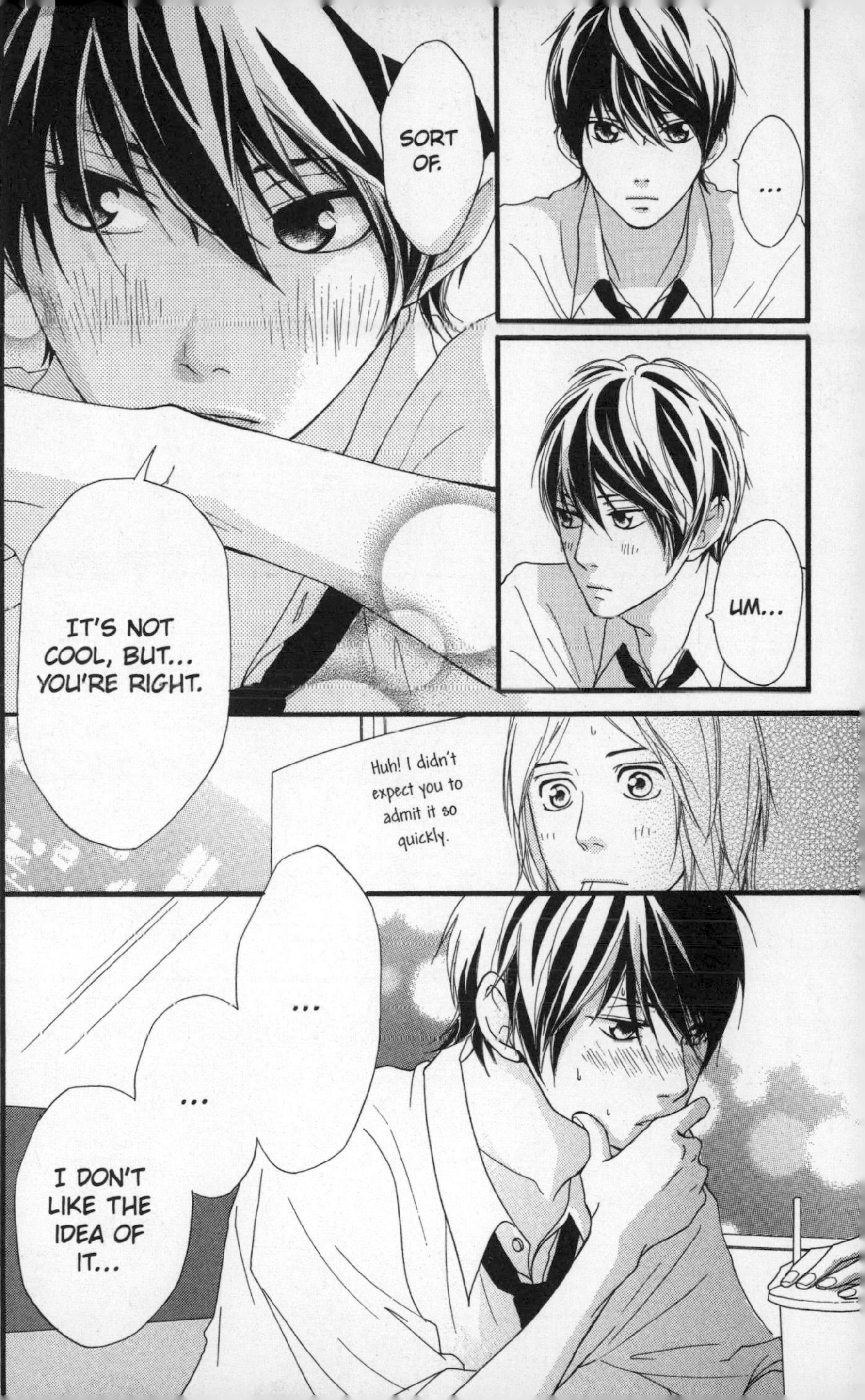
...
UM...
SORT OF.
IT'S NOT COOL, BUT... YOU'RE RIGHT.
Huh! I didn't expect you to admit it so quickly.
...
...
I DON'T LIKE THE IDEA OF IT...

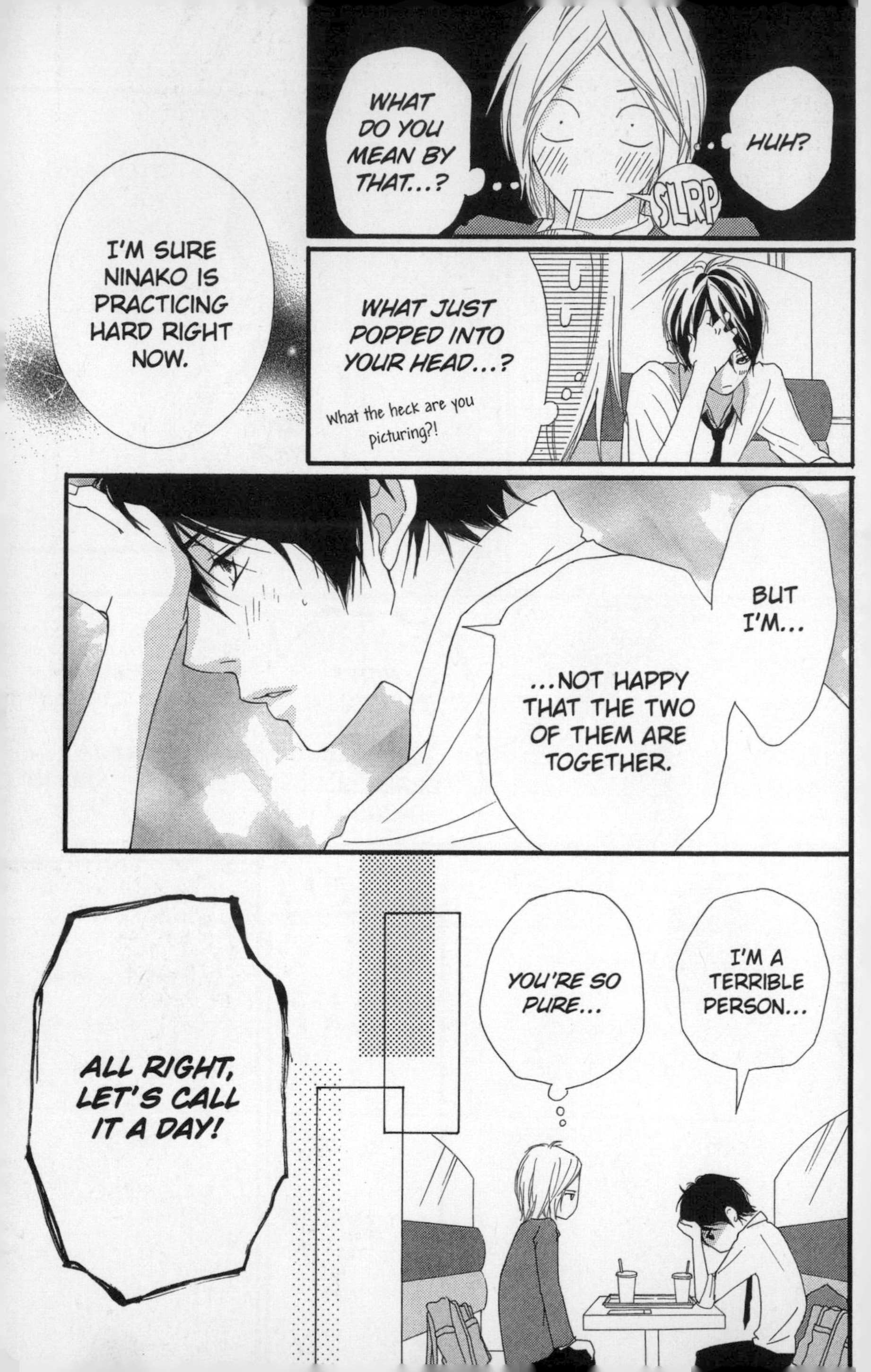
HUH?
SLRP
WHAT DO YOU MEAN BY THAT...?
WHAT JUST POPPED INTO YOUR HEAD...?
What the heck are you picturing?!
I'M SURE NINAKO IS PRACTICING HARD RIGHT NOW.
BUT I'M...
...NOT HAPPY THAT THE TWO OF THEM ARE TOGETHER.
I'M A TERRIBLE PERSON...
YOU'RE SO PURE...
ALL RIGHT, LET'S CALL IT A DAY!

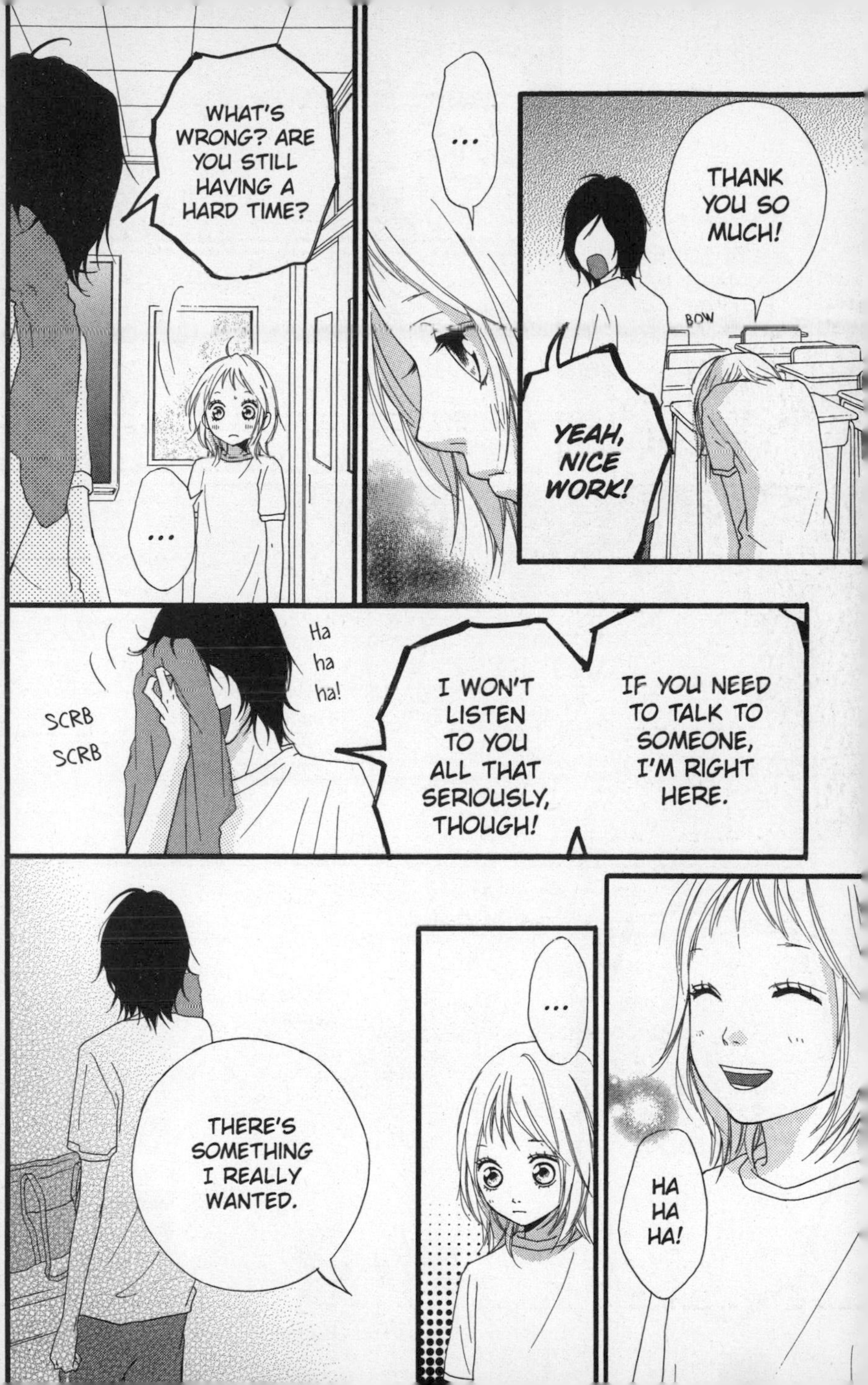
THANK YOU SO MUCH!
BOW
YEAH, NICE WORK!
...
WHAT'S WRONG? ARE YOU STILL HAVING A HARD TIME?
...
IF YOU NEED TO TALK TO SOMEONE, I'M RIGHT HERE.
I WON'T LISTEN TO YOU ALL THAT SERIOUSLY, THOUGH!
Ha ha ha!
SCRB SCRB
HA HA HA!
...
THERE'S SOMETHING I REALLY WANTED.

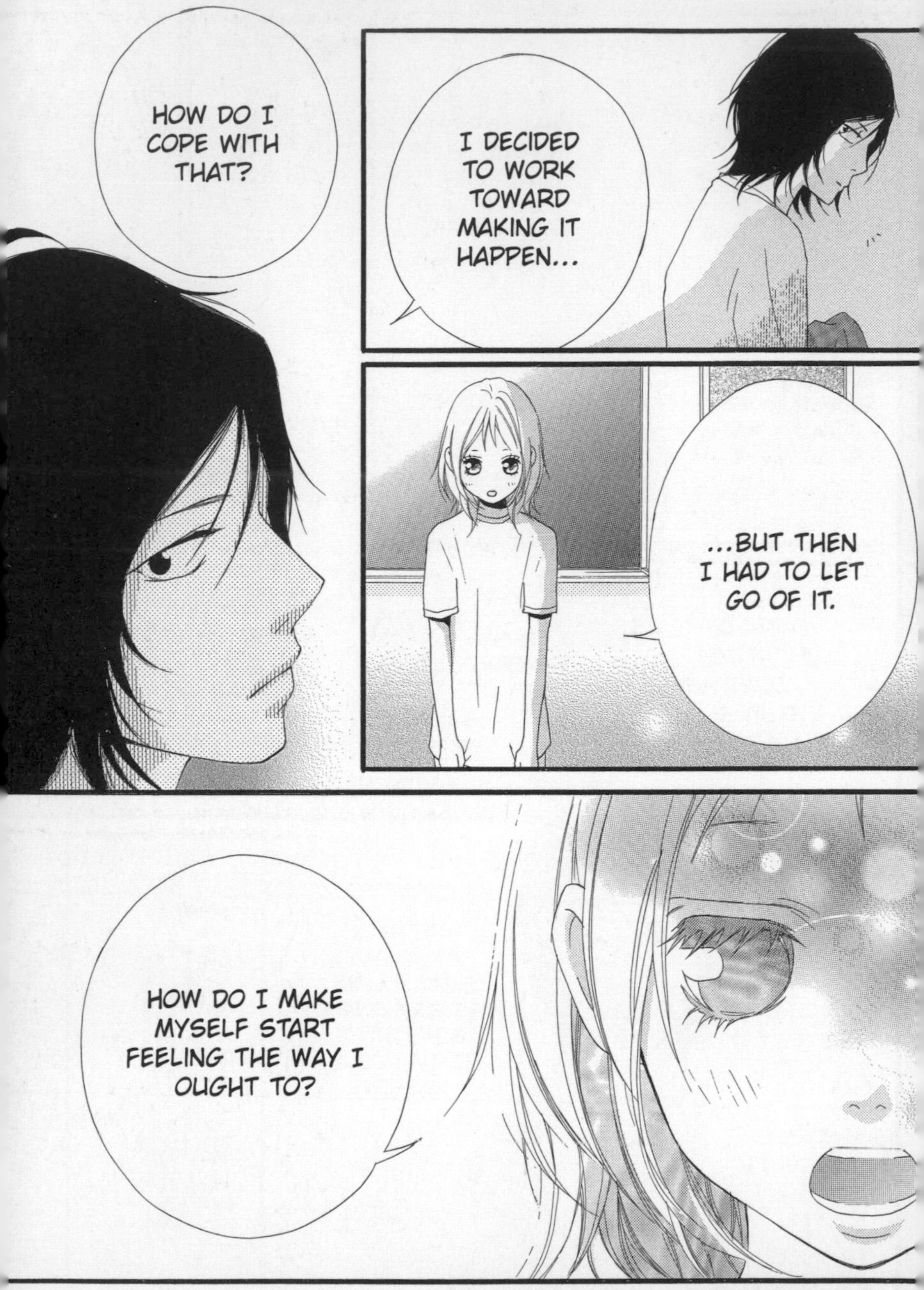
I DECIDED TO WORK TOWARD MAKING IT HAPPEN...
...BUT THEN I HAD TO LET GO OF IT.
HOW DO I COPE WITH THAT?
HOW DO I MAKE MYSELF START FEELING THE WAY I OUGHT TO?

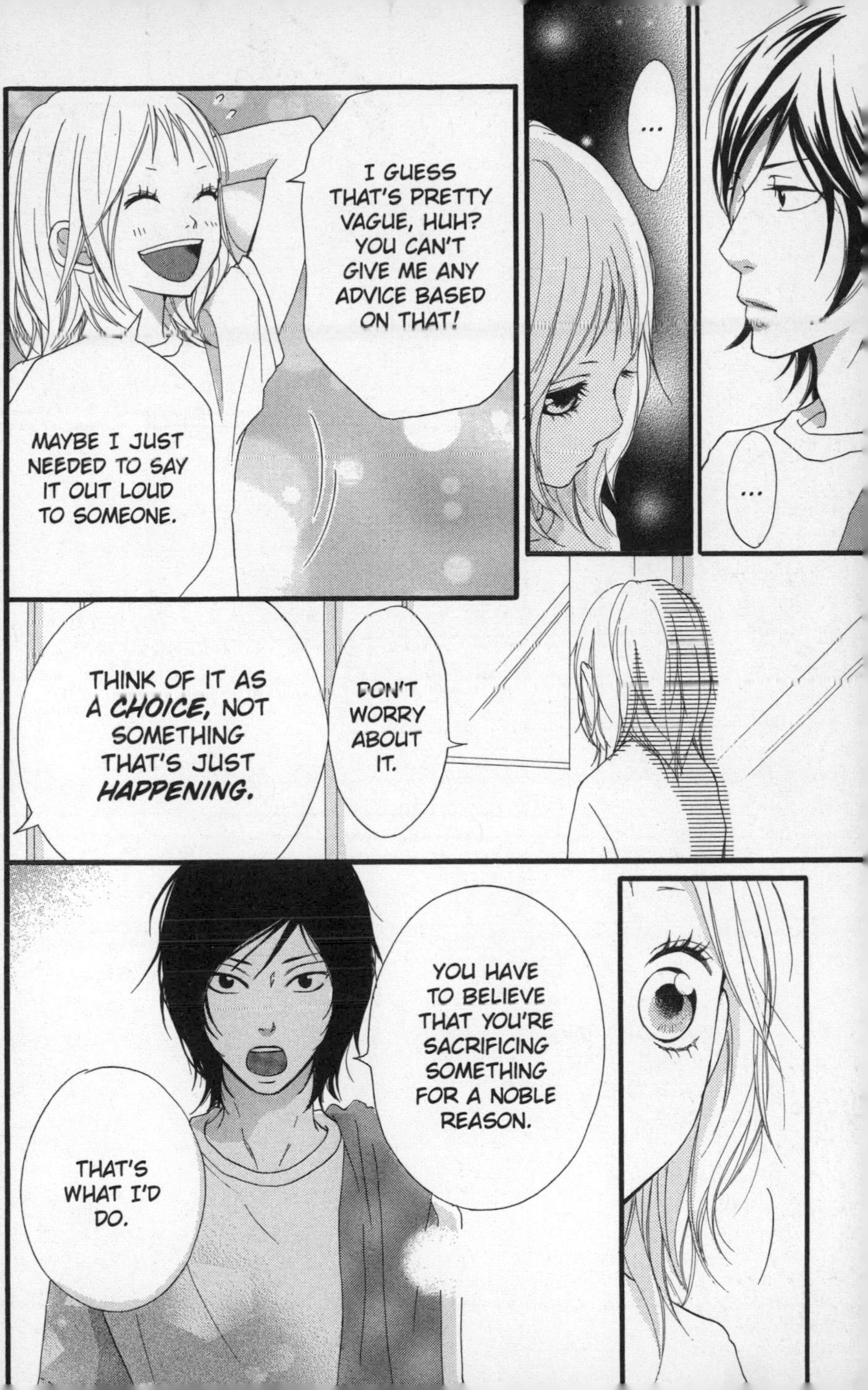
...
...
I GUESS THAT'S PRETTY VAGUE, HUH? YOU CAN'T GIVE ME ANY ADVICE BASED ON THAT!
MAYBE I JUST NEEDED TO SAY IT OUT LOUD TO SOMEONE.
DON'T WORRY ABOUT IT.
THINK OF IT AS A *CHOICE,* NOT SOMETHING THAT'S JUST ***HAPPENING.***
YOU HAVE TO BELIEVE THAT YOU'RE SACRIFICING SOMETHING FOR A NOBLE REASON.
THAT'S WHAT I'D DO.

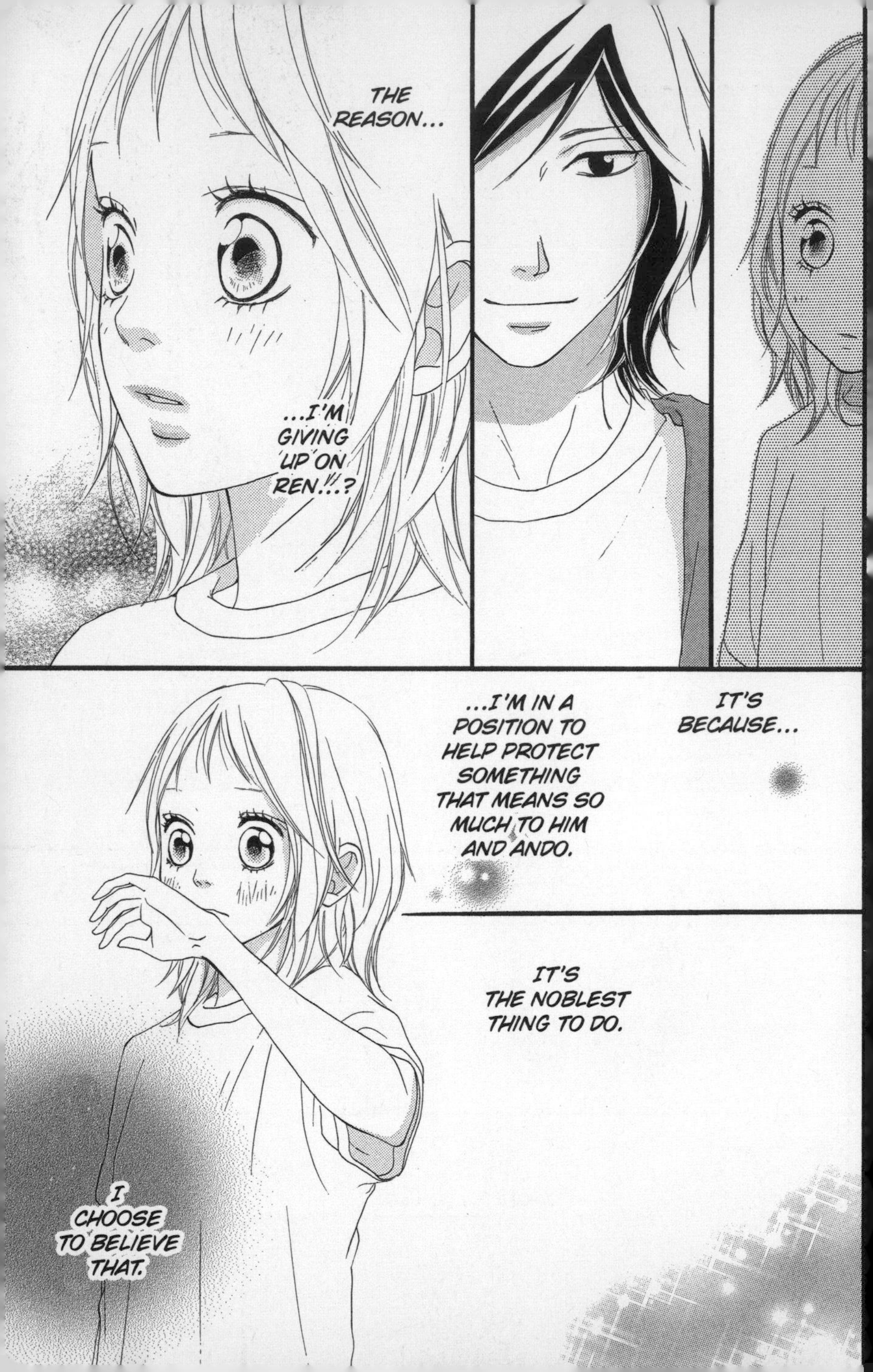
THE REASON...
...I'M GIVING UP ON REN...?
IT'S BECAUSE...
...I'M IN A POSITION TO HELP PROTECT SOMETHING THAT MEANS SO MUCH TO HIM AND ANDO.
IT'S THE NOBLEST THING TO DO.
I CHOOSE TO BELIEVE THAT.

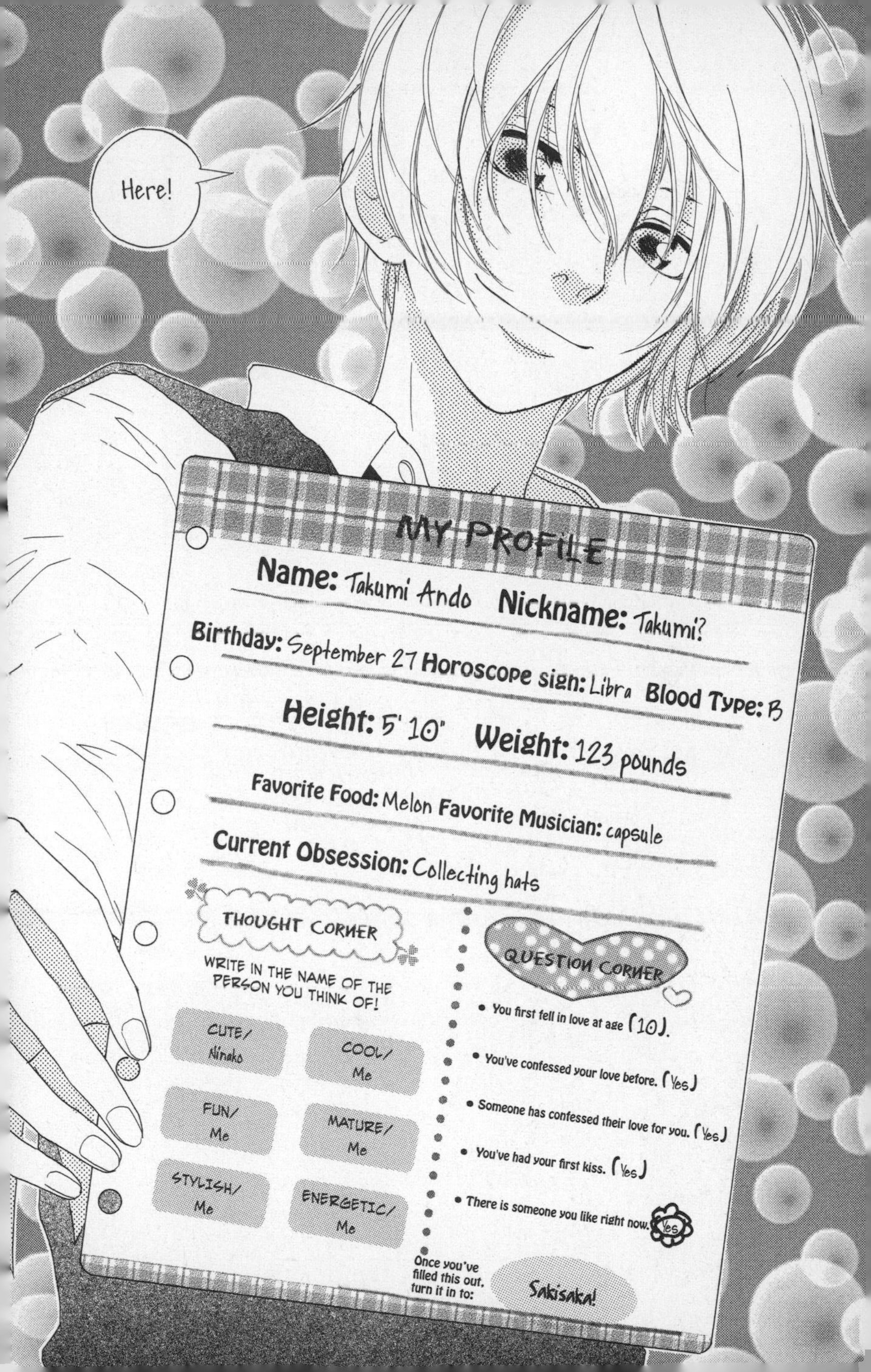
Here!
MY PROFILE
Name: Takumi Ando Nickname: Takumi?
Birthday: September 27 Horoscope sign: Libra Blood Type: B
Height: 5' 10" Weight: 123 pounds
Favorite Food: Melon Favorite Musician: capsule
Current Obsession: Collecting hats
THOUGHT CORNER
WRITE IN THE NAME OF THE PERSON YOU THINK OF!
CUTE/ Ninako
COOL/ Me
FUN/ Me
MATURE/ Me
STYLISH/ Me
ENERGETIC/ Me
QUESTION CORNER
• You first fell in love at age (10).
• You've confessed your love before. (Yes)
• Someone has confessed their love for you. (Yes)
• You've had your first kiss. (Yes)
• There is someone you like right now. (Yes)
Once you've filled this out, turn it in to:
Sakisaka!

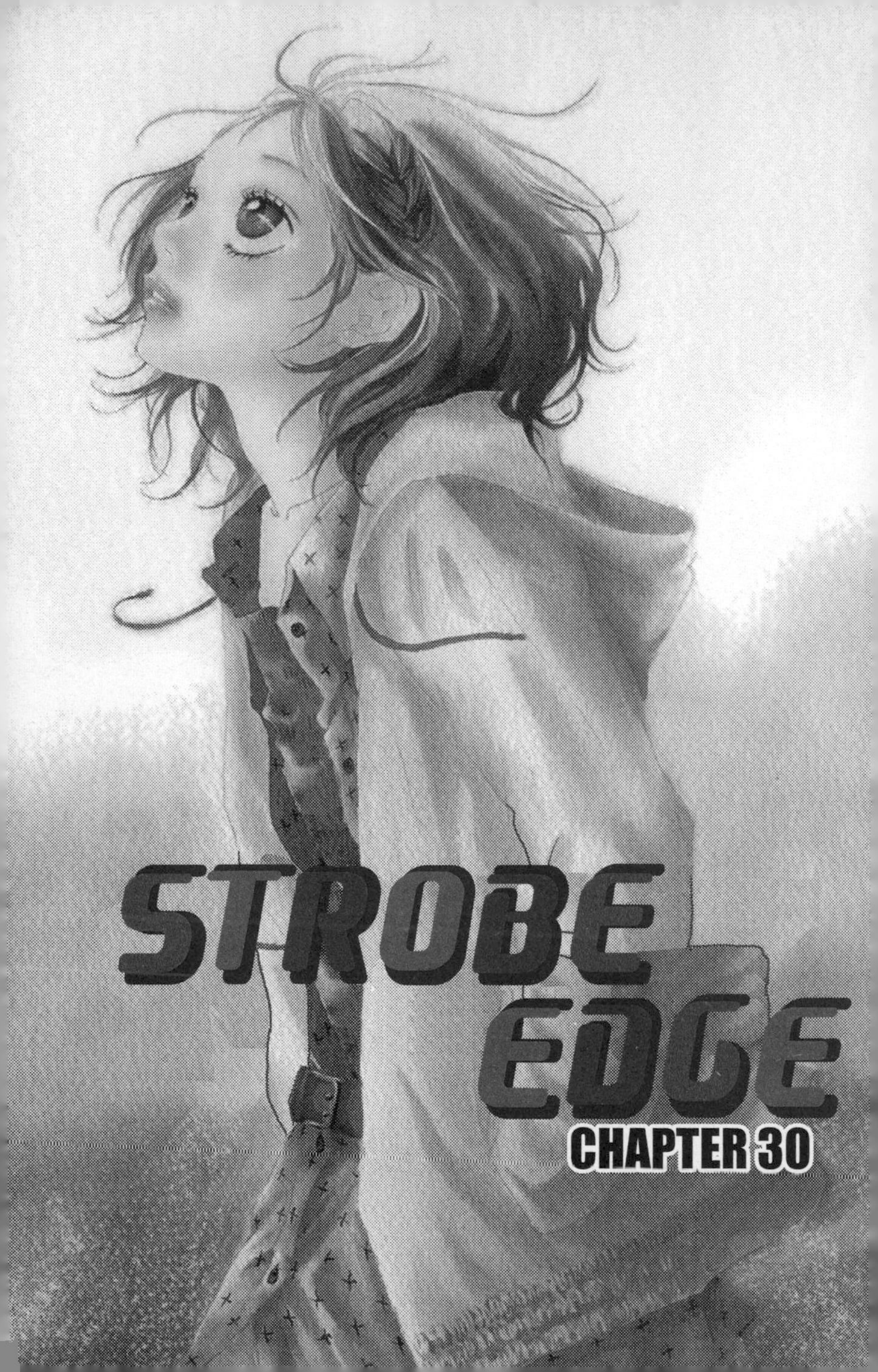
STROBE EDGE
CHAPTER 30

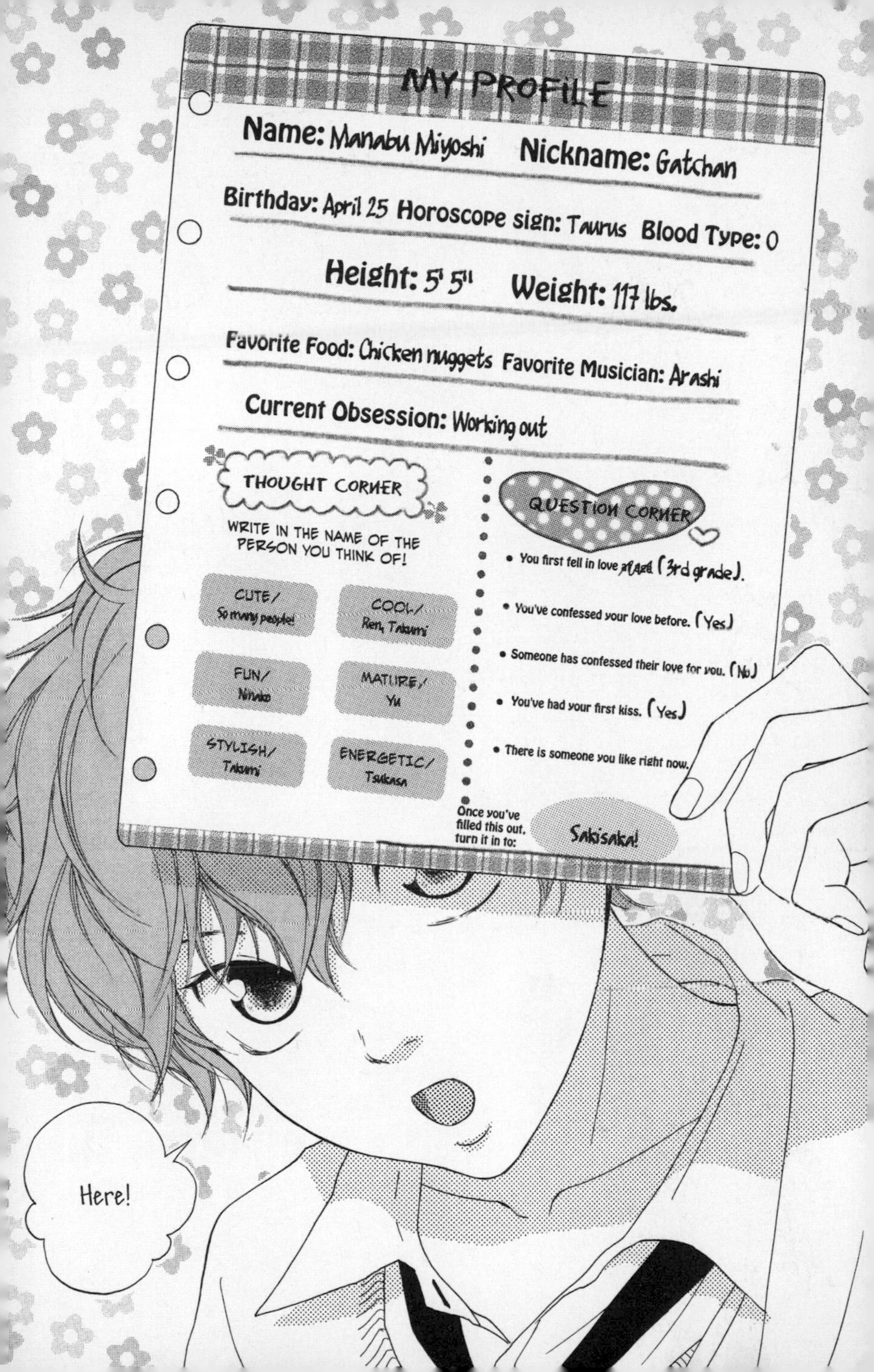
MY PROFILE
Name: Manabu Miyoshi
Nickname: Gatchan
Birthday: April 25
Horoscope sign: Taurus
Blood Type: O
Height: 5' 5"
Weight: 117 lbs.
Favorite Food: Chicken nuggets
Favorite Musician: Arashi
Current Obsession: Working out
THOUGHT CORNER
WRITE IN THE NAME OF THE PERSON YOU THINK OF!
CUTE/ So many people!
COOL/ Ren, Takumi
FUN/ Ninako
MATURE/ Yu
STYLISH/ Takumi
ENERGETIC/ Tsukasa
QUESTION CORNER
• You first fell in love (3rd grade).
• You've confessed your love before. (Yes)
• Someone has confessed their love for you. (No)
• You've had your first kiss. (Yes)
• There is someone you like right now.
Once you've filled this out, turn it in to:
Sakisaka!
Here!

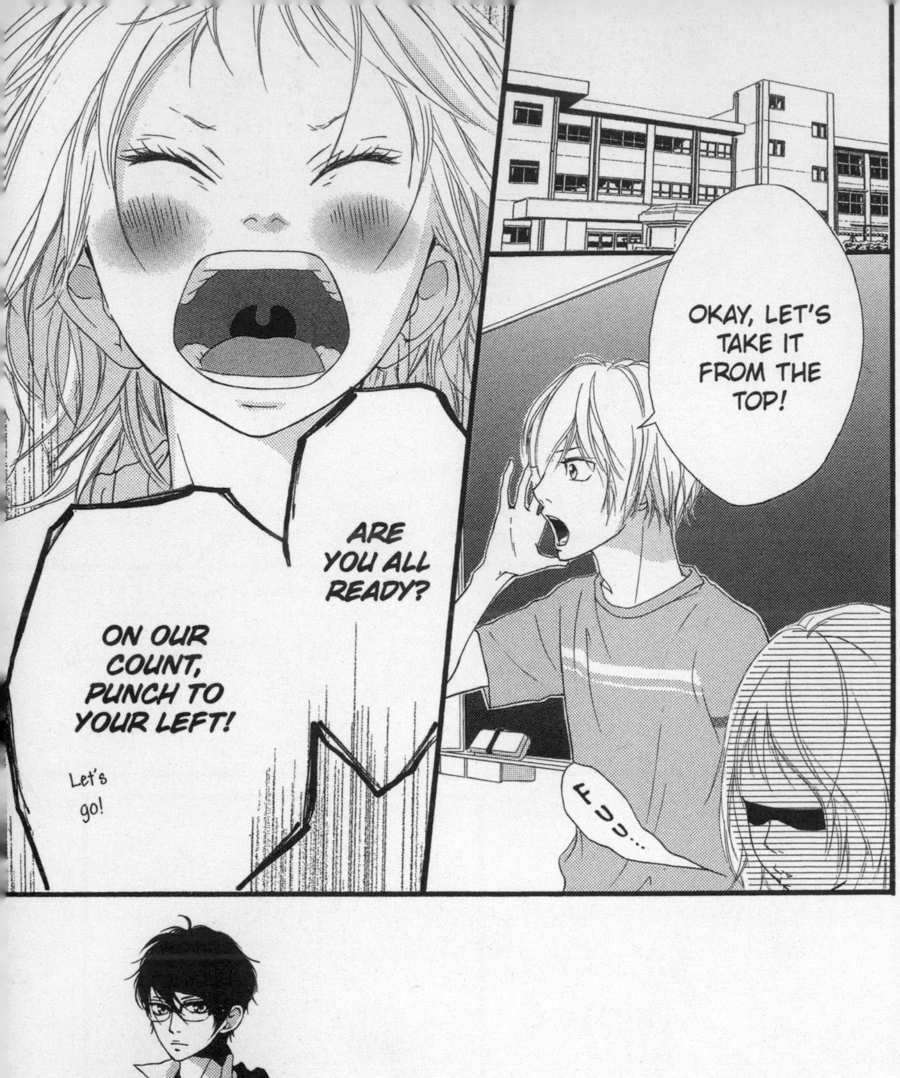
OKAY, LET'S TAKE IT FROM THE TOP!
ARE YOU ALL READY?
ON OUR COUNT, PUNCH TO YOUR LEFT!
Let's go!

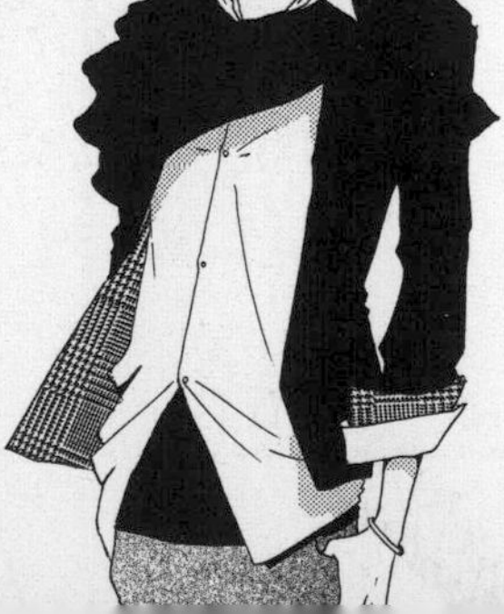

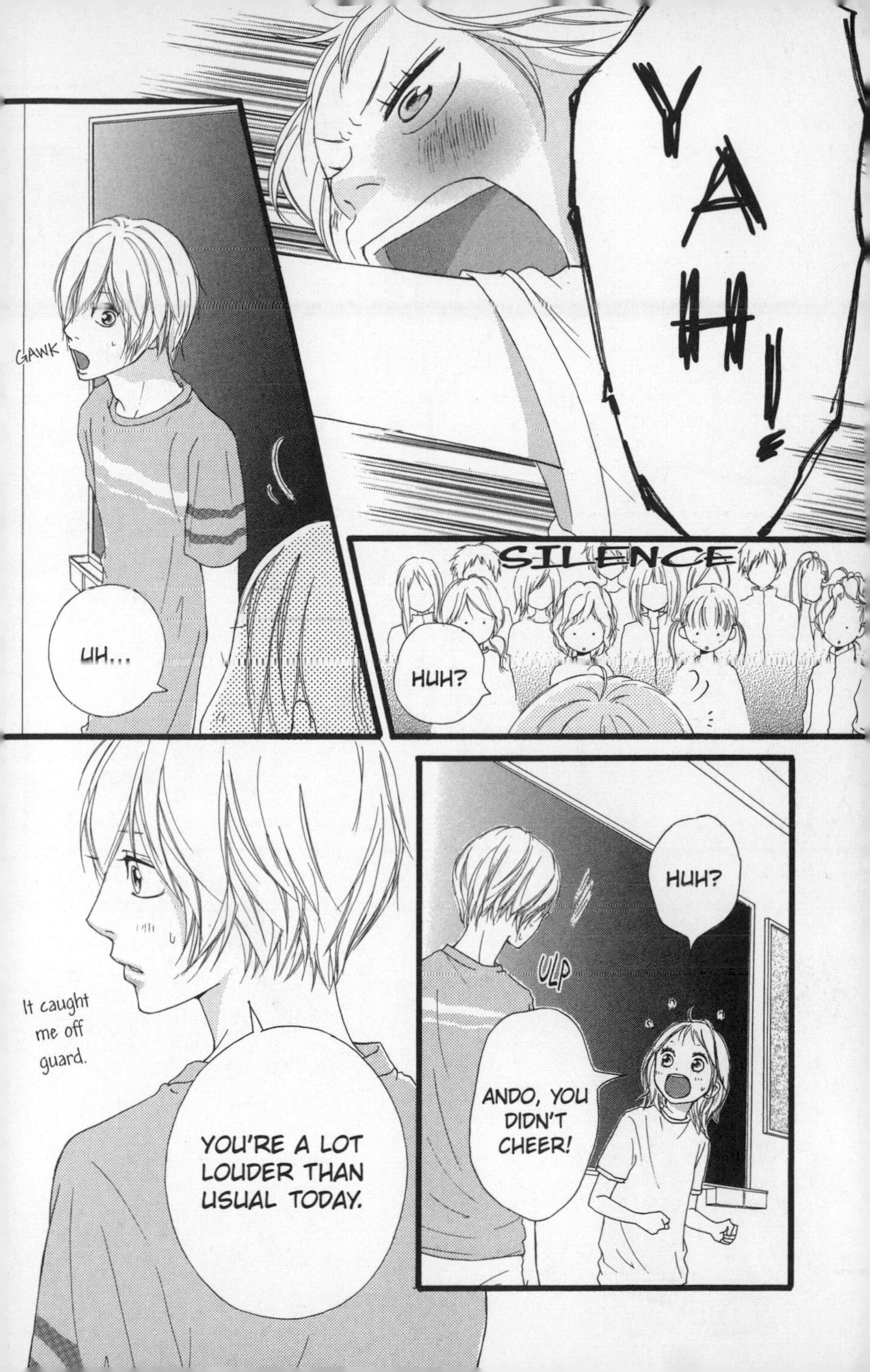
YAH!
SILENCE
HUH?
GAWK
UH...
HUH?
ULP
ANDO, YOU DIDN'T CHEER!
It caught me off guard.
YOU'RE A LOT LOUDER THAN USUAL TODAY.

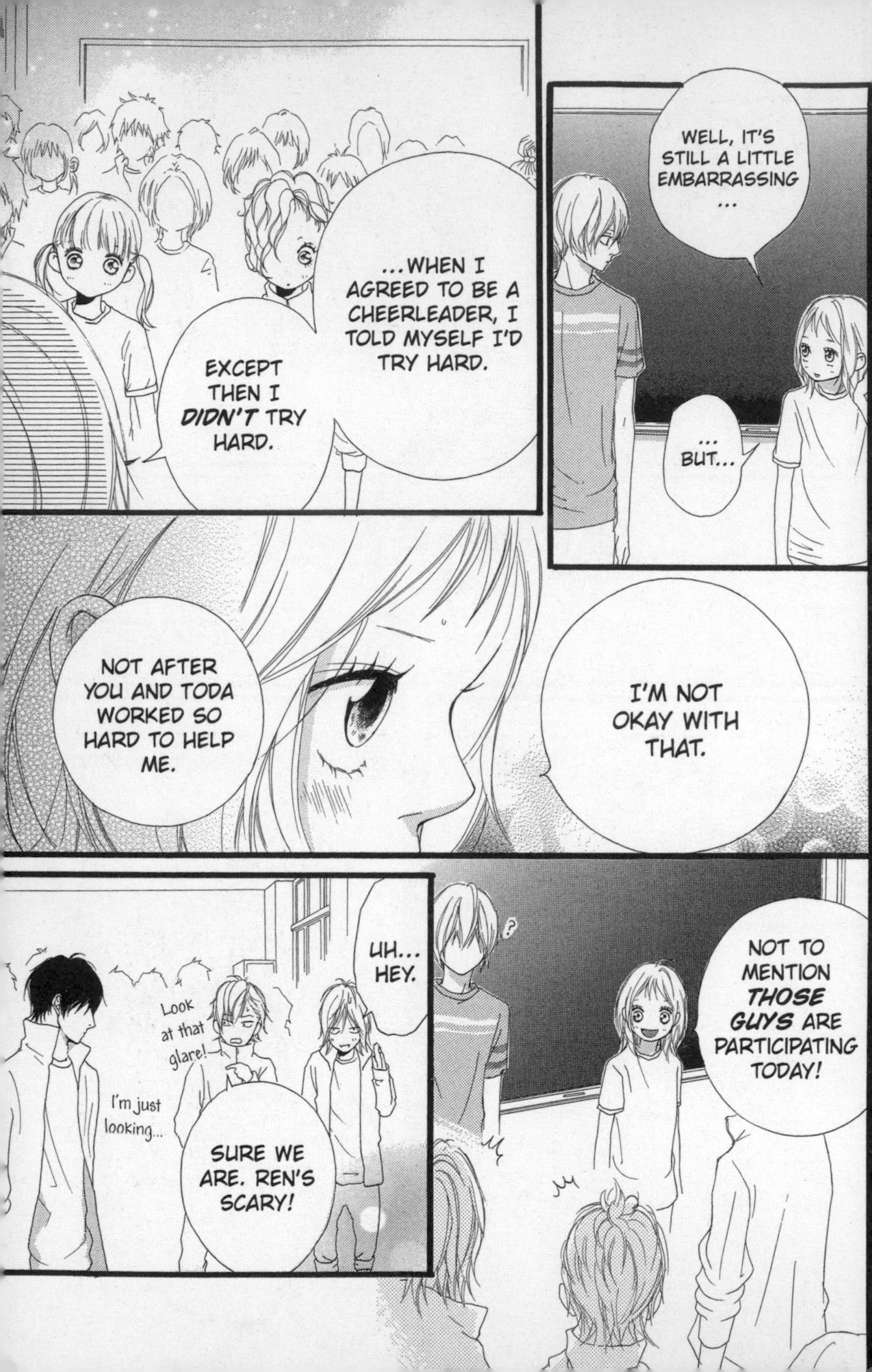
WELL, IT'S STILL A LITTLE EMBARRASSING ...
... BUT...
...WHEN I AGREED TO BE A CHEERLEADER, I TOLD MYSELF I'D TRY HARD.
EXCEPT THEN I *DIDN'T* TRY HARD.
I'M NOT OKAY WITH THAT.
NOT AFTER YOU AND TODA WORKED SO HARD TO HELP ME.
NOT TO MENTION *THOSE GUYS* ARE PARTICIPATING TODAY!
UH... HEY.
Look at that glare!
I'm just looking...
SURE WE ARE. REN'S SCARY!

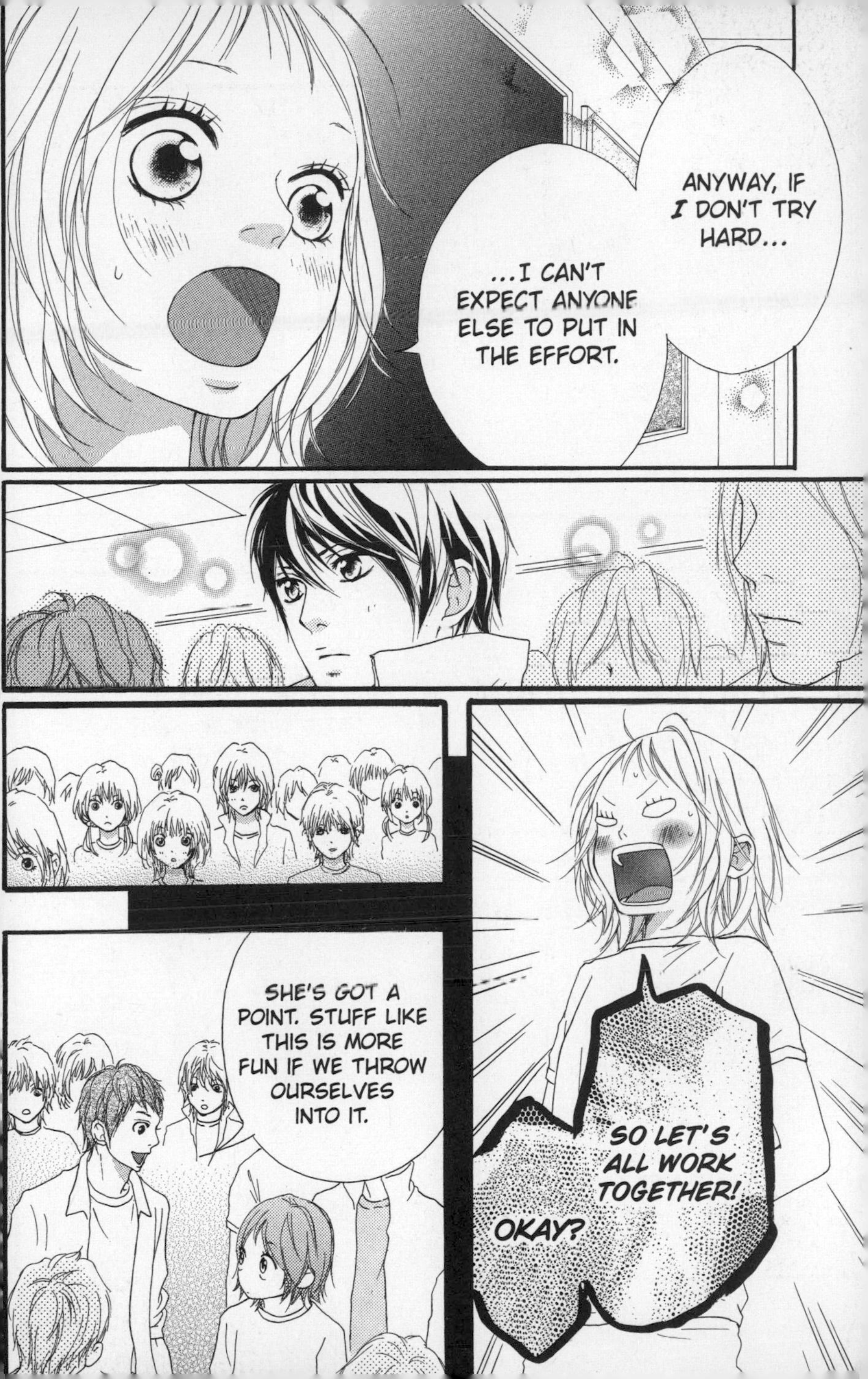
ANYWAY, IF I DON'T TRY HARD...
...I CAN'T EXPECT ANYONE ELSE TO PUT IN THE EFFORT.
SO LET'S ALL WORK TOGETHER!
OKAY?
SHE'S GOT A POINT. STUFF LIKE THIS IS MORE FUN IF WE THROW OURSELVES INTO IT.

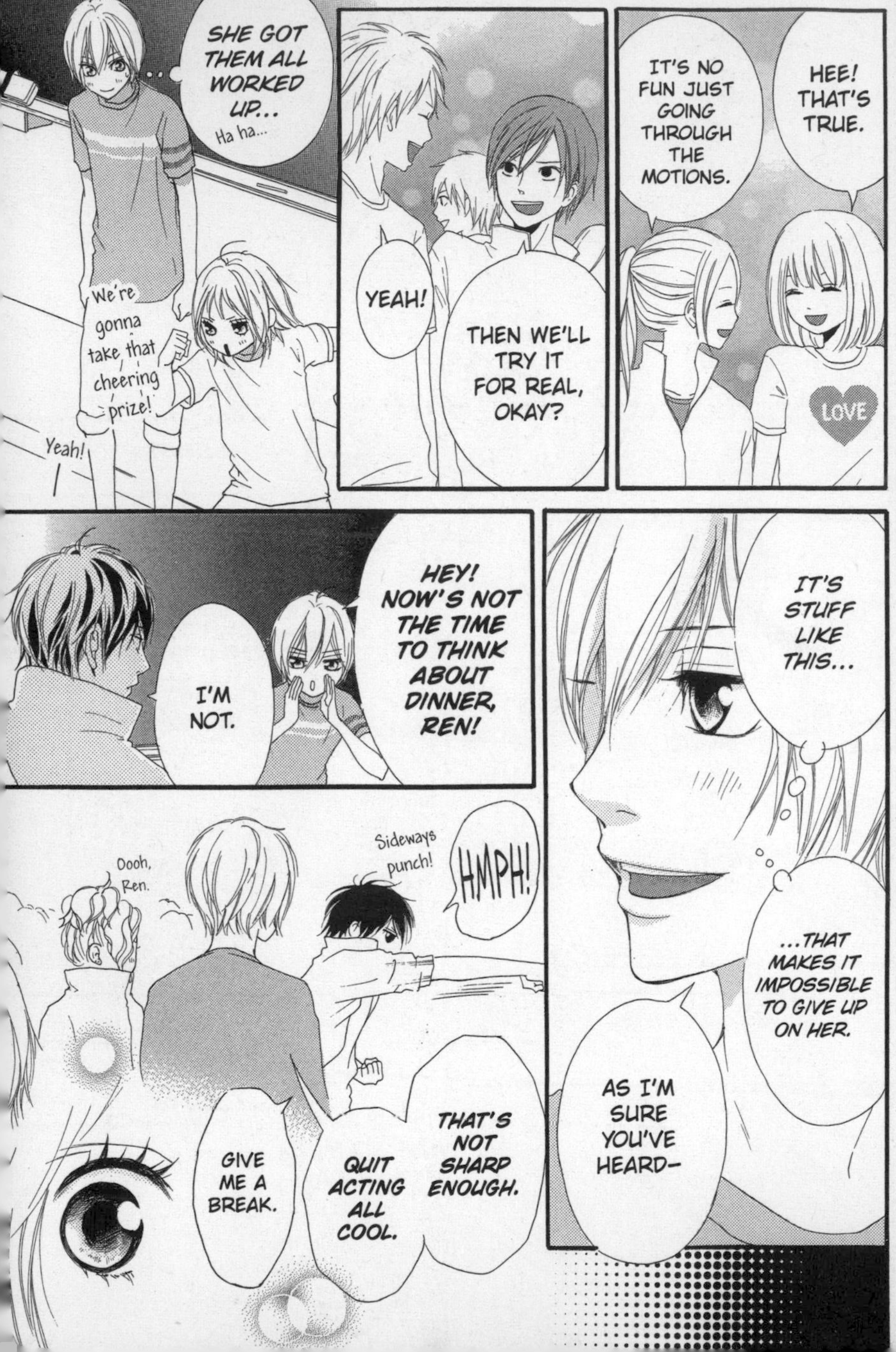
HEE! THAT'S TRUE.
IT'S NO FUN JUST GOING THROUGH THE MOTIONS.
THEN WE'LL TRY IT FOR REAL, OKAY?
YEAH!
SHE GOT THEM ALL WORKED UP...
Ha ha...
We're gonna take that cheering prize!
Yeah!
IT'S STUFF LIKE THIS...
...THAT MAKES IT IMPOSSIBLE TO GIVE UP ON HER.
AS I'M SURE YOU'VE HEARD–
HEY! NOW'S NOT THE TIME TO THINK ABOUT DINNER, REN!
I'M NOT.
HMPH!
Sideways punch!
Oooh, Ren.
THAT'S NOT SHARP ENOUGH.
QUIT ACTING ALL COOL.
GIVE ME A BREAK.

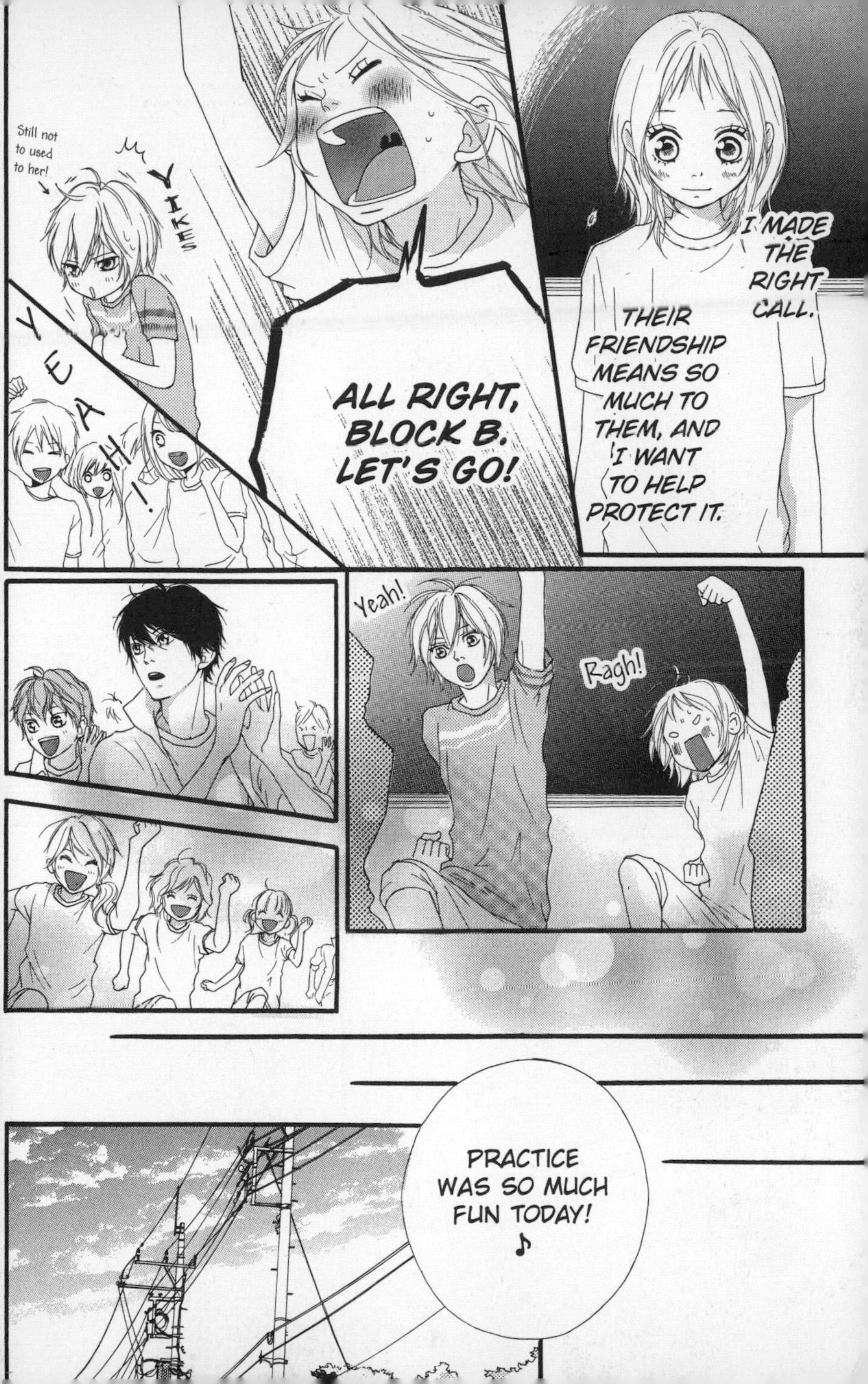
I MADE THE RIGHT CALL.
THEIR FRIENDSHIP MEANS SO MUCH TO THEM, AND I WANT TO HELP PROTECT IT.
ALL RIGHT, BLOCK B. LET'S GO!
YIKES
Still not to used to her!
YEAH!
Yeah!
Ragh!
PRACTICE WAS SO MUCH FUN TODAY! ♪

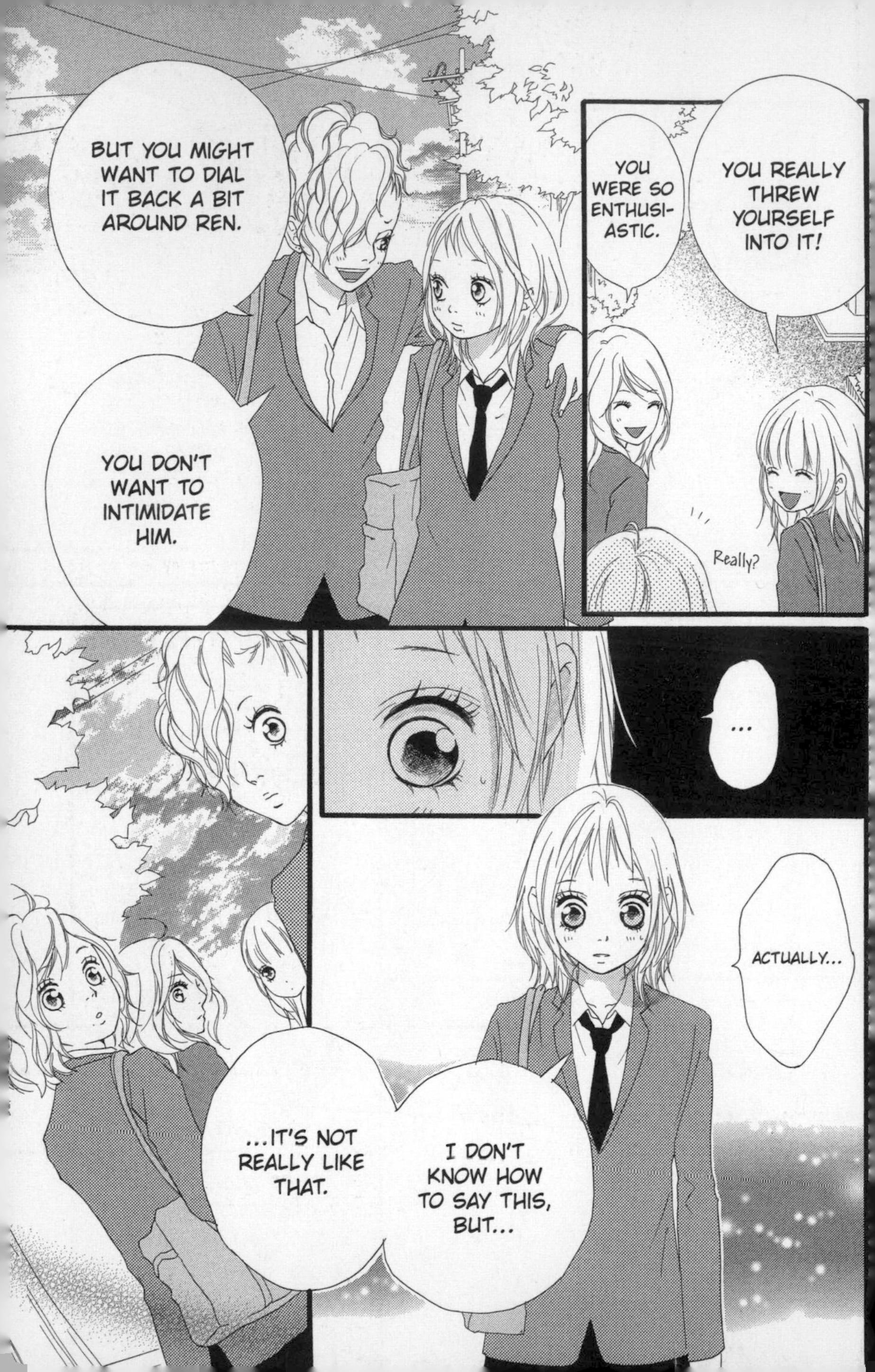
YOU REALLY THREW YOURSELF INTO IT!
YOU WERE SO ENTHUSI-ASTIC.
Really?
BUT YOU MIGHT WANT TO DIAL IT BACK A BIT AROUND REN.
YOU DON'T WANT TO INTIMIDATE HIM.
...
ACTUALLY...
I DON'T KNOW HOW TO SAY THIS, BUT...
...IT'S NOT REALLY LIKE THAT.

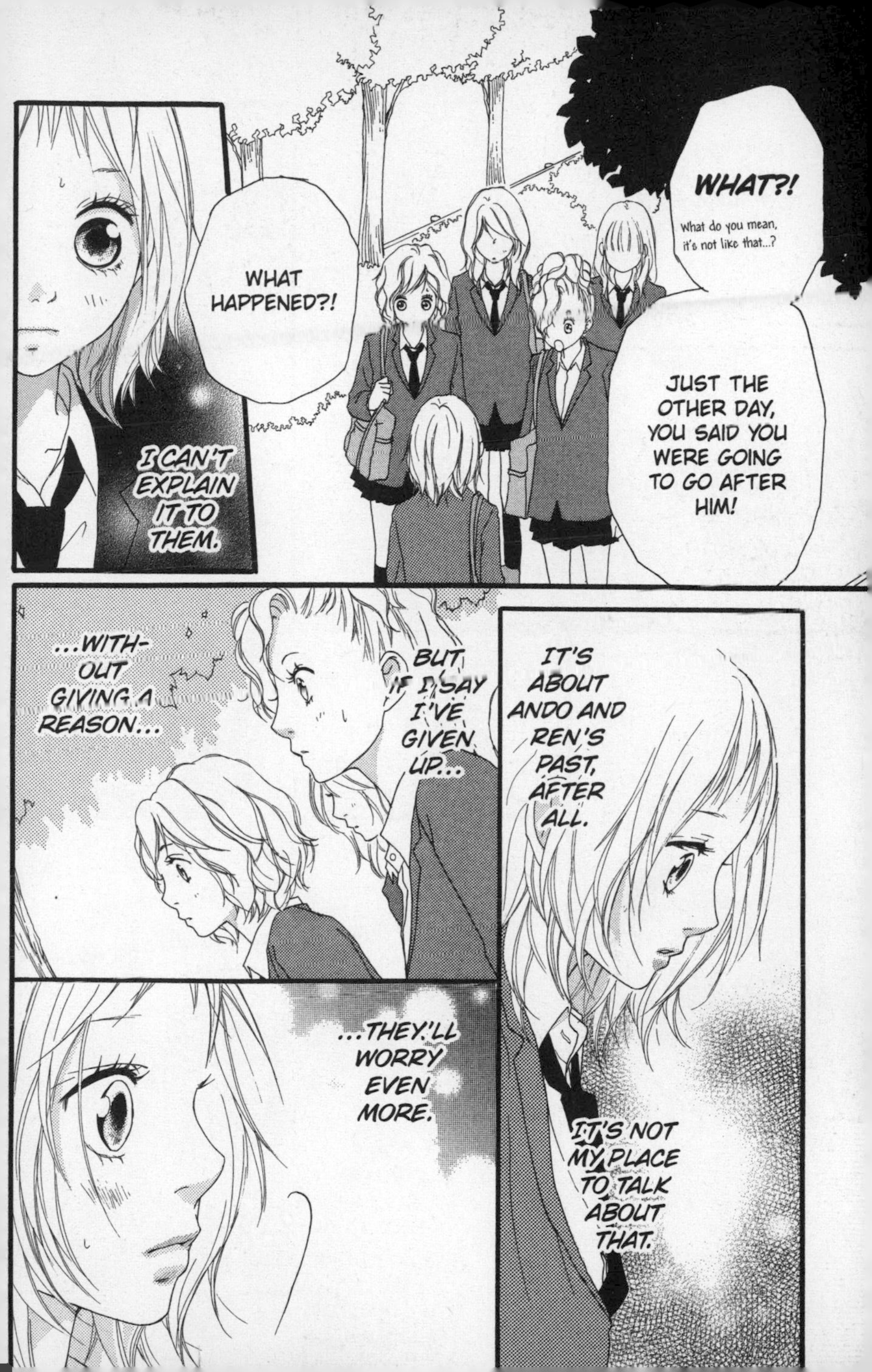
WHAT?!
What do you mean, it's not like that...?
JUST THE OTHER DAY, YOU SAID YOU WERE GOING TO GO AFTER HIM!
WHAT HAPPENED?!
I CAN'T EXPLAIN IT TO THEM.
IT'S ABOUT ANDO AND REN'S PAST, AFTER ALL.
IT'S NOT MY PLACE TO TALK ABOUT THAT.
BUT IF I SAY I'VE GIVEN UP...
...WITH-OUT GIVING A REASON...
...THEY'LL WORRY EVEN MORE.

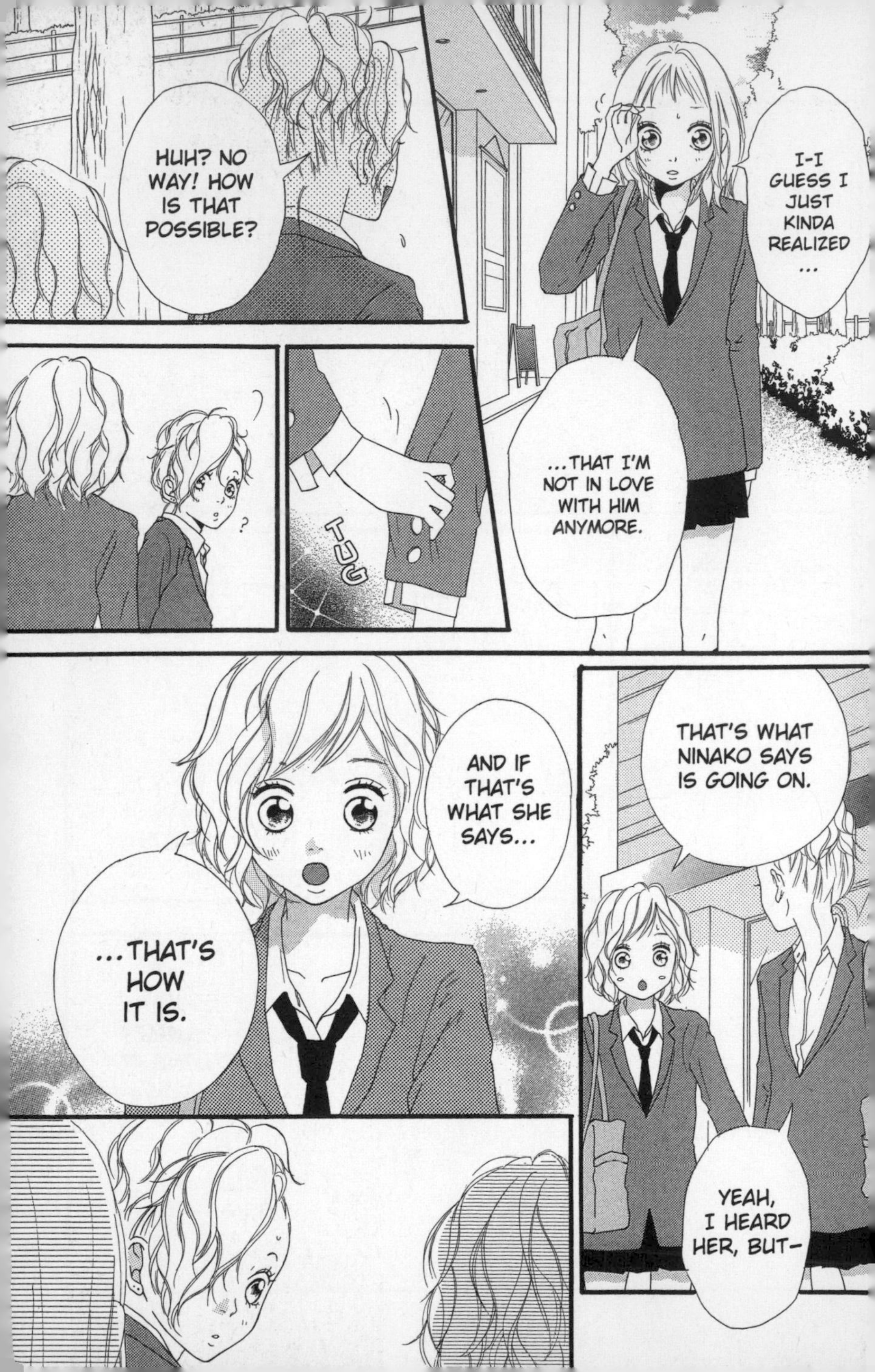
I-I GUESS I JUST KINDA REALIZED ...
...THAT I'M NOT IN LOVE WITH HIM ANYMORE.
HUH? NO WAY! HOW IS THAT POSSIBLE?
TUG
THAT'S WHAT NINAKO SAYS IS GOING ON.
YEAH, I HEARD HER, BUT-
AND IF THAT'S WHAT SHE SAYS...
...THAT'S HOW IT IS.

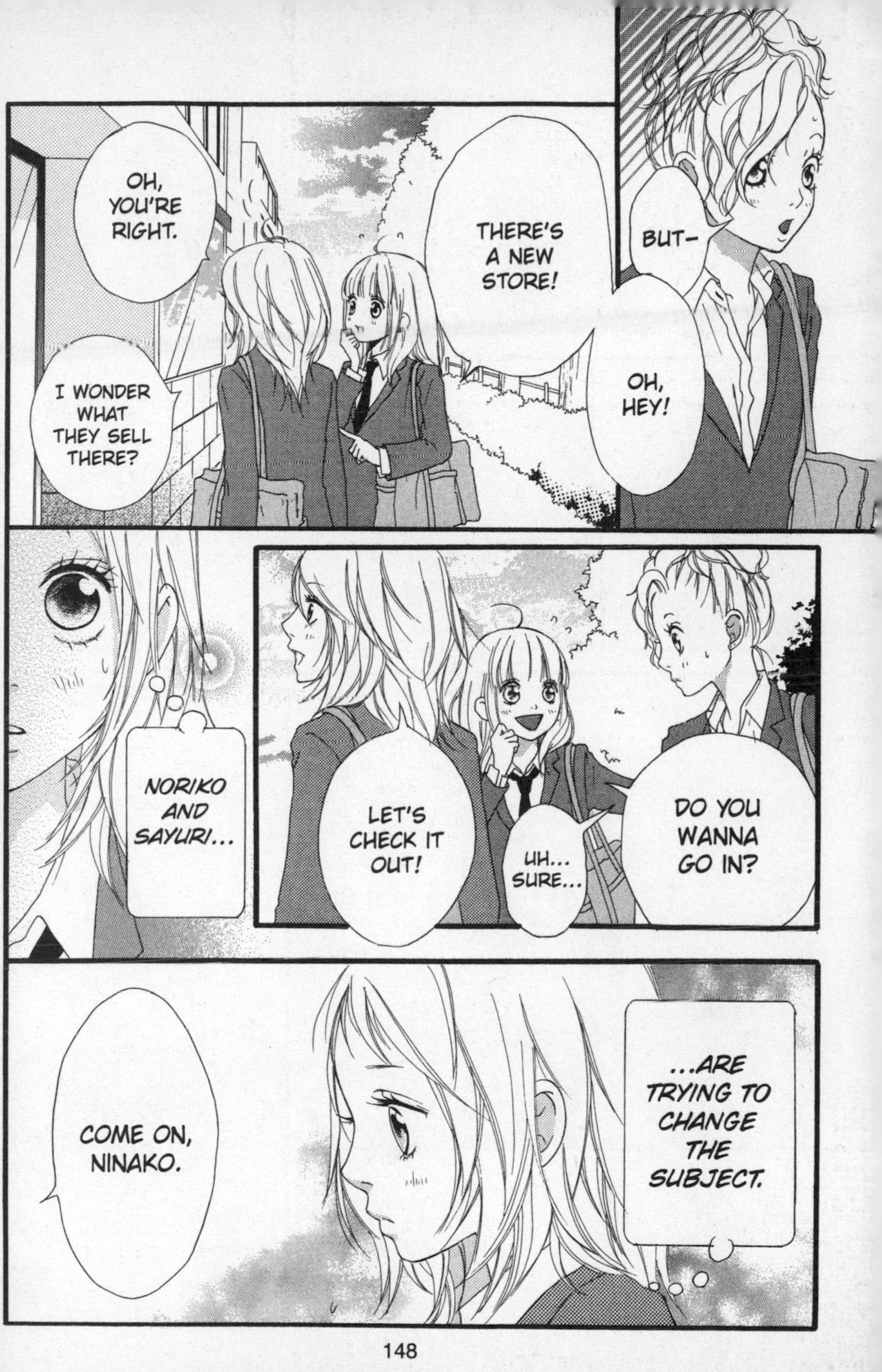
BUT-
OH, HEY!
THERE'S A NEW STORE!
OH, YOU'RE RIGHT.
I WONDER WHAT THEY SELL THERE?
DO YOU WANNA GO IN?
UH... SURE...
LET'S CHECK IT OUT!
NORIKO AND SAYURI...
...ARE TRYING TO CHANGE THE SUBJECT.
COME ON, NINAKO.

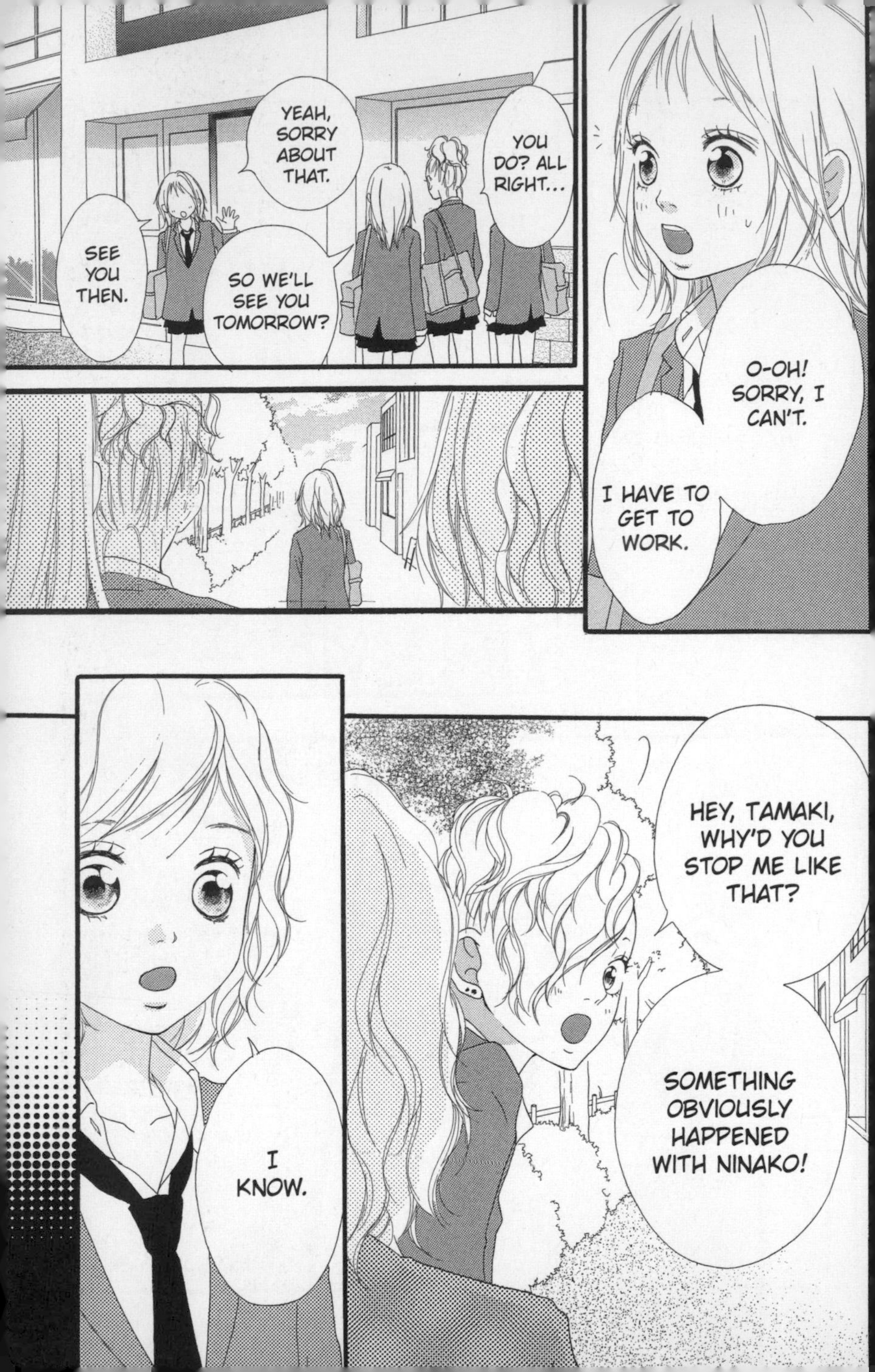

O-OH! SORRY, I CAN'T.
I HAVE TO GET TO WORK.
YOU DO? ALL RIGHT...
YEAH, SORRY ABOUT THAT.
SO WE'LL SEE YOU TOMORROW?
SEE YOU THEN.
HEY, TAMAKI, WHY'D YOU STOP ME LIKE THAT?
SOMETHING OBVIOUSLY HAPPENED WITH NINAKO!
I KNOW.

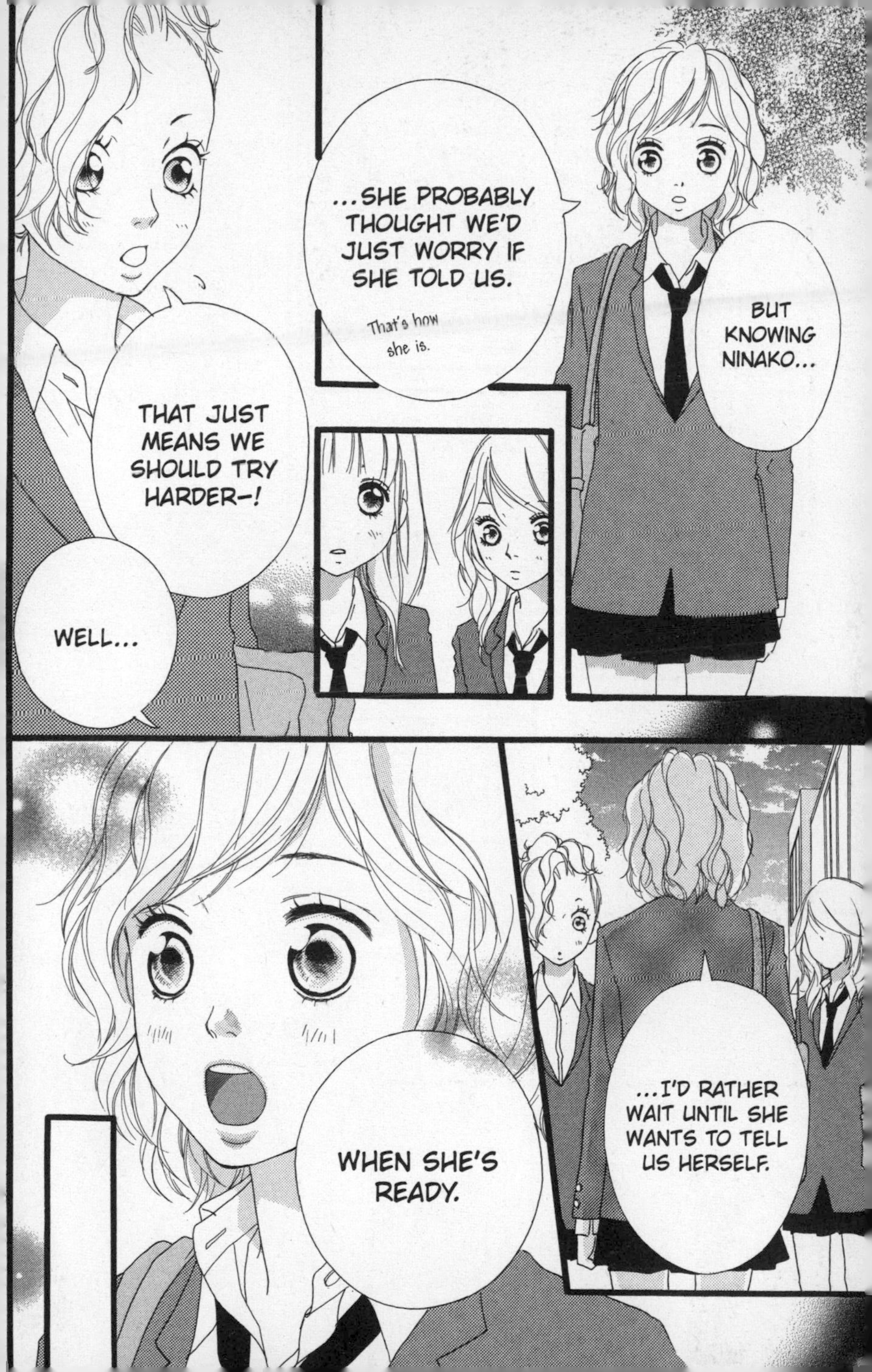
BUT KNOWING NINAKO...
...SHE PROBABLY THOUGHT WE'D JUST WORRY IF SHE TOLD US.
That's how she is.
THAT JUST MEANS WE SHOULD TRY HARDER—!
WELL...
...I'D RATHER WAIT UNTIL SHE WANTS TO TELL US HERSELF.
WHEN SHE'S READY.

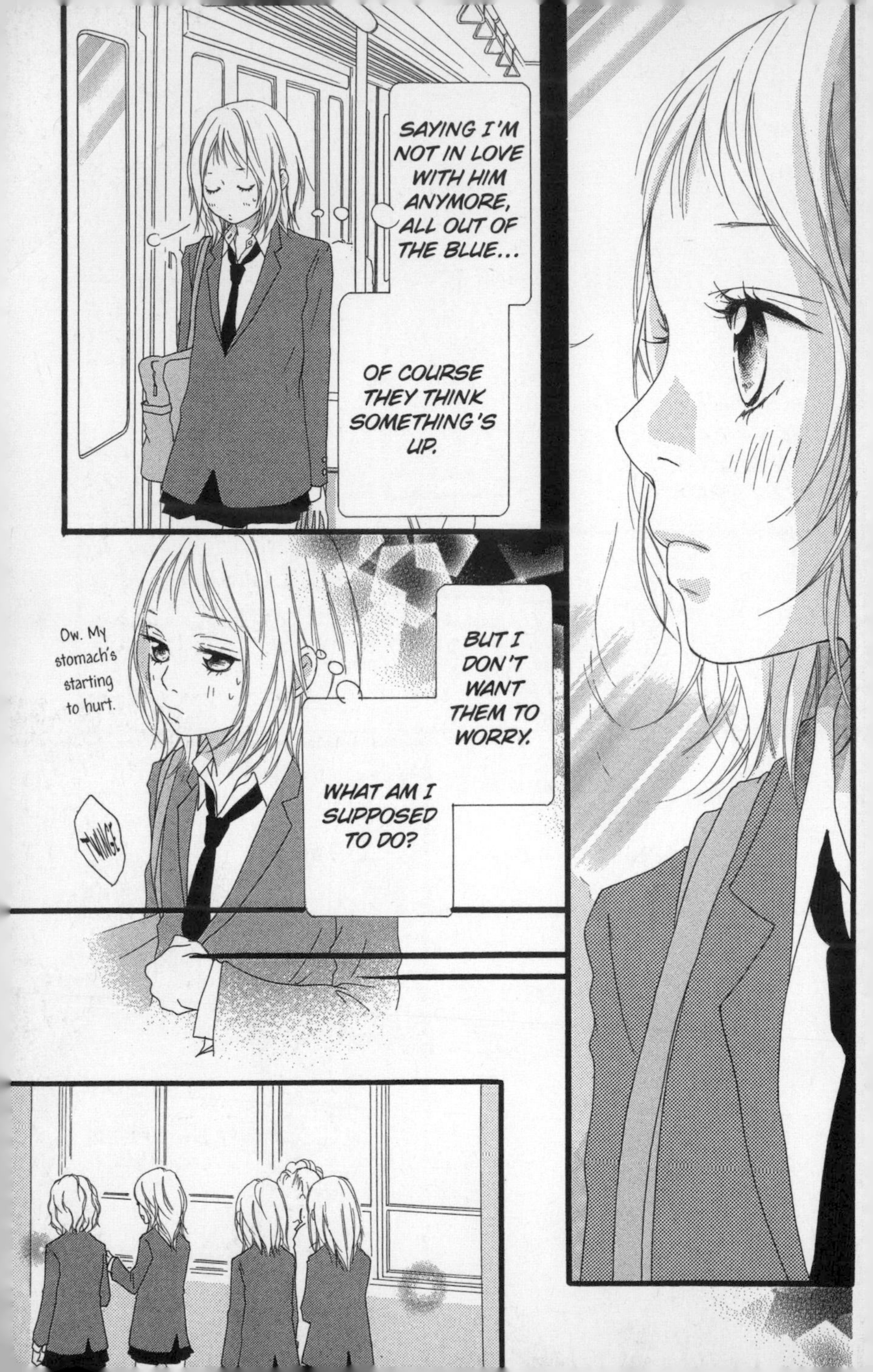
SAYING I'M NOT IN LOVE WITH HIM ANYMORE, ALL OUT OF THE BLUE...
OF COURSE THEY THINK SOMETHING'S UP.
BUT I DON'T WANT THEM TO WORRY.
WHAT AM I SUPPOSED TO DO?
Ow. My stomach's starting to hurt.
TWINGE

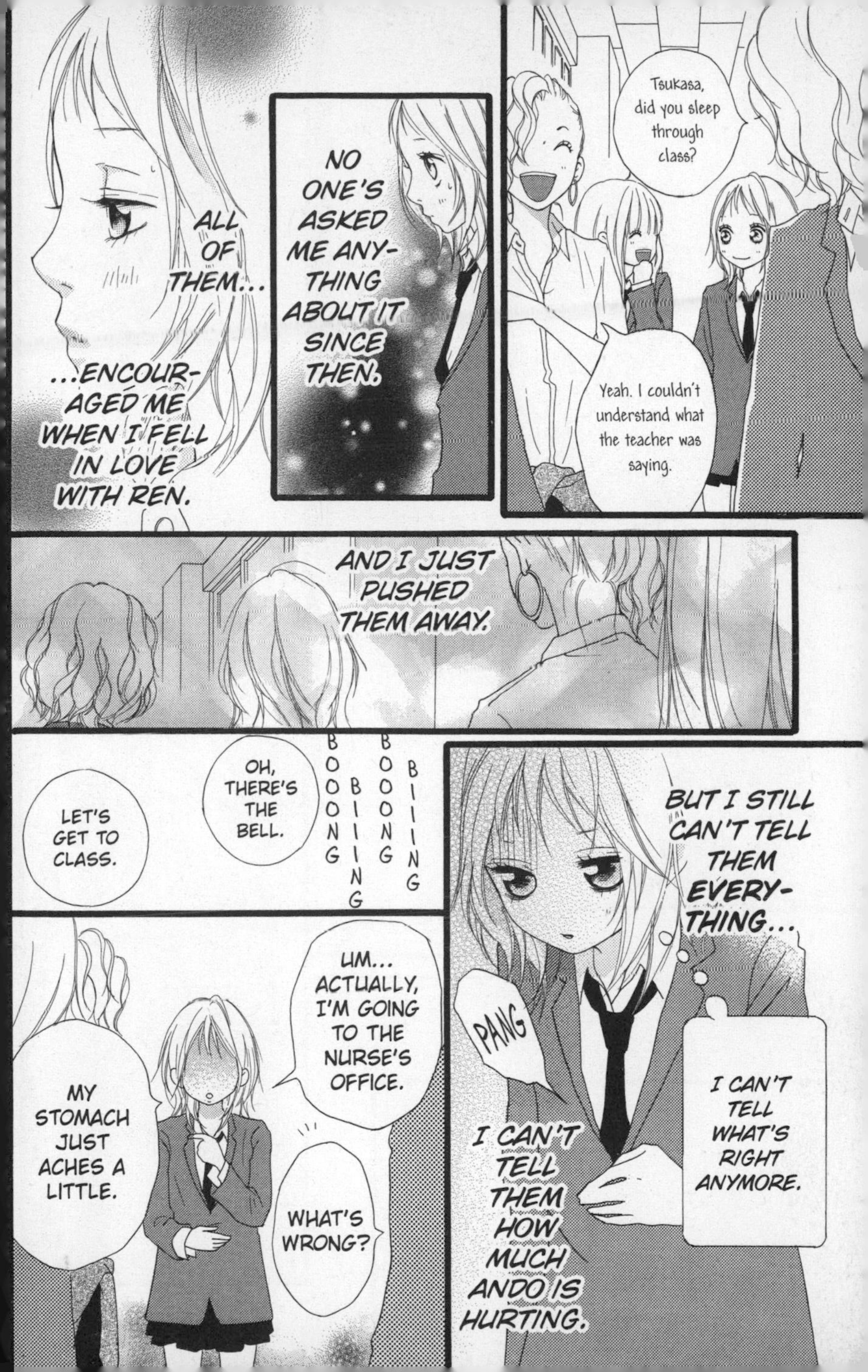
Tsukasa, did you sleep through class?
Yeah. I couldn't understand what the teacher was saying.
NO ONE'S ASKED ME ANYTHING ABOUT IT SINCE THEN.
ALL OF THEM...
...ENCOURAGED ME WHEN I FELL IN LOVE WITH REN.
AND I JUST PUSHED THEM AWAY.
BUT I STILL CAN'T TELL THEM EVERYTHING...
PANG
I CAN'T TELL WHAT'S RIGHT ANYMORE.
I CAN'T TELL THEM HOW MUCH ANDO IS HURTING.
BIIING BOOONG BIIING BOOONG
OH, THERE'S THE BELL.
LET'S GET TO CLASS.
UM... ACTUALLY, I'M GOING TO THE NURSE'S OFFICE.
WHAT'S WRONG?
MY STOMACH JUST ACHES A LITTLE.

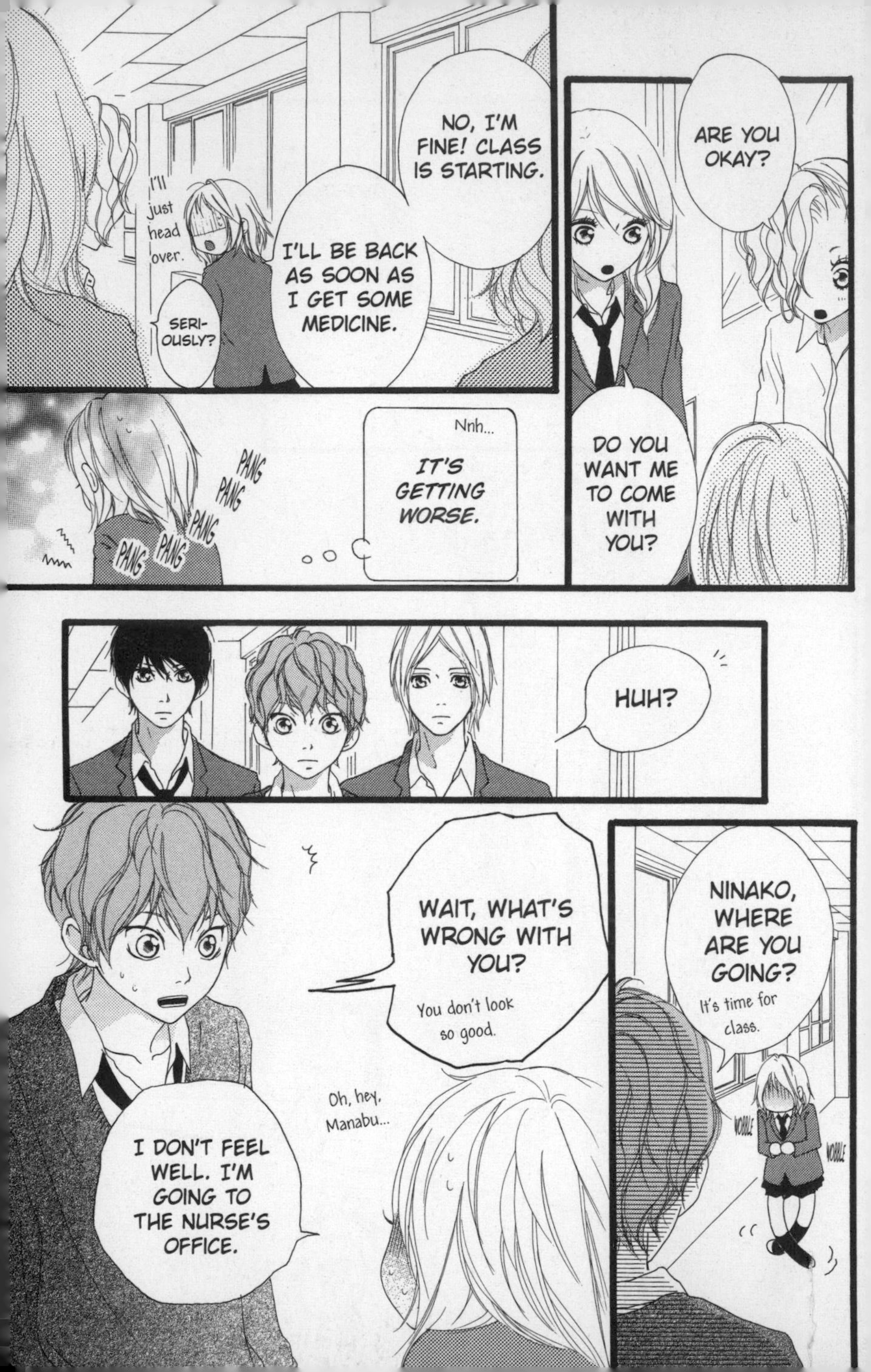
ARE YOU OKAY?
DO YOU WANT ME TO COME WITH YOU?
NO, I'M FINE! CLASS IS STARTING.
I'LL BE BACK AS SOON AS I GET SOME MEDICINE.
I'll just head over.
SERI-OUSLY?
Nnh...
IT'S GETTING WORSE.
PANG PANG PANG PANG PANG
HUH?
NINAKO, WHERE ARE YOU GOING?
It's time for class.
WOBBLE
WOBBLE
WAIT, WHAT'S WRONG WITH YOU?
You don't look so good.
Oh, hey, Manabu...
I DON'T FEEL WELL. I'M GOING TO THE NURSE'S OFFICE.

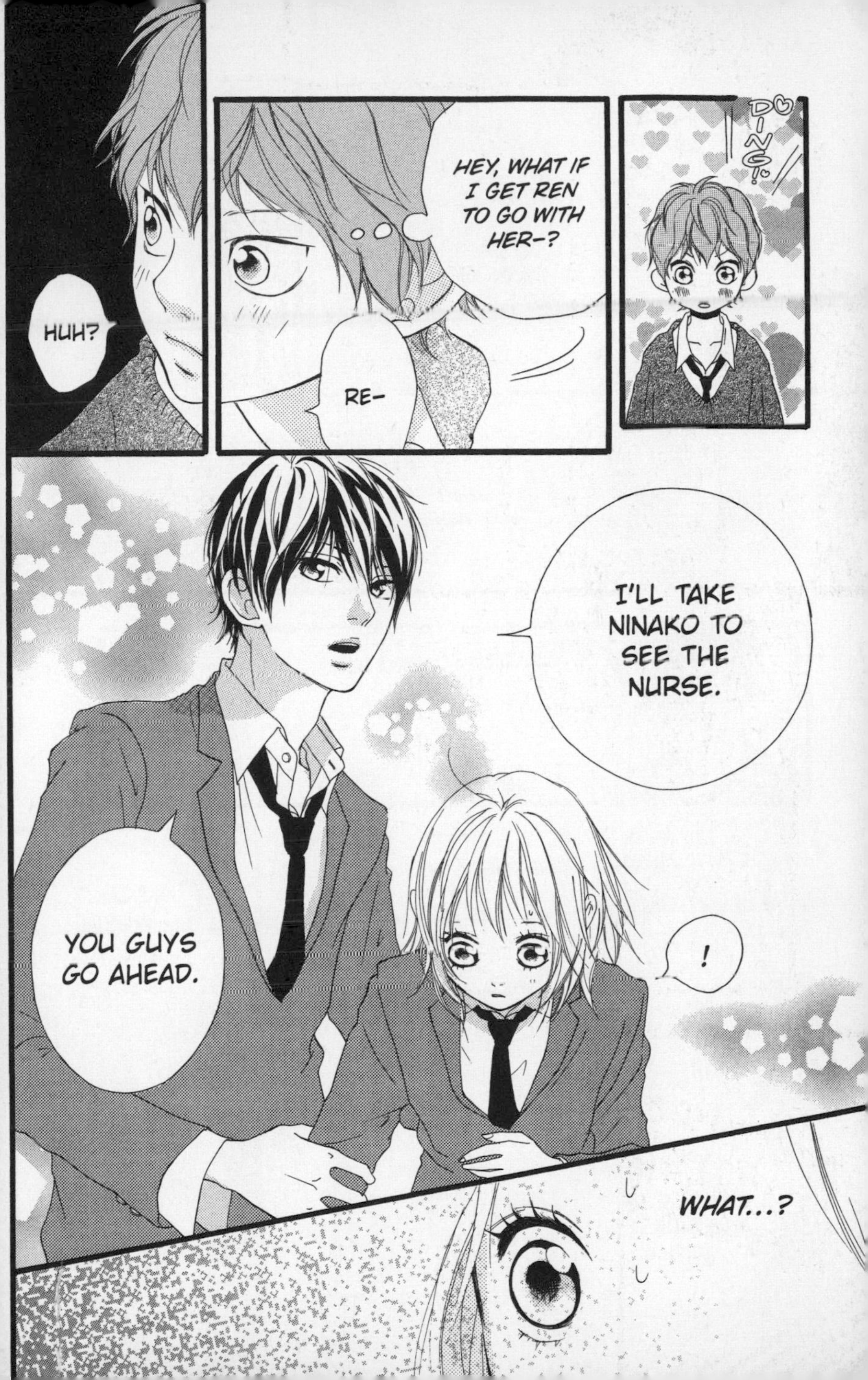
DING!
HEY, WHAT IF I GET REN TO GO WITH HER-?
RE-
HUH?
I'LL TAKE NINAKO TO SEE THE NURSE.
!
YOU GUYS GO AHEAD.
WHAT...?

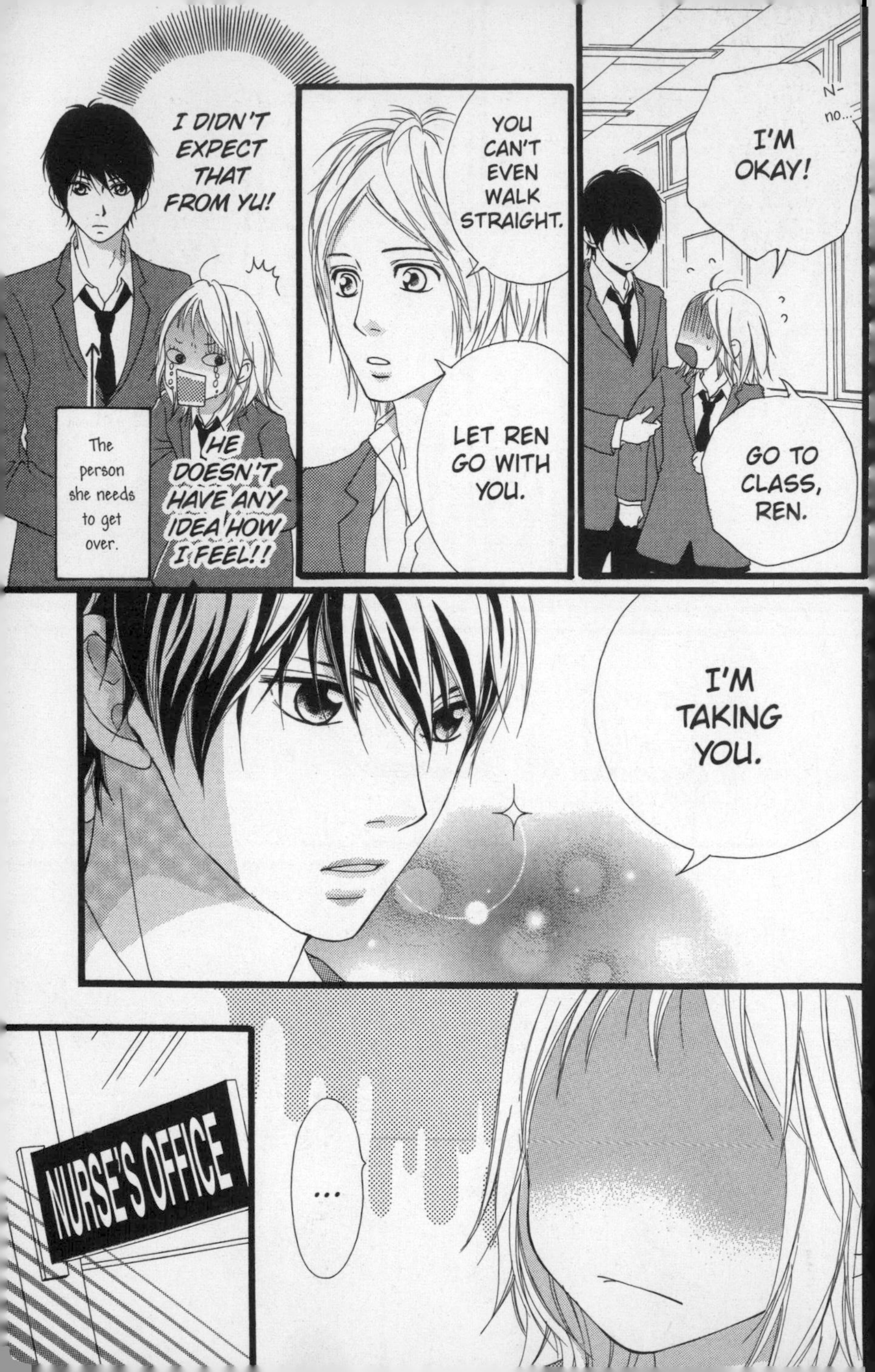
N-no...
I'M OKAY!
GO TO CLASS, REN.
YOU CAN'T EVEN WALK STRAIGHT.
LET REN GO WITH YOU.
I DIDN'T EXPECT THAT FROM YU!
HE DOESN'T HAVE ANY IDEA HOW I FEEL!!
The person she needs to get over.
I'M TAKING YOU.
...
NURSE'S OFFICE

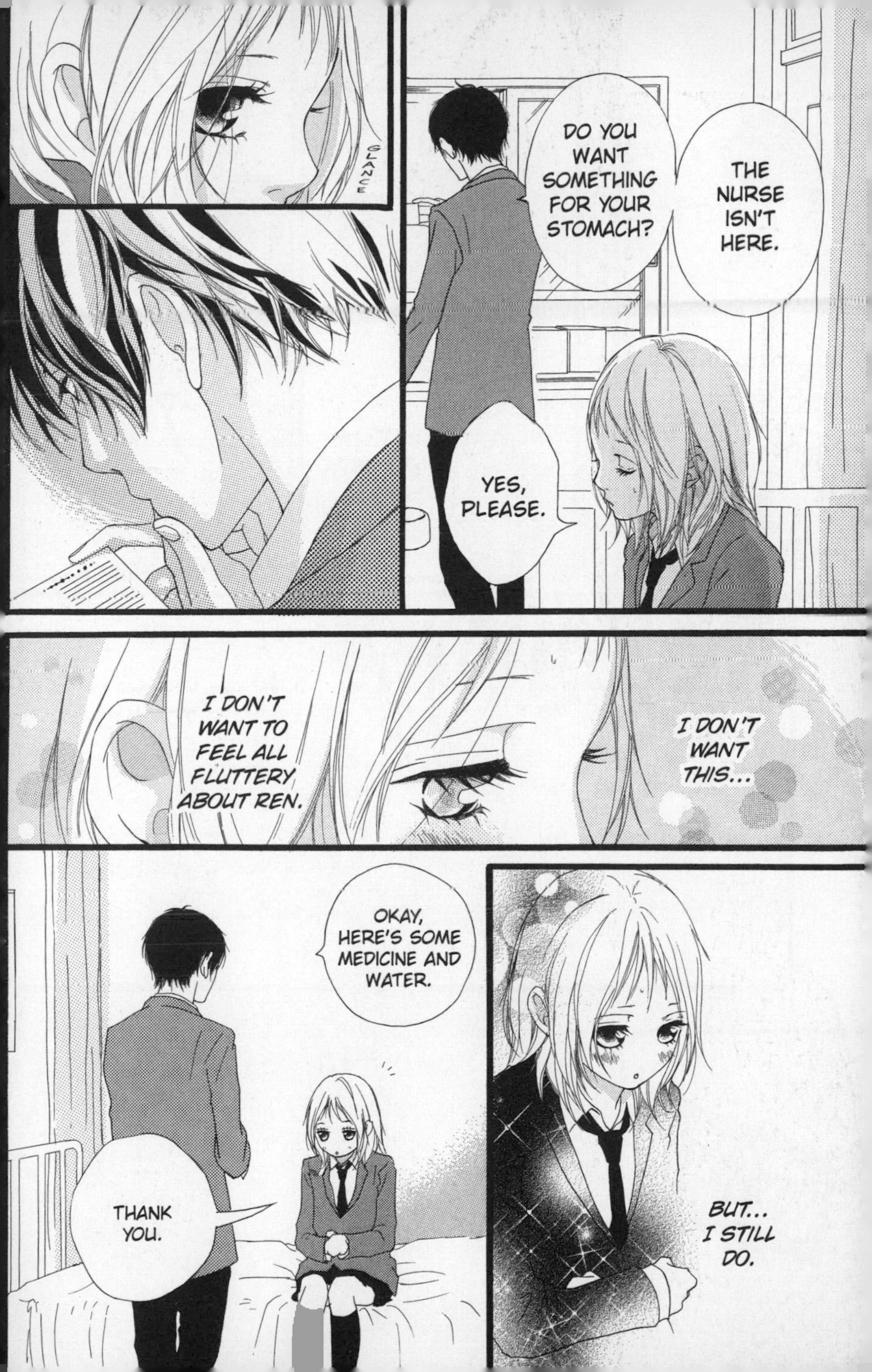
THE NURSE ISN'T HERE.
DO YOU WANT SOMETHING FOR YOUR STOMACH?
YES, PLEASE.
GLANCE
I DON'T WANT THIS...
I DON'T WANT TO FEEL ALL FLUTTERY ABOUT REN.
BUT... I STILL DO.
OKAY, HERE'S SOME MEDICINE AND WATER.
THANK YOU.

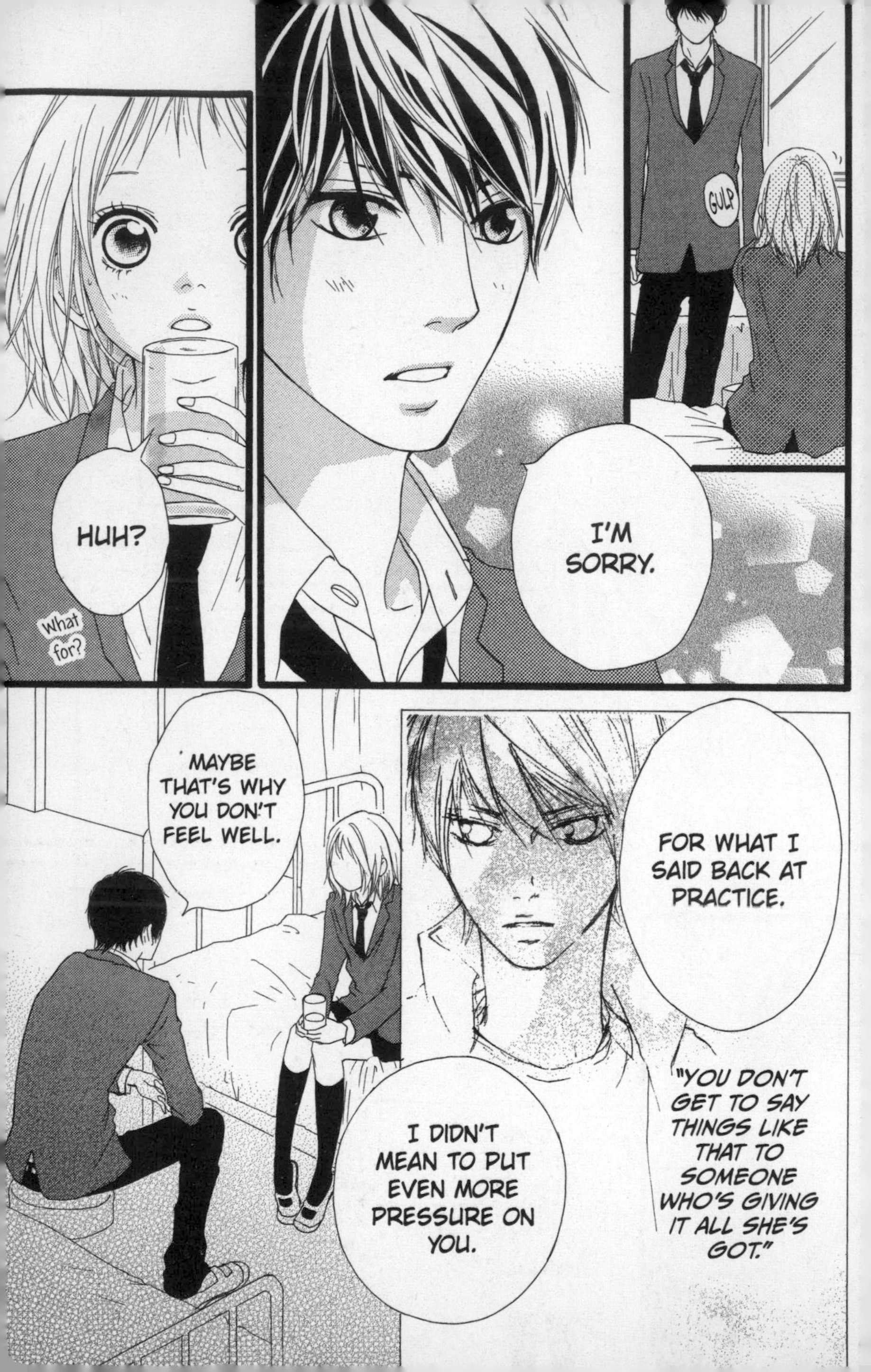
GULP
I'M SORRY.
HUH?
What for?
FOR WHAT I SAID BACK AT PRACTICE.
"YOU DON'T GET TO SAY THINGS LIKE THAT TO SOMEONE WHO'S GIVING IT ALL SHE'S GOT."
I DIDN'T MEAN TO PUT EVEN MORE PRESSURE ON YOU.
MAYBE THAT'S WHY YOU DON'T FEEL WELL.

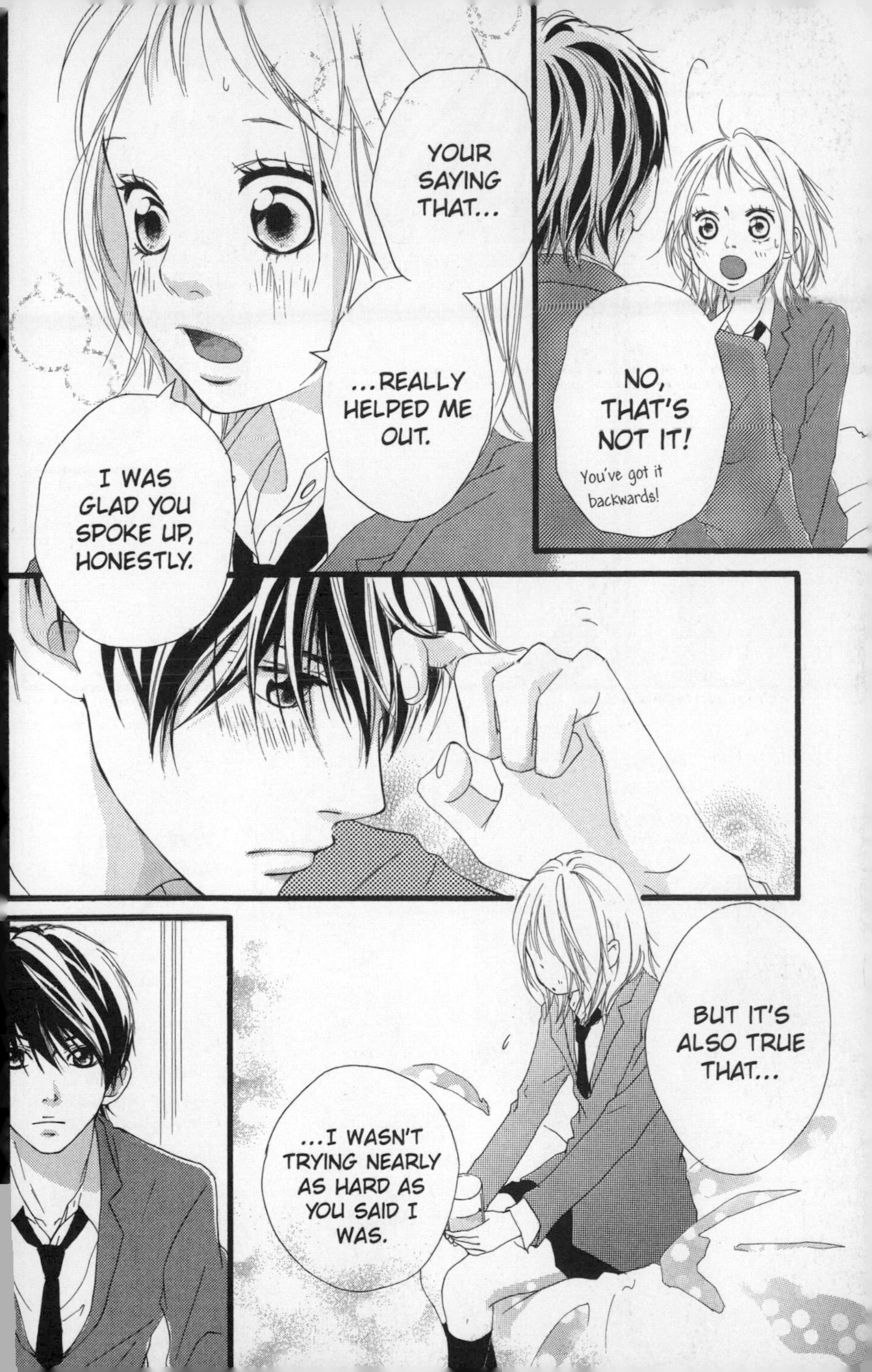
NO, THAT'S NOT IT!
You've got it backwards!
YOUR SAYING THAT...
...REALLY HELPED ME OUT.
I WAS GLAD YOU SPOKE UP, HONESTLY.
BUT IT'S ALSO TRUE THAT...
...I WASN'T TRYING NEARLY AS HARD AS YOU SAID I WAS.

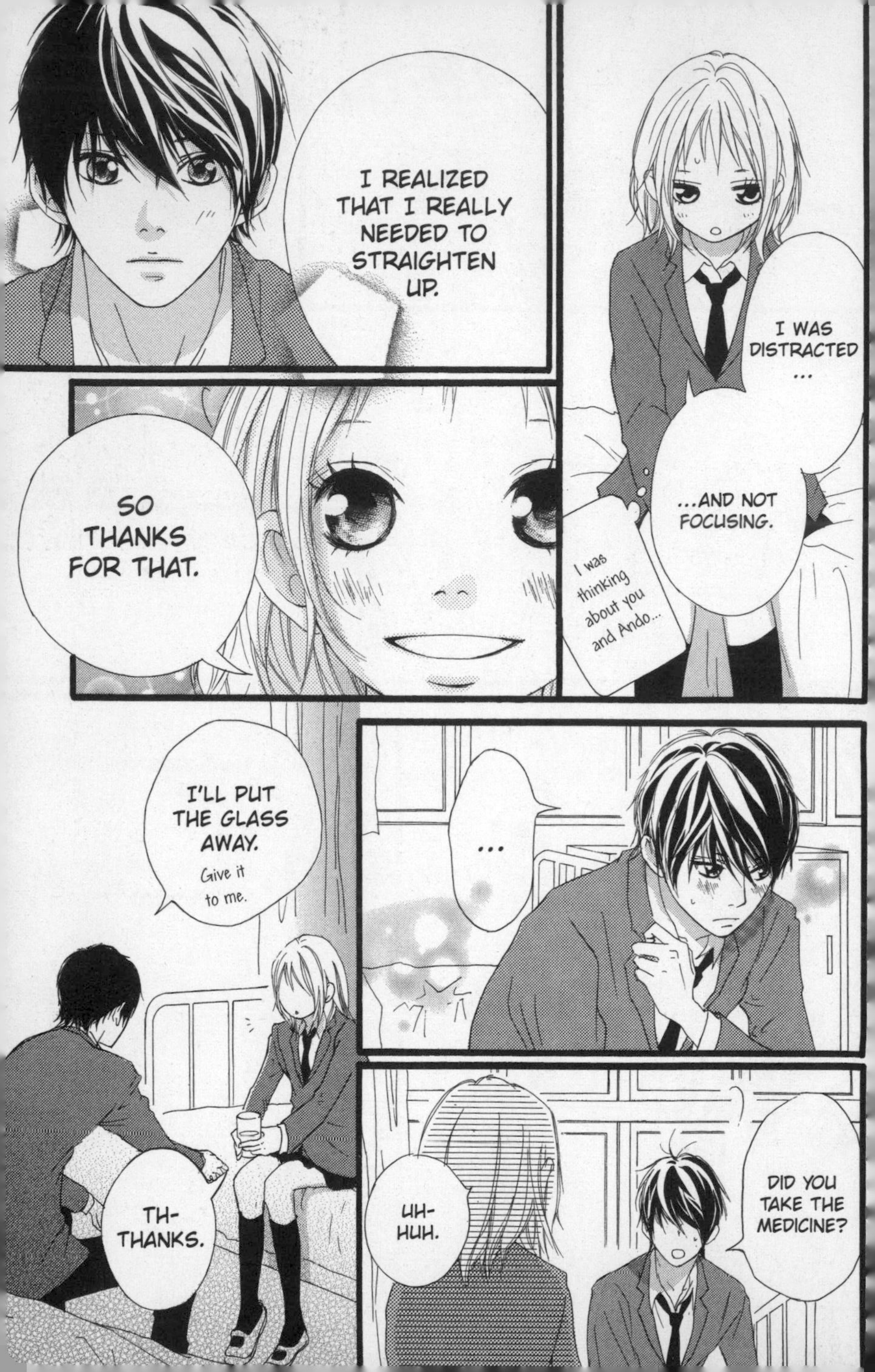
I WAS DISTRACTED ...
...AND NOT FOCUSING.
I was thinking about you and Ando...
I REALIZED THAT I REALLY NEEDED TO STRAIGHTEN UP.
SO THANKS FOR THAT.
...
DID YOU TAKE THE MEDICINE?
UH-HUH.
I'LL PUT THE GLASS AWAY.
Give it to me.
TH-THANKS.

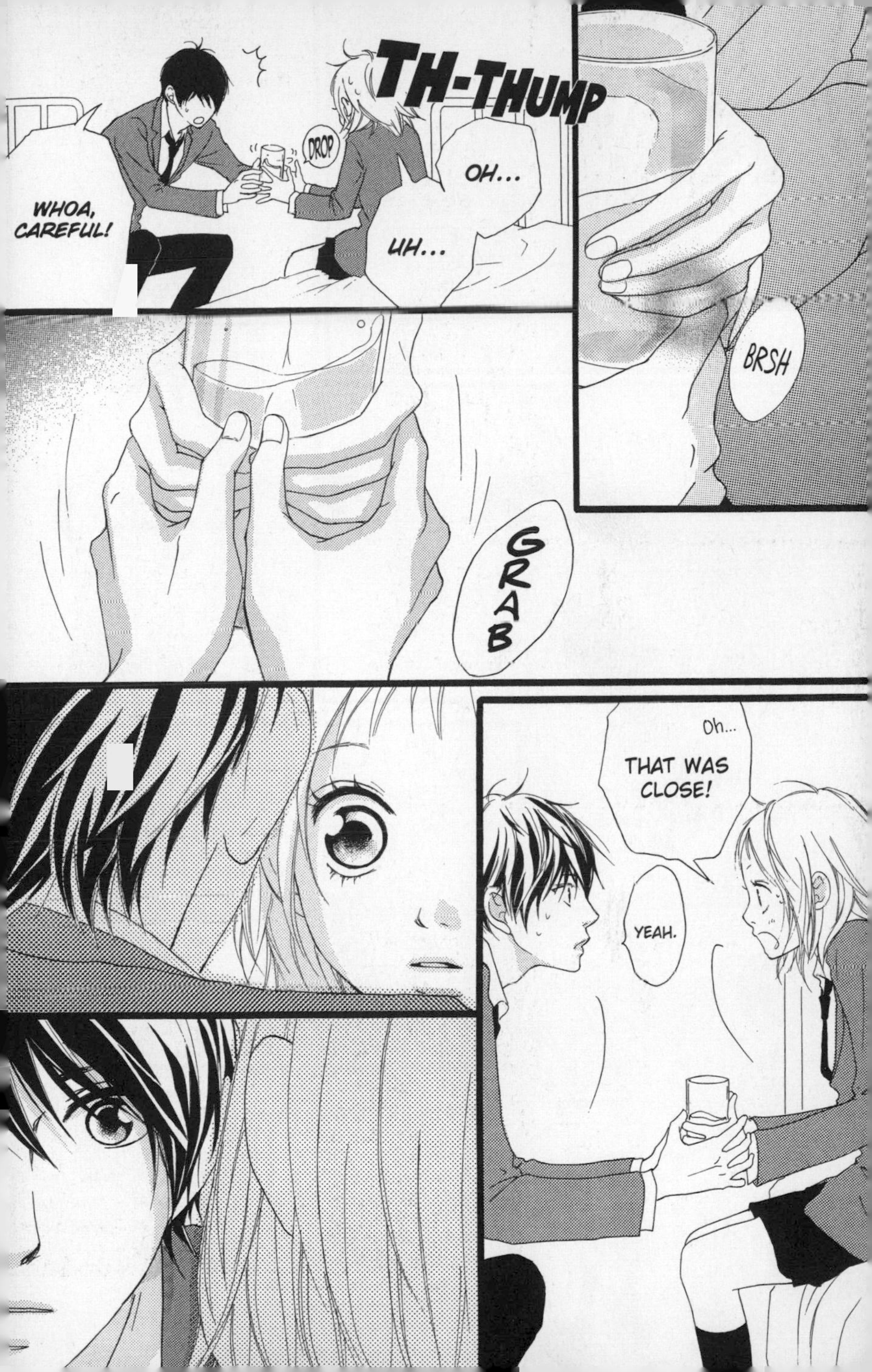
BRSH
TH-THUMP
OH...
UH...
DROP
WHOA, CAREFUL!
GRAB
Oh... THAT WAS CLOSE!
YEAH.

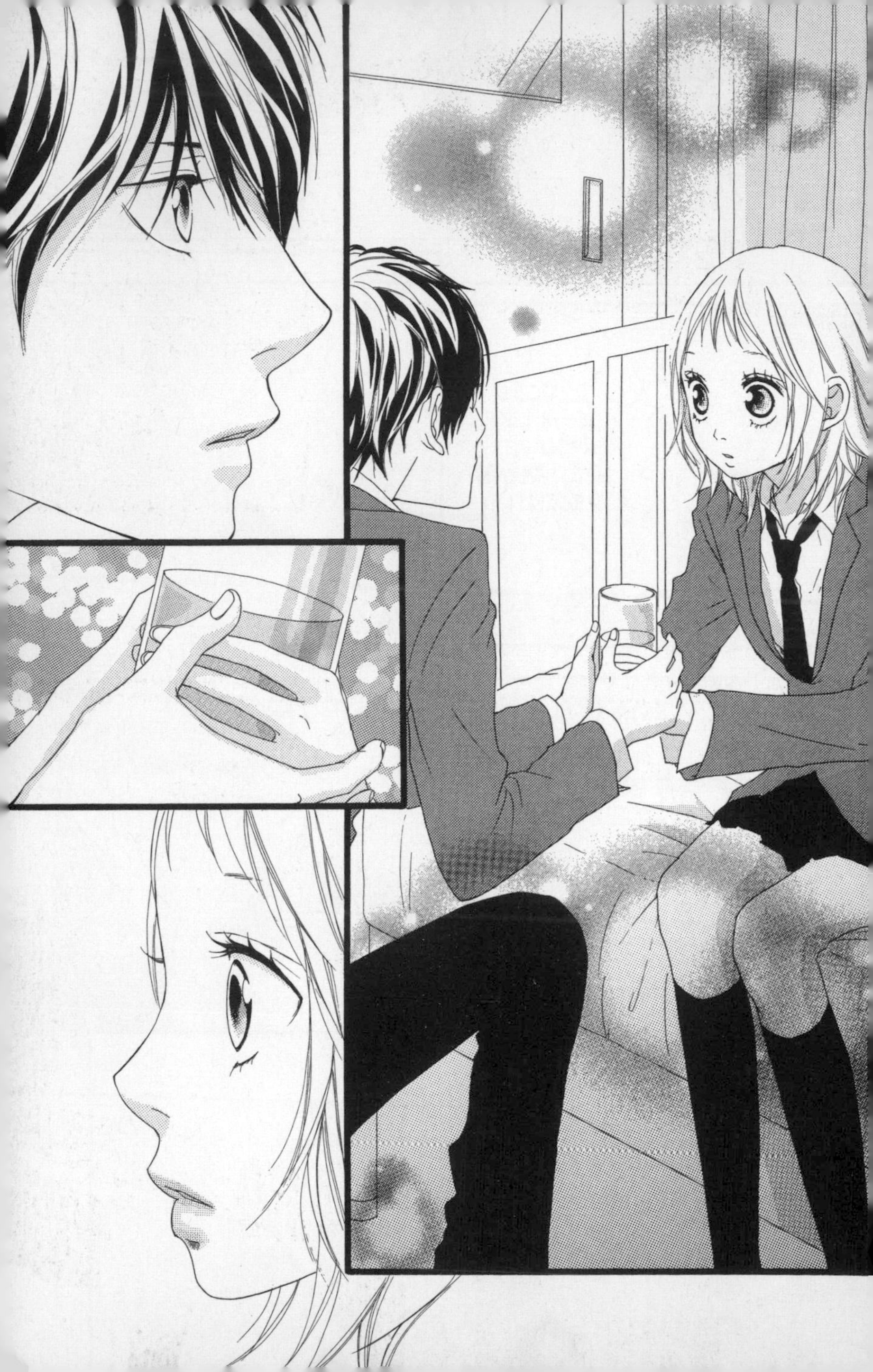

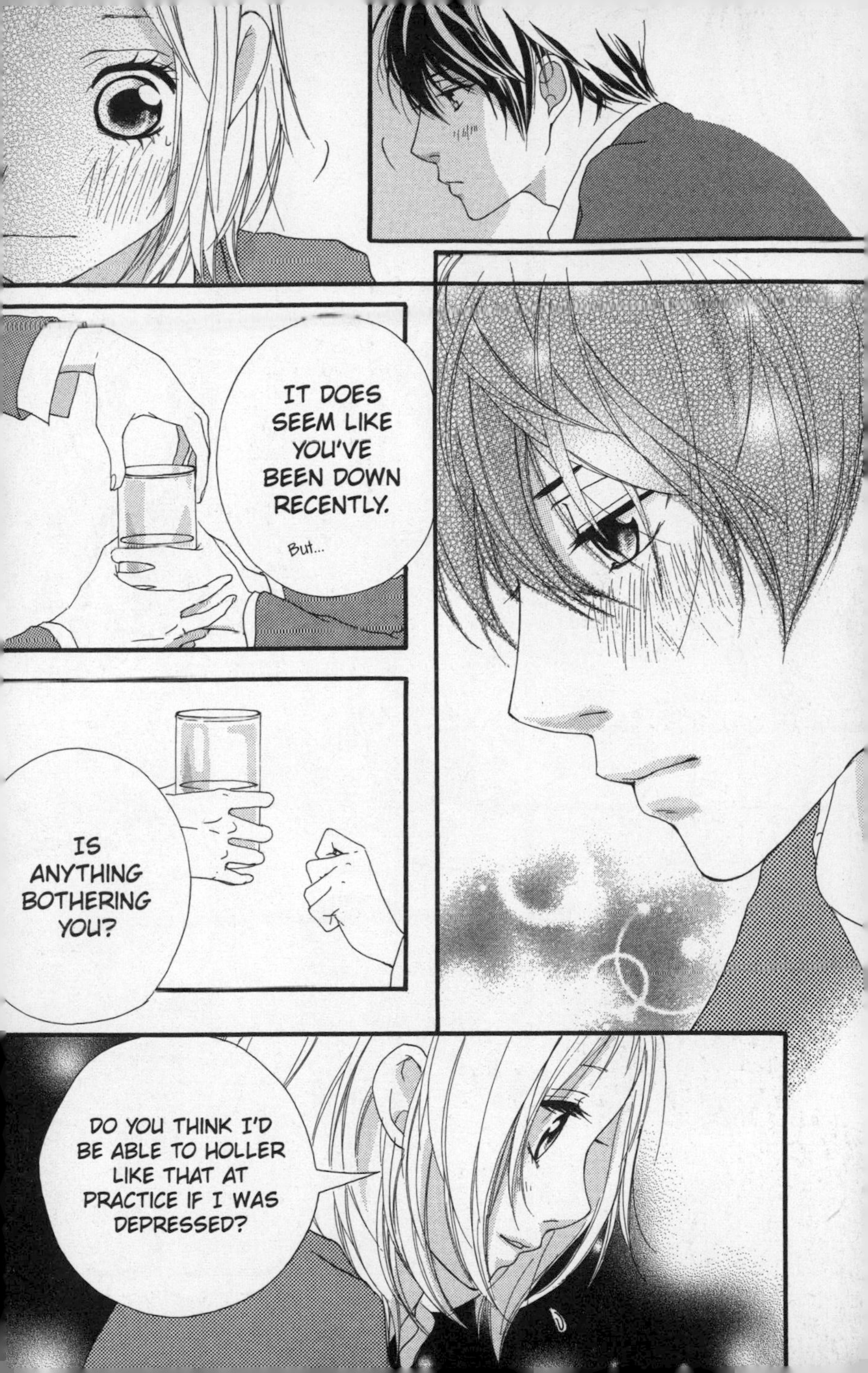
IT DOES SEEM LIKE YOU'VE BEEN DOWN RECENTLY.
But...
IS ANYTHING BOTHERING YOU?
DO YOU THINK I'D BE ABLE TO HOLLER LIKE THAT AT PRACTICE IF I WAS DEPRESSED?

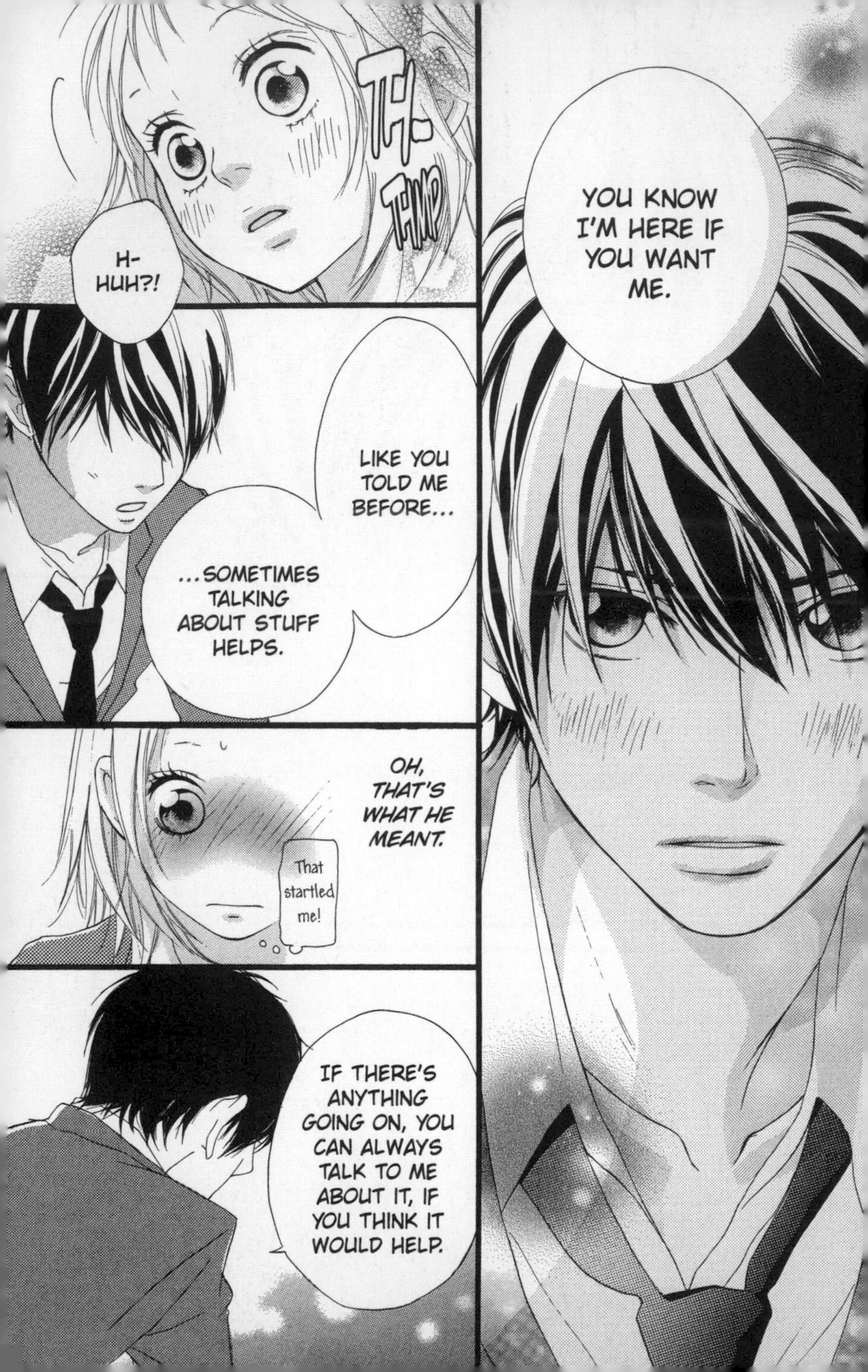

YOU KNOW I'M HERE IF YOU WANT ME.
TH- THMP
H-HUH?!
LIKE YOU TOLD ME BEFORE...
...SOMETIMES TALKING ABOUT STUFF HELPS.
OH, THAT'S WHAT HE MEANT.
That startled me!
IF THERE'S ANYTHING GOING ON, YOU CAN ALWAYS TALK TO ME ABOUT IT, IF YOU THINK IT WOULD HELP.

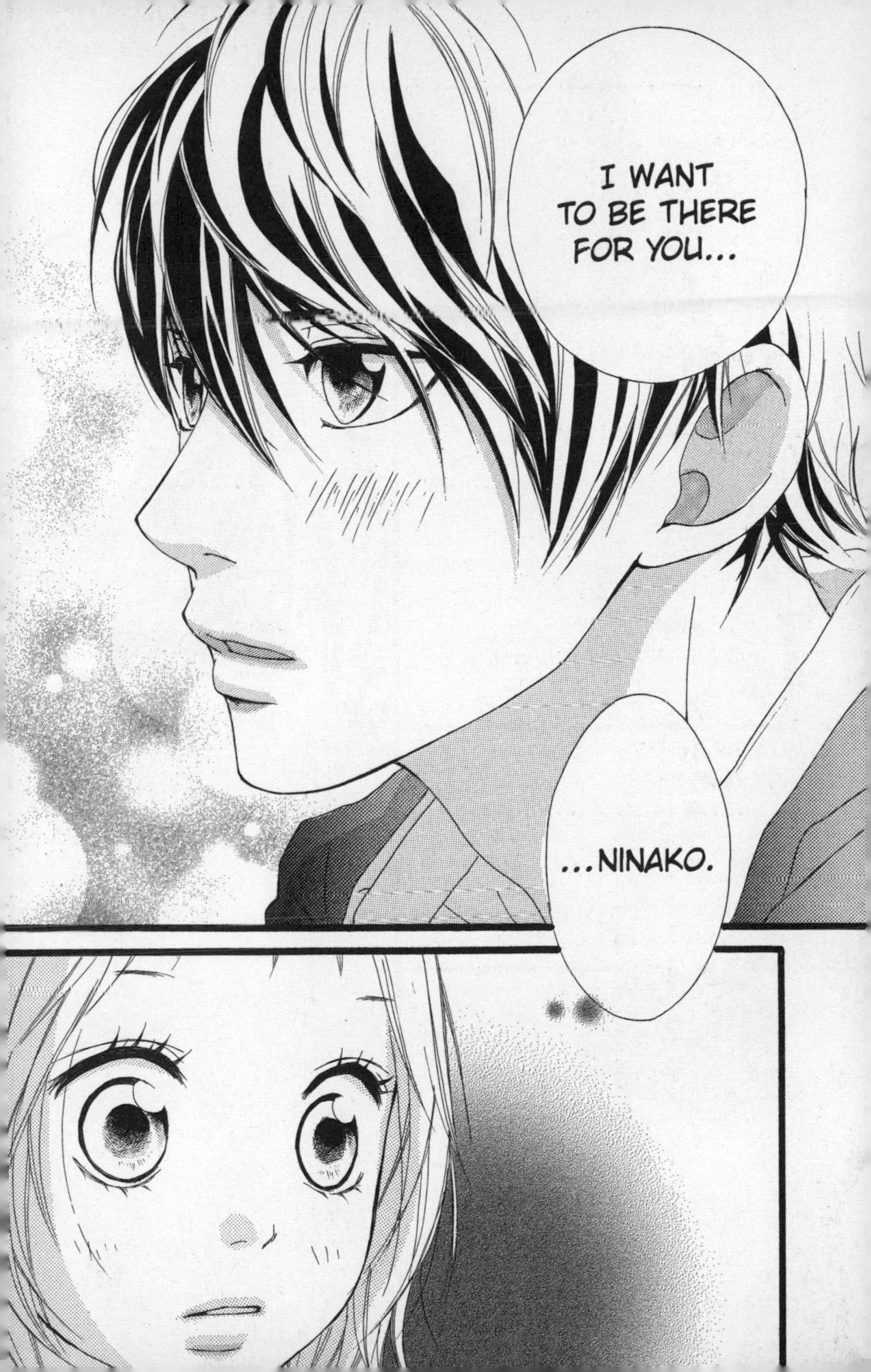
I WANT TO BE THERE FOR YOU...
...NINAKO.

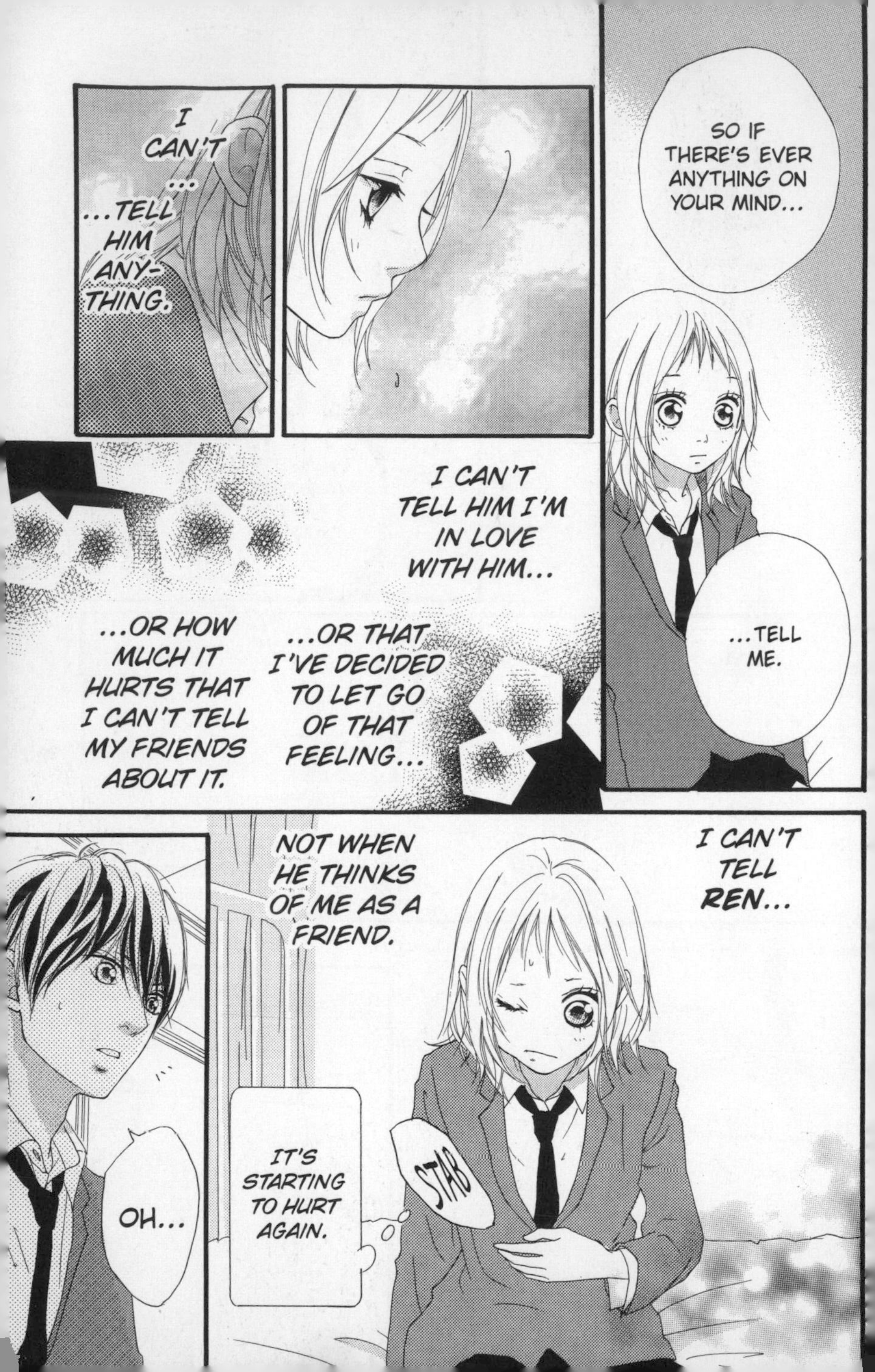
SO IF THERE'S EVER ANYTHING ON YOUR MIND...
...TELL ME.
I CAN'T ... ...TELL HIM ANYTHING.
I CAN'T TELL HIM I'M IN LOVE WITH HIM...
...OR THAT I'VE DECIDED TO LET GO OF THAT FEELING...
...OR HOW MUCH IT HURTS THAT I CAN'T TELL MY FRIENDS ABOUT IT.
I CAN'T TELL REN...
NOT WHEN HE THINKS OF ME AS A FRIEND.
STAB
IT'S STARTING TO HURT AGAIN.
...
OH...

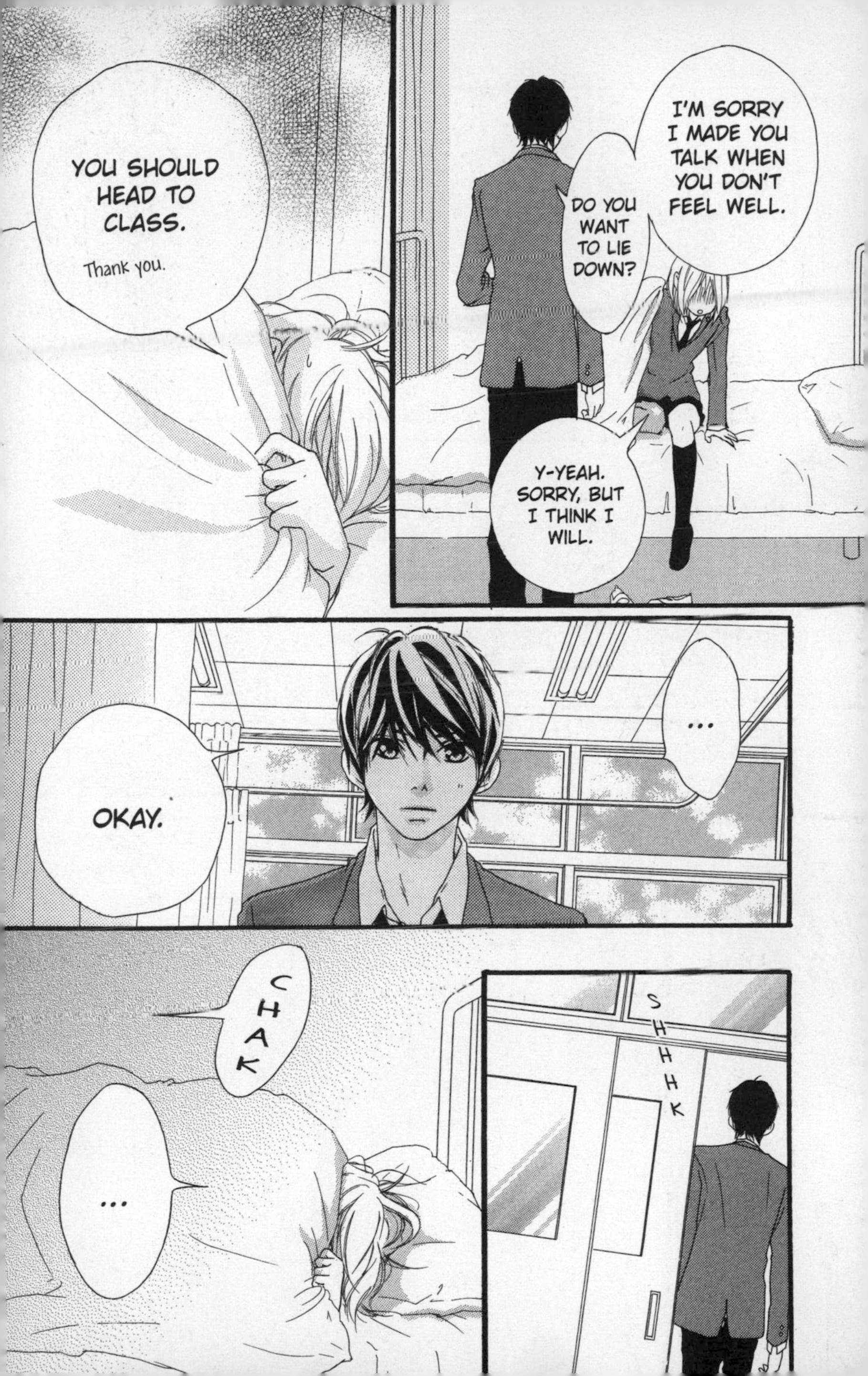
I'M SORRY I MADE YOU TALK WHEN YOU DON'T FEEL WELL.
DO YOU WANT TO LIE DOWN?
Y-YEAH. SORRY, BUT I THINK I WILL.
YOU SHOULD HEAD TO CLASS.
Thank you.
...
OKAY.
SHHHK
CHAK
...

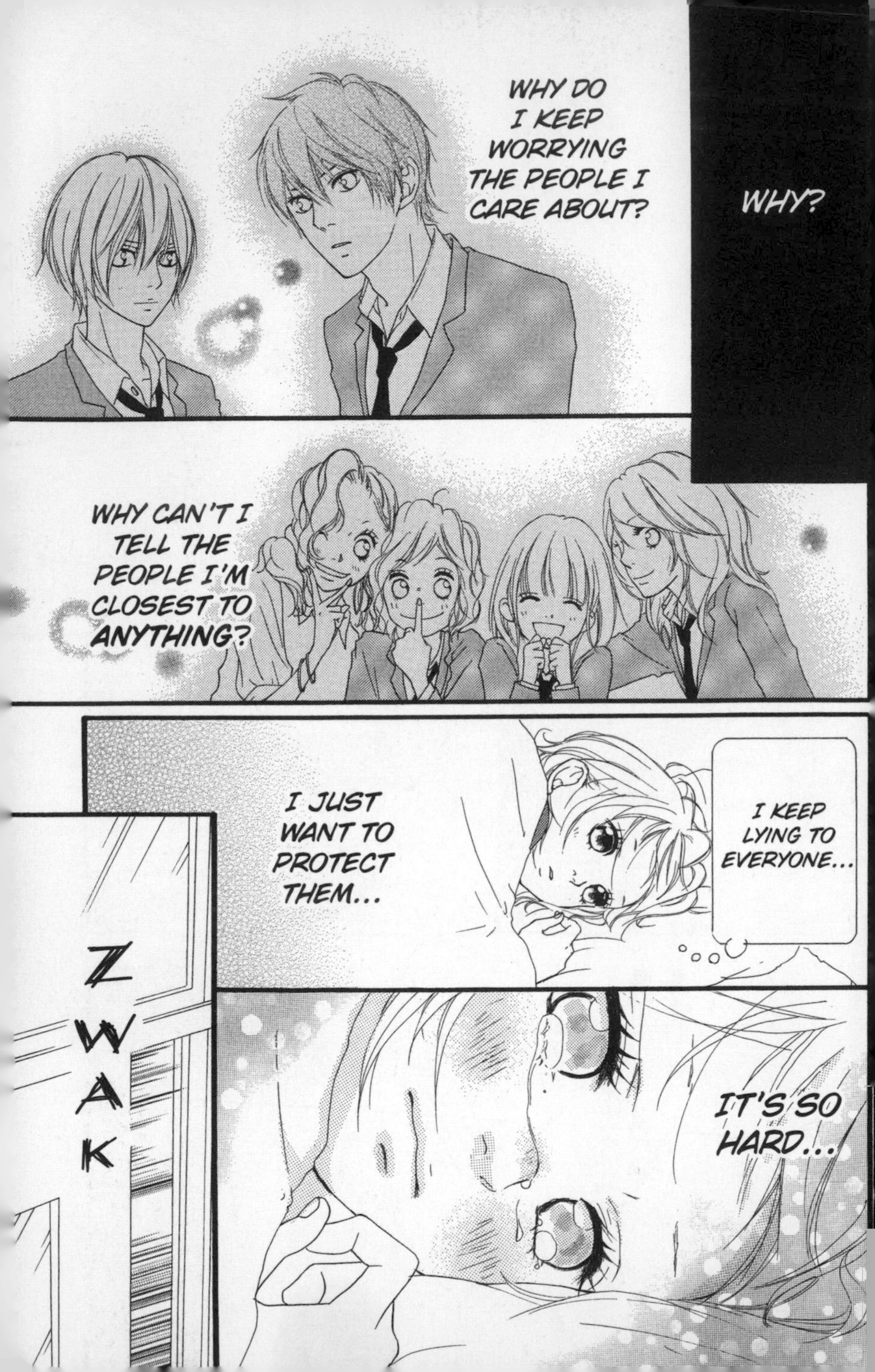
WHY?
WHY DO I KEEP WORRYING THE PEOPLE I CARE ABOUT?
WHY CAN'T I TELL THE PEOPLE I'M CLOSEST TO ANYTHING?
I KEEP LYING TO EVERYONE...
I JUST WANT TO PROTECT THEM...
IT'S SO HARD...
ZWAK

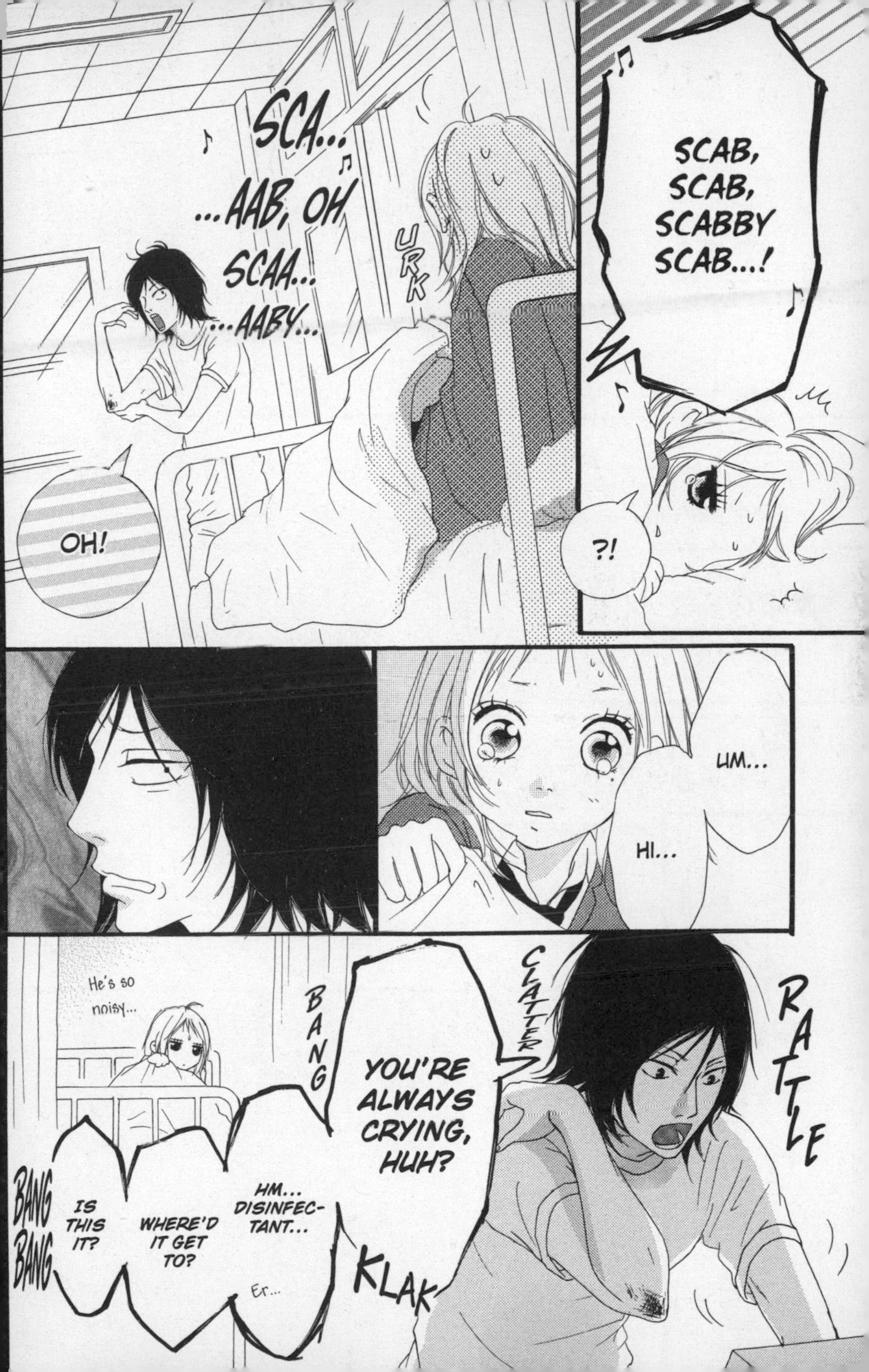
SCAB, SCAB, SCABBY SCAB...!
?!
URK
SCA...
...AAB, OH SCAA...
...AABY...
OH!
UM...
HI...
RATTLE
CLATTER
YOU'RE ALWAYS CRYING, HUH?
BANG
KLAK
HM... DISINFEC-TANT...
Er...
WHERE'D IT GET TO?
IS THIS IT?
BANG BANG
He's so noisy...

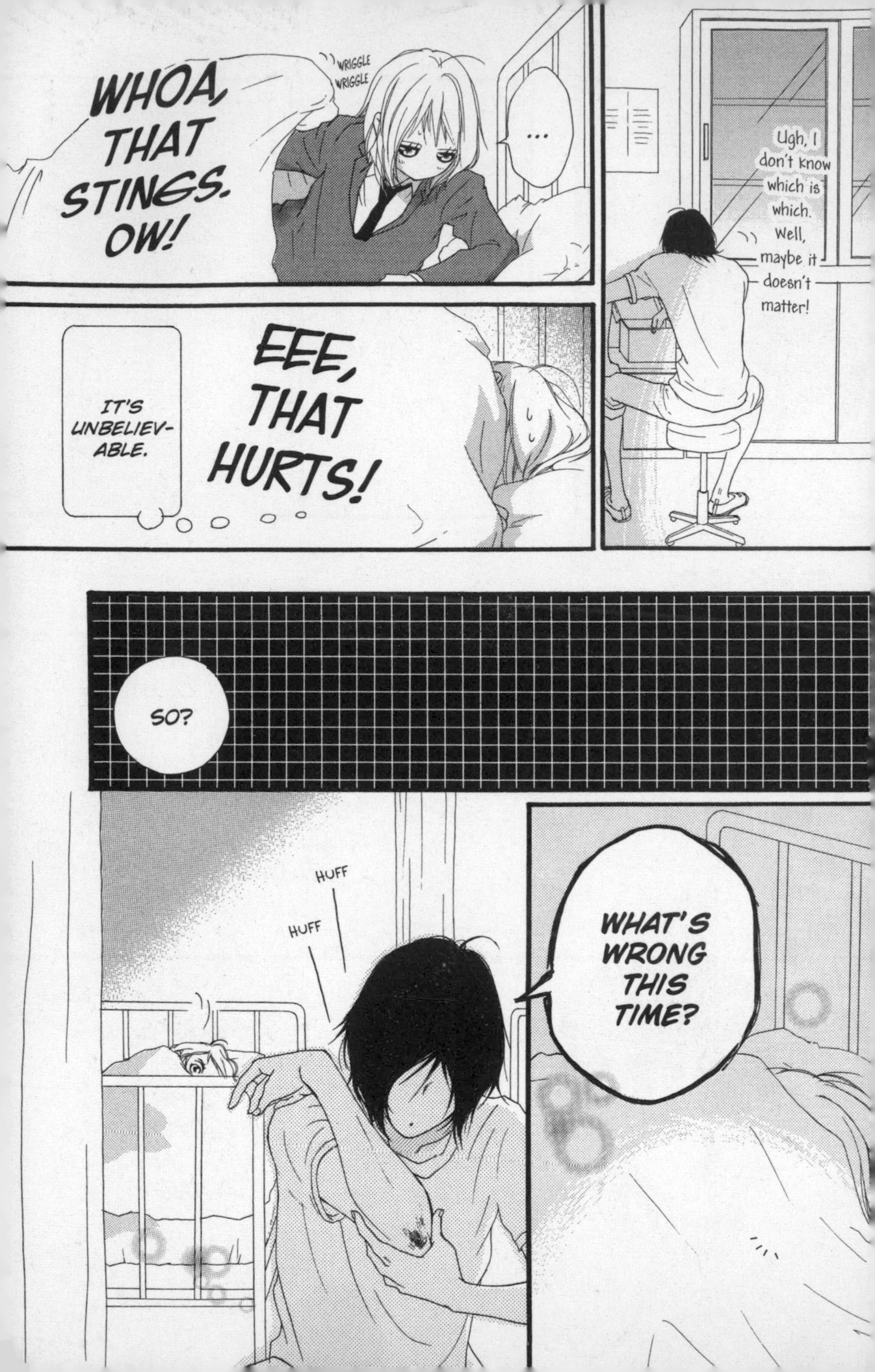
Ugh, I don't know which is which. Well, maybe it doesn't matter!
...
WRIGGLE WRIGGLE
WHOA, THAT STINGS. OW!
EEE, THAT HURTS!
IT'S UNBELIEVABLE.
SO?
WHAT'S WRONG THIS TIME?
HUFF
HUFF

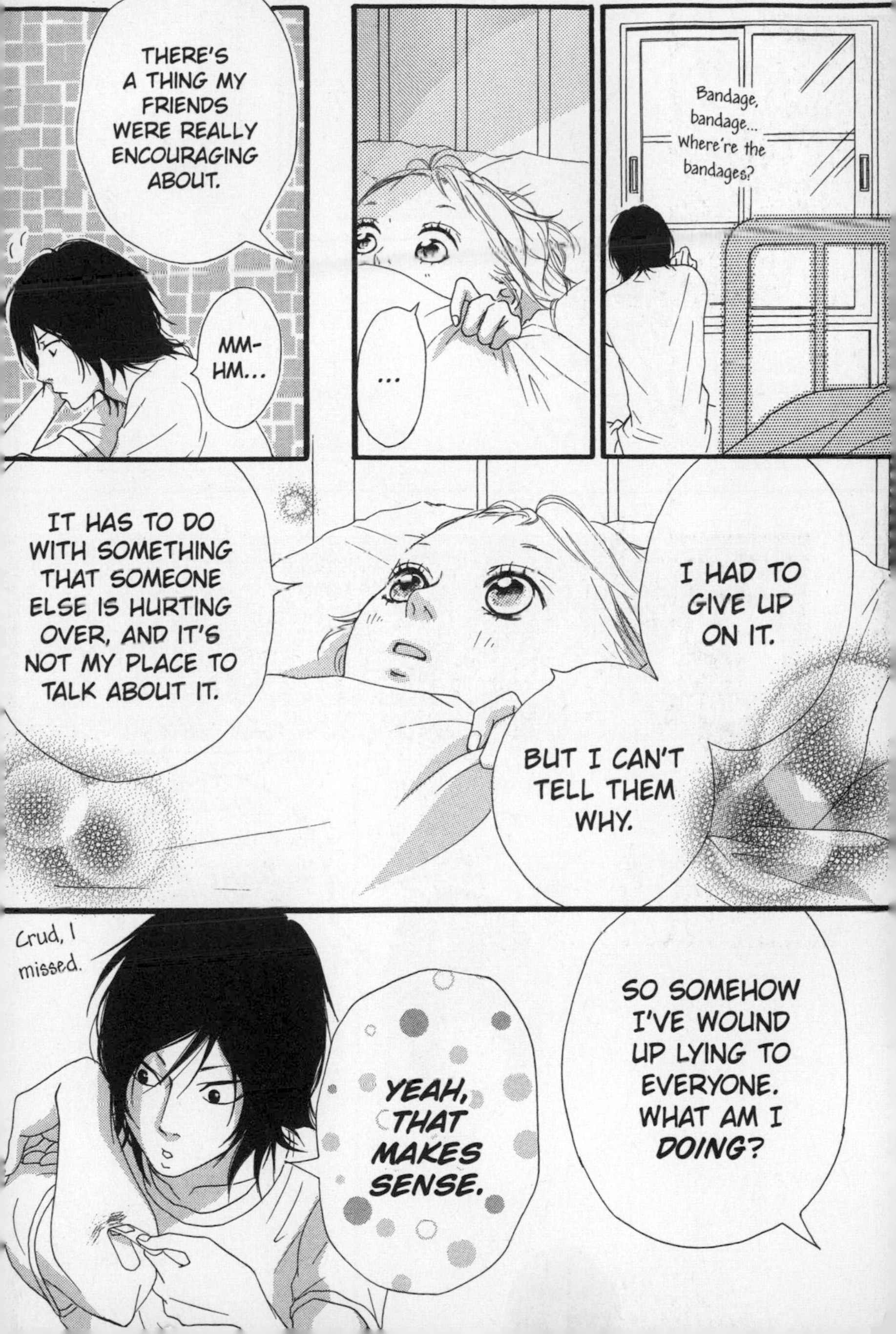
Bandage, bandage... Where're the bandages?
...
THERE'S A THING MY FRIENDS WERE REALLY ENCOURAGING ABOUT.
MM-HM...
I HAD TO GIVE UP ON IT.
IT HAS TO DO WITH SOMETHING THAT SOMEONE ELSE IS HURTING OVER, AND IT'S NOT MY PLACE TO TALK ABOUT IT.
BUT I CAN'T TELL THEM WHY.
SO SOMEHOW I'VE WOUND UP LYING TO EVERYONE. WHAT AM I *DOING*?
YEAH, THAT MAKES SENSE.
Crud, I missed.

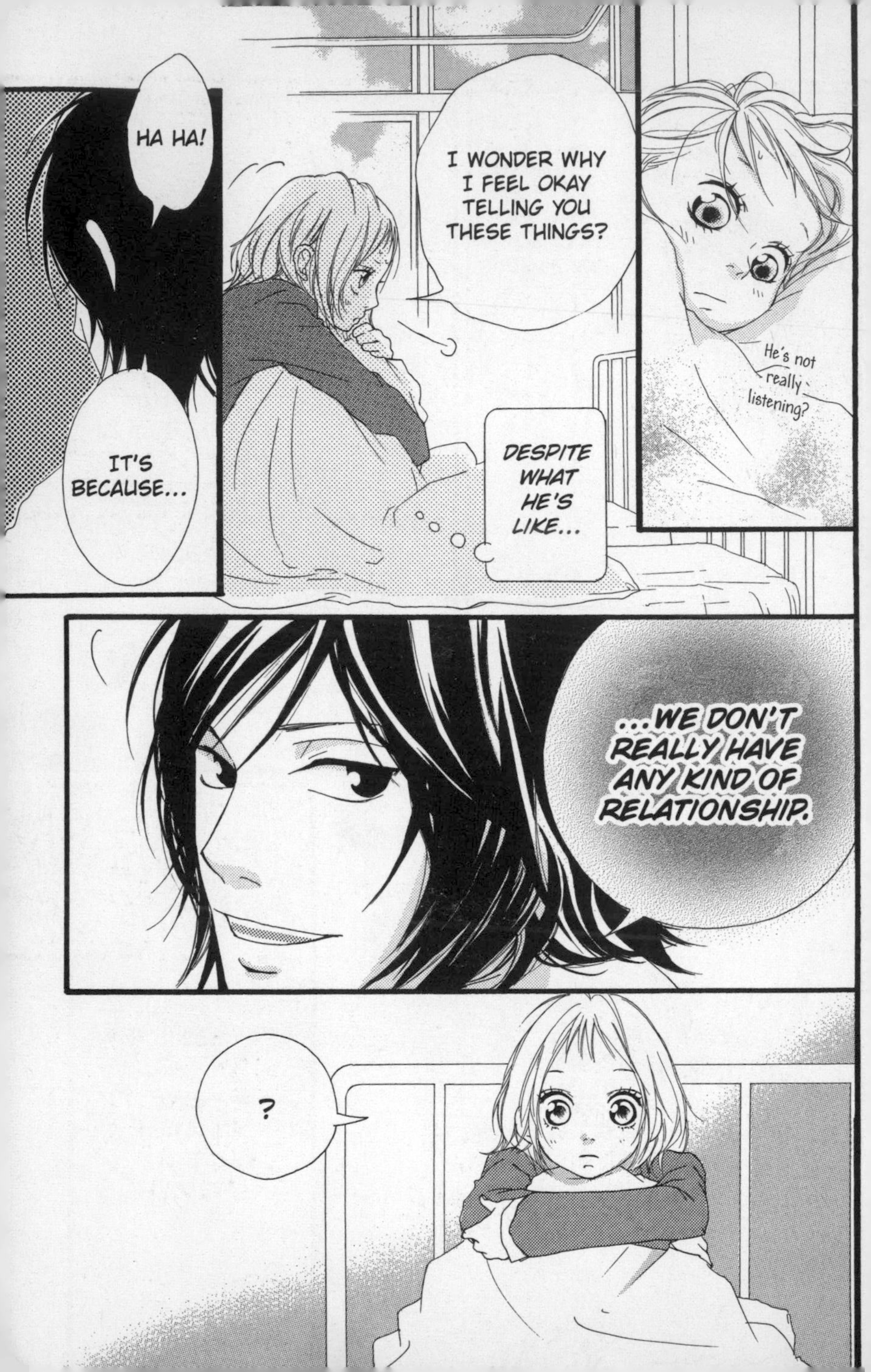
He's not really listening?
I WONDER WHY I FEEL OKAY TELLING YOU THESE THINGS?
DESPITE WHAT HE'S LIKE...
HA HA!
IT'S BECAUSE...
...WE DON'T REALLY HAVE ANY KIND OF RELATIONSHIP.
?

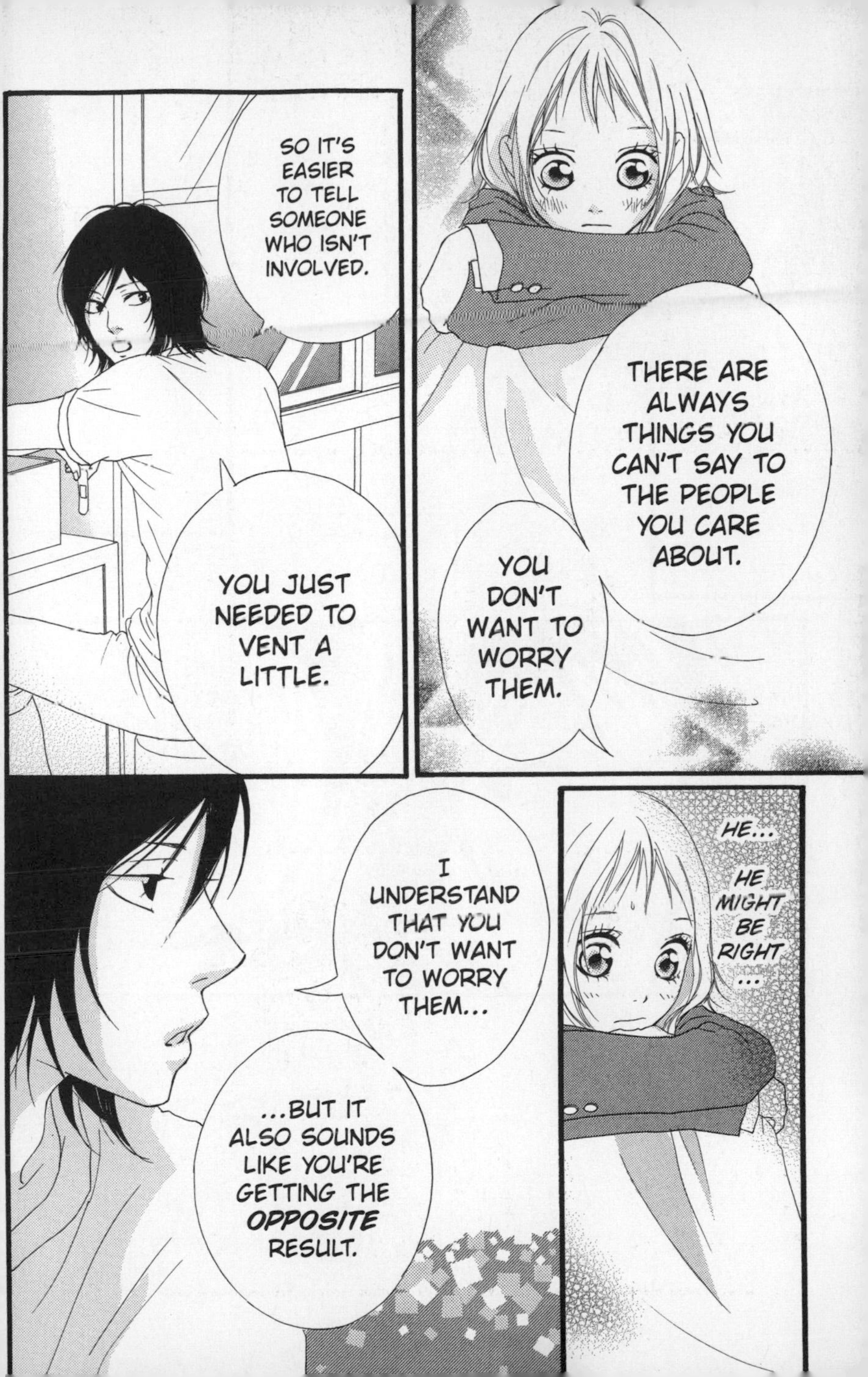
THERE ARE ALWAYS THINGS YOU CAN'T SAY TO THE PEOPLE YOU CARE ABOUT.
YOU DON'T WANT TO WORRY THEM.
SO IT'S EASIER TO TELL SOMEONE WHO ISN'T INVOLVED.
YOU JUST NEEDED TO VENT A LITTLE.
HE...
HE MIGHT BE RIGHT...
I UNDERSTAND THAT YOU DON'T WANT TO WORRY THEM...
...BUT IT ALSO SOUNDS LIKE YOU'RE GETTING THE *OPPOSITE* RESULT.

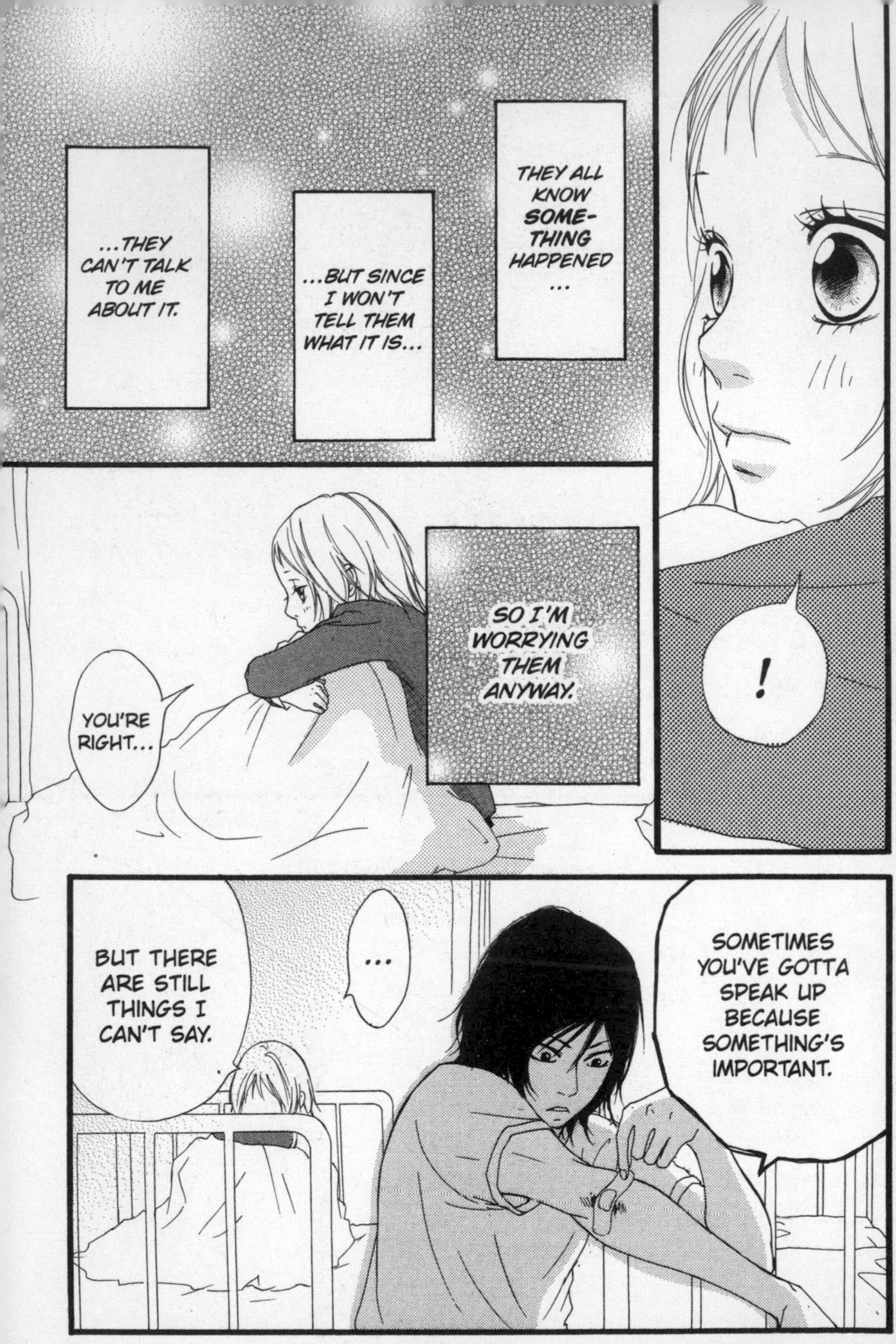
!
THEY ALL KNOW SOMETHING HAPPENED...
...BUT SINCE I WON'T TELL THEM WHAT IT IS...
...THEY CAN'T TALK TO ME ABOUT IT.
SO I'M WORRYING THEM ANYWAY.
YOU'RE RIGHT...
SOMETIMES YOU'VE GOTTA SPEAK UP BECAUSE SOMETHING'S IMPORTANT.
...
BUT THERE ARE STILL THINGS I CAN'T SAY.

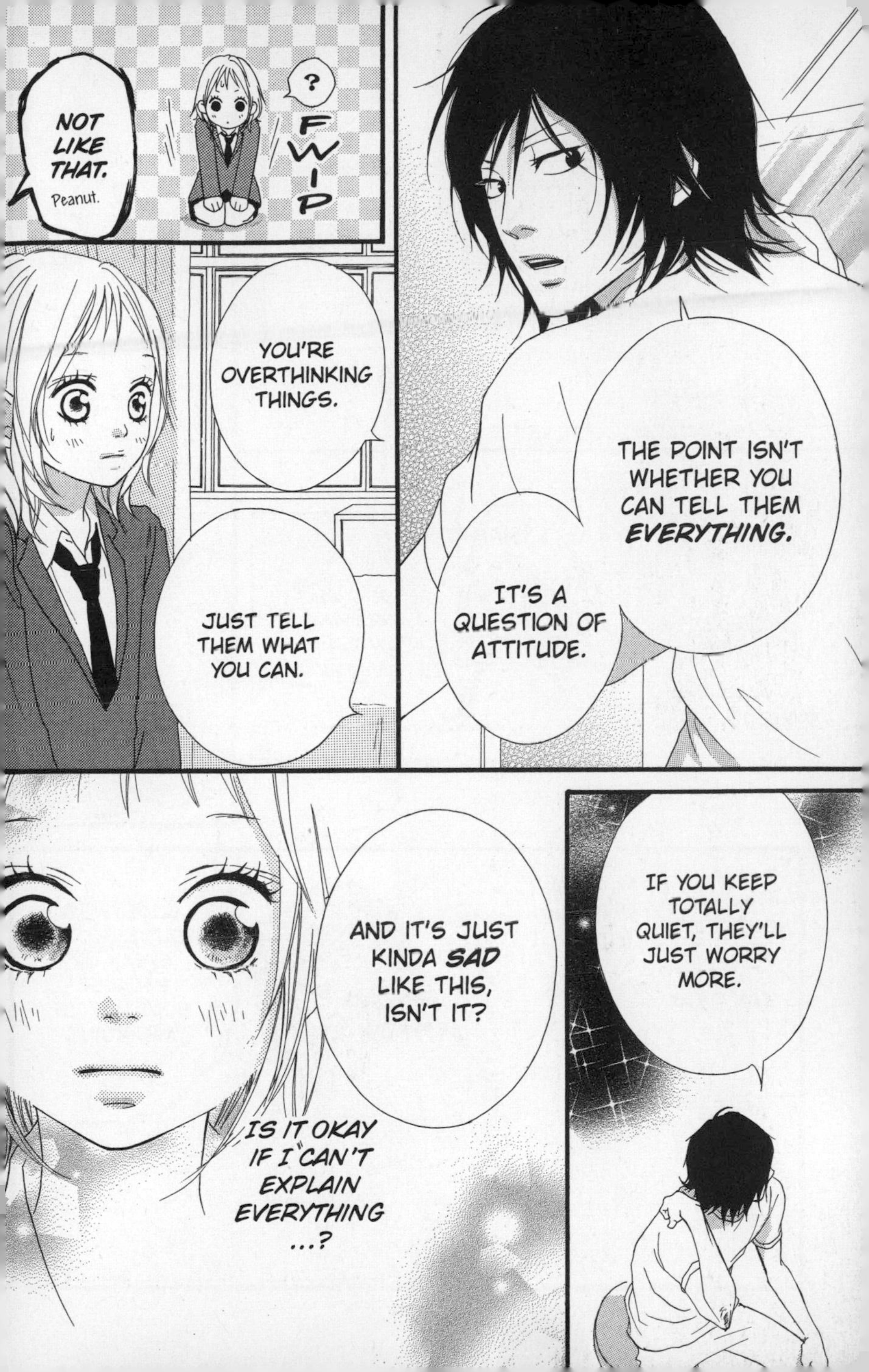
THE POINT ISN'T WHETHER YOU CAN TELL THEM EVERYTHING.
IT'S A QUESTION OF ATTITUDE.
?
FWIP
NOT LIKE THAT.
Peanut.
YOU'RE OVERTHINKING THINGS.
JUST TELL THEM WHAT YOU CAN.
IF YOU KEEP TOTALLY QUIET, THEY'LL JUST WORRY MORE.
AND IT'S JUST KINDA SAD LIKE THIS, ISN'T IT?
IS IT OKAY IF I CAN'T EXPLAIN EVERYTHING ...?

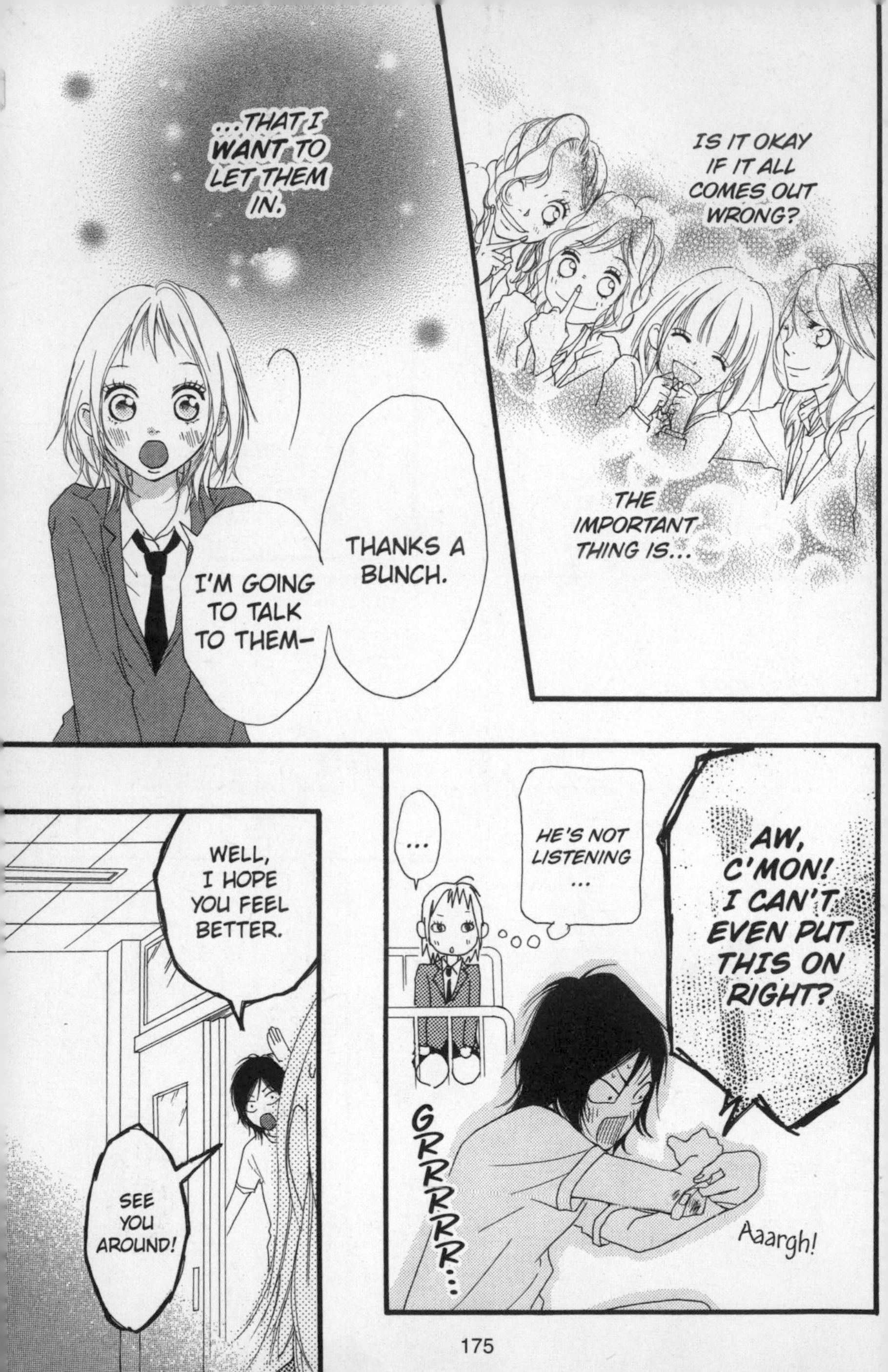
IS IT OKAY IF IT ALL COMES OUT WRONG?
THE IMPORTANT THING IS...
...THAT I WANT TO LET THEM IN.
THANKS A BUNCH.
I'M GOING TO TALK TO THEM-
AW, C'MON! I CAN'T EVEN PUT THIS ON RIGHT?
HE'S NOT LISTENING...
...
GRRRRRR...
Aaargh!
WELL, I HOPE YOU FEEL BETTER.
SEE YOU AROUND!

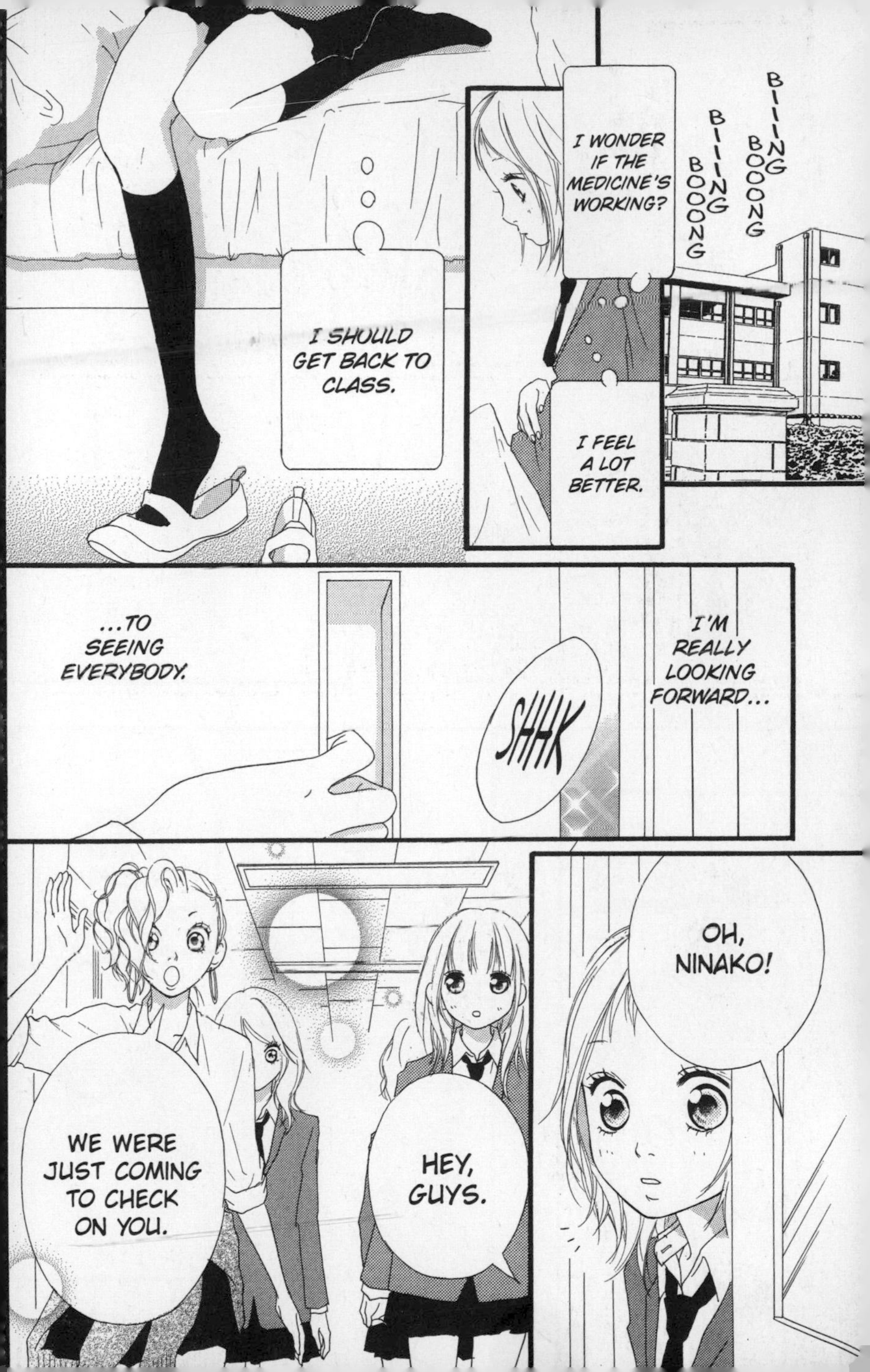
BIING BOOONG
BIING BOOONG
I WONDER IF THE MEDICINE'S WORKING?
I FEEL A LOT BETTER.
I SHOULD GET BACK TO CLASS.
I'M REALLY LOOKING FORWARD...
SHHK
...TO SEEING EVERYBODY.
OH, NINAKO!
HEY, GUYS.
WE WERE JUST COMING TO CHECK ON YOU.

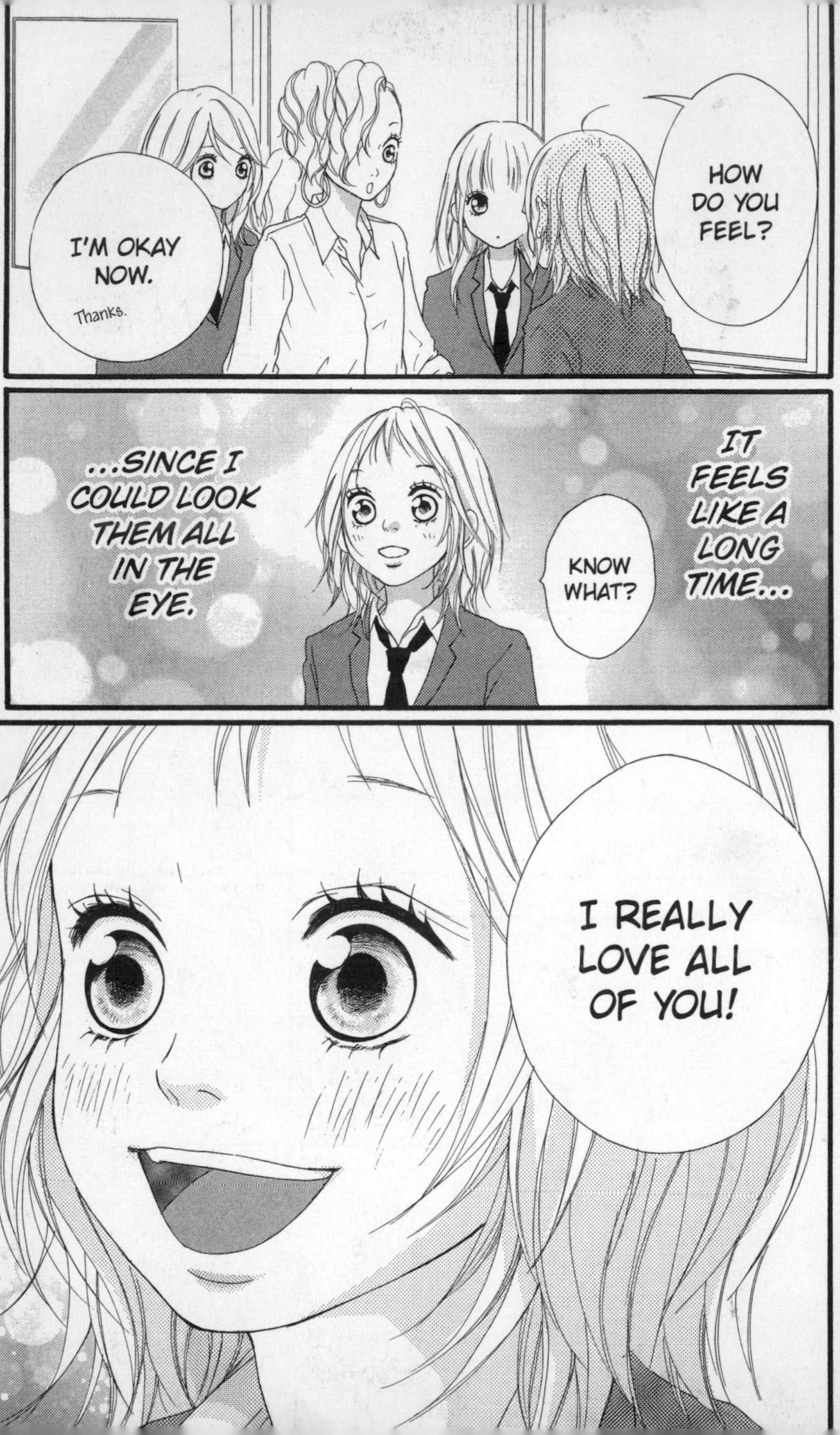
HOW DO YOU FEEL?
I'M OKAY NOW.
Thanks.
IT FEELS LIKE A LONG TIME...
KNOW WHAT?
...SINCE I COULD LOOK THEM ALL IN THE EYE.
I REALLY LOVE ALL OF YOU!

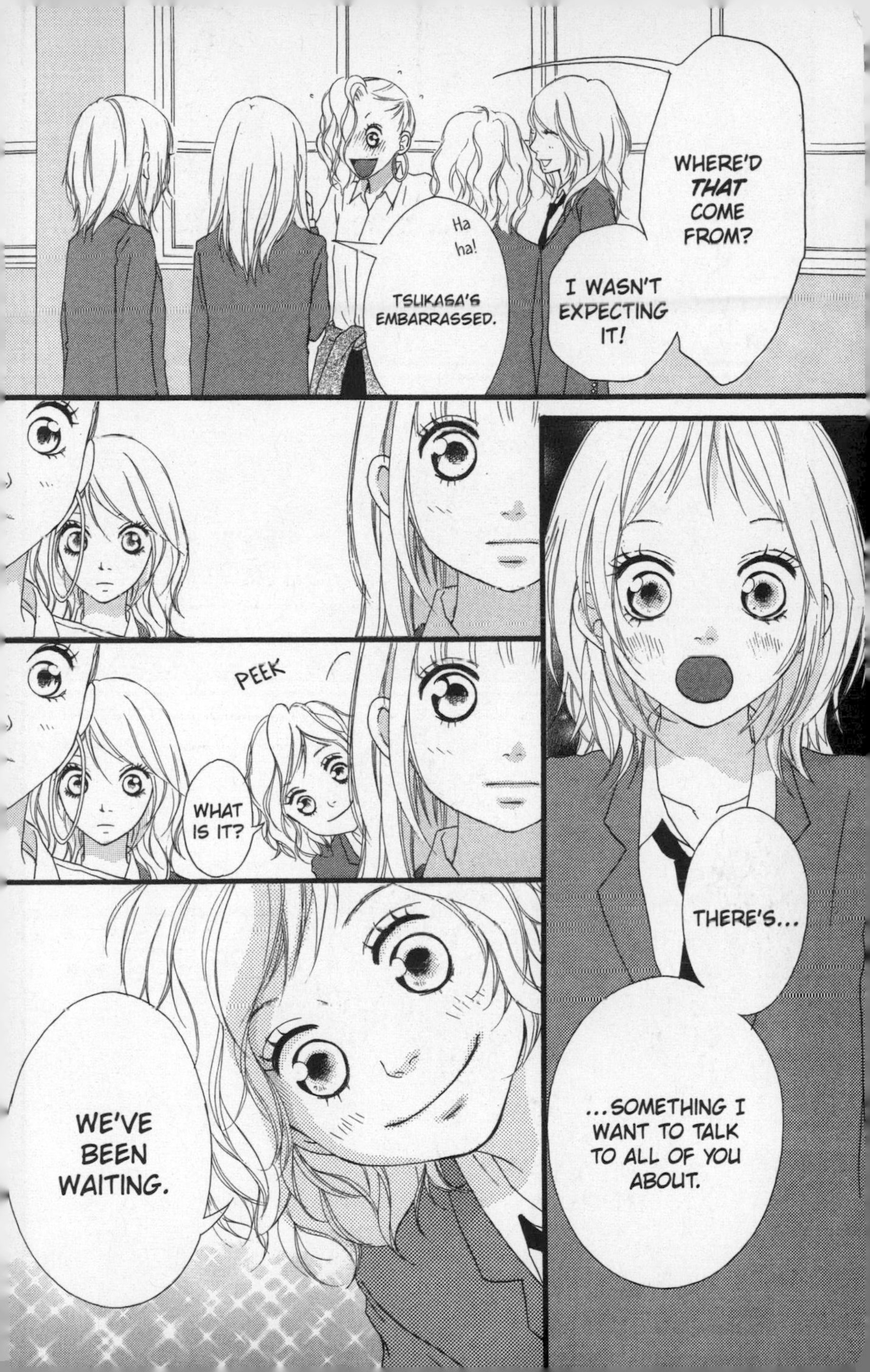
WHERE'D *THAT* COME FROM?
I WASN'T EXPECTING IT!
Ha ha!
TSUKASA'S EMBARRASSED.
THERE'S...
...SOMETHING I WANT TO TALK TO ALL OF YOU ABOUT.
PEEK
WHAT IS IT?
WE'VE BEEN WAITING.

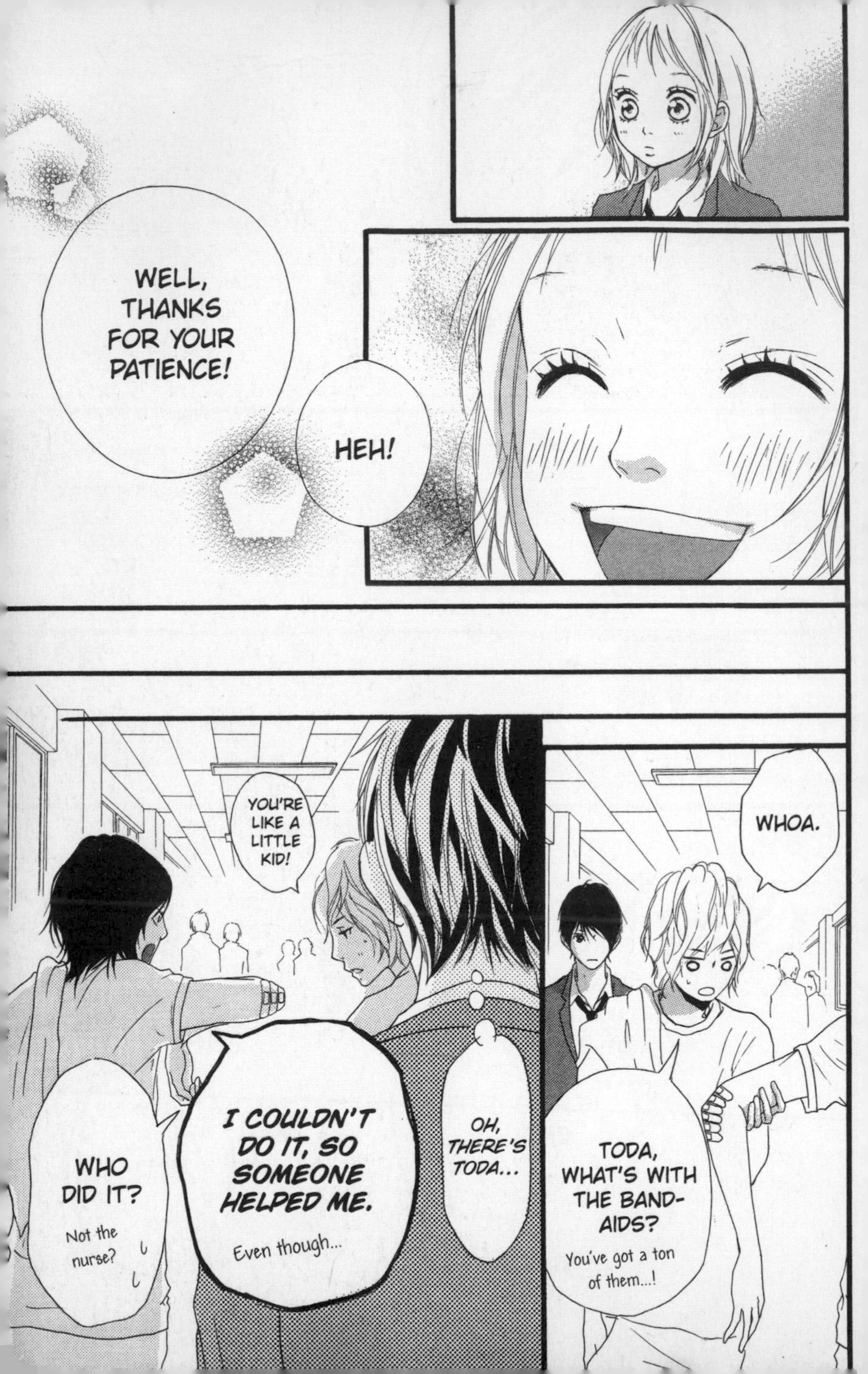
HEH!
WELL, THANKS FOR YOUR PATIENCE!
WHOA.
TODA, WHAT'S WITH THE BAND-AIDS?
You've got a ton of them...!
YOU'RE LIKE A LITTLE KID!
OH, THERE'S TODA...
I COULDN'T DO IT, SO SOMEONE HELPED ME.
Even though...
WHO DID IT?
Not the nurse?

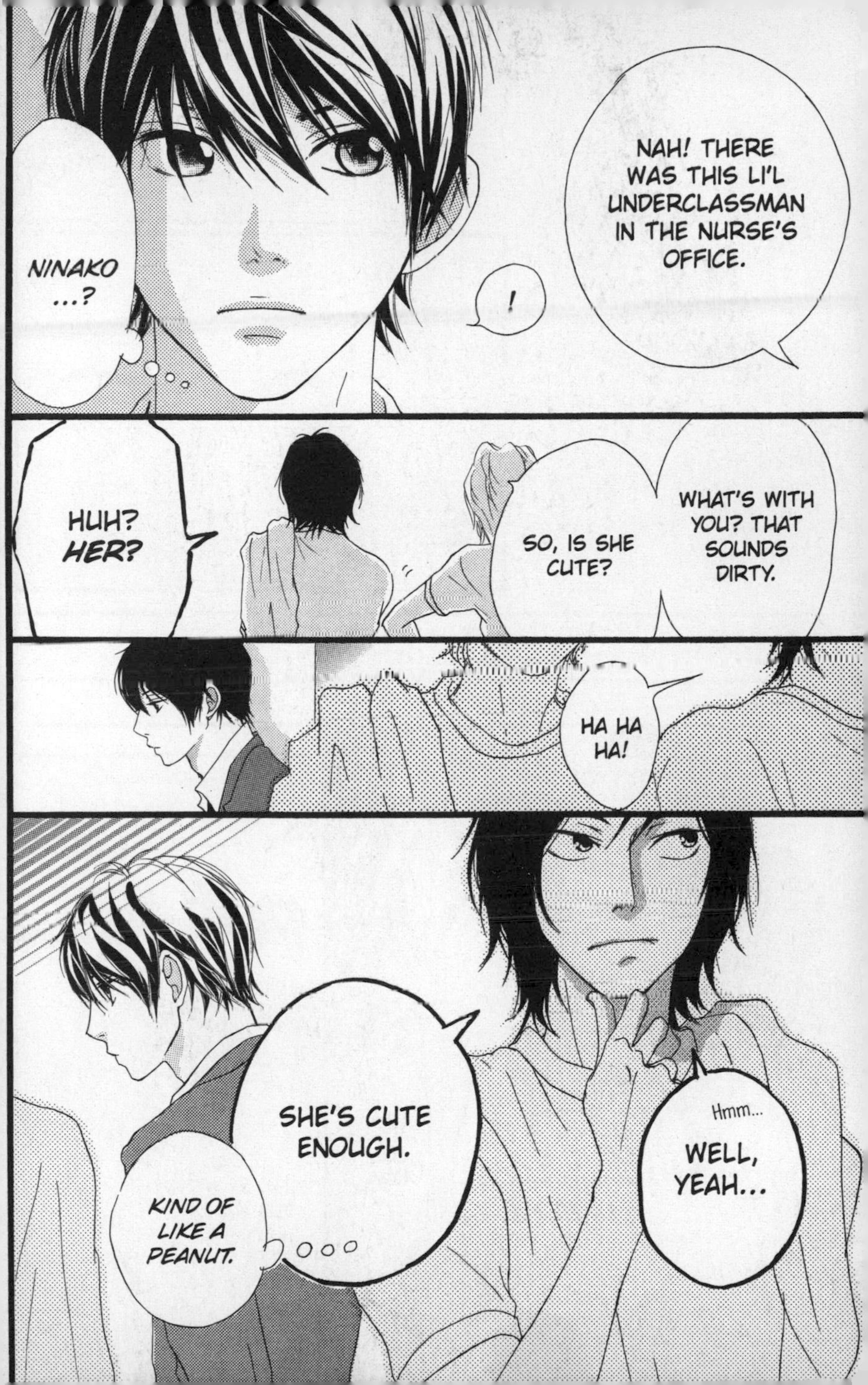
NAH! THERE WAS THIS LI'L UNDERCLASSMAN IN THE NURSE'S OFFICE.
!
NINAKO ...?
WHAT'S WITH YOU? THAT SOUNDS DIRTY.
SO, IS SHE CUTE?
HUH? HER?
HA HA HA!
Hmm...
WELL, YEAH...
SHE'S CUTE ENOUGH.
KIND OF LIKE A PEANUT.

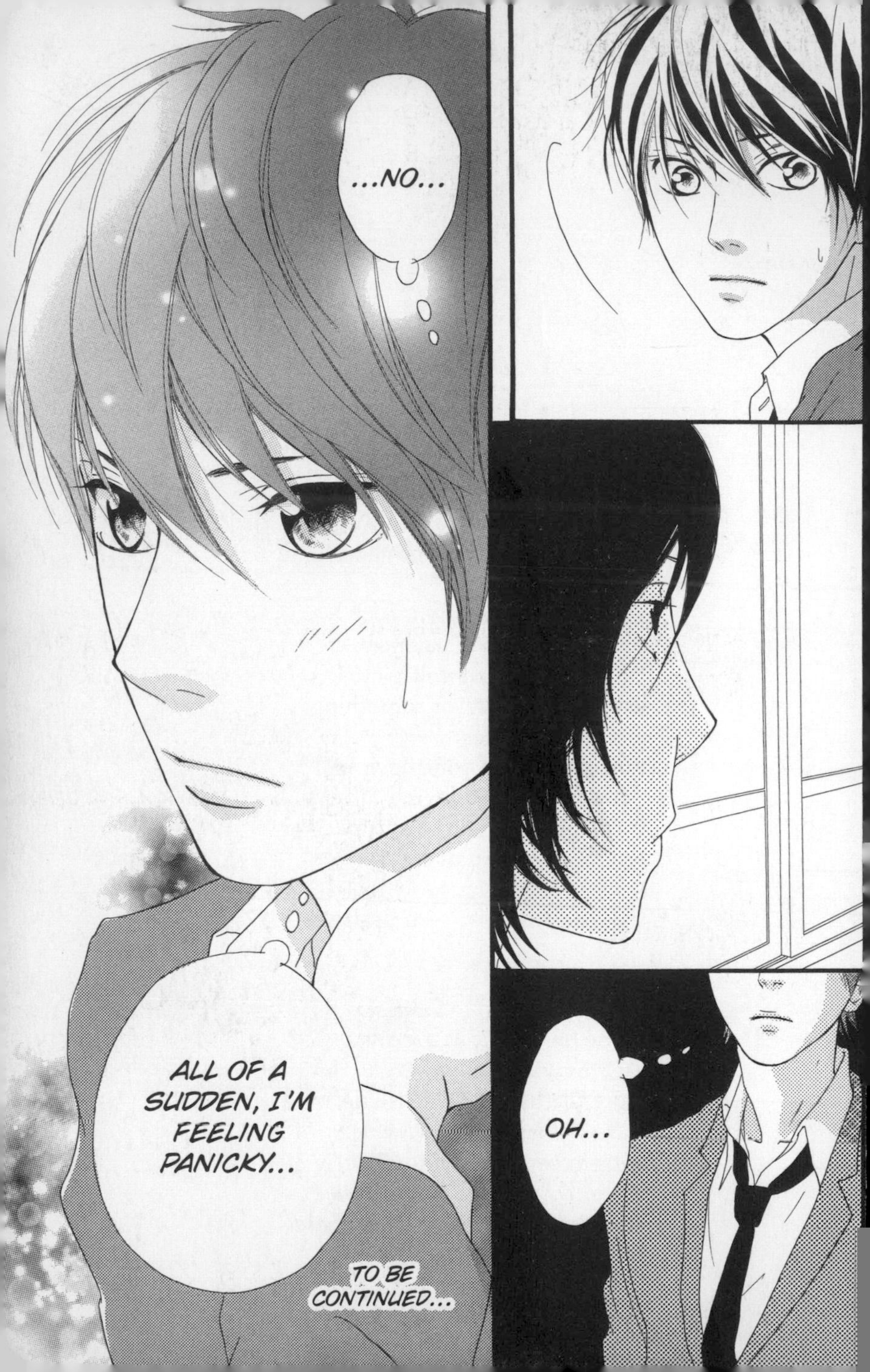
OH...
...NO...
ALL OF A SUDDEN, I'M FEELING PANICKY...
TO BE CONTINUED...

To be continued in volume 9!

Convinced that we should speak and behave in a more feminine manner, a few of my assistants and I formed a "Cutesy Girl Club."
So going forward, when eating, instead of saying, "That's good" we will try to say, "Yummy!♥" or something along those lines.
Personally, I've gone beyond "That's good" to saying "That's frickin' good," so I have a long, hard road ahead of me.

— Io Sakisaka

Born on June 8, Io Sakisaka made her debut as a manga creator with *Sakura, Chiru*. Her works include *Call My Name*, *Gate of Planet*, and *Blue*. Her current series, *Ao Haru Ride*, is currently running in *Bessatsu Margaret* magazine. In her spare time, Sakisaka likes to paint things and sleep.

STROBE EDGE
Vol. 8
Shojo Beat Edition

STORY AND ART BY
IO SAKISAKA

English Adaptation/Ysabet MacFarlane
Translation/JN Productions
Touch-up Art & Lettering/John Hunt
Design/Yukiko Whitley
Editor/Amy Yu

STROBE EDGE © 2007 by Io Sakisaka
All rights reserved.
First published in Japan in 2007 by SHUEISHA Inc., Tokyo.
English translation rights arranged by SHUEISHA Inc.

The stories, characters and incidents mentioned in this publication are entirely fictional.

Printed in the U.S.A.

Published by VIZ Media, LLC
P.O. Box 77010
San Francisco, CA 94107

10 9 8 7 6 5 4 3 2 1
First printing, January 2014

www.viz.com   www.shojobeat.com

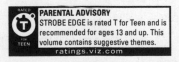

D1096892

Surprise!
You may be reading the wrong way!

It's true: In keeping with the original Japanese comic format, this book reads from right to left—so action, sound effects, and word balloons are completely reversed. This preserves the orientation of the original artwork—plus, it's fun! Check out the diagram shown here to get the hang of things, and then turn to the other side of the book to get started!